Understanding
Intellectual
Development

UNDERSTANDING INTELLECTUAL DEVELOPMENT

THREE APPROACHES TO THEORY AND PRACTICE

William D. Rohwer, Jr.
University of California, Berkeley

Paul R. Ammon
University of California, Berkeley

Phebe Cramer
Williams College

The Dryden Press
901 North Elm Street
Hinsdale, Illinois

Cover design by Robert Bausch

Library of Congress Catalog Card No.: 73–22554
International Standard Book Number: 0–03–089028–4 Cloth Edition
International Standard Book Number: 0–03–089543–x Paper Edition
Printed in the United States of America
 6789   090   9876543

CONTENTS

PREFACE

The process of intellectual development in children has been a topic of lively interest in recent years. Its relevance to the field of education is obvious, and its importance in a general psychology of development has become increasingly clear. Yet, in teaching courses on developmental and educational psychology, we have found it difficult to provide students with a book that presents various theories of intellectual development at an introductory level. The search for a solution to this problem eventually led us to write a book of our own. The book grew out of discussions among the three of us during the summer of 1968, and has developed over the last five years.

An obvious exception to the unavailability of introductory readings is the large number of references that summarize the work of Jean Piaget. However, Piaget's theory represents just one approach to the study of intellectual development—the cognitive approach. We feel that a more complete understanding of intellectual development can be obtained by studying several different theoretical approaches. Thus we have endeavored to write a book in which the process of intellectual development is considered in turn from the perspectives of stimulus-response learning theory, cognitive theory, and psychoanalytic theory. Each of these approaches is set forth in a systematic fashion, with an emphasis on the basic ideas underlying each one and on their relevance to education.

Because it is written primarily for beginning students of developmental or educational psychology, this text does not require previous course work in psychology. Nevertheless, we believe the book will be useful to advanced students as well because of its systematic nature. After an introductory chapter, the book consists of three parts, each devoted to an uninterrupted and coherent account of one theoretical approach. Stimulus-response theory is presented in Part 1, cognitive theory in Part 2, and psychoanalytic theory in Part 3. The advantage of this format is that it allows the reader to achieve a firm grasp of each theory in its own right, without being distracted by the competing contentions of other theories.

Even so, to fully understand any single theory, one must know its distinctive characteristics, and this knowledge can best be obtained by comparing each theory with the others. To facilitate such comparisons, yet preserve the integrity of the three approaches, we have used a parallel organization in all three parts. Each part consists of six chapters and the sequence of the chapter titles is the same: every chapter in Part 1 has a corresponding chapter in Parts 2 and 3. With this parallel organization, the reader can easily locate comparable aspects of the three approaches in order to appreciate fully the distinctive flavor of each one.

In putting this book together, each of us served as the primary author on one of the theoretical approaches: Rohwer on S-R theory, Ammon on cognitive theory, and Cramer on psychoanalytic theory. However, we also criticized each other's work at every stage of the writing, so that each part of the book is, to some extent, a product of our joint efforts.

Many people deserve our thanks for helping make this book a reality. Our debt to other scholars in the field of intellectual development will be evident from the notes for each chapter in the back of the book. Early reviews of the manuscript by William Kessen and Alfred L. Baldwin were particularly useful. In addition, many of our students have shaped our thinking and, in some instances, our writing. We are grateful to Roger Williams, our publisher, for his enduring confidence in us and to Brian Williams for his sensitive and skillful editing. Mrs. Grace O'Connell and Mrs. Angie Giusti were most helpful in typing the manuscript.

Most of all, we wish to thank those closest to us for their patience and encouragement: Carol Rohwer, for the typing of early drafts and for a painstaking critique that forced a major revision of Part 1, and David, Page, Chad, and Bret for providing a personal cause worth the pain of writing this same part; Mary Sue Ammon, for making many important contributions to the style and content of Part 2 and for giving up a summer vacation; and John K. Savacool, whose love and care made it possible to complete Part 3 and bring into the world a daughter, Mara Elena, all in one summer. All the people we have thanked deserve credit for any success we might achieve in helping our readers understand the process of intellectual development.

William D. Rohwer, Jr.
Paul R. Ammon
Phebe Cramer

Understanding
Intellectual
Development

1
INTRODUCTION

Preview

This book is about intellectual development from infancy to adulthood, and in this chapter we introduce three different approaches to the topic: *stimulus-response, cognitive,* and *psychoanalytic theory.*

The book is divided into three parts, each part devoted to one of the theories.

To help the reader make comparisons, we have organized the chapters of each part in parallel fashion—from an opening chapter describing what makes the theory distinctive to a concluding chapter on the implications for educational practice.

WHY STUDY INTELLECTUAL DEVELOPMENT?

The question of how children come to know and think about the world around them is both intrinsically fascinating and practically relevant. To understand why children behave as they do, and why they change as they do, we must ask how and what they learn and how they use what they already know. And certainly we must ask these same questions if we are concerned with imparting knowledge to children by teaching. Thus, the study of intellectual development is at the crossroads of developmental and educational psychology, and is central to both.

Our purpose in writing this book is to promote greater understanding of intellectual development by examining three theoretical approaches to the field and their implications for education. We will first try to delineate intellectual development as a field of study. Then we will outline our reasons for emphasizing theory in general, and for presenting three alternative theories rather than just one theory or a synthesis of ideas from several. In the course of this discussion, a brief sketch of each theory will be provided. Finally, we will explain how the book is organized in a way that facilitates systematic comparison of the three theories.

THE FIELD OF INTELLECTUAL DEVELOPMENT

Exactly what does the field of intellectual development encompass? An abstract definition of intellectual development would almost certainly be too vague, too narrow, or both. Thus, we will describe instead several events in a child's life and then raise some questions that a theory of intellectual development ought to answer.

Milestones of Intellectual Development

Let us look at the life of a typical child so as to identify milestones that the field of intellectual development would include. We could begin with the start of the child's formal education, usually at about age 5 (earlier in some of today's academic preschool programs). Many people, especially professional educators, see schooling as the primary means by which children acquire knowledge and learn to use their minds effectively. The beginning of school does herald some important events in a child's life, but surely it is too late a point for us to begin a study of intellectual development: children already know a great deal by the time they start going to school.

An earlier milestone is the age of the onset of language, which opens up many new possibilities in the child's intellectual life, allowing him to learn from the words of others and to ask questions. But even language does not mark the beginning of intellectual development. Within the first few months of life, when an infant learns to recognize familiar people and objects, and long before he is talking, he can navigate around his home environment as if he knows where things are and where he is going. This very early progress is also part of intellectual development.

Having established that intellectual development actually begins back in the early months of the child's life, we can now look ahead, from the beginning of school toward adulthood. The great middle part of childhood—the school years preceding adolescence—seems at first to involve no major milestones, but rather a gradual accumulation of information and skills. But actually this period consists of numerous "firsts" for the child, both in and out of school: the first time he reads a new word without help; the first time he goes to the store by himself; the first time he follows the rules of a game; the first time he solves a problem in long division; the first time he sneaks into a movie without paying; and so on. If some of the events do not seem very "intellectual," all reflect the child's increasing knowledge and ability to think and take care of himself.

Everyone is aware that adolescence is characterized by the physical and emotional changes of puberty, but important intellectual changes also occur. The milestone of entering high school is symptomatic of basic developments in knowledge and thought—developments that are often almost entirely extra-curricular. The adolescent experiences a new surge of interest in ideas and values, along with things and events: What kind of person do I want to be? What is the good life? How can people live together peacefully? Traditional ideas about right and wrong are no longer accepted without question; the adolescent generally wants reasons for taking a particular stance. The four-year-old who asks "why" is not looking for a logical answer, but the 14-year-old is. Although adolescent behavior is not always rational, it shows a new appreciation for and competence in the use of reason to solve life's problems.

The adolescent also experiences changes in the formal instruction offered to him, moving from reading, social studies, and science to comparative literature, sociology, and chemistry. In learning such a discipline, whether academic or nonacademic, the adolescent learns a principled way of thinking about a field, not just facts or skills, thus signaling yet another advance in intellectual development. Generally, the knowledge acquired in adolescence and adulthood transcends the kinds of information and skills acquired by children. With this new level of competence, the individual can go places and do things he could not do before. Ultimately, he takes over full responsibility for his own life.

It should be reasonably clear by now what our topic includes. It spans the years from birth to adulthood and covers all changes in knowledge and thought that increase the individual's competence. Thus, intellectual development does not just happen to "intellectuals," nor is it concerned only with academic knowledge. All people increase their knowledge and their ability to think as they grow up, and there is a lot more to be learned than what is taught in school.

Of course, there are many individual and cultural differences as to what is learned and how it is used. Some people never learn to read and others never learn to play poker. Some cultures give children of middle childhood greater freedom to explore the world; others give them more responsibility for working in the household or in the community. But such differences are only variations on the basic themes of intellectual development. Some of these themes are indicated by the questions that follow.

Questions about Intellectual Development

Why do developmental milestones occur when they do? Are the minds of children "programmed" by nature to develop in a particular pattern, or do the milestones simply reflect the kind of environment in which a child is brought up? Can the sequence or timing of certain milestones be altered? For example, could children learn the basic discipline of a school subject earlier than they usually do now? Alternatively, could formal instruction in such basic skills as reading and arithmetic be postponed until adolescence? Is it necessary to "teach" certain ways of thinking, or will they develop spontaneously if only given a chance? What conditions cause children to acquire a particular type of knowledge or a new way of thinking?

The intrinsic interest and practical importance of such questions are obvious, but the answers are not. And because the present facts of developmental and educational psychology do not yield any definitive answers, we must go beyond such facts and make some educated guesses about the essential nature of intellectual development. In other words, we have no choice but to get into the realm of theory. That is why this is a book about theories of intellectual development.

THE USE OF THEORY

A psychological theory is a set of guiding principles that gives us a framework for understanding human development. This kind of understanding differs from a mastery of specific rules or particular procedures in that the general principles that constitute a theory are not specifically applicable to any one situation but are relevant to a wide range of events. In contrast, knowledge of specific procedures is often of little help when one is faced with a new problem for which no specific rule has been learned. Thus, a theory is not as "practical" as a set of specific rules—it will not provide detailed instructions for dealing with specific occasions—but it is more useful than such rules because it has wider applicability.

To understand intellectual development, we believe, one must have some theory, or set of guiding principles, that will provide an overall orientation or way of looking at the topic. But now the question is—what theory? The field of psychology has several different theories directly relevant to understanding intellectual development, and there is considerable disagreement as to which one gives the best explanation. Unfortunately, empirical means—that is, concrete, experimental tests—will not tell us which theory most adequately predicts the child's intellectual functioning. The answer to that question depends on which aspect of intellectual functioning one studies.

If one wants to know the best rate for presenting new materials for learning or the most beneficial instructions teachers can give to help a child learn a new task, then the first theory to be discussed in this book, *stimulus-response theory,* is probably the most successful. If one wants to know when children can best understand the ideas of number, measurement, or proportion, then the second theory, *cognitive theory,* may be the most adequate. If one wants to know why a child who was active, curious, and imaginative at age four is listless and uninterested now that he has entered school, then the third approach, *psychoanalytic theory,* may give the most satisfactory answer.

The point is that some theories are better equipped than others to deal with particular aspects of intellectual development, and thus the most complete understanding of intellectual development can be had through a knowledge of several theories. In this way, areas of development that are excluded or ignored by one approach will be dealt with by another, and thus the range of developmental issues covered will be considerably enlarged.

Our program is not without its dangers. First, the theories do not necessarily use the same language to refer to the same phenomena, so the reader must learn different vocabularies and guard against confusion by multiple terminologies. Second, the theories do not always agree even on factual matters. For example, stimulus-response theory may suggest that if the environment (materials, instructions, rewards, and so on) is arranged in a particular way, and if the child's previous learning is appropriate, he will be able to learn task X; but cognitive theory may state that, despite environmental manipulations, the child will not learn the task until he has reached the appropriate stage of development. Third, what one theory may stress as important, may be totally ignored by another. For instance, the concept of instinctual drive is central to psychoanalytic theory but missing from stimulus-response and cognitive theory; the concept of equilibration, central to cognitive theory, is absent from stimulus-response and psychoanalytic theory.

Given these possible difficulties for the reader, wouldn't it be better to try to extract out of these three different theories some common principles and to present these shared ideas in a kind of eclectic amalgam? We believe not. To fully understand a principle, one must see it in the context of its theory. Just as cutting out and gluing together the most beautiful portions of three famous paintings would be unlikely to produce a significant work of art, so putting together parts of different theories in hopes of arriving at an improved "general" theory seems to us fruitless.

Rather, we have chosen to present three distinctly different theoretical approaches to intellectual development. We have chosen these three because, at the present time, they can provide the most extensive and inclusive treatment of the topic. Also, they represent three quite different currents of thought within the field of psychology, and each of these currents has had a different kind of influence on thinking about child development. Finally, we have chosen these three approaches because we feel that each has its unique strengths for explaining intellectual development, just as each has its particular weaknesses. We firmly believe that no single theory, at least at present, is able to deal adequately with all the important issues.

THREE THEORETICAL APPROACHES TO INTELLECTUAL DEVELOPMENT

Let us briefly describe some of the unique features of each of the three approaches.

Stimulus-response theory (also known as learning theory) approaches intellectual development the way it approaches the study of behavior in general; that is, developmental change is regarded as a special case of behavioral change. The stimulus-response view is that intellectual development consists of a large collection of gradual changes in specific performances. Further, it is believed that the character of the changes that take place in one period of a child's life are no different, qualitatively, from the character of changes that occur in any other period.

The stimulus-response theorist attempts to explain a child's level of intellectual performance by identifying, first, the current *environmental* circumstances and, second, the results of *previous learning* that are related to this performance. *Current* environmental circumstances might include such conditions as the way in which the child was asked to solve the task, the amount or kind of information he is given about the adequacy of his approach, the nature of the task itself, or the presence or absence of extraneous stimuli in the situation. The results of *previous learning* might include the amount of prior practice the child has had in performing similar tasks and the kind of reward or punishment he has learned to expect under similar conditions. The stimulus-response theorist believes that if a child cannot perform at a given intellectual level, he should be provided with appropriate environmental conditions and prerequisite learning experiences that he is lacking.

The cognitive theorist agrees that development is in some respects a gradual, cumulative process but he believes it also proceeds through a series of qualitatively different stages. Each stage is characterized by a different way of thinking or type of "cognitive structure." These structures set limits on what a child can and cannot learn at a particular stage. Each succeeding stage incorporates the cognitive structures developed in the previous stage and, at the same time, opens up new possibilities for learning and thinking.

According to cognitive theory, the child himself is the source of change in cognitive structures from one stage to the next. Although the environment and innate structures have some effect on development, most such change occurs because the child "constructs" new ways of thinking from his own activity in relation to the environment.

Psychoanalytic theory is similar to cognitive theory in that it assumes that intellectual development results from both innate givens and environmental experiences. Likewise, it also assumes that the quality of behavior differs at different stages of development. It differs from cognitive theory, and from learning theory, however, in the nature of the innate and environmental factors it considers relevant.

At the base of psychoanalytic theory is the concept of drive and the need for drive gratification. The concept of drive refers to a psychological need that causes a person to do something—that is, that motivates either psychological or physical activity. Intellectual development is understood to result from the need to gratify the drive. Only by developing his intellect can the child take care of himself and satisfy his needs, and until such development has occurred, he must depend on someone else—generally his mother—for survival. Because the mother is such an important person in the child's life (she satisfies his needs and ensures his survival), this relationship strongly influences his intellectual development. It is this stress on motivational and emotional factors that most clearly differentiates the psychoanalytic theory of intellectual development from the cognitive and stimulus-response theories.

This is a very brief overview of the three approaches to intellectual development to be discussed in this book. Within each of these three general theories themselves there are, of course, disagreements about specific developmental occurrences. However, it is not our intention to focus on these differences, though the reader should be aware that they exist. Rather, what we have tried to do is present a form of each general theory that is self-consistent, and that, to our minds, portrays those aspects of the theory most important for understanding intellectual development.

ORGANIZATION OF THE BOOK

Our aim is to portray each of the theories on a separate canvas rather than together as a patchwork. Thus, the book consists of three parts—Part 1, stimulus-response theory; Part 2, cognitive theory; and Part 3, psychoanalytic theory. The topics covered by the six chapters in each part are as follows.

Point of View. The opening chapter of each part characterizes the essential features of the theory described in detail later—how it is distinctive in the way it views the psychology of human beings, what it asks us to look at, and what methods its adherents use to evaluate its utility. This chapter also describes some of the background of the theory—for example, its roots in philosophy, initial formulations, reformulations, and present versions.

Basic Concepts and Principles. Each theory includes concepts and principles that are the basic tools used to describe and explain intellectual development. The second chapter in each part introduces, defines, and illustrates the terms that refer to these concepts and principles. For stimulus-response theory, these are terms such as *stimulus, response, mediation,* and *reinforcement;* for cognitive theory, *cognitive structure* and *equilibration;* for psychoanalytic theory, *instinctual drive* and *reality testing.* Besides providing a glossary of basic terms, this chapter organizes the material so as to give preliminary shape to the theories themselves.

Model of Behavior.   Each theory also contains an explicit statement of the relationships among the concepts and principles, and in this third chapter these relationships are summarized in a model or flow chart. The model is meant to provide a hypothetical picture of the ways in which human behavior is produced and maintained. The three models provide the reader with an organized scheme for remembering the fundamentals of each theory and for using them to view behavior.

The Character and Causes of Development.   This chapter focuses on the two central questions of the book: What is intellectual development? and, What makes it occur? Each theory offers a distinctive way of identifying, describing, and explaining intellectual development: it is a collection of changes in specific performances or it is an unalterable sequence of coherent stages. It is the result of learning or of one's own cognitive activity or of an innate plan interacting with environmental experience. In presenting a systematic account of the three approaches to development the chapter offers generalizations that are applicable to many areas in which development occurs.

Some Major Areas of Intellectual Development.   This chapter applies the generalizations of the previous chapter to some major areas of intellectual development. These areas vary from part to part according to the emphases of each theory. Part 1 describes developmental changes as they occur for eight different varieties of learning, such as the learning of *discriminations* or the learning of *rules.* Part 2 explicates developmental change in the individual's *understanding of the physical world* and his *logical thinking.* Part 3 shows how the development of *semantic communication* and of *judgment* are outgrowths of feeding experiences during the first year of life, and how the development of the intellectual abilities for *abstraction* and *objectivity* are related to the reemergence of strong instinctual drives during adolescence. This chapter cannot cover all major areas of intellectual development in each theory, but it describes enough to show how the theory can explain other aspects of intellectual development.

Implications for Education.   The final chapter discusses the implications of the theory for educational practice. Preceding chapters emphasized how the theory could be used to understand intellectual development. This chapter shows how it can be used specifically to understand developmental changes in the classroom and how the teacher can facilitate the development of the children. Examples of such implications are the importance of planning instruction in accordance with the learning it requires, of tailoring instruction to the child's developmental stage, and of recognizing that some learning difficulties originate in emotional problems. Thus, the closing chapter in each part demonstrates the practical power of systematic theories.

SUMMARY

The purpose of this book about intellectual development is to present some ways of viewing and understanding the milestones of development from infancy to adulthood. Acting on the assumption that a good theory is the most powerful tool for achieving such understanding, we present theories of intellectual development. Since no one theory to date is comprehensive enough to encompass all of the aspects of intellectual development, and since there is no objective way at present of making a conclusive choice among contending theories, we offer three different approaches: stimulus-response theory, cognitive theory, and psychoanalytic theory. An entire, uninterrupted part of the book is devoted to each approach so as to provide coherent, systematic accounts that do justice to the theories. To assist the reader in comparing major facets of the theories, the sequence of chapters is parallel throughout the three parts.

Part 1

The STIMULUS-RESPONSE Approach to Intellectual Development

2

THE STIMULUS-RESPONSE POINT OF VIEW

Preview

This first part of the book is concerned with stimulus-response psychology, which focuses on behavior and its two determinants, environmental conditions and past learning. In the S-R view, intellectual development is a product of the accumulated results of learning. In this chapter we identify some hallmarks of the S-R view of human beings; explore the historical contributions to the approach, from Locke through Pavlov, Thorndike, and Watson; and explain the methods of detailed description and experimental manipulation used to test the validity of S-R hypotheses.

HALLMARKS OF THE
STIMULUS-RESPONSE APPROACH

A child changes because he learns. Over time, what he learns accumulates, making the changes noticeable. When we notice these changes, and when they appear to be widespread, we conclude that the child has *developed*. This proposition—that the cumulative effects of learning produce development—shapes the entire approach of stimulus-response (S-R) theories to understanding human development.

Some hallmarks of an S-R approach to understanding human beings are apparent in the kinds of questions an S-R psychologist might ask about intellectual development. Does the behavior of children differ from that of adults when they are learning a new concept? If so, what specifically are the differences? What conditions affect the behavior of children and adults when they are learning concepts? Are these conditions the same for both? Are the results the same? If differences in behavior between children and adults are observed, what differences in their environments and in their previous learning histories explain them?

Three features of these questions should be emphasized. First, they focus on *behavior*. It is differences in behavior that must be explained: Why, for example, can adults learn to identify examples of a new concept more readily than can children? Second, these questions assume that behavior is determined by the *environmental conditions* in which it occurs. Third, the questions assume that behavior is determined by *past learning*. These three features are hallmarks of the S-R approach to understanding human intellectual development.

For clarification, here are two questions that are *not* characterized by these features: How and why does the structure of the child's mind change as he grows into adulthood? What determines the development of conscious thought as he grows? Such questions are important and interesting, but the problem with them, to the S-R psychologist, is their *form*: they do not refer to *behavior*, to aspects of persons that other persons can observe. Hence, it is difficult to obtain agreement about what the questions mean or about the character of the developmental changes theories are supposed to explain. For S-R theory, it is developmental changes in behavior that are the prime objects of explanation.

Not everyone accepts these commitments about the form of questions about children's intellectual development. Some people, for example, believe agreement can be obtained about the meaning of a phrase like "the structure of a child's mind." Indeed, such language is used frequently among educators, parents, and non-S-R psychologists. Although questions about the "structure of a child's mind" are asked in other parts of this book, they are not acceptable here. In fact, many kinds of questions thought respectable by many persons are flatly rejected by S-R psychologists. Thus, it should be asked, how did S-R psychologists come to adopt such a strong position about the form in which phenomena should be described? Here is one answer.[1]

HISTORICAL BACKGROUND

Among the philosophers heeded by psychologists who were to form the S-R tradition of psychology in the United States, the British Empiricists were probably the most influential. In particular, two positions advanced by John Locke (1632–1704) shaped the commitments of many psychologists interested in learning: first, that the contents of the mind are the product of *experience* and not of the nature of the mind itself; and, second, that the arrangement of the elements that form the contents of the mind is determined by principles of *association* rather than by an inherent structure of the human brain. Two specific principles of association posited by Locke also survive in present S-R theories. One is *contiguity*—elements will be associated if they occur together in experience. The other is *repetition*—the association between elements is stronger the more often they occur contiguously. For example, infancy is a time when an association is formed between the two elements of mother and nourishment, because infants experience the two elements together—that is, contiguously—and the association is strengthened because this contiguity occurs repeatedly.

S-R psychologists warmly embraced Locke's principles of association but coldly rejected his methods for validating those principles. Locke used the methods characteristic of his discipline: logical analysis and verification by reference to his own mental experience. But S-R psychologists find these methods too subjective and private. If the conclusions of one person's reflections on his experience differ from those of another person, there is no way to choose between them because it is not possible to communicate to others personal experiences that are entirely subjective. Thus, to the S-R psychologist, the method of personal reflection has the effect of preventing clear communication.

At the turn of the twentieth century, two men were using scientific methods rather than the method of reflection to evaluate Locke's principles of association. In Russia, Ivan Pavlov (1849–1936) was amassing evidence that he would use to build a theory of classical conditioning. In the United States, E. L. Thorndike (1874–1949) was developing a theory that would complement Pavlov's.[2] Their theories formed the dominant stream of psychological thought about learning for the next half century. Both emphasized the principle of contiguity and both focused on questions about behavior and on the conditions in which particular behavior occurred. Moreover, both tested possible answers by experimenting with subhuman animals, so descriptions of the results referred almost exclusively to observed overt behavior.

Pavlov's procedures are widely known. For example, he would fix a dog in place with a harness, then have a bell rung at intervals, followed immediately by the appearance of meat powder close enough so the dog could see and smell it but not eat it. The focus of Pavlov's observation was on how much saliva the dog secreted when the meat powder was present compared to when it was not present. After the bell and the meat powder had been presented contiguously several times, the bell was rung but the meat powder was not presented. Again, the amount of saliva was compared with the amount produced when the meat powder was present. The results showed that the ringing of the bell was followed by salivation even in the absence of the meat powder.

Pavlov called the meat powder an unconditional stimulus and the salivation behavior that occurred in its presence an unconditional response. The term "unconditional" was used because the meat powder evoked increased salivation without any prior training. He called the bell ring a conditional stimulus and the salivation behavior that accompanied it in the absence of the meat powder a conditional response. "Conditional" meant that the power of the bell ring to increase salivation depended on, or was conditional to, prior training in which the bell had been presented contiguously with the meat powder. The terms used in the United States are slightly different: the meat powder is an *unconditioned stimulus* (abbreviated UCS), the salivation behavior evoked by the meat powder is an *unconditioned response* (UCR), the bell ring is a *conditioned stimulus* (CS), and the salivation behavior evoked by the bell ring is a *conditioned response* (CR). The word *stimulus* refers to aspects of the animal's immediate environment arranged by the experimenter —the meat powder and the bell ring—and the word *response* refers to the animal's observable behavior, the amount of saliva produced. Pavlov was interested in the relationship between the UCS and the CS, in the events that established an association between the bell ring and the meat powder. The critical feature of Pavlov's method was that he reached conclusions about associations by observing the animal's behavior, saliva production, not by personal reflection. Thus, Pavlov was like Locke in emphasizing association but unlike him in his method of arriving at conclusions about the principles of association.

Thorndike was also interested in how associations are formed between stimuli and responses. In one widely known experiment he put a hungry cat in a small cage and placed food immediately outside, in full view of the animal. The cat could open the cage door by pulling a string loop hanging inside. What Thorndike wanted to know was how the cat behaved in the time an association was formed between being placed in the cage (the stimulus) and batting the string loop to open the door (the response). Besides observing how the cat behaved in the cage, Thorndike paid particular attention to how much time elapsed between insertion of the cat into the cage and his escape from it. He noted that the time gradually decreased when a cat was repeatedly placed in the cage; that is, with practice, the cat became faster at making the response that permitted escape.

To account for this kind of behavior—often called trial-and-error learning—Thorndike evolved two laws of association. The *law of exercise* was similar to Locke's principle of repetition, except that the connections were between stimuli and responses rather than between ideas. According to this law, a particular response has a greater chance of occurring in the presence of a particular stimulus the more times these events have occurred together previously. The law of exercise, of course, is similar to Pavlov's conclusion that the more times a neutral stimulus is presented contiguously with an unconditioned stimulus, the greater chance the stimulus will evoke a conditioned response when presented alone.

But Thorndike believed that a full account of how connections are formed between stimuli and responses required a second law. This *law of effect* had two parts: first, the more satisfaction resulting from a response to a stimulus, the stronger the association between the response and that stimulus; second, the more discomfort resulting from a response, the weaker the association. In other words, rewards strengthen associations and punishments weaken them.

In advancing the law of effect, Thorndike raised an issue that psychologists have been disputing ever since—namely, whether satisfiers or rewards are necessary for the establishment of associations. Do the aftereffects of a response determine whether the response will be connected with the stimulus to which it was made? This issue is like the philosophical question whether man acts so as to maximize pleasure and avoid pain. Indeed, psychoanalytic theory (Part 3) uses a related notion, the pleasure principle, to account for the early development of human behavior.

For S-R theorists the law of effect poses the problem of how to define satisfiers in a way that is not completely circular. The law of effect asserts that satisfiers increase the chances that responses will be made. But satisfiers are defined as events that an organism seeks after—that is, events that increase the chances that an organism will make responses. Thus, the definition is almost entirely circular and so it is difficult to test the validity of the law of effect.

Pavlov's and Thorndike's principles of learning have proven very durable. Their assertions that associations are strengthened by contiguous repetition and by rewarding aftereffects of responses survive in many current theories. Their methods of investigation also survive; their clear, specific descriptions of environmental conditions and of the behavior of animals in them were based not on methods of personal reflection but on methods of direct observation that others could repeat and agree on.

Although Pavlov's and Thorndike's methods and theoretical principles emerged early, and would influence S-R psychologists for the rest of the century, in the first two decades of the 1900s, many psychologists adopted alternative theories and methods—chiefly structuralism and Gestalt psychology. In the United States, E. B. Titchener (1867–1927) was the chief proponent of *structuralism*, a school of psychology that was consistent with Locke in its theoretical principles and methodology. The object of study was human mental processes, which usually meant the study of associations between sensations and ideas. The method was that of personal reflection or *introspection*: persons were asked to give verbal descriptions of their own mental processes. These descriptions were characterized by extraordinary amounts of detail and were analytical in the extreme.[3]

Gestalt psychologists, discarding the analytical approach, insisted that human perception and thinking could be understood only in terms of wholes

—that is, entire patterns or *Gestalten*—and not in terms of parts or the individual components of patterns. The Gestaltists shared with S-R psychologists a methodology that consisted of observing the behavior of organisms in response to stimulus patterns or to problem-solving tasks. They differed from S-R psychologists, however, in their distaste for analyzing stimuli into their components and for analyzing behavior into its component responses. For example, the process of problem solving was characterized as the emergence of insight rather than as the gradual establishment of stimulus-response connections.[4]

The popularity of the structuralist position provoked one American psychologist, John B. Watson (1878–1958), to publish in 1913 a manifesto for S-R psychologists, "Psychology as the Behaviorist Views It," in which he stated:

> Psychology as the behaviorist views it is a purely objective experimental branch of natural science. Its theoretical goal is the prediction and control of behavior. Introspection forms no essential part of its methods, nor is the scientific value of its data dependent upon the readiness with which they lend themselves to interpretation in terms of consciousness. The behaviorist, in his efforts to get a unitary scheme of animal response, recognizes no dividing line between man and brute.[5]

The effect of these dicta, which clearly followed the traditions of Pavlov and Thorndike, was to rule out of order reference to any aspect of human beings other than their behavior. The ensuing era was dominated by the theories of Thorndike, Pavlov and Watson. The major assumptions of these theories were that behavior is determined by environmental conditions and that behavior differences could be explained by environmental differences. During this period, many S-R psychologists hoped that all human behavior could eventually be explained without any reference to conditions inside the human being. Thus, the S-R image of man was that he was relatively *passive,* devoid of conscious, willful, seeking characteristics, and highly *impressionable*, automatically subject to the effects of contiguities between stimuli and the responses that chanced to occur with them. In principle, at least, the behavior of such an organism would be completely predictable and even controllable, given a knowledge of past experience (the organism's learning history) and present environmental circumstances (stimuli).

CONTEMPORARY STIMULUS-RESPONSE THEORIES

Today's S-R psychologists generally retain the heritage of Thorndike, Pavlov, and Watson, but their ideas about learning have changed. They continue to emphasize that explanations must be verified by experimental methods and that communication be concrete and well specified, but they no longer insist on ignoring the interior of the organism. S-R psychologists currently assume the operation of numerous processes inside the person in order to explain his external behavior. In fact, for all but the simplest forms of learning, it is now thought that behavior is determined as much by internal conditions as by current external conditions.[6]

The idea that internal conditions determine a person's behavior is consistent with the traditions of S-R theory (even though such conditions are not open to direct observation), for internal conditions are defined as being the persisting effects of past learning. Previous learning can determine behavior that will occur in the presence of particular external conditions or stimuli. Whether a dog salivates when a bell is rung depends on his having a previous history of associating the bell ring with access to food. If this internal condition is absent—the persisting effects of prior conditioning—salivation behavior will not occur in response to the external stimulus. Thus, contemporary S-R theorists see behavior as the product of a combination of both internal and external conditions.

This shift to include internal as well as external conditions in explanations of learning makes it more difficult than it once was to contrast S-R psychology with, for example, cognitive psychology. Differences persist, but they are not as stark as in earlier theories.

Nevertheless, contemporary S-R theorists still believe that learning essentially consists of making connections, or associations, between particular stimuli and responses. Internal conditions of learning, they believe, strongly influence current behavior and new learning, but these conditions consist mainly of what has been learned before; they are not imposed by the inherent structure of the mind. External conditions by themselves do not determine behavior, it is thought, but still behavior change is best accomplished by providing the external conditions that will ensure learning occurs. A child's development, then, consists of progressive changes in his behavior produced by a crystallization of all the learning events in his life. Thus, the S-R psychologist believes, to understand intellectual development, one must specify what the child has learned.

Today's S-R theorists do not believe man is a completely passive or easily impressionable organism, for past learning makes him resistant to change. But he is still a product of past learning. This view is not entirely pessimistic: it recognizes that the child may be changed by the arrangement of external conditions for learning—just what the educator can provide.[7] But this optimism entails responsibility: if a child's intellectual life is determined by the arrangement of learning conditions, the result can be either salutary or disastrous; when a child fails intellectually, it is not because of his inherent problems but because of inadequate external conditions.

METHODS OF TESTING HYPOTHESES

The methods S-R psychologists use to check their assumptions have two characteristics: *descriptive detail* and *manipulation of conditions*.

Descriptive details clarify communications to others, increasing the chances of reaching informed agreement about the truth of conclusions. The

S-R psychologist believes that one effective way to convince himself of the truth of someone else's conclusion is to experience the events that led the other person to his conclusion. For example, if a friend tells you a particular restaurant is a superb place to eat, how do you decide whether his assertion is true? You try it yourself, of course. But if you try it with no more information than your friend's statement that it is a superb place to eat, you might conclude that your friend did not communicate clearly, for he did not provide enough information to allow you to engage in the process that led him to a gratifying meal. He did not, for example, say what night he dined there, and so you might go on a night when the restaurant was closed or overly crowded. You need more detailed information before you can dine in such a way as to judge the validity of your friend's conclusion. Similarly, the S-R psychologist insists that the procedures followed in reaching conclusions about intellectual development should be described in detailed, specific terms that can be communicated to others in such a way that they can decide for themselves whether the conclusions are true.

The method S-R psychologists use more than any other to verify their conclusions is the experimental method, which we will examine closely. The observations that S-R psychologists make can be made in free situations—that is, situations where the observer does not try to control the environmental conditions—or, using the experimental method, in situations where the observer can control and intentionally modify one or more environmental conditions.

Consider an example. Suppose you knew that eight-year-old children on the average could read more proficiently than four-year-old children, and you wanted to know why this is so. One answer might be that the older children have had four more years of reading instruction than have the four-year-olds. Is this explanation true? A count of the number of years of reading instruction for children from the two age groups would probably show it is— but true in a weak sense because there are so many other experiences that eight-year-olds have more of than have four-year-olds. For instance, eight-year-olds have eaten more breakfast cereal, and a count of the amount of the cereal eaten in the two age groups would show that this apparently nonsensical idea is at least as true an explanation of differences in reading proficiency as the reading instruction explanation. Such an explanation is weak because it does not persuade us that it designates the factor really responsible for the observed age difference in reading proficiency.

The experimental method of testing explanations is stronger. The method consists of designating a factor as responsible for a phenomenon and then manipulating that factor to determine its effect on the phenomenon. In the present example, a relevant experiment might be as follows. If it is the amount of reading instruction that is responsible for the superior proficiency observed in eight-year-olds, then providing the same amount of instruction to four-year-olds should eliminate the difference. To evaluate this idea, we might randomly divide a set of four-year-olds into two groups—the first undergoing an intensive program that condenses into six months the reading instruction usually given in the first three grades of school, the second being given a similar program of schooling but with no reading instruction. We would have as a third group some eight-year-olds given the normal amount of reading instruction, which we can compare with the two four-year-old groups. Ordinarily, the instructed four-year-olds would be called the *treatment* or *experimental* group, the uninstructed four-year-olds would be called the *baseline* group, and the eight-year-olds would be called simply a *comparison* group.

At the end of the six months, all groups would be observed in the same situation, each child asked to read aloud the same five pages of a reading text. We might observe the number of errors made in reading the selection and the amount of time required to complete the reading. If the specially instructed four-year-olds read as well as the eight-year-olds (and, of course, better than the four-year-olds in the baseline condition), it would be persuasive evidence that the difference between four- and eight-year-olds in reading proficiency is due to the greater amount of reading instruction usually given the eight-year-olds.

Observations made in this manner fall in the domain of the experimental method because the factor designated as responsible for the phenomenon is *manipulated* and because all other factors are held constant. Here the factor manipulated was amount of reading instruction: the experimental group received the instruction, the baseline group did not. Other factors were held constant in two ways: first, the children in the baseline group were given a program of schooling exactly like that given the treatment group, except for the reading instruction itself; second, the four-year-olds in the two groups were assured of being initially equivalent by being randomly assigned. Thus, the treatment and baseline groups differed only in the factor manipulated, reading instruction, while in all other factors they were the same.

The comparison group of eight-year-olds permits us to decide whether or not the ordinary differences in amount of reading instruction between four- and eight-year-olds provides a full explanation of their differences in reading proficiency. If the results of the experiment show that the treatment group of four-year-olds performs as well as the eight-year-olds, the explanation will have been verified. If the treatment group performs no better than the baseline group of four-year-olds, the explanation will have been falsified. Without the comparison group of eight-year-olds, however, we could not tell whether reading instruction accounts for all or only part of the difference between four- and eight-year-olds. The treatment group of four-year-olds might perform substantially better than the baseline group of four-year-olds but not as well as the comparison group of eight-year-olds. In the case of this outcome, we might conclude that differences in reading instruction explain part of the original difference but not all of it. For example, to be fully effective, reading instruction might have to be spaced more slowly than it was in the intensive six-month program given to the treatment group. Or it might be that no amount or type of reading instruction can make four-year-olds into eight-year-old readers because there is no way to provide experimentally the maturation or growth that takes place normally during that four years of the life span.

These possible explanations of the results of one experiment suggest other experimental studies to verify them. The point of the example is that learning psychologists use the experimental method, in which factors are manipulated and held constant, in order to test the validity of their ideas for explaining interesting phenomena.

These two features of the methods used by S-R psychologists—detailed description and experimental manipulation—are largely responsible for the contributions of S-R theory to understanding human behavior.

SUMMARY

This chapter described the S-R point of view for understanding human beings, a view that focuses on behavior and its two determinants—environmental conditions and past learning. In applying this viewpoint to the problem of understanding intellectual development, we emphasized the principles of learning because intellectual development is seen as a product of the accumulated results of learning.

Stimulus-response theory began with the British Empiricists, who provided the philosophical background for the formulation of learning principles in terms of processes of association. In the early 1900s Pavlov identified the contiguity of external stimuli and Thorndike identified the after-effects of responses as major determinants of associations. These contributions, along with Watson's insistence that behavior is the object of understanding in psychology, formed the major propositions of early versions of S-R theory. In this period, environmental conditions were believed to be the principal determinants of behavior. Today it is believed that internal conditions, the results of previous learning, also profoundly influence behavior. Throughout these periods, S-R psychologists have used experimental methods to evaluate hypotheses drawn from their theories.

3

BASIC CONCEPTS AND PRINCIPLES IN STIMULUS-RESPONSE THEORY

Preview

This chapter introduces many S-R terms useful in understanding human behavior. The basic elements are stimuli and responses, of which there are many kinds: overt–covert, conditioned–unconditioned.

One important class of stimuli is the reinforcers, positive or negative, primary or secondary. We will describe respondent and operant conditioning, two ways of forming associations. We will distinguish between learning and performance and discuss extinction and the related concepts of unlearning, inhibition, and interference. Finally, we will show how past learning affects performance and subsequent learning, using the concepts of generalization (primary and secondary), and transfer (positive–negative, specific–generalized, vertical–horizontal).

PRIMARY UNITS: STIMULI AND RESPONSES

The two fundamental S-R concepts of *stimulus* and *response* are difficult to define in simple terms. Loosely, a stimulus is an event that an outside observer can *designate* and that he *hypothesizes* has an effect on the behavior of the person he is observing. Both parts are important. *Designatability* limits the events to those the observer can specifically point to, either directly or by a procedure that can be followed to point to the event. For example, to designate the stimulus for a campus riot as "something in the air" would not be acceptable, whereas "the report of a rifle shot" would be, since it is designatable.

But the number of designatable events that occur in the vicinity of any response is usually enormous, and the event designated the stimulus must be selected from this pool according to some criterion. Choosing a criterion is a problem because of the relationship of the term "stimulus" to the term "response": if a stimulus is defined solely according to whether a response is associated with it, then the terms stimulus and response end up referring to the same thing. Thus, events designated as stimuli are those hypothesized by the observer to occasion a response—that is, a change in the behavior of the person being observed. Whether the hypothesis is correct can then be assessed by experiments in which the presumed stimulus is made present or absent. If the response occurs when the stimulus is present but not when it is absent, the hypothesis is supported; if the response occurs when the presumed stimulus is absent, the hypothesis is shown to be wrong. In summary, stimuli are *designatable* events that have either a demonstrated or a hypothesized *effect on responses.*

Overt versus Covert Stimuli

The views of Watson imply that those stimuli of concern to S-R psychologists are mainly external to the organism being observed. But it is now recognized that events that control behavior may be internal as well—indeed, for human behavior, probably a large proportion of them are internal.

For example, you may have had the experience of sitting down to write a long-overdue letter to a friend in the absence of any external event that could be identified as the direct occasion or stimulus for your decision. Nevertheless, you may be able to identify an internal stimulus, such as recalling the letter you received from him four months ago. (The problem of designatability raised by the concept of internal stimuli will be discussed shortly.) Although this recollection may have been the direct stimulus for your action, the stimulus for the recollection may have been something external, such as hearing a song containing your friend's name played on the radio.

S-R psychologists call external stimuli, such as the song, *overt* stimuli and internal stimuli, such as the recollection of the friend's letter, *covert* or *mediating* stimuli. *Covert* means that such stimuli are not open to direct observation by an outside observer. The adjective *mediating* is used to reflect the presumption that internal stimuli such as memories act as links, or *mediators,* between overt stimuli and behavior.

Overt versus Covert Responses

Defining the concept of response is as difficult as defining "stimulus." A response is an act, reaction, or specific piece of behavior of the person being observed. Like stimuli, responses must be designatable, either directly or indirectly. Unlike stimuli, however, a response can often be identified without reference to the event that occasions it. In contrast, a stimulus is not a stimulus unless it occasions a response. An outside observer could easily identify your writing a letter of reply to your friend as a response, although he might have great difficulty designating the stimulus that prompted it.

Responses are *overt* if they are identifiable through direct observation and *covert* or *mediating* if they are not. This classification is similar to that for stimuli because responses are thought to serve often not only the function of a response but also the function of a stimulus. In the letter-writing example, the recollection of your friend's old letter may be classified as a response to the stimulus of the song containing the friend's name. But, as we noted, this recollection may also be construed as a stimulus for the response of writing a reply. Thus, if it is internal or covert, the same event may serve two functions —a response function and a stimulus function.

By admitting that stimuli and responses can be covert, S-R theorists shoulder a heavy burden, owing to the criterion of designatability. They must be careful to designate overt stimuli and responses in such a way that outside observers can agree on their identity; even greater care is needed when the stimuli and responses are covert. To appreciate this, consider again the letter-writing example. The hypothesis was that the overt stimulus, your friend's name in a song, evoked the covert response of recalling his recent letter, and that this response stimulated you to the act of replying to the letter. Note that the hypothesis posits two links or connections: one between hearing your friend's name and your recall of his letter; the other between your recall of his letter and your writing a reply. The S-R psychologist's task is to verify independently that these links exist—that is, to determine whether you recall your friend's letter when you hear his name and to show that your recalling the letter is a sufficient stimulus to make you write a reply. For instance, another way of prompting you to recall the letter would be to show you the letter. If seeing it did not result in your writing a reply, the hypothesis that recall of the letter stimulated writing a reply would be implausible. Thus, the criterion of designatability applies to covert, as well as to overt, stimuli and responses.

The two terms stimulus and response, and all their modifiers, are the primary units of analysis in S-R theory. When an S-R psychologist sets out to understand a phenomenon, his first task is to identify the *behavior,* that is, the *responses,* that comprise the phenomenon, and to identify the *stimuli,* that is, the *conditions* that affect the behavior. For example, a statement like "Children learn more from movies than from books" would not be acceptable to an S-R theorist. It would require several steps to convert that statement into a form so that he could identify the behavior and the conditions that make up the phenomenon. First, he would have to translate the phrase "Children learn more" into specific responses, such as reactions to test questions about the contents of specific books and movies. Then he would have to analyze the essential characteristics of movies and books presumed to be responsible for differences in responses to the test questions. He would then formulate hypotheses about how these essential characteristics of the stimulus materials relate to performance on the test, specifying the conditions in which books would produce more correct responses and the conditions under which movies would produce more correct responses. Finally, he would test these hypotheses by performing experiments in which he would manipulate the essential features of the stimuli (and probably the character of the test questions as well) to determine which ones were responsible for differences in the number of correct responses made. Thus, for any phenomenon, the S-R psychologist believes he can achieve understanding only by *defining, specifying, analyzing, hypothesizing,* and *verifying* experimentally his analyses and hypotheses.

ASSOCIATIONS

Stimuli and responses are the primary units into which an S-R psychologist analyzes a phenomenon. But as we showed, to understand a phenomenon, one must do more than simply specify its components as stimuli and responses; he must specify the relationships among these units. In the simple case of a single stimulus and a single response, the relationship is the direct connection between the two. This connection is termed an *association.* When an association is established, the designated response will occur when the stimulus occurs. Stated another way, the stimulus *controls* the response when they are associated: when the stimulus is present, the response is made; when the stimulus is absent, the response is not made. For example, when the bell is rung, the dog salivates; when it is not rung, he does not.

We will shortly discuss some principles of S-R theory that greatly qualify this simple single stimulus–single response case, but it illustrates the fundamental notion that behavior is the product of connections between stimuli and responses. Note that the concept of an association is mainly a definition, one that is tightly bound up with the definitions of a stimulus and a response. In contrast, the concept we turn to next is not entirely definitional

—it has the status of a factor that is believed by many to determine the formation of associations.

REINFORCEMENT

Stimulus, response, and association are useful concepts regardless of the particular kind of S-R theory espoused, but a fourth concept, *reinforcement,* is important in some theories but not in others. We have already discussed a closely related concept in Thorndike's contributions to S-R psychology.

In Thorndike's view, the after-effects of a response determine the strength of an association between a stimulus and the response. Thorndike identified two classes of after-effects: satisfiers and annoyers. Satisfiers were believed to strengthen associations; annoyers were believed to weaken them. Reinforcement has much the same meaning, although its current definitions are more sophisticated than were Thorndike's.

Reinforcers are events that affect the probability that a particular response will be made again. If an event increases the probability that a response will be repeated, it is a positive reinforcer. For example, suppose a kindergarten child points to the larger of two triangles, whereupon the teacher praises him and the child proceeds to designate the larger triangle again; if the teacher does not praise him, he points to the smaller triangle. In this example, the event of being praised is a positive reinforcer because it increases the probability that the initial pointing response will be made again.

Positive Reinforcement, Negative Reinforcement, and Punishment

Much of our knowledge about reinforcement comes from B. F. Skinner,[1] who identified a number of different reinforcers, including positive and negative reinforcers. If the *occurrence* of an event increases the probability that a response will be repeated, it is called a positive reinforcer. If the *termination* of an event increases the probability that a response will be repeated, the event is called a negative reinforcer.

The difference between positive and negative reinforcers can be illustrated as follows. Suppose the kindergarten teacher praises the child whenever he selects the larger figure from the pair of triangles. If the child then selects larger figures more frequently, the teacher's praise is a positive reinforcer. But suppose the child is forced to stand in front of the class until he selects the larger triangle, and only then is he allowed to sit down. If he selects larger figures more frequently thereafter, the termination of the demand that he stand before the class is a negative reinforcer.

Negative reinforcement is often confused with punishment, but the concepts differ in an important way: a negative reinforcer is an event that *increases* the probability that a response will be repeated; a punisher is an event that *decreases* the probability a response will be repeated. To force the kindergarten child to stand in front of the room would be punishment if it was done *after* he chose the wrong figure and if it *decreased* the frequency with which he subsequently selected wrong figures. Notice that a punisher does not increase the probability that the correct response will be made—it simply *inhibits* the response it follows. If the punisher is not coupled with a reinforcer for the correct response, the child might simply inhibit all responses. In contrast, terminating the requirement that the child stand before the class would be regarded as a negative reinforcer, not a punisher, because it results in an increased probability that the child will repeat the response of choosing the larger figure.

Another issue about reinforcers is how they originate—that is, how initially neutral events acquire reinforcing power. Some events are natural reinforcers—they increase the probability of responses they follow—for example, food when a person is hungry or water when he is thirsty. With human intellectual behavior, however, we usually cannot identify natural reinforcers that are affecting the probability of a particular response. In fact, one difficulty in understanding intellectual behavior is the unpredictability of the character of reinforcing events. For example, it is not obvious that the probability of the kindergartener's choosing the correct figure should be increased by terminating the requirement that he stand in front of the room. Indeed, for some children, being allowed to stand before the class might act as a positive reinforcer. To understand how such differences between children might occur, it is necessary to understand how events become reinforcers. According to S-R theory, an event becomes a reinforcer because of learning. Thus, to explain how reinforcers originate, we must first examine two fundamental learning processes.

FUNDAMENTAL LEARNING PROCESSES: OPERANT AND RESPONDENT CONDITIONING

The two fundamental learning processes in S-R theories are *operant* conditioning and *respondent* conditioning. In operant conditioning, the principal cause of learning is the *aftereffect* of a response; that is, the probability a response will occur is determined by its *consequences*—does it or does it not lead to reinforcement? In addition, in operant conditioning, the response is *not directly caused* or elicited by a stimulus. Even so, such responses can be *controlled* by stimuli. For example, the kindergarten child will not make the response of pointing to the correct figure unless some stimulus containing the two figures is available for pointing. But, given the presence of such a stimulus, the issue of whether the child will make the pointing response is decided by the reinforcing effects the child has previously experienced for making the response. Another feature of operant conditioning is that the responses that are conditioned are usually voluntary in nature—figuratively speaking, the person can control them.

In respondent conditioning, by contrast, the responses are usually involuntary—they are difficult to bring under voluntary control. One reason is that such responses are caused by stimuli: a puff of air to the eye elicits an eyeblink; the presence of food evokes increased salivation. Respondent conditioning is the form of learning extensively investigated by Pavlov; as he demonstrated, an event that is initially neutral, such as a bell ringing, can come to be a conditioned stimulus for a response, such as salivation.

Now we can apply these fundamental learning principles to the problem of how reinforcers are made. Some events already have reinforcing power at the beginning of a person's life; they are, in effect, universal satisfiers, evoking unconditioned responses in virtually all infants regardless of environmental circumstances. One example is the event of an infant's ingesting milk: if he cries and as a result is given milk, it is likely he will cry more frequently. Thus, the milk is a reinforcer; it is a consequence of the crying response.

But note that the milk is also an unconditioned stimulus: it automatically evokes several responses such as salivation, swallowing, and, eventually, satiety. Therefore, these responses can be conditioned to other stimuli repeatedly presented in contiguity with the milk. For example, infants are typically held in such a way that they continually view their mother's face while they are drinking. The responses to the milk, such as the termination of stomach contractions caused by hunger, can thereby be conditioned to the stimulus of the mother's face. When this happens, the mother's face can begin to function like a positive reinforcer; the probability of a crying response can be increased by seeing the mother's face as well as by being fed.

This same analysis applies to the example of the kindergartener who was more apt to point to the larger of two figures when this was praised by his teacher. Such praise may be viewed as a positive reinforcer. Suppose now that the teacher gives the child a workbook of pairs of geometrical forms and tells him to circle the larger figure in each pair. Suppose also that every time the child circles the larger figures in all the pairs on a page, the teacher not only praises him but also draws a star at the top of the page. In time, the child's responses to praise should be conditioned to the teacher's marks on workbook papers, so that the marks become a substitute for spoken praise. By this process, the marks have become positive reinforcers in their own right; they too can increase the probability of the pointing response, even in the absence of spoken praise.

An alternative outcome is to imagine a teacher who feels that children should be supported emotionally when they make erroneous responses. Thus, if the kindergartener mistakenly circles the incorrect figure, the teacher, wishing to reassure him while helping him learn his response was incorrect, would praise him profusely for trying hard and finish by saying, "But that was the wrong one, Chuck." If Chuck continues to make incorrect choices precisely because it produces a positive reinforcer (the praise), and if the teacher repeatedly delivers praise and the sentence, "But that was the wrong one, Chuck," the sentence itself might come to be a positive reinforcer. The teacher's verbal correction, far from helping Chuck make the right response, would increase the probability he would make the incorrect response. To carry the example another step, imagine the bewilderment of Chuck's next teacher, who finds that telling him he has made an incorrect response actually increases the frequency of the behavior she intends to weaken. To deal with this situation, the teacher would need to be aware that what is poison to her is candy to the child.

As we will see, the S-R concepts of stimuli, responses, associations, and reinforcement, and the principles of operant and respondent conditioning, are inadequate to describe many important phenomena, such as the following: what a child is known to have learned does not always show in his behavior, having learned one association sometimes affects the ease of learning another one, and when a child has learned one association, it often appears that he has learned other ones as well.

LEARNING VERSUS PERFORMANCE

Consider the fact that learning an association does not guarantee that the response will invariably be made to the stimulus. For example, suppose we know that kindergartener Chuck has formed an association between the instruction to select the larger of the pair of figures, the presence of two figures differing in size, and the response of pointing to the larger one. We know this because we have repeatedly observed him standing before the class, under these conditions, selecting the larger figure. Now imagine that for the next several days the teacher gives Chuck the instruction and displays of figures at his seat, and that during this period he does not consistently select the larger figure. A new observer might not believe us if we told him Chuck had learned to discriminate larger from smaller figures. This kind of inconsistency has prompted S-R psychologists to distinguish *learning* and *performance.* Simply put, the distinction recognizes that people learn more than they often act like they have learned. It emphasizes that a child exhibits what he has learned under some circumstances and does not under others. Thus, one must always be cautious in stating what a child has or has not learned; one must specify the conditions under which the child will show what he has learned. This distinction is similar to one you will encounter in Part 2 between competence and performance—that is, between what a child knows and the knowledge he exhibits in his behavior.

The distinction is really very familiar, as mothers show when they answer a compliment like "Your daughter's an angel" with "Yes, she is here, but you should see her at home." A teacher shows his awareness of the distinction when he complains a standardized test is bad because one of his students scored poorly on it, when he knows, from the child's behavior in class, that he has learned what the test says he has not. But sometimes persons who deal with children are not aware of the distinction—as when a teacher says she is shocked by the news that a child who has never read proficiently in class has constructed a bomb by reading a chemistry lab manual.

S-R theory explains inconsistencies between learning and performance in three ways—by extinction, inhibition, and incentive stimuli. *Extinction* means that associations can not only be learned but also unlearned. *Inhibition* means that a learned association may survive intact but the responses involved may fail to occur. *Incentive conditions* means that the apparent stimulus in an association may not be the only stimulus necessary for the response to occur.

We will consider each explanation in turn.

Extinction

Learned associations are thought to be strengthened by reinforcement and weakened by the cessation of reinforcement. Extinction refers to the process of associations being weakened by the cessation of reinforcement.

In respondent conditioning, a conditioned response can be extinguished by the repeated presence of the conditioned stimulus without the presence of the unconditioned stimulus. An operant response becomes extinguished if it is made repeatedly but never followed by a reinforcing event.

For example, respondent conditioning is the process that established the mark of a star on Chuck's worksheet as a reinforcer—the mark was presented repeatedly in contiguity with praise from Chuck's kindergarten teacher, the original reinforcer. If the teacher then continues to mark stars on worksheets, but never again along with praise, the association between the two events will extinguish and the stars will lose their reinforcing power. In operant conditioning, Chuck's response was to circle the larger of two figures on worksheets. If he makes this response but his teacher consistently fails to reinforce it through praise, the probability of the response will decrease and eventually the association will extinguish. If so, judging by Chuck's performance, it will appear that he has not learned to discriminate larger from smaller figures.

A common way to describe extinction of responses is to say that the responses have been forgotten. In fact, extinction is one way the phenomenon of forgetting is explained in S-R theories. Suppose a child learns to spell *doctor* incorrectly as *d-o-c-t-e-r*. If he misspells the word repeatedly but the response does not lead to reinforcement, it will eventually extinguish—that spelling of the word will be forgotten. In effect, he has unlearned a previously learned association.

Inhibition

If learning does not show in performance, it may not be lost or extinguished but inhibited. That is, an association can remain intact but the response involved may still fail to occur. An inhibited response can occur again, without further learning; an extinguished response cannot.

One factor believed to produce inhibition is *punishment*. If a well-learned response is followed by punishment, it may inhibit the response; when no longer followed by punishment, it will probably occur again. For instance, a first-grade child might be punished so severely for talking in class without permission that he would avoid making such responses again so long as the teacher is present. But when he enters another class where talking is not punished, he might well begin to talk again. Here the punishment is thought to inhibit responses, not to weaken associations. To S-R theorists the reason is that associations are weakened only by the repetition of responses in the absence of reinforcement. In contrast, when punishment is successful, responses are not even made; thus, the relevant associations cannot be extinguished.[2]

A second factor believed to produce inhibition is *interference*, which is thought to occur (1) when there are previously established associations between a single stimulus and two different responses, but (2) only one of the two responses can be made in the presence of the stimulus. If the two responses are incompatible, the occurrence of the response more strongly associated with the stimulus tends to inhibit the occurrence of the other response. For example, suppose the child who has learned to spell doctor incorrectly as *d-o-c-t-e-r* then learns to spell it correctly. Provided he does not make the old response (*d-o-c-t-e-r*) while learning the new spelling, the old association will not extinguish or be unlearned. So when he takes a spelling test a week later, the two spellings will interfere with one another, and he will give only the stronger of the two. If the stronger of the two is the older one, the new spelling will be inhibited. Thus, from what can be observed in the child's spelling test performance, it can appear that he has not learned the new response. In fact, however, the child has simply forgotten the new response in the sense that the old spelling inhibits the new one by means of interference.

Incentive Conditions

Whether a learned association will show up in performance often depends on *incentive conditions*, which tell a person when there will be a payoff for his behavior.

Suppose a child learns to read aloud in front of his parents who, despite his errors, praise him for his renditions. Suppose in school the child fails to receive this kind of praise from his teacher when he reads aloud. Then, given a common set of stimuli—a printed page in a book and the question, "David, do you want to read aloud?"—the child might respond differently in the presence of the teacher than in the presence of his parents. His parents' presence will signal that reinforcement will follow his reading performance, whereas the teacher's presence will signal it will not. The printed page and the request are stimuli, the responses are reading aloud, and an association has been learned between these stimuli and responses. Even so, this learning does not always show in performance: David's responses occur in the presence of the parents but not in the presence of the teacher. In short, the parents are incentive stimuli for the responses of reading aloud, the teacher is not.

An event is thought to acquire the power of an incentive stimulus by respondent conditioning. For example, because David invariably associated his parents with the reinforcer of praise, his responses to praise could be conditioned to his parents' presence. The parents thereby became incentive stimuli. David's learned associations between the book and reading aloud were exhibited when these incentive stimuli were present but not when they were absent. Thus, discrepancies between learning and performance can often be explained by incentive conditions.

Clearly, we cannot use a child's performance as an infallible guide to determine whether he has learned the associations necessary for the performance. The child may have accomplished the learning, but the associations may have been extinguished, or the associated responses may be inhibited, or the incentive conditions may not be sufficient to elicit the performance.

GENERALIZATION

Sometimes responses are made to stimuli even though direct associations between them have not been learned. For example, if we make a tone become a conditioned stimulus by repeatedly presenting it to a dog in contiguity with food powder, not only will the original tone come to evoke a salivation response, but other tones, of different pitch, will also evoke such a response—even though they have not been specifically presented with either the food powder or the original tone. S-R theorists call this kind of phenomenon *generalization.*

Generalization is of two kinds. *Stimulus generalization* means the same response is made to other stimuli that are different from the stimulus the response was originally connected to. *Response generalization* means that a stimulus evokes not only the response originally learned with it, but other, similar responses as well. For example, by a process of operant conditioning, Chuck formed a strong habit of pointing to the larger of pairs of geometric figures. But if he also circles larger figures, under the same circumstances that he points to them, we can say that response generalization occurred.

S-R psychologists make a further distinction between primary and secondary generalization. In the example of the salivating dog, the bells differed in the frequency of the tone they emitted but were otherwise the same. The set of stimulus events that all evoked the same response were similar in a way that can be specified easily; they all fell on the same physical dimension. Stimulus generalization of this kind is called *primary* generalization: the more similar a new stimulus is to one already associated with a response, the more likely the new stimulus will also evoke the response. The key term is "similar"; similarity is easy to define for primary stimulus generalization: it refers to the physical proximity of two stimuli, such as the frequency of two tones. Two high-frequency tones are more similar than a high- and a low-frequency tone.

Secondary generalization is more complicated to explain because no clear physical dimension can be used to gauge the similarity of stimuli. For example, if a child learns to make certain responses to his mother, he may for a time also make the same responses to other adults, without additional learning. Here we cannot specify the degree of similarity among the stimuli in this set—that is, adult human beings—with reference to particular physical dimensions. S-R theory explains such phenomena by events internal to the learner. Such events and their links are called *mediation.*

MEDIATION

Mediation is the mechanism through which past learning determines the responses that will be evoked by new stimuli. A stimulus can evoke more than one response, and some of these responses are peculiar to that stimulus, but others are not. For example, some of the overt responses of gripping a ball to throw it are the same with many different balls—for example, the exertion of finger pressure on the surface of the ball. But other responses vary with the type of ball to be thrown—a baseball is grasped more tightly than a basketball.

Similarly, a single stimulus can evoke many covert responses—responses that cannot be observed directly—and some may vary from stimulus to stimulus, but others may be the same. Thus, several covert responses evoked by two different stimuli may be identical, even though the objective characteristics of the stimuli may differ widely. For instance, the praise a child receives from his mother and the praise he receives from a new adult acquaintance may evoke in him some of the same covert responses, such as feelings of warmth.

Identical covert responses to different stimuli *mediate* secondary stimulus generalization; that is, they bridge the gap between an original stimulus and other related ones. In secondary generalization, similarity does not mean physical proximity but the amount of overlap between the responses to two different stimuli. In other words, the larger the proportion of responses that are identical, the more similar are the two stimuli, and the greater the probability of generalization. For example, the covert responses of the child to the praise of his mother and to the praise of a new acquaintance are similar in this sense, and it is likely that an overt response the child has learned to make to the mother will generalize to the acquaintance. Thus, when the acquaintance is about to leave after a visit, the child might want to kiss her goodbye, just as he does with his mother when she leaves. The child's identical covert responses (feelings of warmth) to the two adults mediate the generalization, so that an overt response (kiss) is given to a stimulus (acquaintance), even though a direct association between the acquaintance and the kiss has never been learned.

Mediation is an important element in another set of S-R principles known as *transfer,* which are related to secondary generalization.

TRANSFER

The principles of transfer deal with the effects of previous experience on later learning and thus are particularly important for those concerned with the success of education.

All of us must learn a large number of skills and a great deal of information in order to manage the enormous variety of life's problems. There simply would not be enough time for all of this if every attempt at learning skills of a particular type required as long as the learning of the first skill of that type. A child may be given specific practice at solving a particular type of arithmetic problem, and he may master the skills involved very slowly. Yet subsequently we can readily observe the child learning to solve another type of arithmetic problem much more rapidly than the first type. In such a case, the task for the psychologist is to explain why the student performs better in learning to solve the second kind of problem than he did on the first. The concept often used to refer to such a phenomenon is that of *positive transfer* from past learning. In other cases, a student might perform more poorly than would be expected on the basis of previously learned associations. The concept that designates this phenomenon is *negative transfer* from past learning.

As mentioned, transfer and generalization are related. Both concern the effect of previous learning on performance in the presence of new stimuli. In addition, explanations of both phenomena depend on the assumption that the effects of previous learning are mediated by *identical elements*. As we have seen, the secondary generalization of a response to a new stimulus is mediated by identical covert responses to the two stimuli. In one important respect, however, the two principles are different. The principles of stimulus generalization are applicable to the occurrence of a previously learned response to a new stimulus, *in the absence of additional learning*. The principles of transfer are applicable to cases where previous learning exerts effects *on subsequent learning*.

Specific versus Generalized Transfer

Another important distinction is the difference between *generalized* and *specific* transfer. Specific transfer refers to cases where particular associations learned previously affect the learning of another association. For example, suppose we ask two children to learn to pronounce the printed word *COWBOY,* and that one student has previously learned an association between the printed word *COW* and the vocalization response "cow," while the other has not. If the first student then learns the response "cowboy" to the stimulus *COWBOY* more rapidly than does the second student, it might be explained as a case of positive specific transfer: the previously learned association between *COW* and "cow" has transferred to the connection between *COWBOY* and "cowboy."

The concept of specific transfer is of little help in explaining how the learning of the skills to perform one task affects the learning of skills to perform a different task. Thus, we have the concept of *generalized* transfer, which refers to cases where persons learn skills applicable to more than single associations. For example, in the course of learning to play a particular athletic game, such as baseball, a person not only learns the movements associated with that game but also skills that assist him in learning the movements required for other related games, such as tennis. He learns how to coordinate the movement of his arm muscles with the information from his eye about the distance, speed, and trajectory of an oncoming ball. More broadly, he learns techniques for conditioning himself physically for the exertion that is required in playing a demanding sport. In learning to perform one task, a person often acquires skills that are essential components in learning to perform a variety of other tasks. The application of such skills to the task of learning new associations is called generalized transfer.

Generalized transfer is appropriate for describing the higher order skills required to learn school subjects as well as athletic games. Educators usually hope that instruction in specific subject matter contents will assist the student to develop skills for learning other subject matters. In other words, the teacher hopes that the student will learn skills as well as content.

Horizontal and Vertical Transfer

Most examples of transfer we have discussed so far represent *horizontal transfer*—they refer to cases where a skill or an association learned in one task or context is used in another task or context. The critical feature of this kind of transfer is that the order of learning makes little difference: there is as much reason to expect transfer from tennis to baseball as there is to expect transfer from baseball to tennis.

In contrast, *vertical* transfer refers to cases where the order of learning is crucial, where one association or skill is literally prerequisite for learning another, as algebra is a prerequisite for calculus. A precise example is when a child must learn to discriminate between figures having different numbers of sides before he can learn concepts such as square and triangle.

SUMMARY

This chapter introduced many S-R concepts that are useful in understanding human behavior. The basic elements are stimuli and responses, of which there are many kinds: overt–covert, conditioned–unconditioned. One important class of stimuli are the reinforcers, positive or negative, primary or secondary. We also distinguished between respondent and operant conditioning, two ways connections or associations are formed. We emphasized the fact that a person may have learned more than he demonstrates in his behavior at any one time. We distinguished between learning and performance and discussed extinction and the related concepts of unlearning, inhibition, and interference. Finally, we showed how past learning affects performance and subsequent learning, using the concepts of generalization and transfer and their subvarieties: primary and secondary generalization; positive and negative transfer; specific and generalized transfer; vertical and horizontal transfer. We explained that the mechanism by which these effects of past learning come into play in new situations is mediation.

4

A STIMULUS-RESPONSE MODEL OF BEHAVIOR

Preview

An S-R model of behavior has three components: (1) behavior, consisting of responses; (2) external conditions, consisting of initiating and reinforcing stimuli; and (3) internal conditions, consisting of the results of previous learning.

We will show how these components are related.

We will also explore, using an extended example of children's problem-solving behavior, a learning hierarchy consisting of eight types of learning, in order to show how each level of performance depends on prior learning of a lower type.

THE BASIC STIMULUS-RESPONSE MODEL

In order to organize S-R concepts and principles into a coherent picture of the processes that result in behavior, we need to use the concepts and principles to construct a model of behavior. Here we will describe the ways the model can be used to understand behavior that occurs in a given segment of time.

As we describe the model, let us think of an example that illustrates the components of the model. Imagine a schoolroom where the children are busy with a project—arranging for the cultivation of a tomato plant. Each child has a plant in a flower pot filled with soil and a small jar to use in watering and fertilizing the plant. Since the children brought their jars from home, they vary widely in size and shape. Suppose now that the teacher produces a large bottle of liquid fertilizer and directs the children to transfer equal amounts from the bottle to their jars so that they can mix it with water and pour it on their plants. The teacher then poses a problem: how can the class make sure that every child receives an equal amount of the liquid fertilizer? Some children suggest that all jars be placed on the table and the fertilizer poured into each one until it reaches the same level in every jar. Other children suggest that a single jar be used to transfer the fertilizer from the bottle to each individual jar so that the amount in each is always a transfer-jar full. The elements in this example are illustrated in Figure 4.1. Both methods are tried and for each one some of the children complain that they have not been given their fair share. What is the framework offered by S-R theory for explaining the children's behavior?

Figure 4.1. Objects and containers used for cultivating tomato plants.

Behavior

We must first describe the phenomena in very specific behavioral terms. In an S-R model, the primary units for such behavioral designations are, of course, responses. Here at least five responses are of interest: (1) voicing the judgment that two amounts of liquid in containers of varying shape are equal when their heights are equivalent; (2) the judgment that they are unequal under these circumstances; (3) the judgment that the two amounts are equal when poured from the single transfer jar; (4) the judgment that they are unequal under these circumstances; and (5) the response of voicing the suggestion that a transfer jar be used. Thus, an S-R model of behavior leads us initially to focus on the task of analyzing behavior into the responses that compose it.

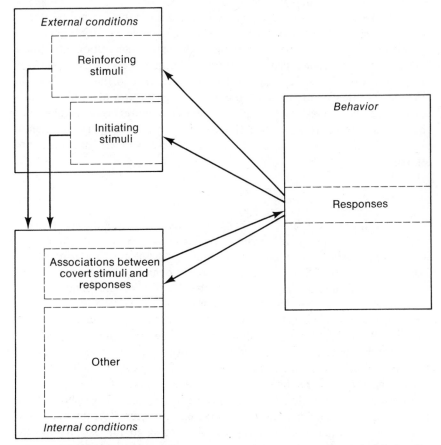

Figure 4.2. Schematic diagram of a stimulus-response model of behavior.

In Figure 4.2 an S-R model is represented schematically. Three components of the model are displayed: behavior, external conditions, and internal conditions. Each component can be further analyzed; behavior, for example, is composed of responses. The arrows represent ways the three major components are related. Shortly we will examine these relationships, but first let us discuss the remaining two major components, *external conditions* and *internal conditions*.

External Conditions

Just as behavior can be analyzed into the responses that compose it, so external conditions can be analyzed into the stimuli that compose them. In Chapter 3, we saw that such stimuli can be classified in a number of ways, including both conditioned and unconditioned varieties. For the model, we must emphasize another distinction among the stimuli that define the external conditions for behavior, namely, stimuli that *occasion* the behavioral response and stimuli that are the *aftereffects* of the responses.

Consider the fertilizer-jar example. The stimuli that form the external conditions of the five responses we have listed include *initiating* ones—the tomato plants, fertilizer container, the jars, the teacher's question, and so on. The external conditions also include the consequences of the responses— *reinforcing stimuli* provided by the teacher's reaction to the responses, the reactions of other children, and the amount of fertilizer a child obtains as a consequence of his responses. Thus, the external conditions consist of stimuli that occasion responses—whether they evoke them or simply initiate them— and of stimuli that occur as the aftereffects of responses, that is, reinforcing stimuli.

Internal Conditions

The internal conditions for behavior mainly consist of the accumulated residue of past learning. As Figure 4.2 indicates, these internal conditions include previously learned associations among covert stimuli and responses. For some versions of S-R theory, the model is complete; for others it is not, and this is indicated in the figure by "Other" in the internal conditions.

Referring to the fertilizer-jar example, let us make some inferences about what kinds of internal conditions would occasion the responses observed. In the S-R model, this means that we must identify internal stimuli and responses that have been associated because of previous learning. Recall that the external conditions included the stimuli of the jars, the liquid fertilizer bottle, and the teacher's direction that equal amounts of fertilizer should be transferred to every child's jar. One observable response of the children was to suggest that all jars be placed on the table and the fertilizer poured so that it reaches the same level in every jar. According to the S-R model, this response is produced by a combination of the external conditions—the external stimuli—and internal conditions, that is, internal stimuli and responses. Stated another way, the external stimuli do not produce the response directly but only by activating internal stimuli and responses that have been associated in previous learning.

What might these internal associations be? The implication of S-R theory is that the children have already learned to react to containers of liquids and the direction "to pour" by lifting and tilting the container; possibly these associations were originally learned in connection with bottles of juice, soft drinks, cartons of milk, and so on, in combination with the instruction "to pour" given by a parent. The theory also leads us to expect that the response of lifting and tilting such containers would generalize to a container of liquid fertilizer, even though the children may never have seen one before. Thus, one of the internal responses evoked by the external conditions consists of some representation of previously encountered stimuli—containers of liquid and the instruction "to pour." In turn, this covert response would be expected to stimulate an internal representation of the lift and tilt response. Finally, we must assume that the children have previously learned associations between internal representations of previous stimuli and responses and overt verbal utterances describing those responses, especially when asked a question. Thus, they say aloud, "Pour the liquid into the jars."

Thus far we have described a process that would account for only part of the children's response. They also said that the fertilizer should be poured into every jar until the height of liquid in every jar is equal. Without describing all of the stimulus-response links involved, we can say that they would be similar to those already described. That is, the external stimulus of the jars, the liquid, and the word "equal" would evoke internal responses representing past experience by means of the process of generalization.

Some versions of S-R theory would lead us to assume that all of the children's responses could be accounted for by individual stimulus-response connections of the kind we enumerated. But such a description would be very unwieldy; that is, we would have to specify a great many individual stimulus-response connections in order to explain the response suggesting that a transfer jar be used to equalize the amount in all the jars. Thus, we will shortly consider another version of S-R theory, which may help us understand responses that seem to depend on more complicated past learning than simple associations.

Relationships in the Basic Model

Let us now underline aspects of the basic model of behavior that are common to most versions of S-R theory. Figure 4.2 shows that the major components —behavior, internal conditions, and external conditions—are interrelated. It is important to repeat that external conditions, that is, stimuli, are related to behavior only indirectly—they must first activate internal conditions before their presence can occasion an observable external response. Also note that behavior affects both the internal conditions and the external conditions that prompted it. A response has aftereffects, thereby changing the external conditions from what they were at the outset, and it also may change the initial stimuli as well. For example, the stimulus of a full fertilizer bottle will be changed radically if the response is to empty it or to drop it on the floor.

According to S-R theory, it is also true that a response, especially in combination with its aftereffects or reinforcers, can affect the internal conditions of behavior. If a response leads to positive reinforcement, associations will be strengthened between the stimuli and responses in the chain that led to the overt response. Learning will have occurred and the internal conditions for behavior will have changed precisely because they consist of what has been learned.

The assumption in the S-R model that a response can change the internal conditions of behavior highlights the importance of the question, "What is learned?" If internal conditions are major determinants of behavior and if internal conditions largely consist of what has been learned, then it is critical to identify the content of learning. Up to now, we have implicitly accepted S-R theorists' idea that the content of learning is associations. In Chapter 3 we distinguished two kinds of associations, those brought about by operant conditioning and those brought about by respondent conditioning. We also found it necessary to accept the idea that associations between individual stimuli and responses can be chained together and can occur covertly, mediating between external conditions and behavior. But even if we understand both these kinds of learning, their elaboration by means of chaining, their augmentation by the concept of generalization, and the principle of mediation, we find it difficult to describe in a satisfactory way the complex behavior in the fertilizer-jar example. How did the children solve the problem of ensuring that each of them should obtain equal quantities of liquid fertilizer? Thus, we need to examine a version of S-R theory that answers the question "What is learned?" by specifying a variety of learning types.

EIGHT TYPES OF LEARNING

Robert Gagné, a psychologist trained in the S-R tradition, has proposed a framework that distinguishes eight different types of learning.[1] Gagné's framework names each type of learning, describes the kind of performance each type of learning makes possible, specifies the external conditions that promote each type of learning, and specifies the internal conditions necessary for each type of learning. In addition, Gagné has proposed that there are hierarchies in the various types of learning.

Table 4.1 summarizes Gagné's eight types of learning. Note how the various types differ. When the learner completes a given type of learning, it enables him to engage in a distinctive kind of performance. For example, if he learns multiple discriminations (Type 5), he can respond uniquely to each one of a set of different stimuli, whereas if he learns a concept (Type 6), he can make the same response to all of the stimuli in a particular class.

The types of learning also differ in the way external conditions promote them. Signal learning or respondent conditioning (Type 1) is promoted by repeated presentations of a neutral stimulus in contiguity with an unconditioned stimulus; stimulus-response learning or operant conditioning (Type 2) is promoted by reinforcing aftereffects of the response.

Table 4.1. Summary of Eight Types of Learning

TYPE	CONTENT OF LEARNING	CHARACTERISTIC PERFORMANCE	INTERNAL CONDITIONS	EXTERNAL CONDITIONS
8	Problem Solving	Combining two or more rules in novel way to solve a problem	Previously learned rules	Problem statement; prompts for recalling relevant rules; prompts to combination of rules
7	Rules—relationship between two or more concepts	Responding to various specific stimuli as if controlled by a rule	Previously learned concepts	Verbal statement of rule; prompts for recalling component concepts; various specific instances exemplifying rule
6	Concepts	Common response to many different stimuli that belong to same class	Previously learned discriminations	Prompting a response chain in the presence of each of many stimuli that differ in appearance but belong to same class
5	Discriminations	Distinctive response to each of two or more stimuli	Previously learned motor or verbal chains	Prompting recall of appropriate response chains; emphasizing features of stimuli that distinguish among them
4	Verbal Associates	Sequence of verbal responses to one or more stimuli	Previously learned stimulus-response connections	Presenting stimuli; prompting in sequence responses to each stimulus; reinforcement
3	Motor Chains	Sequence of motor responses	Previously learned stimulus-response connections	External stimuli as prompts for each response in chain; repetition; reinforcement
2	Stimulus-Response connections	Habitual single response in presence of stimulus	Attention to stimulus; available response	Presenting stimulus; attracting attention; immediate reinforcement
1	Signals: Respondent Conditioning	Evocation of set of responses by a previously ineffective stimulus	Previously established connection between unconditioned stimulus and unconditioned response	Repeated, contiguous presentation of unconditioned stimulus and initally ineffective stimulus

Finally, each type of learning requires a different kind of prior learning. One must learn rules (Type 7) in order to solve problems (Type 8), and he must learn concepts (Type 6) in order to learn rules, and so on. Thus, the various types of learning are distinguished by the performance they make possible, by the external conditions that promote them, and by the kind of prior learning they require.

The idea of prior learning is the key to the idea of a learning hierarchy. Except for the first type of learning, signal learning, each type depends on another type. This dependence among the types is called hierarchical because it operates in only one direction and because it is a total kind of dependence. For example, Type 6, concept learning, depends on one's having learned discriminations. But the reverse is not true; discrimination learning depends not on concept learning but on the prior learning of chains, either motor (Type 3) or verbal (Type 4). The dependency among the types is very stringent: Type 5 learning is *prerequisite* for Type 6 learning; a concept can be learned only if the relevant discriminations have been learned first. Stated another way, the learning of any one type will transfer to learning of the next higher type.

Let us now examine the types of learning and their interdependence. Using the fertilizer-jar example, we will begin at the highest level, problem solving, and trace its prerequisites to the lowest level, signal learning.

Type 8: Problem Solving

When a person solves a problem, he is jointly applying several rules to a single situation. Many different kinds of performance can result, but they have in common the fact that they would not be possible on the basis of applying a single rule. Thus, problem solving involves the combination of rules.

Clearly, to combine and apply rules to solve a problem, one must first have learned the rules; that is, the internal conditions necessary for problem solving consist of previously learned rules. The external conditions include the problem, reminders or prompts to assist the learner to recall the rules he has previously learned, and suggestions to assist the learner in combining the rules in a workable way.

How can the bottle of liquid fertilizer be divided among all the children so that each receives an equal amount? The problem is complicated by the fact that the children's jars for containing the liquid vary widely in shape and size. What rules are needed to solve this problem? One is a rule that defines amounts of liquid—that is, the rule for determining the volume of a container. Another is the rule that equal quantities result when a constant quantity is added to two or more other quantities that are initially equal. Still another is the rule that a constant is a value that does not vary, such that every instance of a constant is identical with every other instance. To apply these rules to the problem, we must, first, identify every child's jar as initially being equal in containing none of the fertilizing liquid; second, use as a transfer jar a single container that, when filled with the fertilizer and poured into the other jars, will thereby add a constant amount to them; and, third, recognize that the result will be equal amounts of fertilizer. The rule on how to determine amount is important since the height of liquid may vary so much in individual children's jars. If the child knows that volume is determined by all of the dimensions of a container, he can judge that amounts are equal even though their appearance varies with the shape and size of the jars.

The Gagné framework insists that these rules must be previously learned in order to solve the liquid fertilizer problem, but it does not mean the child must be able to state the rules verbally. So long as he behaves *as if* he knows the rules, according to the S-R view, we can infer he has learned them. Of course, he may have learned the rules but be unable to solve the problem, because he either forgot the rules or does not combine them properly. This possibility makes the external conditions for problem solving important for ensuring that learning is adequately realized in observable performance. Thus, the teacher may wish to prompt the children by reminding them of the rules for adding constants to zero and by providing a transfer jar.

Type 7: Rule Learning

In the simplest case, rule learning consists of learning a relationship between two or more concepts. In more complicated rules, the content of learning may be relationships between concepts and rules or even between simpler rules. Learning a rule enables a person to respond to a wide variety of specific situations with behavior that is controlled by a single set of concepts and their interrelations. The internal conditions necessary for learning a rule consist of the prior learning of the concepts that comprise the rule. The external conditions that promote rule learning include prompts to recall the component concepts and providing a wide variety of concrete instances that exemplify the rule.

One important rule for solving the fertilizer problem is that for determining the volume of a liquid. If the jars have a cylindrical shape, the rule for volume is made up of a relationship between two simpler rules and a concept. The simpler rules are (1) that for determining the area of a circle and (2) that for multiple addition or multiplication. The concept is that of height. Then the rule for determining the volume of liquid in a cylindrical container is to multiply the height of the liquid by the area of a circle produced by taking a horizontal slice through the cylinder. In turn, the rule for determining the area of a circle is made up of the relationship between the rule for multiplication and the concept of the radius of a circle. Similarly, the rule for multiplication is made up of the combination of the rule for addition and the concept of repetition.

The important point about rule learning is that once learned, a rule can be applied across widely differing situations, even to situations that have never been experienced before. Thus, one distinguishing characteristic of rule learning is that it exhibits transfer, horizontally, to many instances other than those present when the rule was initially learned. As we will see, this same character-istic also holds for concepts, since a rule is a combination of concepts. In the example, the children had never seen a bottle of liquid fertilizer, but they could nevertheless apply the rule for volume even though it may have originally been learned in connection with containers of milk or juice.

Type 6: Concept Learning

In Gagné's framework, one demonstrates concept learning when he makes a single response to a variety of stimuli that belong to the same class, for example, by identifying many different animals—shepherds, collies, span-iels, labradors, setters—as dogs. One important feature of concept learning is that a person does not make the response to stimuli that fall outside the class, for example, to call a horse, a cat, and a cow, "dogs." In the performance made possible by concept learning, one makes an identical response to several stimuli in a class and a different response to stimuli outside the class.

One internal condition necessary for concept learning is the prior learn-ing of discriminations (Type 5). For example, if a child cannot discriminate between a Siamese cat and an Irish Setter, he cannot learn the concept of dogs. Another precondition is the prior learning of a covert stimulus-response chain (Type 4). To learn the concept of "dogs," one must be able to discriminate between stimulus objects (for example, a spaniel and a setter) and make an association of each with the response "dogs." The response need not be verbal; it could as well be a pointing response.

Among the external conditions that promote concept learning, perhaps the most important is that there be many stimuli exemplifying the concept. In addition, as the various such examples appear, the teacher might prompt the child to make a common response; for example, the teacher encourages the child to say "dog" to each of various dogs shown him. The external conditions should also include stimuli that do *not* belong to the class defined by the concept, so as continually to remind the learner of the discriminations he has previously learned.

The heart of concept learning is that a person acquire a common internal response to many different external stimuli. He must acquire an association that can *mediate* between very different external stimuli and an overt response that is the same for all of them. A child might encounter large dogs and small dogs, black dogs and red ones, some ferocious and some gentle. He might respond differently to each: "That's Harold's"; "That one is mean." But if he also makes a common response in every case, the association neces-sary for learning the concept "dogs" can be acquired.

Sometimes it is difficult to distinguish between concept learning and rule learning, because the two often shade into one another. The main distinc-tion is that a rule requires the prior learning of the separate concepts that compose it, whereas a concept can be learned without learning any prior ones.

The difficulty with this definition can be illustrated thus: A child's everyday behavior in relation to dogs probably demonstrates concept learning—members of the category are simply identified by a common response ("dogs"). But to precisely distinguish dogs from many other animals, the child probably must learn one or more rules. That is, to precisely define dogs, the child must know terms that refer to concepts—for example, legs, ears, diet, habitat. Thus, the definition of "dog" involves relationships among concepts; "dog" is not a single concept itself.

The fertilizer-jar example shows a large number of concepts that are prerequisites for the rule-governed behavior shown by the children who solved the problem. We mentioned many concepts under rule learning: height, radius, circle, repetition. All these the child must learn in order to solve the problem, and to learn each one he must learn the underlying discriminations. This analysis shows a key feature of the S-R approach: to understand complex behavior, one must divide it into components and trace the probable past learning of these components.

As we describe Type 5 learning, discrimination, think of the circle concept in the liquid-fertilizer example. Recall that, in the rule for cylindrical volume, the area of a circle is multiplied by the height of the container. For the child to see this, he must have learned the concept of circle and must respond to the circular aspect of the cylinder. If he has learned circle, he can identify it in many circumstances—in the moon, wheels, balls, light bulbs, TV dials, toothpaste caps, and telephone poles, but not in doors, drawers, match books, and yardsticks. So how can learning the concept of circle be brought about? Through the prior learning of discriminations.

Type 5: Discrimination Learning

When a person learns a concept, he can make a common response to many different stimuli; when he learns a discrimination, he can make a different response to each different stimulus. Before a child learns the concept of circle, for example, he must learn to respond differently to figures that are circular, ellipsoid, rectilinear, and otherwise angular—learn different responses to different stimuli.

To illustrate, let us suppose a kindergarten teacher wants his students to be able to discriminate between circles, squares, and triangles. He might show drawings of each figure and tell the children, "Point to the circle," "Now point to the triangle," "Now point to the square." Or he might point to each figure successively and ask the children to apply the appropriate verbal labels. When a child is able to make these responses correctly, he is showing a performance made possible by discrimination learning. In the Gagné framework, he has learned a discrimination.

What internal conditions are necessary for a person to learn discriminations? The main one is that he has previously learned stimulus-response chains. In the above example, one such chain is when a child can discriminate the circular figure, make a covert response to it (such as think of the word "circle"), associate that response with an internal stimulus for evoking the necessary overt response (either by pointing or by saying "circle"), and make the overt response.

This distinction between learning a chain and learning a discrimination may at first seem trivial. But performance of a discrimination is more complex than performance of a chain. A young child shown only a circle will quickly learn to designate it as a circle, if he has previously learned the word "circle" and the connection between the figure and its representation. If he is then shown a square and learns to call it a "square," he may have some difficulty learning the chain but will still do so rather quickly. But suppose he is shown both figures simultaneously and asked to pick the square. Very likely he will be confused, and may even point to the circle. This is because this learning (verbal chains) is vulnerable to interference from other learning. In effect, the chain learned for the stimulus-response, circle-"circle" competes with the chain learned for the sequence, square-"square." The child's work in learning a discrimination is, in fact, rather arduous.

If the child's difficulty in discrimination learning is interference, then, we might guess, for each stimulus he must form chains distinctive from one another. The external conditions for successful discrimination learning, then, should prompt a child to form distinctive internal responses to the stimuli. In our example, one way to prompt such responses is to help the child notice the distinguishing features of the figures—the corners of the square versus the curve of the circle, the four angles of the rectangle versus the three angles of the triangle. Another way to prompt is to repeat the task so the child can practice forming distinctive responses.

Once a child has learned discriminations and is able to distinguish circles from ellipses and other curvilinear figures, he can learn the concept for which the discriminations are prerequisite. For example, if he has learned to discriminate among particular squares, triangles, circles, and so on, he can now learn the concept of circle. Such learning can be promoted if the child has been exposed to a variety of circular forms, so that he has a common response to them—in fact, an internal response he learned to make when discriminating a particular circle from a square and a triangle.

Types 3 and 4: Motor Chains and Verbal Associates

Chains are either motor or verbal or both, and so are discussed together. At their simplest, chains are the learning of associations between two previously learned stimulus-response associations. We can show this in the fertilizer-jar example by analyzing the children's behavior into its components and then following these components back in the children's learning history to the previous learning that forms their prerequisites. We started by apportioning the fertilizer with a transfer jar; delineated the rules necessary for the solution; focused on the rule for determining volume; noted one of the concepts involved in that rule, the concept of "circle"; specified the discrimination learning prerequisite for learning the concept; and now the example has been reduced to learning a chain of stimulus response associations to the circular figure by itself.

The circular figure is one end of the chain and the overt response (for example, saying "circle") is the other. What are the other links? One might be a visual response in which the child traces the outline of the figure with his eyes. Another might be an association between such visual tracing and the response of translating that into a word such as "round." This word, in turn, might be associated with another word like "circle." If we imagine that these stimulus-response links occur internally in the child, then the internal response "circle" must be linked up with the overt motor response of physically producing the utterance "circle."

Obviously, the internal conditions necessary for chain learning consist mainly of the prior learning of the individual associations involved. The three external conditions that promote such learning seem to be prompts that evoke each link in the proper sequence, reinforcement following the performance of the entire chain, and repetition of the chain. There are many everyday examples of chain learning—driving a car, playing the piano, reciting a poem—but S-R psychologists have not yet found a satisfactory explanation as to how it occurs. The principal puzzle is that the stimulus for each link in the chain is very difficult to specify. Indeed, it may be that once a chain is well learned, it behaves like a single response rather than like a sequence of individual stimulus-response connections.

Type 2: Stimulus-Response Learning

Stimulus-response learning is essentially the same as what we called operant conditioning in Chapters 2 and 3. The difference is that a particular stimulus controls the occasion of the response. Thus, for example, the learner makes the response of saying "round" in the presence of visual stimuli that are circular, not in the presence of just any stimulus. In this sense the stimulus controls the response—the response is made only when the stimulus is present. The internal conditions for this form of learning are: that the person have the ability, first, to make the response (in our example, to say the word "round") and, second, to pay attention to, or orient himself toward, the stimulus so that its presence can be registered. The three external conditions that promote such learning consist of gaining the learner's attention, presenting the stimulus, and delivering reinforcement immediately after the response is made.

In human behavior, stimulus-response learning in a pure form rarely occurs. Most human behavior consists of a chain of responses rather than of a single response. We would have to strain the fertilizer-jar example to illustrate Type 2 learning. The best we can do is point to the individual stimulus-response associations involved in the chain from the circular figure to the response "circle."

Type 1: Signal Learning

In Gagné's framework, respondent conditioning is called signal learning. As noted, such learning is particularly important, first, for improving the behavior often called "paying attention" and, second, for creating reinforcers. In the fertilizer-jar example, the children clearly could not solve the problem presented by the teacher if they did not even register the message because they did not pay attention. Thus, it may be presumed that in their history of prior learning, the children acquired a conditioned response of listening when the teacher speaks. In fact, the conditioning of this attending response may have begun when the children were infants and the mother's voice was presented

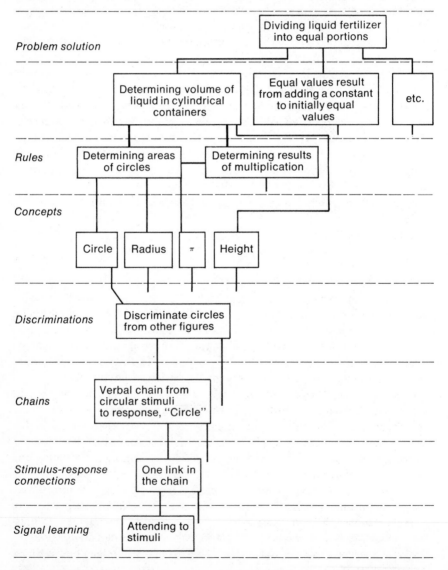

Figure 4.3. Diagram of the learning hierarchy relevant to the liquid-fertilizer example.

in contiguity with food. Similarly, the teacher's praise for problem solving probably gained the status of a reinforcer because of its prior presentation along with unconditioned stimuli that evoked feelings of well-being in the children. Accordingly, in both ways, even Type 1 learning is an important prerequisite in the complex problem-solving behavior the children exhibited.

Figure 4.3 reviews the Gagné framework for identifying the content of learning. As the diagram shows, complex behavior requires an enormous amount of prior learning. This prior learning is necessary for us to produce intellectual behavior. In the fertilizer-jar illustration, we traced an example through a learning hierarchy, from problem solving at the top to signal learn-

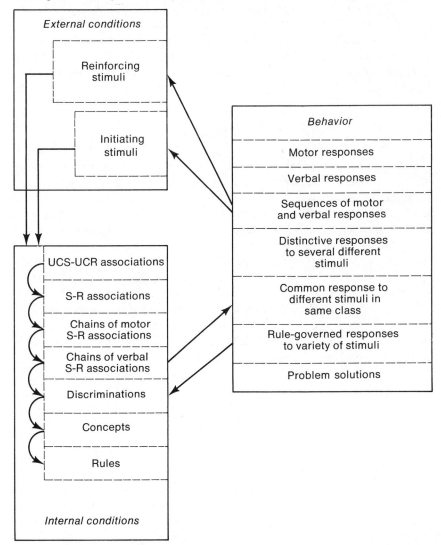

Figure 4.4. Schematic diagram of an elaborated stimulus-response model of behavior

ing at the bottom. But we did not trace the entire hierarchy; we followed only single branches of it to illustrate the eight types of learning. We can see that literally hundreds of specific chains would have to be learned to permit a child to solve the problem of apportioning the fertilizer. Had we followed to its origins one of the other rules necessary for solving the problem, we would have encountered some of these other chains. The S-R approach to complex behavior emphasizes the enormity of this prior learning in order to provide an explanation of the fact that many kinds of complex behavior are not within the capability of young children; in other words, this is the approach S-R theory takes to explain development.

We are now prepared to use the S-R model, and the Gagné framework, to understand the way S-R theory views the causes and the character of intellectual development. As we do so, it will be useful to have a representation of the model as elaborated by the Gagné framework. This elaboration is shown in Figure 4.4, a revised version of the model of behavior presented earlier in Figure 4.2.

SUMMARY

This chapter presented a model of behavior offered by the S-R approach. The three principal components of the model are (1) behavior, consisting of responses; (2) external conditions, consisting of initiating stimuli and reinforcing stimuli; and (3) internal conditions, consisting of the results of previous learning. These components are related so that external conditions activate the results of previous learning internally and this activation results in the overt responses of behavior. The behavior in turn alters the external conditions and the internal conditions as well by causing learning to occur.

We explored intensively Gagné's framework of eight types of learning and applied this framework to an example of problem-solving behavior in children in order to show how each level of performance depends on prior learning of a lower type. In the course of exploring this learning hierarchy, we emphasized the impressive amount of very specific prior learning that is required for a person to engage in complex behavior.

5

THE CHARACTER AND CAUSES OF DEVELOPMENT

Preview

This chapter extends the S-R model to developmental phenomena. We show that development is incremental and specific.

Learning is also shown to be cumulative, so that through transfer, a child gains more proficiency in more intellectual performances as he grows older.

We see that as a person gets older, his performances reflecting higher-level learning increase and the rapidity of new learning increases. The principal causes of developmental change are learning, generalization, and two kinds of transfer, horizontal and vertical.

A DEFINITION OF DEVELOPMENTAL
CHANGE

S-R theorists view developmental change as being the same as other changes in behavior. Thus, we can extend the model presented in Chapter 4 to understand phenomena of intellectual development. Actually, we already know how S-R theory will explain development; what we need to answer first is the question, "What is the character of development?"

For S-R theorists, the character of development can be described in terms they use to describe behavioral change. In the S-R model of behavior, the relationships among the components—behavior, external conditions, and internal conditions—almost guarantee change. When responses are made, that is, when behavior occurs, it affects both the external conditions and the internal conditions that provoked it in the first place. Since external and internal conditions are responsible for behavior, changes in them should result in changes in behavior. Consider when a person learns stimulus-response (Type 2) connections: he makes a designated response to an initiating stimulus, which leads to reinforcement, and this aftereffect changes the probability he will make the response again. In general, according to S-R theory, we can characterize behavioral change as changes in the kinds of performances we can observe in a person and changes in the probabilities that he will make the responses that comprise these performances.

Does this description of behavioral change also characterize developmental change? To answer this we first need to clarify the concept "developmental change."

Obviously, the concept of development implies observable changes in behavior; but does it refer to all varieties of behavioral change? If an adult accountant learns a new skill such as computer programming, so that his behavior would show a change from an incapacity to a capacity to write computer programs, would this behavior change be an example of developmental change? Probably not. But if it was a child who between ages ten and twelve became able to write computer programs, the behavior change probably would be regarded as developmental. This example illustrates a key aspect of development—namely, that it consists of behavior changes that occur at the same time as changes in chronological age.

By itself, however, a correlation between age changes and behavior changes is not enough to define development. After all, the adult accountant presumably aged at least a little while he was learning computer programming. Why does the change in his behavior fail to qualify as developmental? Because his behavior change did not *depend* on his change in age. If he learned to write computer programs at age 32, he could probably have learned it as well at age 30. There is no consistent relationship between adults' chronological age and their ability to learn to write computer programs. But among children there is such a relationship—more seven-year-olds can probably write computer programs than can six-year-olds, and more eight-year-olds than seven-year-olds, and so on. Thus, development refers to behavior changes that are correlated with age in a special way: the changes must by *typical* in the age range specified. This is the reason why psychologists interested in development concentrate on the age range 0 to 18 years. Within this range are many typical correlations between age change and behavior change; beyond this range are few such correlations.

It is tempting to further qualify the definition and say these behavior changes are always moving in the direction of adulthood or in the direction of greater competence. But these qualifications break down quickly. For example, the behavior of an adult reading will resemble more the behavior of a child who has not learned to read than it will that of a first-grade child who is learning to read. The adult is apt to sit quietly, looking at the pages, as will the prereading child, whereas the child learning to read will not only look at the pages but utter aloud oral translations of the print before him. The idea of increasing competence can also be misleading. In some behavior younger children are more competent than older children. For example, it appears that younger children accomplish signal learning (respondent conditioning) more readily than older children.

Another way to qualify the concept of development is to use a three-part definition. Developmental change includes those behavior changes (1) that are correlated with changes in chronological age; (2) that are typical for the members of any given age group; and (3) that are progressive—that is, moving in the direction of behavior typically exhibited by the next older age group. By this definition, if behavior characteristic of four-year-olds changes in the direction of behavior characteristic of five-year-olds, the change is developmental.

S-R theorists would feel this definition is useful but rather arbitrary, for to say that behavioral change is typically correlated with age and that it is progressive does not imply that distinctly different processes are involved. For example, S-R theorists would regard the changes for an adult and for a ten-year-old in learning to write computer programs as essentially the same. Even so, our definition is useful because it emphasizes that there are some regularities about many, many behavioral changes and these regularities are often correlated with age. Given our working definition of developmental change, let us now characterize the general course of intellectual development.

THE CHARACTER OF DEVELOPMENT

To S-R theorists the character of development can be summarized as being *incremental, cumulative,* and *specific.* Developmental changes in behavior are gradual in that they occur in small steps or *increments* rather than in large abrupt alterations. Development consists of small-step changes building on preceding small-step changes—that is, it is *cumulative.* Finally, developmental change arises from learning particular entities rather than from changes in general capacities—that is, it is *specific.*

This view creates a challenging explanatory task for S-R theorists because developmental changes often appear to be dramatic, abrupt, and general, emerging with little apparent relationship with what has gone before. Most of us have experienced the surprise that comes in meeting a child we have not seen for two or three years and finding him to be an entirely different person from the one we remembered. Indeed, the impression that developmental changes occur in bunches and appear to span across a wide range of behavior when they do occur leads to conceptions that emphasize distinct stages or periods of development. Children at one stage of development are regarded as being qualitatively different than they are at another stage. Such a conception is very appealing because it accords rather well with our casual observations of the ways children change. But S-R theorists reject this conception and so must demonstrate that development is incremental, cumulative, and specific.

There are two arguments in favor of the S-R view. First, usually when we are surprised by the magnitude of change in a child, it is because we have not seen him in a long time. If we watched him hourly or daily, we would probably see numerous and varied small changes that, when accumulated over months or years, would appear to be an abrupt change from his past behavior. Second, we sometimes mistake the changes that flow from the child's having acquired a single skill for changes in his general maturity, especially when that single skill is the capstone of his learning of a variety of other skills. For example, a child's parents may suddenly begin permitting him to go several blocks away to play in a park between dinner and bedtime. Such a shift can dramatically increase the range of optional activities open to the child and his apparent maturity, but it may arise because he added only a single skill to a number of other skills he had acquired previously. Previously he might have learned to find the way to the park, to cross streets safely, to manage conflicts with other children, and so on, but have been unable to read a clock so his parents could not rely on his returning home punctually. Then, on learning to tell time, he is suddenly allowed to go about his neighborhood with more freedom than before. The change might appear to be dramatic and general whereas in fact it was quite specific. Thus, the apparent abruptness of developmental changes is partly due to the gaps in our observations but also to the cumulative character of learning that underlies development.

Precisely because S-R theorists view development as being gradual, cumulative, and specific, they cannot easily offer a description of how children in general develop. Instead, the theorists suggest that observations should be made that take special note of behavioral changes over time so as to produce a detailed description of particular developmental changes. Then the theory can offer a way of investigating how those changes were brought about, that is, their possible causes. But the theory, by itself, can provide little information in advance about what all children will be like at certain ages or even in certain age ranges. In fact, the theory explicitly implies that what children will be like depends on what they have learned; and what they have learned will depend on what they have learned previously and on the external conditions of learning.

At this point let us offer some broad generalizations about how the character of behavior should change as children grow older and older. These generalizations follow from the Gagné framework in Chapter 4, which contained eight types of learning arranged hierarchically. This hierarchy has two implications for the character of developmental change.

First, since every higher level type of learning requires prior learning of relevant lower types and since the child, as he ages, is more likely to have completed more lower-level learning, then *the older the child, the more often he will successfully complete performances that require higher-level learning.* Thus, the older child would probably learn the rules necessary for performing scientific inference more readily than the younger child—not because his general intellectual capacity is qualitatively different but because he has had more chances to engage in the prerequisite lower-level learning. Notice that this generalization does not guarantee that every kind of rule-governed performance will increase with age nor that any particular rule-governed performance will be observed more often for older than for younger children. This is because any specific rule-governed performance depends entirely on prior learning of specific, relevant prerequisites. Thus, a young child might be able to play chess whereas an older child could not—because the younger one had learned the necessary prerequisites for this particular set of rule-governed behaviors, and the older one had not.

The second implication of the Gagné hierarchy for developmental change concerns transfer: *the older the child, the more rapidly he should be able to complete the learning for any new performance.* Any given performance requires the prior learning necessary for prerequisite, lower-level performances. But if a person has already learned some of these prerequisites—say, for some other performance—then they will transfer to the new performance and only the missing components must be learned. Because older children are apt to have learned more, they probably have more transfer advantage than do younger children who have to start from scratch to learn all the prerequisites for a particular performance. For example, suppose a child is asked to convert yards to feet to inches. An older child should have an easier time than a younger child because he has already learned the rules for performing division and so only needs to learn the rules defining yards, feet, and inches. The younger child, however, might also have to learn the rules for performing division.

Despite this example, S-R theorists maintain there is an exception to this generalization that older children will learn more rapidly than younger children. The exception is that the more a child has previously learned, the more likely his subsequent learning will be retarded by *negative* transfer. That is, not only will he have available much more appropriate information than will the younger child, but he will also have learned much more that is inappropriate for accomplishing certain new performances. For example, in learning the route to a friend's house in another part of a city, a child will often have less difficulty than an adult. The child has previously learned fewer chains of associations between his home and the area of the city in which the friend's house is located. So he suffers less interference from past learning than does the adult and can give the adult directions during the journey. Thus, unless the external conditions of learning are such as to diminish the likelihood that inappropriate prior learning will be recalled in connection with a given performance, in particular situations the older child or an adult may learn more slowly than a younger child.

Let us summarize the S-R view of the character of change. To S-R theorists development consists of changes in performance that are correlated with chronological age and that are in the direction of performances typical of the next older age level. These changes are specific, occur gradually, and are accumulated with preceding changes. In the Gagné framework, the further development progresses, the more readily the person will (1) perform tasks that require higher-level learning types (concept learning, rule learning, problem solving) and (2) be able to complete additional learning. The S-R view emphasizes that both these characteristics are true on the average and not necessarily for any particular skill.

THE CAUSES OF DEVELOPMENT

In Chapters 2 through 4 we discussed most of the S-R concepts needed to explain development. We will now review these concepts, principal among which are *learning, generalization,* and *transfer,* and use them to try to understand how development occurs.

A fundamental proposition in S-R explanations of development is that, *apart from the effects of physical growth, development results from learning.* To be sure, many developmental changes are caused by generalization and by transfer, but both these processes themselves depend on learning. Thus, if we are curious about developmental changes in performance as the child grows older, S-R theory implies that we should look for the cause in what the child has learned.

One complication of this proposition is in the clause on the effects of physical growth. Physical growth contributes to developmental change in two major ways. The first is that physical growth determines the availability of many kinds of responses. If a response (or a sequence of responses, such as that involved in a motor chain) is not within a person's physical capability, then the response is simply not available for association with stimuli—it is not available for learning. Infants are incapable, for demonstrable physical reasons, of a number of performances—walking, running, figure skating, and so on. A person also needs physical growth to provide him with the capability to perform less gross motor acts; an infant's nervous system probably has not developed enough to permit the fine motor coordination required in fluent speech. The second way physical growth contributes to developmental changes is that it modifies the reinforcing power of certain stimuli. For instance, the physical changes in reproductive capacity that occur during puberty might well contribute to marked changes in the reinforcing power of certain kinds of sexual stimuli.

To S-R theorists both ways that physical change can affect intellectual development are indirect. That is, changes in response availabilities and in reinforcing power must be combined with learning in order to bring about developmental changes in performance. Thus, the growth of a person's physical capacity to make the responses needed to do figure skating will not by itself produce the performances of figure skating—numerous motor chains involving these responses must be learned as well.

Since learning is required even when physical growth is a prerequisite for intellectual development, we can concentrate on the principles that govern learning in order to understand the causes of intellectual development. As we proceed, however, we should bear in mind that physical and neurological growth also affect intellectual development, especially in childhood.[1]

As noted, S-R theorists regard developmental changes as being in the general class of performance changes. To be called developmental, such performance changes must be correlated with chronological age and they must be in the direction of behavior typical of the next older age level. Since developmental changes are performance changes, in the S-R view, they can obviously be caused by learning. If a child learns a new rule or a new concept, he becomes capable of engaging in performances he could not attain previously. Thus, some developmental changes in performance are caused by accomplishing new learning.

But some performance changes can be brought about without learning from scratch everything necessary for the change. S-R theorists identify three mechanisms responsible for such changes: *generalization, horizontal transfer,* and *vertical transfer.*

Generalization

In Chapter 3, we used the term generalization to describe cases where a response learned to one stimulus is also made to other physically similar stimuli not present when the initial learning took place. In the case of signal learning, a salivation response conditioned to a tone of a certain frequency will also be made, without additional learning, to a tone of another similar frequency. Generalization also occurs in connection with stimulus-response learning. For example, suppose a child has learned an association between the response of the word "circle" and the stimulus of a particular circular figure. He can generalize this response to new instances of physically similar circles, even though they were not present when he initially learned the association.

Can we assume that the older the child is, the more he will generalize? Actually, as the next chapter will show, the older the child, the *less* he generalizes from a particular stimulus to physically similar ones. If an older and a younger child have both learned an association between the word "circle" and a circular figure, the younger child is *more* likely than the older to generalize this learning broadly—to the extent that he might identify many curved figures, like ellipses, as circles. The older child is more likely to exhibit narrow generalization—that is, to limit the response "circle" to figures that are truly circular. Nevertheless, we can assume that older children will generalize more *often* than younger children, simply because they have learned more that can be generalized. Thus, the older the child, the more learning he has to generalize but the narrower will be the range of his generalization for any specific learning.

Horizontal Transfer

Another way performance changes of a developmental sort can occur is through transfer. For example, suppose a child is converting feet to inches, and he has already converted yards to inches. Since he has this latter skill, we know he has learned: multiplication rules; the definitions (rules) of "yard" and "inch"; the concepts, such as distance, prerequisite for learning the definitions; the principle of equivalence; the concept of a unit; and so on. So, except for the definition of foot and the rule relating feet to inches, he has previously learned everything he needs to convert feet to inches. Because of this, he will not have to learn all of these prerequisite rules and concepts from scratch. This previous learning is expected to *transfer* to the new task. That is, if the child is given reminders to prompt his recall of the relevant rules and concepts he has previously learned, he should be able to learn the additional rules necessary for the performance, since he already possesses most of what he needs. We expect transfer because many rules and concepts necessary for the new performance are *identical* with those the child has already acquired. That is, the child should exhibit an enormous advantage in learning the rules for the new performance as compared with the learning he had to do the first time in order to perform the task of converting one kind of measurement to another.

In this example the transfer is *lateral* or *horizontal.* This kind of transfer can occur without the child having to learn any higher-level skills other than those already acquired. To define feet in terms of inches has no more prerequisites than to define yards in terms of inches; and the concept of a foot requires no more prior learning than does the concept of a yard—both require a different kind of prior learning but they require no *more* prior learning.

Vertical Transfer

Some performance changes caused by new learning occur through *vertical* transfer. In the example we just discussed, suppose the child has now learned to convert measurements of length (inches, feet, and yards) of one kind of unit to another kind of unit. He should now be able to learn to solve this problem: "How many packages of rope must one buy in order to reach the bottom of a 50-yard-deep well if the length of rope in each package is 360 inches?" To learn to solve this problem, the child must coordinate several rules, including the one for converting measurement units, into a higher-level skill. In such a case, we would expect the previous learning of prerequisite rules to transfer vertically to the learning of the higher-level variety necessary to solve the problem. Here, transfer means that the child will solve the problem more readily if he has previously learned the rules involved than if he has not.

Cumulative Learning

Both horizontal and vertical transfer occur when prior learning is combined with new learning. Taken together, the two types allow us to understand an important aspect of developmental change: some developmental changes appear to occur rapidly and are exhibited in many different performances. Consider again the common experience of observing how dramatically a child seems to change from one time to another. When we last saw him he may have seemed incapable of any performances involved in converting units of measurement. The next time we see him he may be able to make many conversions. In the S-R view, such a broad range of performance changes is possible because learning is *cumulative*. And the heart of the notion of cumulative learning is transfer.

Learning is cumulative in the sense that the products of learning—that is, what is learned—are interrelated hierarchically. Accordingly, many ostensibly different performances can be affected by a single new event of learning. This is because much of the learning that is prerequisite for all the different performances is identical. All of what has been learned by one point in time transfers to the learning that occurs during the next time interval, resulting in rapid and wide-ranging performance changes. Consider the example of converting measurements. Suppost the first time we see him, the child has learned everything necessary for such conversions except the rule for division. At that point, he would be totally unable to make any conversions successfully. However, if he learns the missing component—which he may do quite rapidly if he has previously learned all of the prerequisites—then by the second time we see him he should be able to make the conversions.

Transfer should become more frequent as the child grows older. This follows from the fact that more is learned as the child ages, so more can be transferred. Once again, however, this characterization of development applies only on the average because transfer depends on particular, specific, prior learning. A younger child might exhibit more transfer with respect to a particular performance than an older child if his past learning relevant to that performance had been more extensive than that of the older child. If a young child specializes narrowly—as in the case of a precocious chess player—he may outstrip an older child on tasks within his specialty. Nevertheless, in general, S-R theory leads us to expect that learning will be more rapid and have wider ramifications for older than younger children.

The S-R approach leads to the final conclusion that the causes and the character of developmental change depend entirely on the specific intellectual functions one wants to know about. Prior learning, transfer, external conditions, and new learning are always involved, but their particular relationship must be discovered for the specific developmental changes that we want to understand—it is to some of these that we turn next.

SUMMARY

In this chapter, we have seen that the essentials of the S-R view of intellectual development are as follows:

1. Development is incremental, cumulative, and specific.
2. With increasing age, there is an increase in the proportion of performances that reflect higher-level types of learning.
3. With increasing age, the rapidity of new learning increases.
4. The principal causes of developmental change are learning, generalization, and two kinds of transfer—horizontal and vertical.
5. Learning is cumulative, so that through transfer, a child shows more proficiency in more intellectual performances as he grows older.

6

SOME MAJOR AREAS OF INTELLECTUAL DEVELOPMENT

Preview

Using Gagné's eight types of learning, in this chapter we examine the theory and some evidence as to how a person develops intellectually from infancy to adulthood.

We show how S-R theory accounts for such changes in terms of the kind of relevant previous learning the person has accomplished.

We also show that when individuals differ from each other, it is primarily because they have learned different things before.

INTRODUCTION

S-R theory provides a way of looking at changes in particular kinds of intellectual behavior as children grow older. This method is to describe the major performances children learn to complete and to analyze the previous learning they have accomplished in order to do so.

This extremely large task has not been completed, for research has not progressed far enough. S-R theory was not originated for the purpose of explaining developmental change. Even as recently as 25 years ago, few S-R psychologists were working on phenomena of intellectual development, so only partial information has been accumulated about the character of change in the major areas of this field.[1] Thus, for now we will have to be content with a more modest way of examining specific developmental changes, drawing on the information that has been accumulated so far.

The discussion is organized in terms of the eight types of learning distinguished in the Gagné framework. We will describe the known changes that occur as children grow older, trying to explain them in terms of the causes of development derived from S-R theory in Chapter 5, namely, the effects on internal conditions that are produced by learning, generalization, and transfer. Since our discussion assumes an understanding of the definitions of each of Gagné's learning types, it may be useful to review them in Chapter 3.

TYPE 1: SIGNAL LEARNING

Signal learning is the simplest of the eight types Gagné has distinguished. Responses in signal learning are numerous in that they occur in bunches, reflexive in that they can occur with little or no prior learning, and innately tied to some stimulus such that if the stimulus occurs the responses occur. For example, if you touch your finger to a hot iron, many responses will ensue—you will feel pain, withdraw the finger, probably scream, and undergo several physiological changes, some concerned with delivering fluids to the burn, some with bodily expression of emotions. Pleasant as well as unpleasant reactions share the same characteristics—responses that are numerous, reflexive, and innately tied to some stimulus. These are the *internal* conditions necessary or prerequisite for signal learning to occur. The *external* conditions consist of the following: the stimulus that evokes the set of responses (the hot iron in contact with the finger); some other stimulus that is initially, that is, before training, neutral (sight of the iron); the contiguous occurrence of the two stimuli with the neutral stimulus presented slightly before the unconditioned one (sight of the iron, followed by the heat); and, usually, the repetition of this sequence—neutral stimulus, unconditioned stimulus, unconditioned responses.

The product of these internal and external conditions is that the neutral stimulus comes to evoke the set of responses, or at least some of the responses, that were originally made only to the unconditioned stimulus. The initially neutral stimulus, the conditioned stimulus, comes to serve as a signal for the unconditioned stimulus, and acquires the capacity to evoke the responses itself.

Why do S-R theorists include this so simple and apparently stupid form of learning in their approach to intellectual development? There are three reasons: First, it is a pervasive form of learning, since it can occur simply through repeated contiguity of two stimuli. Second, it is the means whereby an enormous variety of events that can reinforce behavior acquire that kind of function. Third, it is the means whereby initially ineffectual stimuli can become capable of enlisting attention.

To turn now to specifics, the major internal condition necessary for signal learning to occur is the availability of reflex responses that are evoked by unconditioned stimuli. Experiments show that the success of signal learning depends on what kinds of responses are to be conditioned. In these studies, the following responses have been successfully conditioned to initially neutral stimuli: salivation, sucking, mouth opening, head turning, eyeblinks, foot withdrawal, pupil dilation and contraction, heart rate, and respiration rate. The latter two responses are often regarded as signs of emotional activity.[2] This is consistent with the belief that signal learning is important for creating reinforcers and controlling attention.

We can see some developmental changes in signal learning by looking at differences in the effects of external conditions, depending on the age of the child. A principal component of such external conditions is the character of the signal itself—the kind of neutral stimulus to which the response is to be conditioned. Research shows that after infancy, conditioning proceeds most easily when the signal is a visual one. During infancy, however, there are changes in the kind of stimuli that are most effective. Auditory stimuli are effective very early, followed in order by touch, smell, taste, and finally visual stimuli.[3] It is believed that these changes are due to changes in the efficiency of the various sensory systems that result from bodily growth.

Another important kind of developmental change that occurs between ages 0 and 70 is in susceptibility to conditioning. Some research shows that from birth to six years, the older the child, the more easily he can be conditioned, whereas from six to 70 years, the older the person, the more difficult conditioning becomes.[4]

TYPES 2, 3, AND 4: STIMULUS-RESPONSE LEARNING, MOTOR CHAINS, AND VERBAL ASSOCIATES

The next three types of learning occur so rarely in isolation, at least in human subjects, that we will consider them together rather than separately. That is to say, the learning of connections between single stimuli and responses, the learning of single motor chains, or the learning of single verbal associates is uncharacteristic after early childhood. There are two reasons, according to S-R theory: first, after early childhood, the child's environment rarely offers external conditions that involve only single connections, chains, or associates; second, during early childhood, children learn so many of these that they are evoked in most occasions of later learning, become a part of the internal conditions for such learning, and make most later learning more complex than single chains or connections.

In the external conditions for all three types of learning, at least two different stimuli are present and reinforcement is delivered when a response is made to one of these stimuli but not when it is made to the others. An example is the task of learning to select one of two objects that differ in size but are identical otherwise. One object is arbitrarily designated as being correct. When the learner chooses that object, he receives a reward such as candy. A major developmental change has been observed in performance on tasks like this—namely, that performance seems to become more efficient, the older the learner is, until approximately 11 or 12 years of age. Then, as the learner gets older, performance becomes increasingly less efficient, so that by the age of 18 or 19 it is no better than that observed for four-year-olds.[5] The reason for this developmental change has not yet been established but S-R theory suggests that the reinforcement attached to performing well on the task progressively loses its effectiveness after childhood. This explanation fits in well with the common observation that the trinkets inside cereal boxes are sufficient incentive for a child, but not for adults, to learn to distinguish among various brand names.

Figure 6.1. A task used to assess stimulus generalization in the learning of motor and verbal chains.

A second noticeable developmental phenomenon is not concerned with *initial* performance on a learning task but with *generalization* of the performance to other stimuli. This phenomenon has been demonstrated in situations like the one shown in Figure 6.1. A child is seated at a table facing a large backboard mounted vertically on top of the table. Eleven small lamps are spaced equally apart on the board in a horizontal row. The child is told to press a button in the table as rapidly as possible whenever the middle lamp in the row is lighted; he is praised for the rapidity of his response.

Now suppose the child has achieved a stable performance with the displays described, pushing the button when the middle lamp is lighted. Then, without any interruption or further instructions, lamps other than the middle one are lighted, so that sometimes the middle light comes on and at other times each of the peripheral lights comes on. The question is, how many of the lamps, other than the middle one, will the child respond to by pressing the button? How broadly will he generalize? For learners of all ages from 7 to 12, the closer the peripheral lamp to the middle one, the more times they will push the button. But the interesting developmental change is that younger children are more likely than older children to press the button for lamps that are far from the middle one as well as for lamps near it. The older the learner, the *less* generalization he exhibits.[6]

Once again, S-R theory suggests two explanations: First, the total reinforcement (praise) provided for performing well is not as effective for the younger child as it is for the older child. Thus, the younger child does not learn the association between the middle lamp and the button pressing as thoroughly as does the older child. Second, as the child grows older, what he learns in the original task is different. Instead of learning a simple connection between the lights and a response, he learns a chain that begins with the lights but that is connected with a covert response such as "the light in the middle," which in turn stimulates the overt, button-pushing response. In other words, the older child's performance is mediated by a chain of previously learned verbal associates rather than consisting only of learning a connection between the external stimulus and the response of pressing the button; prior learning transfers vertically, making a higher-level type of learning possible. The mediation provided by the chain of verbal associates then has the effect of sharpening the child's discrimination of the stimulus pattern to which the response is appropriate—it sharpens his definition of the pattern to the point that he has learned a simple concept rather than a chain.

This explanation of prior learning transferring to new learning occurs in other forms of intellectual development, as we shall see. *As the child ages, his performance on a task becomes increasingly controlled by internal conditions, as well as by external ones.* The older the child, the more he has learned, and this past learning (internal conditions) affects subsequent learning. In fact, the balance seems to shift from total control by external conditions to substantial control by internal conditions. As a person gets older, what he has learned increases, and as his prior learning increases, it becomes a more powerful determinant of new learning.

Unfortunately, S-R psychologists have not yet fully explored the development of chain learning in such performances as a person's memorizing and reciting long series of verbal units like poetry or the alphabet. We not only lack theoretical explanations of developmental changes in such performances, we even lack adequately detailed descriptions of the changes themselves. There is some minimal evidence that the efficiency of forming longer verbal chains increases with age, from about five to 12 years, but even this descriptive evidence has not been corroborated sufficiently.[8]

TYPE 5: MULTIPLE DISCRIMINATION

Multiple discrimination learning, Type 5, allows a person to perform a task such as to give English equivalents for French words; that is, he can make different responses to each of a set of stimuli. The prerequisites, or internal conditions, are prior learning of each pair of French-English equivalents in isolation as a verbal associate. The prerequisite for learning each pair is the prior learning of a verbal chain for each member of the pair, so that when a person hears the French word, it evokes a short chain of internal stimuli and responses leading him to make the overt response of pronouncing the French word.

Experiments conducted so far tend to validate the importance of these prerequisites for successful multiple discrimination learning. When the person's task is to learn a pair of words in such a way that when he is given one member of the pair he can designate the other, prior learning of verbal chains to each pair member separately improves performance. The importance of this prerequisite seems to be constant at all ages, from early childhood to adulthood. What seems to change with age is the amount of prerequisite learning that has already occurred. For example, suppose we ask a learner to associate pairs of English nouns and that we use two different lists, one of familiar noun pairs and one of unfamiliar noun pairs. By "familiar," we mean words for which verbal chains have been previously learned. When such lists are given to children and adults, results show that the list of familiar word pairs is often learned more easily than the list of unfamiliar ones.[9] Thus, there is good reason to believe that prior learning of verbal chains is an important prerequisite for multiple discrimination learning.

There are two kinds of evidence that prior learning of individual verbal associates is important for multiple discrimination. First, experimenters have tried to examine the effect of prior learning on performing an entire list of noun pairs. For example, in an experiment on whole-part learning, the speed that a subject learns a whole list when he studies it in its entirety is compared with the speed he learns the list when he studies first one half, then the other half, then the two halves together. In both cases, total learning time is about the same.[10] These results suggest that the learning of the individual pairs of associations occurs during the learning of the whole list; or, in terms of Gagné's model, verbal associate learning occurs as a part of multiple discrimination learning. Unfortunately, there is no evidence on developmental differences in the outcome of comparisons between the whole and the part method of learning, since the experiments have not been conducted with children.

The second kind of evidence is based on the use of word-association norms, which are obtained by having many people respond to each of a list of words with the first other word that comes to mind. The assumption is that the first word that comes to mind is one that the person has previously learned, or associated, to the stimulus word. It is then possible to construct lists of word pairs that differ in degree of association between the two members of each pair. High degrees of association are exemplified in pairs of words formed by combining a stimulus word, say, "table," with another word that most people give as a response, like "chair." Low degrees of association are exhibited in pairs consisting of words that very few people give as associates, such as "table"– "rabbit." When comparisons are made between the ease of learning a list made up of high-degree associates and low-degree associates, the usual result is that the former are easier.[11]

The most interesting thing about these comparisons is that differences in ease of learning are more pronounced for children than they are for adults. In fact, degree of association rarely produces differences in adult learning.[12] This suggests that adults have previously learned, to some degree, associations between a great many pairs of words, whereas for children these prior associations are not so numerous. Thus, differences among word pairs in degree of association are very small for adults but much larger for children.

If it is true that previously learned individual associations are important for multiple discrimination learning, then it should also be true that the influence of this prior learning may be either positive or negative. As Gagné has pointed out, the most difficult aspect of multiple discrimination learning is that of overcoming interference or negative transfer from prior learning.[13] Research has not established the validity of this assertion, for the problem is that as people gain more experience at learning multiple discriminations, they become more proficient at it—an example of positive transfer—but with increasing experience, interference also becomes greater. The result is that the more multiple discrimination learning that has taken place, the more efficient is the next attempt at such learning. In contrast, remembering becomes less efficient, for the larger the number of multiple discriminations one has learned, the more difficult it is to remember the most recent one because the previous ones interfere with it.[14]

Developmental trends in multiple discrimination learning are much the same. The older children are, the more rapidly they can learn to perform tasks that require multiple discriminations. For example, older children can learn a list of word pairs much easier than can younger children—such improvement continues to be shown at least up to the age of 17 or 18.[15] But it also seems true that the older the learner, the more rapidly he forgets what he has learned. Research is limited, but it seems to show that such forgetting (that is, forgetting that occurs because of interference from prior learning) is very minimal for four-year-olds, appreciable for six-year-olds, and as marked for eight-year-olds as it is for adults.[16]

To sum up, developmental change in multiple discrimination learning is produced by both positive and negative transfer. The initial learning of any particular discrimination is facilitated by vertical transfer from the prior learning of associates, chains, and connections. In contrast, the task of remembering the product of such learning grows increasingly difficult, once again because of prior learning. The prior learning of associates, chains, and the like, increasingly interferes with the capacity for remembering more recent multiple discriminations. In brief, the more you learn, the faster you learn; but the more you learn, the more you forget.

TYPE 6: CONCEPT LEARNING

The kinds of performances included in concept learning are of an enormous variety, from simple to complex. In addition, concept learning is commonplace—it happens all the time. Before we explore the information that the S-R approach has produced about concept learning, let us recall its defining characteristics. The internal conditions that are prerequisite include the learning of multiple discriminations that permit a person to respond differently to one stimulus than to others, the chains necessary to permit responding in the same way to some aspects of several stimuli that differ in many other aspects, and the connections necessary for those chains. The external conditions include the appearance of, and information about, events that exemplify and that do not exemplify the concept.

The performances of concept learning are characterized by three features: (1) A person makes an identical response to at least two stimuli that differ in appearance but that are members of some common class. (2) He makes a different response to one or more other stimuli that do not belong to the class. (3) He makes the first-mentioned, identical response to still another member of the class, even though it has not been presented before. In other words, when a person gives such a performance he makes multiple discriminations, not to single stimuli, but to classes of stimuli, and transfers that learning, horizontally, to other stimulus members of the class without additional training. In such learning a person responds to selected aspects of stimuli with the same response, so that response is appropriate for all stimuli sharing the same property, not just identical stimuli. For example, the concept of a *book* involves discriminating books from boxes, magazines, newspapers, and so on. Learning the concept "book" allows a person to make a common response to any of several objects that differ in many ways—thickness, color, size—but that share the defining attributes of books.

Studies show that concept learning becomes more efficient with increasing age as a child grows from five to 14 years.[17] But why is this so? S-R psychologists disagree about exactly what causes improved concept learning as children grow older, but one observation is that a child becomes better able to locate and respond to the different aspects of stimuli so that he can better define whether a stimulus is or is not a member of a class. For example, to learn the concept of "triangularity," the child must notice the three angles in any such plane figure. Young children have not learned to do this; when they scan a figure visually, their eyes typically do not fix on these defining attributes, whereas the visual response of older children does do so.[18] It seems that younger children have not learned the stimulus-response connections that are prerequisite for the chains and multiple discriminations required for successful concept learning.

Evidence that children become more proficient in learning concepts with increasing age has been gained in a variety of ways. One simple way is to give a child the task of selecting the larger of two objects, regardless of what the objects are. If he selects the larger object, it is assumed the concept has been learned. At the beginning of the task, the child is shown one set of two objects four times, then another set of two different objects four times, and so on, until he always chooses the larger one. Since the procedure continues in this way until the child can consistently choose the larger object on every presentation of two new objects, he is then thought to have learned the concept. Results show that the greatest improvement in learning efficiency occurs between ages four and eight. After age eight, there is still some improvement up to age 20 but the amount of increased efficiency is very small. An idea of how difficult this kind of learning is at the three ages is given by the number of new sets of objects presented before performance indicates that the concept has been learned. About 20 different sets of objects are required by four-year-olds, only 10 are needed by 10-year-olds, and about six by 20-year-olds.[19]

A slightly more difficult task is one where three objects are presented, two of which are identical and a third that differs from the first two. The objective is to select the "odd" object, regardless of exactly what object it is and of its position relative to the other objects. Once again, successful performance depends on the availability of specific chains for particular aspects of the stimuli. In this case, however, an even more complicated set of chains is required since it must include one that is appropriate for the difference between the objects rather than just some concrete aspect of each object. Evidence about developmental changes in the ease of performing this task is meager, but it appears that the biggest improvement occurs between ages six and 12.[20]

A different method of exploring developmental changes in concept learning allows the S-R psychologist to determine what a child has learned— a concept or simply a chain. For example, a child is asked to select the longer of two pencils that are otherwise identical. After he masters this two-choice task, he is presented again with two pencils; this time the shorter pencil is replaced by a still longer pencil. The child can now select either the same pencil he had been selecting all along, indicating that a chain has been learned to that particular pencil, or he can choose the new pencil, the one that is now the longer of the two, indicating that he has learned the concept of "longer." In general, the older the child, between the ages of three and six years, the more likely he is to learn the concept rather than the chain.[21]

These methods, (and others not described) seem to show that concepts are learned more readily by the older child, especially in the age range of four to seven. But this conclusion is not generally valid if we get down to specifics. For one thing, the more difficult the task, the older the age range when improvement is most marked. Similarly, if a task is made very easy, even young children appear to learn concepts readily and to choose to learn concepts rather than just simple chains. Perhaps the determining factor is whether or not the child has previously learned, and recalls, the specific chains necessary to learn the concept embodied in the stimuli used in the task. For example, if the concept involves color, where the task is always that of choosing the red object regardless of what the object is, even very young children perform efficiently. But if the task involves form, marked improvement in efficiency tends to occur later in the age range. Thus, specific chains linking the *form* aspects of stimuli with responses are learned later than are specific chains for the *color* aspects of stimuli.

With regard to the recall of relevant chains, a similar trend emerges. In an optional task, where the child can succeed either by learning a specific chain or by learning a concept, even very young children will learn the concept, if that is emphasized in the stimuli. For example, in the pencil task, if two pairs of pencils are presented simultaneously, each pair containing a long and a short one, but the pairs being of different lengths, young children will readily learn the concept "longer" whereas they learn a chain when only one pair is used. The S-R interpretation is that the use of two pairs of pencils prompts the recall of the chains necessary for concept learning.[22]

Throughout this discussion of developmental changes in concept learning there has been an important theme—namely, that improvement in the efficiency of such learning is caused by increases in the amount of previous learning that has taken place.

TYPES 7 AND 8: RULE LEARNING AND PROBLEM SOLVING

When a rule is acquired, what has been learned? To Gagné, a person who has acquired a rule has learned a relationship—a chain—between previously learned concepts. But though rule learning requires that one has learned chains, it differs from the learning of verbal or motor chains. In ordinary chain learning, links are established between particular S-R connections; in rule learning, links are established between concepts. The distinctive thing about rules is that they apply to all members of each of the concepts in the chain, not just to single instances. Thus, rule learning is the formation of conceptual chains.

Rule learning is distinct from the memorization of verbal chains. To be able to verbally state a rule does not mean it has been learned, only that a verbal chain has been learned. For example, a child can learn the verbal chain necessary to say, "Two plus two is four," yet be entirely unable to anticipate the result of adding two things to two other things. On the other hand, a person may have learned a rule, in the sense that he can behave consistently in accord with it, but be entirely unable to utter a verbal statement of the rule. For example, it requires a number of rules to describe the grammatical regularity in the speech of a four-year-old, but the child himself cannot state those rules.

Since rule learning consists of chaining concepts together, the necessary internal conditions consist of the prior learning and recall of the concepts to be related. The previous learning of these component concepts is prerequisite to learning the given rule. To S-R theorists, no qualitative change in the character of intellectual processes is required for a person to learn a rule—the necessary thing is the prior learning of the component concepts.

Let us now discuss developmental changes in rule learning. In general, S-R theorists believe that as a child grows older, he will learn more and more rules. He will also usually learn any given rule more efficiently, the older he is. Both expectations are based on the key S-R assumption that as the child grows older, he learns more concepts that are prerequisite for the learning of the rules in which they are involved.

From the S-R perspective, older children (say, 14-year-olds) are able to learn rules with much greater ease than younger children (say, five-year-olds) because of positive transfer, both horizontal and vertical, from prior learning. If a particular concept is a part of a rule to be learned, the learning of that concept will transfer to the learning of the rule. But the learning of that concept will also transfer to the learning of some other rule for which it is also a component. Thus, the learning of one rule can facilitate the learning of another rule if both rules involve one or more of the same component concepts. It is in this sense that the S-R approach views learning as being cumulative and developmental change as being the product of accumulated learning.

If both prior learning and transfer of learning are required, rule learning would seem to be both difficult and easy, depending on how much relevant prior learning has been accomplished. That is, if a child is asked to learn a rule consisting of concepts he has not learned before, his progress may be achingly slow. But if the rule consists entirely of concepts he has learned before, his progress may be surprisingly rapid.

The S-R conception of developmental changes in the child's ability to learn rules applies equally well to the issue of developmental changes in the child's ability to successfully engage in the type of learning called problem solving. In the Gagné model, problem solving consists of the performance of behaviors that are governed by a number of previously learned rules. Its distinctive feature is that the rules are combined or related or chained together in ways *different* from the ways they were learned previously. Developmental changes in this kind of learning depend entirely on the previous learning of relevant rules and the recall of those rules in the context of the problem.

Figure 6.2. Setting and materials for the flotation problem.

Let us consider an example. (This example will also be presented again in Chapter 11, to illustrate the cognitive approach to developmental change.) As Figure 6.2 shows, a child is given several objects varying in size, weight, shape, and materials—a block of wood, a nail, an empty tin can, and so on —and asked to identify those that will float in a tub of water. In other words, he must follow the rule that objects having a density less than the density of water will float. This rule is, of course, very complex, for it combines several simpler rules, each one made up of concepts. For example, one term in the rule for flotation is *density,* which is itself a rule made up of simpler rules: density is the ratio of weight to volume. What conditions, then, are necessary for the child to learn the flotation rule?

We can answer this question by applying the Gagné framework. Gagné does *not* say that to learn the rule the child must have reached a particular developmental stage. But if not, how can we explain the fact that most persons have not learned this rule by age 12? From an S-R viewpoint, it is because most persons have not accomplished the necessary prerequisite learning until approximately this age range. Thus, the main factor is that before a child can learn the rule, he must learn the prerequisite rules, and their prerequisite concepts, and so on; the crucial factor is not whether his mind has developed fully enough to carry out the logical operations involved.

This prior learning may be time consuming, for the rule governing flotation is so complex that it is made up of many other simpler rules, concepts, discriminations, and chains. To see this, recall that one component of the flotation rule, *density,* is itself a rule, and that the flotation rule involves a comparison of the density of the object and the density of the water. An enormous amount of prerequisite learning is required for a person to be able to compare these densities. Many instances of rule and concept learning are involved and for each of the lowest-level concepts there are prerequisite multiple discriminations and chains. In view of this and of the fact that equally complex hierarchies of learning would be required to successfully compare the weights and volumes of two substances, it is not surprising that the task of learning the flotation rule is difficult.

This example can also illustrate horizontal and vertical transfer. Suppose the child has now learned the rule necessary to compare rectangular volumes. Would as much learning be required to compare cylindrical volumes? It would not, for many of the rules and concepts learned in judging rectangular volumes are prerequisite for judging cylindrical volumes. They would transfer, horizontally, and would make learning the cylindrical rules easier.

To illustrate vertical transfer, as well as problem-solving learning, let us suppose the child has learned the flotation rule and that we tell him, "Find a way to float the objects you said will sink." The solution is to combine a sinkable object with another object so as to increase volume more than the sum of the weights—for example, by putting the nail on a block of wood. To solve this problem, the child must have previously learned the rule for flotation and a higher-level rule for combining the densities of two objects. These previous learnings transfer, vertically, to the performance of solving the problem, that is, to the learning of a higher-order rule than either of the two component rules learned separately.

We have now reviewed for each one of eight types of learning the information available about developmental changes. In every case we have seen that changes do occur, that they are very specific, and that they can be explained by prior learning, generalization, and transfer. Thus far, however, we have assumed that the changes observed are characteristic of all children. If this assumption were valid, the mysteries of intellectual development would probably be much simpler to unravel than they actually are. The problem is that developmental changes are not the same for all children.

INDIVIDUAL DIFFERENCES

Our main purpose in discussing individual differences is to show how they are important for understanding development and to examine how S-R theory might explain them.

When any two persons are given the same intellectual task, their performance will be similar in some ways and different in other ways. The study of individual differences is not primarily the study of individuality or uniqueness. Instead it is the attempt to define properties of persons that determine the degree to which they are similar or different. The problem is to decide how to classify persons, that is, how to select which traits to use in defining categories. There are two possible ways. One is simply to observe and catalog, for any given task on which prople differ, all of the other ways these same people are similar and different. Then the next step is to select those traits that seem to relate to level of performance on the task. A second and better way is to use knowledge of what determines performance differences to construct a scheme for classifying people. In S-R theory, previous learning is the major determinant of performance, suggesting that persons should be classified by what they have learned previously.[23]

Suppose we want to know which persons in a sample can solve the problem of making objects float that usually sink. Whatever our theory, we must ask for information about the persons sampled. How old are they? What stage of development have they attained? S-R theorists, especially Gagné, would ask, "What have the persons already learned?" In particular, we would want to know which persons had learned to compare the density of water with the density of objects and to combine the densities of objects. To the S-R psychologist trying to classify individuals so as to explain individual differences in performance, knowing the extent of learning of prerequisite skills is more important than other information such as age, sex, socioeconomic status, nationality, or developmental level. In the S-R view, persons differ in the ways they perform intellectual tasks because they differ in what they have learned.

A problem for the S-R view of individual differences is that even when all persons in a sample are equal in what they have previously learned, they may still differ in learning the next skill in a hierarchy. For example, in the problem of floating sinkable bodies, suppose all persons had previously learned to compare and combine densities. Some persons might still solve the problem more rapidly than others; even if previous learning were equal, there would still probably be differences in performance on intellectual tasks. Thus, the S-R psychologist is forced to admit that some individual differences cannot be explained by S-R theory. Perhaps these residual differences are due to genetic or biological differences.

Finally, let us state explicitly the S-R view of individual developmental differences. As mentioned, one way persons can be categorized is by their chronological age, so that, other things being equal, the older the child, the larger the number of intellectual tasks he can perform. To S-R theorists, however, this phenomenon is attributable to differences in what children have learned previously—a view consistent with the way S-R theory views other kinds of individual differences, namely, that their primary source is in what has been learned. But note that it is exactly this view that we found when we examined the S-R approach to developmental change itself: development toward greater and greater competence at more and more intellectual tasks is attributed to the completion of more and more relevant learning.

SUMMARY

In this chapter we discussed the development of many specific intellectual functions. For each of Gagné's eight types of learning, we examined the theory and some evidence as to how a child develops from infancy to adulthood. Some changes are rather obvious, some rather unexpected, but in each case we showed how S-R theory accounts for the changes in terms of the kind of relevant previous learning the child has accomplished. Finally, we explored individual differences, pointing out once again that the S-R view leads to the conclusion that individuals differ from one another and resemble one another precisely to the extent that they have learned the same things before.

7

IMPLICATIONS OF STIMULUS-RESPONSE THEORY FOR EDUCATION

Preview

This chapter shows how S-R theory may be applied in the classroom.

We will distinguish three phases of instruction: planning, implementation, and evaluation. The first phase sets performance objectives and, using Gagné's framework, constructs the learning hierarchy needed to achieve them. The second implements the first, from gaining attention to increasing memorability. The third evaluates the success of the instruction in achieving the performance objectives.

We also describe some ways of reducing undesirable behavior. Throughout, we emphasize that intellectual development results from learning.

In this chapter, we change emphasis. Until now, we discussed how S-R theorists explain intellectual development, how they view phenomena that seem to occur naturally as persons grow from childhood to adulthood. But now we must ask, can S-R theory help us facilitate intellectual development? Can we change development so that it is more rapid or so that it results in higher achievement? Thus, we shift from a neutral interest in natural phenomena to a concern with how we can improve on the usual course of development.

This concern with improving intellectual development is shared by many people—parents, government policy makers, businessmen, and so on. Parents worry about their children's future, policy makers want a citizenry that can support government and make society function, businessmen need trained manpower to achieve economic success. The institution most directly concerned is the school, whose prime objective is to foster intellectual development. Thus, in this chapter our major emphasis is on the implications of S-R theory for the structure and conduct of schooling.

Earlier we noted that S-R theorists believe that intellectual development consists of changes in performance that are correlated with age. These performance changes are directed toward the learner's achieving capabilities characteristic of the next higher age level. To S-R theorists, such changes occur because of *learning,* the *generalization* of learning, and the *transfer* of learning. It is transfer, both horizontally and vertically, that makes learning cumulative and that is responsible for the kind of performance changes that we call developmental. S-R psychologists assert that learning is controlled by two kinds of conditions—those external and those internal to the learner, the products of his past learning.

This model of behavior and of the causes of developmental change implies that the course of development can be altered if the conditions of learning, both internal and external, can be controlled. Since intellectual development is caused by learning, we can promote it by determining what is to be learned and by instituting conditions favorable for accomplishing the learning.

These implications are straightforward, but the S-R approach complicates matters by insisting that developmental objectives be described in specific ways. For the theory to help us promote intellectual development, we must specify what changes in performance constitute the desired objectives. Without this description, we cannot identify what types of learning are necessary for the performances, what prerequisites (internal conditions) must be designated for these types of learning, or what external conditions will promote them. Thus, if we adopt an S-R approach to fostering intellectual development, we are obliged to begin with a description of performance objectives.

DEVELOPMENTAL PERFORMANCE
OBJECTIVES AND VALUE JUDGMENTS

Suppose a board of education hires an S-R psychologist to help establish procedures for promoting the intellectual development of the children in its jurisdiction. He asks the board what performances it wants the children to exhibit. The board responds by asking the psychologist what such objectives *should* be. But S-R theory offers very little assistance in identifying desirable objectives for intellectual development—for three reasons.

First, the theory assumes that development depends on what is learned. It does not specify absolute endpoints of development: performance changes are developmental if they increasingly resemble the performances of the next older age group. So, to the S-R psychologist, the endpoint of development depends on what people typically learn. If the board wants to know what people *should* learn, beyond what they usually learn, the theory is of little help.

Second, too little information is available about the performances typical of particular age groups. The theory says more about the causes of developmental change than about the character of intellectual development. To formulate developmental performance objectives, the S-R consultant would probably have to fall back on information from standardized school achievement tests or IQ tests. Such tests describe performance typical for advancing age groups, but the performances are in the small range tapped by the tests.

Third, and probably most important, to set developmental performance objectives, the board of education must make value judgments according to certain standards about the desirability of particular behavior. But S-R theory does not categorize performances as good or bad. Thus, it cannot be used to select performance objectives.

STATING AND COORDINATING DEVELOPMENTAL OBJECTIVES

Once the board of education has selected its objectives in promoting intellectual development, the S-R consultant can help. He could insist that the selected objectives be formulated in terms of explicit, concrete behavior. This demand would oblige members of the board to translate statements like "Appreciates literature" or "Understands Newton's laws of motion" into statements like "Demonstrates an appreciation of fiction by writing reviews of five novels per month in clear and simple English" and "Exhibits an understanding of Newton's laws of motion by correctly stating them verbally and mathematically and by solving a series of problems entailing applications of the laws." Note two features of these performance objectives: (1) they are stated in terms of what the person can do; (2) they refer to specific content. The first feature is an obvious consequence of insisting on *performance* objectives. The second reflects the idea that development is the product of learning. The only way S-R theory can be useful is by specifying what needs to be learned, and to do this the content of desired performances must be specified.

The S-R consultant can also help the board coordinate objectives. Suppose the board has decided that all children should accomplish these two objectives by the end of their fourth-grade year: (1) master calculus (perform as well as the average college mathematics major after completing a first course in calculus); and (2) master Newton's laws of motion (as defined above). By analyzing the performances required in these objectives, the consultant could specify for the board the magnitude of the child's task in achieving them. He could specify all the learning prerequisite to attaining the performances, formulate the learning hierarchies necessary to reach the objectives, and make some estimate of the time required to accomplish all of the learning. Suppose five years appeared reasonable. But also suppose that the objectives could be accomplished in this period only by allotting all available learning time to their pursuit. Then the consultant would have to report to the board that the objectives were attainable, but only at the cost of discarding or delaying learning in other areas such as social studies and literature.

The board would then again be faced with a decision: Is mastery of calculus and the laws of motion worth the cost of ignoring all other topics for five years? Because this question calls for a value judgment, S-R theory offers little direct guidance in answering it. But, an S-R approach would lead the consultant to emphasize that objectives must be coordinated if they are to be reached—any commitment to learning of one kind means that that portion of time cannot be devoted to learning of another kind. Even though this consideration does not force the board to make one decision rather than another, it is relevant to their deliberations.

Note that S-R theory does *not* claim that fourth-grade children are too young or mentally immature to attain the objectives of mastering calculus and the laws of motion by the stated time. Instead it leads the consultant to point out the cost involved. Since the theory holds that intellectual development depends on what has been learned, the obstacle to achieving a developmental objective is only whether enough time can be cleared so that all the necessary learning can be accomplished.

In summary, S-R theory can help in some parts of the task of selecting objectives for intellectual development, but not others. The theory cannot state what developmental objectives *should* be; this must be decided by other agencies.[1] The reason for this modest position is that S-R theory regards intellectual development as the product of learning, so that there are no fixed limits on what intellectual development can consist of by any particular ages. However, the theory does demand that whatever objectives are chosen must be stated in terms of performances so that they can be analyzed for the kinds of learning prerequisite to attaining them. The theory also implies that a total plan for intellectual development must be considered when any particular objectives are set. Otherwise, the work required to attain one set of objectives may make it impossible to attain others that may also be desired.

STIMULUS-RESPONSE THEORY AND INSTRUCTION

Although S-R theory provides some help in stating and coordinating developmental objectives, its major contribution is to planning and carrying out instruction. Even though we usually think of instruction in connection with school, it of course takes place in many other settings as well—in the home, the neighborhood, on the job, and so on. Instruction is a set of external events intentionally arranged to promote an internal event—learning. This definition may seem to make instruction most applicable to formal education, but to S-R theorists instruction applies in whatever context promoting intellectual development occurs. The reason is that for S-R theory both intellectual development and education refer to changes that are brought about by learning. Given the goal of promoting intellectual development in children, the S-R approach would be to design conditions that will facilitate the learning that produces the kinds of developmental changes desired.

The rest of this chapter outlines a way of organizing the events of instruction so as to promote intellectual development. We should not, however, be concerned only with facilitating the learning necessary for some specific performances and forget that our focus is on intellectual development. We often think of development as something different from, more than, or deeper than changes brought about by particular kinds of learning. If a child completes the learning necessary to perform addition and subtraction, for example, we readily agree he has learned something, but it is not as natural to think that he has developed intellectually—this way of describing the change in the child is not the first way that occurs to us. But to S-R theory, changes brought about by learning that advance the child toward performances characteristic of older children are exactly what is thought of as intellectual development: it is the cumulative effects of learning, through generalization and vertical and horizontal transfer. Thus, as we outline the steps of instruction, keep in mind that even though they pertain to specific instances of learning, if such instruction facilitates learning it thereby promotes intellectual development.

Instruction consists of three phases: *planning, implementing,* and *evaluating.* We may think of these phases as steps to follow when we want learning to take place: designing the instruction, conducting the instruction with students, and evaluating the success of both the instructional plan and the way it was conducted.[2]

PHASE 1: PLANNING INSTRUCTION

To begin the first phase of instruction, we should state as objectives the performances a child should exhibit if instruction is successful, as we illustrated in our board of education example. The second step is to analyze these terminal performances to determine what the child must learn in order to accomplish them. Usually the learning necessary for a terminal performance will require prior learning, and the prior learning will require still other previous learning, and so on. Thus, our analysis must specify a hierarchy of learning, from higher level to lower level, in which a succession of prerequisites is identified. The third step is to specify, for each learning event we identified, a performance or set of performances that prove the learning has taken place. The final step is to designate the external conditions that will facilitate each of the specific learning events in the hierarchy that are prerequisite to the terminal performance. We will discuss these four steps in turn.

Stating Objectives as Terminal Performances

Using the example from Chapter 6, suppose we decide that one developmental objective for a child is to understand Archimedes' principle of floating bodies. The first question to ask is, "What kinds of behavior would lead us to decide that a child had understood the principle of floating bodies?" There are many answers appropriate to this question and we would probably wish to state the objective in at least the following ways: (1) If shown a demonstration in which one of two objects floats in water while the other does not, the child can give a verbal explanation of this difference in terms of relative densities. (2) If given a collection of objects, the child can determine and accurately predict which ones will float. (3) When asked, the child can utter a verbal statement of Archimedes' principle or give an equivalent symbolic or mathematical statement. These three versions of the objective all refer to performances of the child that we can directly observe, and a child who could accomplish these performances would persuade most of us that he understood the principle of flotation.

Analyzing Performances and Constructing Learning Hierarchies

Although the three performances are related, it is conceivable a child could do one but not the others. For example, he might be able to memorize a verbal statement of the principle, but be unable to determine the flotability of each of a set of objects; or he might be able to determine flotability but be unable to state the principle verbally. Thus, we will need to construct three learning hierarchies, one for each of the performance objectives, and we know they will be related—that is, they will probably share some prerequisites in common.

To begin to analyze final or *terminal* performance objectives, we may identify the types of learning they require in terms of the Gagné framework. Consider performance (2), that of determining and predicting the flotability of various objects. From Chapter 6, we know that this performance presupposes the learning of a complex rule involving the notion of specific gravity: objects float if their density is less than the density of water. This rule is complex because it is made up of other rules and concepts; density relates the weight of material to the volume the material occupies—in other words, density is weight per unit of volume. Once we have identified the learning necessary for the terminal performance—in this case, a complex rule—we then analyze that learning into its prerequisites, namely, other, simpler rules. Each of these rules must next be analyzed into its components, namely, still other simple rules and concepts. If we continue to work in this fashion, we will eventually produce a large, complicated hierarchy of learning that designates all of the prerequisites for the terminal performance and the prerequisites of the prerequisites. In addition, we must identify, in Gagné's terms, the type of each learning accomplishment in the hierarchy so as to help us complete our next two steps: specifying performances for each learning event, and specifying the external conditions that promote each learning event.

Specifying Performances for Prerequisite Learning

Just as developmental objectives are stated in terms of performances, so it is important to designate, for each learning event in a hierarchy, a performance or set of performances that the child should be able to exhibit when learning is completed. The reason for this is that, in the implementation phase of instruction, we will want to be able to determine whether the child has accomplished each prior learning event in the hierarchy before we ask him to proceed to the next event.

The Gagné framework will help, since for each type of learning, the framework describes the general behavior that is produced. In constructing the hierarchy we have identified the type of each learning event—rule learning, concept learning, discriminations, and so on. Thus, the performance that shows the child has learned the rule for density should be when he responds to various situations in a systematic way, as if behaving according to a rule. A person who has learned the so-called "density rule" will be able to determine the density of many objects in many situations by relating two properties of the objects, weight and volume. Similarly, a person who has learned the so-called "volume rule" will be able to determine the volume of many objects by relating the properties of area and extent. In turn, a person who has learned the concept of length will be able to identify this feature of objects across a wide spectrum, referring to them with the same response, "length," regardless of differences in their appearance. Thus, to complete this first step of the planning phase, one must designate performances like those just mentioned for every component of the hierarchy leading to the terminal performances.

External Conditions to Promote Prerequisite Learning

We have identified the internal conditions necessary for a learning event to occur by specifying the lower-level learning that is prerequisite. We must now describe the external conditions that should be instituted during the implementing phase to promote each particular type of learning in the hierarchy.

Once again, the Gagné framework is of help because it describes the external conditions that promote the completion of each type of learning. For example, when the student is learning the concept "length," the instructor can create three external conditions that should be helpful: (1) stimulate in the learner recall of the relevant discriminations he had previously learned (between length and width, for instance); (2) present a variety of stimuli having the dimension of length; (3) choose those stimuli or objects presented initially so that the feature of length is very prominent in them and prompt the learner to attend to that dimension and to identify it (by pointing or by saying "length"). As the learner's performance becomes better, these prompts should be gradually withdrawn until he can make the length response in the absence of external assistance. Finally, objects should be introduced that have not been shown previously and the learner should be able to identify their length dimension, exhibiting horizontal transfer of learning.

As this example shows, the fourth step of the planning phase requires a lot of work, drawing both on Gagné's framework and on the results of research. For many particular kinds of learning, such as concept learning, experiments have been conducted precisely to determine what external conditions promote high levels of performance. To develop an effective plan for instruction, the teacher should incorporate the results of these experiments.[3] External conditions appropriate for one type of learning may not be relevant to another type, so a complete instructional plan should describe specific external conditions appropriate for each component in the learning hierarchy.

We have seen that the planning phase of instruction includes four major steps: stating objectives in terms of terminal performances; analyzing these performances to construct a learning hierarchy; specifying performances that indicate whether or not each component in the hierarchy has been completed; and identifying external conditions that will promote the learning of each component in the hierarchy. Equipped with a plan that describes in detail the aspects of instruction designed to promote a particular kind of intellectual development, let us now turn to the second phase.

PHASE 2: IMPLEMENTING INSTRUCTION

Gagné has proposed a way of dividing up the implementation phase which we can adapt for our purposes.[4] In Gagné's proposal, this phase has nine parts: (1) gaining and maintaining the learner's attention; (2) informing him of the outcome he can expect at the end of learning; (3) stimulating his recall of relevant prior learning; (4) presenting stimuli; (5) providing guidance or prompting; (6) providing feedback; (7) encouraging self-appraisal; (8) providing for transfer; and (9) increasing the memorability of learning.

The order in which these parts are accomplished can vary from one type of learning to another and the importance of each one also varies, depending on the particular type of learning that is to be accomplished. Even so, this outline can be used as a kind of implementation checklist to ensure that essential features of instructions are not omitted. As we discuss each of the steps, remember that they are all applicable, to some degree, to each type of learning in the hierarchy; that is, all steps have to be taken for each type if it is to be accomplished.

Gaining and Maintaining the Learner's Attention

Gaining and maintaining attention is obviously essential, for if this step fails, all remaining steps will also fail, since the learner will not register the stimuli they provide. If, for example, a teacher tries to present recorded passages from musical selections as the stimuli for learning the concept of fugue, while at the same time an airplane is crashing just outside the classroom windows, the attention of the learners will, of course, be so diverted that probably no learning of the concept of fugue will be accomplished.

For S-R theory, the behavior of attending to some specified event is produced by learning. In the Gagné framework, it is signal learning (Type 1) the learning of connections (Type 2) and of chains (Type 3). Thus, some principal determinants of attending behavior are the external conditions of reinforcement. If the response of attending to relevant events during instruction is reinforced, it will be repeated. If attention is not reinforced, it will diminish; instead, attention will be given to other events. Thus, to gain and maintain attention, the instructor must control the reinforcers available to the learner.

There are four aspects to controlling reinforcement. One is to *identify* those events that are reinforcing for a particular learner. Another is to find ways of *delivering reinforcers* when desired responses are made and of withholding them when the responses are not made. A third is to choose a *schedule* of delivering reinforcers that will be most effective in maintaining the desired behavior. A fourth aspect is to *promote generalization* of attending responses. We will examine each aspect in turn.

Identifying Reinforcing Events. Different children have different histories of experience. So they differ widely in the particular events that effectively reinforce their behavior. For one child, praise from an adult may reinforce the behavior that preceded it. For another child, criticism may be reinforcing. For a third child, being ignored or left alone may be reinforcing. One child's poison may well be the other's reinforcer. Thus, one of the instructor's principal tasks is to identify for each child what is and is not reinforcing.

Delivering Reinforcers. In choosing the reinforcer to use with a child, a major consideration is whether it can be delivered when he makes a desired response and withheld when he does not. For example, suppose Harold finds it reinforcing to make Tim, assigned to a seat nearby, angry by hitting him with paper wads. To change Harold's attending behavior, the teacher must find a way to end the reinforcement Harold receives for attending to Tim. Perhaps she could station herself near Harold's seat, having noticed before that when she recognizes Harold by being near him, he attends to his work and does not harass Tim. But obviously this option would restrict her mobility in the classroom. Another option would be to assign the two boys to widely separated places in the room, thus eliminating the possibility that Harold would receive reinforcement for attending to Tim. In addition, knowing that her recognition of him was also reinforcing to Harold, she could verbally praise him whenever he attends to instruction. When he does not attend to instruction, she could simply ignore him.

This example illustrates three important S-R principles on gaining and maintaining attention: First, the teacher must identify and eliminate the reinforcements a student is receiving for behavior that interferes with the behavior desired. Second, the teacher must choose an event reinforcing to the child that can be delivered adequately and without excessive cost to the teacher or other students. Finally, the teacher must *reinforce the behaviors desired and ignore other responses.* For many teachers, this last principle is the most difficult to adhere to, even though from an S-R viewpoint it is one of the most important. Many are tempted to punish responses in order to assist children in eliminating undesirable behavior and to encourage them in learning to make desired responses. But the S-R view is very clear on this point. To extinguish undesirable behavior, it is much more effective to ensure that reinforcement does not follow such responses than to deliver punishment for them. Similarly, to increase desired behavior, it is much more effective to reinforce the component responses than to punish deviations from them.

Schedules of Reinforcement. Once effective reinforcers have been identified and ways found to deliver them, the instructor must decide on a schedule for delivery. In general, reinforcers are most effective if they are delivered immediately after a child makes a desired response. In the above example, the teacher would be well advised to praise Harold as soon as he begins attending to instruction. Thus, the contention is that reinforcement should be immediate.

Another issue about schedules of delivery, however, is more complicated: Should reinforcement be continuous or intermittent? Reinforcement is *continuous* if it is delivered each and every time a desired response is made. It is *intermittent* if it is not delivered on some occasions when a desired response is made. In general, continuous reinforcement should be used when a desired behavior is weak, and a shift should be made to intermittent reinforcement when the behavior has strengthened to a desired level. At the outset Harold rarely attended to the material presented during school instruction, and this is the point when the teacher should use continuous reinforcement, praising him every time he pays attention. After a time, Harold would exhibit regular attending behavior and so the teacher should shift to a schedule of intermittent reinforcement.

The shift to an intermittent schedule must be *gradual,* or there will be substantial weakening of attending behavior. For example, the teacher might begin the shift by praising Harold four out of every five times he exhibits attending behavior. Although she should expect some weakening of the behavior, the behavior will persist, and shortly it will be as strong as it was on the continuous schedule. At this point she can shift again to a lower ratio of delivery to desired responses, and so on, until the schedule consists of rather infrequent occasions of reinforcement for the desired behavior while still maintaining the child's tendency to pay attention.

There are, of course, good reasons for shifting from a continuous to an intermittent schedule. One is that a continuous schedule, if prolonged, results in *satiation*—the reinforcer no longer works as well because the child has received too much of it. Another is that prolonged, continuous reinforcement places a great burden on the teacher and can actually interfere with other instructional steps. If the teacher is constantly delivering reinforcement for attention to a number of children in the room, she cannot present the stimuli the children are to learn from.

Still another advantage of an intermittent schedule is that the desired behavior will be maintained at full strength for a much longer time when a shift is made to a complete withdrawal of reinforcement. If, for some reason, the teacher is unable to deliver reinforcers to a child for an extended period, he will continue to pay attention longer if he has been on an intermittent schedule than if he has been on a continuous schedule.[5]

Promoting the Generalization of Attending Responses. Suppose the teacher notes that Harold is consistently attentive during reading instruction, provided she praises him on a schedule of intermittent reinforcement. How can she improve the chances of his behavior generalizing to instruction in other settings—in another class or with respect to another subject such as arithmetic? Such a generalization sometimes occurs even when the instructor has not planned it. However, a teacher can use other known properties of stimulus-response and chain learning to exert some control over generalization.

The principle that will help achieve this aim is this: the more the stimuli in the original setting resemble the stimuli in the setting to which generalization is desired, the more likely such generalization will occur. Thus, the teacher should seek to maintain stimuli in, say, the arithmetic lesson that are identical with stimuli present in the reading lesson, where the child may already be highly attentive. For example, the two lessons might be conducted in the same room. Harold might be assigned to the same seat during both kinds of lessons. And the same teacher might be in charge of both kinds of lessons. Since the stimuli are virtually identical in the two settings, they should facilitate generalization of attentiveness from reading instruction to arithmetic instruction. Note that the teacher has sought to increase the chances of generalization, first, by introducing identical stimuli in the two settings, and, second, by emphasizing the common elements in the two settings.

These, then, are the four principal aspects of controlling reinforcement in order to gain and maintain a learner's attention during instruction: (1) identify events that are reinforcing; (2) select reinforcers that can be delivered and withdrawn as the desired response is and is not made; (3) schedule reinforcement to increase the strength of behavior and then to maintain it with a minimum frequency of delivery; and (4) introduce stimuli that are identical from one setting to another in order to promote generalization of the desired attending behaviors.

Informing the Student of Expected Outcomes of Learning

The second step in the implementation phase of instruction is to describe and give examples to the student of the responses he will be able to make when he accomplishes the learning to be done. At present, little is known about the effects of this step except that it seems to work. Possible reasons for its success are that it gives the learner an incentive to know what he will be able to do; it saves time since he does not have to discover for himself the aim of his activity; and it suggests which aspects of the material to be presented are relevant and require his attention.

The meaning of this step can be seen most easily in examples. Suppose the instructor wants to help learners correctly identify and pronounce all four-letter English words ending in the letters ILL. Having gained the students' attention, he might say, "After you complete this lesson, you will be able to recognize and pronounce all four-letter words that end with *ILL;* words like *will, sill, till, mill, bill, kill,* and so on." In another example, suppose the objective is for students to be able correctly to add and record the sum of pairs of single-digit numbers. The instructor could say, "After you complete the work in class today and in your workbook, you will be able to add numbers like 8 and 4 to obtain the sum 12."

Stimulating Recall

In virtually all instruction, the learning required depends on the accomplishment of prerequisite learning. But even if the instructor knows that the prerequisites have been learned, he cannot assume that students will automatically recall them. Since some prerequisites may have been learned days or weeks before instruction in the new material begins, it is useful to remind students of previous learning and to stimulate their recall of it.

Recall may be stimulated in a variety of ways. One way is a simple reminder: "Remember that this word, *K-I-L-L* [printing it on the chalkboard], is *kill.* The first part of the word is *k* and the second part is *ill.*" The purpose of the reminder is to reinstate the chains learned to the stimuli *K, ILL,* and *KILL.*

The instructor could then extend the reminder technique to stimulate the recall of the chains to each of several consonants—*S, W, M,* and so on,—and the multiple discriminations learned among them. A different technique is to require the student to reproduce the responses previously learned. In this case, rather than presenting the responses, the instructor would ask the learner to supply them: "[printing *K-I-L-L* on the chalkboard] What is this word? What is the first part [pointing to *K*]? What is the second part [pointing to *ILL*]? What are each of these [pointing in turn to each of the several consonants that will be the initial letters in the words to be learned]?" This second technique will require the student himself to recall and reproduce the sounds associated with the letters. It has the advantage that the instructor can check to be sure that the previously learned chains and discriminations are actually available to the students. If not, the teacher can choose to begin the new lesson with a period of *relearning,* assisting each child to regain mastery of the prerequisites for the current lesson.

Choices among techniques for stimulating recall should be made according to this simple rule: use a technique that ensures that prerequisites are readily available to the learners in the current setting. Otherwise, the students will have difficulty reaching the current learning objective and be unable to use effectively the instruction provided to assist them.

Presenting Stimuli

For virtually every kind of instructional objective, stimuli should be presented that the learner can respond to. These stimuli vary with the type of learning to be accomplished. For signal learning (Type 1), the stimulus consists of some kind of physical event. For the learning of connections and motor or verbal chains, the stimuli are of two kinds: external and internal. If the child's task is to print the letter *B*, for example, the instructor must not only present the letter (or give the direction to print it) but also ensure that the child experiences the self-produced stimulation of actually making the marks of printing the letter. These internal stimuli *mediate* the overt responses. They are necessary because the connections involved in this learning include internal stimuli that are produced only by the act of printing itself.

For a child to learn multiple discriminations, the instructor must present several stimuli to be discriminated so that the child can make a distinctive response to each one and can learn to inhibit a response appropriate to one stimulus in the presence of another stimulus. For example, suppose the child's task is to learn the sounds usually associated with each of several consonants that *ill* words begin with, such as *k, s, w, m,* and so on. The instructor should present each consonant in close succession so that the child can make the distinctive response associated with it and so that he can learn that each sound is associated with one and not others of the letters.

The stimuli to be presented in concept learning are objects or events that represent the class to which a *single* response is to be learned. If the objective is for a student to learn the concept of "triangle," the stimuli will consist of several different triangular forms. Obviously, the instructor will have to present more than one triangle so as to ensure that the child is learning a concept rather than a chain.

In rule learning (as well as for defined concepts), the stimuli are frequently verbal statements of the rule to be learned—for instance, "Objects of a density greater than that of water will not float." Other stimuli may be presented along with such verbal statements to illustrate the operation of the rule—here a variety of objects differing in density and other properties, and a container of water.

The choice of the stimuli to be presented will be partly dictated by the type of learning to be accomplished. But additional choices must be made as well. For example, some stimuli can be represented in different media—words, pictures, diagrams, or actual objects. Unfortunately, S-R research and theory have not yet progressed far enough to yield unequivocal rules for making choices among these various alternatives. It appears that the best medium for presenting stimuli depends very much on the age of the student, the type of learning to be accomplished, and the particular content of the learning. Accordingly, when planning instruction on a specific topic, the teacher should try out various modes of presenting stimuli to determine which is best for the individual learner involved.

Providing Guidance or Prompting

Generally, guiding and prompting (1) emphasize relevant aspects of the stimuli presented and (2) provoke the desired response by presenting auxiliary stimuli. The first class of acts is illustrated in the teacher's pointing to the three sides and angles of geometric forms when the objective is the learning of the concept of triangle. The second class of acts is exhibited when the teacher physically guides the hand of the child as he attempts to print the letter *B;* or in pronouncing the word *kill* immediately before asking the child to pronounce it when presented with the printed letters *K-I-L-L.* These instructional acts, prompting and guiding learning, are pervasive in the school setting and are important for the fact that they considerably facilitate the student's work.

Providing Feedback

Feedback refers to events that tell the learner whether his responses are adequate. Reinforcement is one form of feedback; it is delivered only when a desired response is made, thus informing the learner of the adequacy of his response. But feedback takes other forms too. Sometimes the learner sees it in the direct consequences of his response. To the would-be golfer it is the results of his swing: watching the ball hook, slice, dribble, or never leave the tee gives him information about the adequacy of his responses. Often feedback is provided by an instructor or by instructional materials, as when a teacher says, "Right!" when a student correctly spells a word.

We cannot say with certainty that feedback is necessary for successful learning, but most psychologists believe it helps. Some believe feedback has the same effect as reinforcers in general. Others think it enables the learner to correct his erroneous responses. Still others believe feedback tells the learner how close his performance is to what will be possible when he completes the learning he is engaged in. Whatever the reason, feedback is widely believed to be an important part of the implementation phase of instruction.[6]

Encouraging Self-Appraisal

Self-appraisal allows the learner to produce feedback for himself. Tests, for instance, allow him to check his performance against the standard he is striving to reach. Thus, he can determine for himself the adequacy of his responses, the extent of his learning, and the aspects of the task that need more work. Tests used for self-appraisal have three positive effects in instruction. First, they allow the student to acquire the skills of managing his own learning. Second, they give him further practice in learned skills, so that he better retains what he has learned. Third, since self-appraisal is very motivational for many students, tests may maintain attention to the learning required for successful performance.

Providing for Transfer

Just as generalization of attending behavior should not be left to chance, likewise transfer should also be provided for in instructional plans. The importance of transfer is obvious: no amount of direct instruction in a skill can ever cover all the instances in which the person will need to apply that skill. Thus, whatever means will help him use the skill in settings other than the one he learned it in are valuable indeed. For example, if a student learned the skill of long division in school, we would hope he could apply it also in collecting money from customers on his paper route who have been subscribers for only part of a month.

Unfortunately, not much information is available about methods of increasing the probability of transfer of academic skills. At present, the most trustworthy general principle is that the greater the degree a skill has been learned originally, the greater the degree of transfer. Another, more controversial principle is that in concept and rule learning, the wider the variety of instances encountered during initial learning, the greater the transfer of the concept or rule to the new instances. A third principle is that transfer is also better if adequate learning hierarchies have been formed; that is, if all of the skills prerequisite for transfer have been learned previously.

Increasing the Memorability of Learning

If there is no transfer, a student's skills are severely limited to the settings and stimuli he originally learned them under. He is even more severely limited if he has forgotten learned skills. Since forgetting is a pervasive fact of human existence, we must find ways of increasing the memorability of learned skills important to the student, so he can achieve a performance that will be demanded of him or so they will be available as prerequisites for later learning.

Knowledge about forgetting is far from complete, but two principles for increasing memorability are rather widely accepted at present. The first principle is that what determines memorability the most is the extent to which something was learned initially. If one thing is easy to learn and another is difficult to learn, they will be remembered equally well provided only that they were mastered to the same degree originally. This principle has two implications—(1) that any material that is important should be learned to a high degree; (2) that one should periodically relearn important material so that he can achieve again the same high degree of mastery.

The second principle of memorability is that the distinctiveness of skills learned should be enhanced. A principal source of forgetting is apparently interference, either from material learned prior to the learning of a given skill or from material learned afterwards. Furthermore, the more similar the two sets of learned material, the more likely interference will occur. Accordingly, whenever similar materials or skills are being learned, it is worthwhile to establish conditions that are distinctively different during the learning of each.

These nine parts, then, constitute the major features of the implementation phase of instruction. As we noted at the outset, they are not steps in a sequence; they occur in different orders depending on what topic the instruction is concerned with. To illustrate this point, and to summarize the implementation phase, we present in Table 7.1 the various parts of this phase, expressed as an example formulated by Gagné.[7]

PHASE 3: EVALUATING INSTRUCTION

In the evaluation phase, the teacher determines the effectiveness of the planning and implementation phases. The evaluation phase can be relatively straightforward, if the planning phase has been executed well: if the objectives of instruction are designated and stated in specific behavioral terms, the evaluator's task is simply to find out if the objectives have been met. But evaluation can become complicated, especially if the teacher determines that instruction has not met the objectives. Thus, we should take a look at some *types, methods,* and *consequences* of evaluation.[8]

Types of Evaluation

Here we are concerned with evaluating *instruction,* as opposed to evaluating *students,* so the methods we will discuss are not appropriate for answer-

Table 7.1. Instructional Process for Exercise on "Inferring the Presence of Water Vapor in the Air."

INSTRUCTIONAL EVENT	FUNCTION
1. Teacher directs attention to clouded windows on cold day; ring of water left by glass of ice water; cloud left by breathing on a mirror. Questions students about why these events happen.	1. *Achievement motivation,* established based on child's curiosity and desire to display knowledge to other children and to parents.
2. Children given tin cans and ice cubes.	2. *Stimulus objects* provided.
3. Students told to put ice cubes in the cans, and to watch what happens to outside of cans.	3. Completion of stimulus situation. *Verbal directions* to focus attention.
4. Students asked to describe what they see—"fog"; "water drops"; "large drops running down"; "ring of water at base of can."	4. *Verbal directions* to stimulate *recall* of previously learned concepts. *Feedback* provided.
5. Students asked what they can infer from their observations—"Liquid is water from the air."	5. Learning of a principle by discovery; for some students this may be recall. *Feedback* provided.
6. Other alternatives pointed out to students. Could it be some other liquid or come from metal of can? *How can one test an inference?*	6. *Verbal directions* to inform the learner of the expected *outcome* of instruction (how to test this inference).
7. "How can we tell whether this liquid is water?" ("Taste it.")	7. *Verbal directions* requiring *recall* of previously learned principle.
8. "If water comes out of the metal, what should happen when it is wiped off?" ("Can should weigh less.")	8. *Verbal directions* requiring *recall* of previously learned principles.
9. Students asked, if the water comes from air, what happens to weight of can after water collects on it. ("Can should increase in weight.") Direct observation is made of increase in weight of can from ice, by weighing on an equal-arm balance.	9. *Verbal directions* requiring *recall* of previously learned principles.
10. Students asked to recall that steam consists of water droplets and water vapor (an invisible gas). Air can contain water vapor.	10. *Verbal directions* requiring *recall* of previously learned principles.
11. Students asked to state what they observed, what they inferred, how they checked their inference.	11. Learning of the principles of distinguishing observation and inference, and of operations required to check inferences. *Feedback* provided.

Table 7.1. (cont.)

INSTRUCTIONAL EVENT	FUNCTION
12. Students asked to make and test inferences in two or three other new situations and to describe the operations and reasoning involved. These might be water evaporation, the extinguishing of a candle in a closed cylinder, the displacement of water by gas in an inverted cylinder.	12. Additional *examples* of the principles learned, to ensure recall and generalization.
13. Students presented another new situation and asked to describe what they observed, what they inferred, how they checked their inference.	13. *Appraisal* providing *feedback*.

ing questions about individual students—whether Cora is more intelligent than Robert or whether Annie has learned more than Sarah. But these methods can answer the question of whether instruction has helped students attain designated objectives.

Individual and instructional evaluation differ in the standard used to make a decision. For individual evaluation, the standard is usually the performance of other individuals. Tests used for such evaluation are called *norm-referenced* tests because the performance of an individual is compared with the norm, or average, performance of other individuals in his group. Most standardized school-achievement tests, such as IQ tests, are of this type. Richard's performance on a reading achievement test will be reported as a grade-equivalent score, which purports to tell what grade students are in when the average of their test performances is the same as Richard's. If Richard receives a grade equivalent of 4.5, this score means that his performance is the same as the average performance of children when they are midway through the fourth grade of elementary school. Similarly, the IQ score represents the performance of an individual in terms of how far it is above or below the average performance given by all other persons of the same chronological age. Both these tests are of the norm-referenced type.

In contrast, tests evaluating instruction are keyed to objectives rather than to the average performance of groups of individuals. The standard for performance on such tests is the criterion provided by the behavioral statement of the objectives of instruction. Thus, these tests are commonly called *criterion-referenced*. When such tests are used, instruction is regarded as successful only if student performance meets the criterion.

For example, if an objective of instruction is that students understand Archimedes' principle, a behavioral statement of this objective would specify that students be able to: (a) give a verbal explanation of the fact that some objects float in water whereas others do not, referring to the variables that determine the densities of objects and their relation with the density of water;

(b) predict which of several objects will and will not float, given the resources necessary to determine the density of each object; and (c) give a verbal or symbolic statement of Archimedes' principle. Given these ways of stating the instructional objective, evaluation would consist of constructing a test containing items that would ask students to exhibit these three performances, both with materials that had been used in the course of instruction and (to assess the extent of transfer) with new materials—that is, objects and containers not used during instruction. If students did exhibit the designated performances, instruction would be judged a success.

Another important distinction among types of evaluation is the point at which evaluation is made. Evaluation can take place *during* or *after* the planning and implementation phases. Evaluation during the planning phase is useful for improving instruction before it is implemented. For example, if the evaluator examines closely the initial formulation of a learning hierarchy for instruction in Archimedes' principle, he may find it faulty in designating the types of learning involved or incomplete in identifying all the prerequisites for the terminal performances. Thus, the instructor can modify the plan before implementation begins. Evaluation made during the implementation phase allows the instructor to give the student feedback and guidance where needed. Evaluation made at the end of both phases can help the teacher decide whether and how to revise the instructional plan.

Methods of Evaluation

To the S-R theorist, the evaluation method best designed to promote intellectual development is an *empirical* method, such as tests. How students perform on tests provides empirical evidence as to whether the instructional objectives have been met. To the teacher, the main tasks of empirical evaluation are, first, to formulate the test items and, second, to decide how many items must be passed by how many students before students can be considered to have learned the unit of instruction. In formulating items, he must consider whether to complete them successfully the student must turn in a performance that represents the objectives. A successful performance is *not,* for example, a correct answer to a single true-false question about Archimedes' principle, since this could be achieved by luck as well as by having accomplished the learning intended in the instructional plan.

Ideally, all students should pass all items before instruction is judged a success, but in practice, of course, this ideal can rarely be met. Test items are not always reliable indicators of the success of learning—a student may pass or fail an item for reasons other than the success or failure of his prior learning. Yet it seems fair to conclude that if he fails all the items, he did not meet the objective, and if he passes them all, he attained the objective. Thus, though there are no firm rules, some decision must be made about how many items a student must pass so that we can consider that instruction has succeeded.

It is optimistic to suppose that an instructional plan will succeed for all students. Since students differ in prior learning and physical functioning, including different handicapping conditions, a teacher must decide how general the effectiveness of an instructional plan must be for it to be judged a success. Should it be effective for both blind and sighted students? For both first graders and fourth graders? Again, there are no hard and fast rules about what is acceptable instructional effectiveness. But the teacher should beware of setting his standard too low, or he will succeed only in accepting poor instructional units.

Consequences of Evaluation

The results of *individual* evaluation are used to assess how one person's attainments compare to other persons' in the same group. The results of *instructional* evaluation are used to assess the adequacy of instruction. If instruction is found inadequate, either or both the planning and implementation must be revised. Evaluation is most profitable when it improves instruction—a view consistent with the S-R approach to intellectual development. When a student does not accomplish an instructional objective, just as when a person does not develop intellectually, it is due to a failure of learning; and a failure of learning occurs because the conditions of learning, or of instruction, are inadequate.

To be most useful, evaluation should provide information about what specifically should be modified when instruction is found inadequate. Thus, the teacher should not rely entirely on terminal student performance to evaluate instruction. Because there are many parts of an instructional unit, if judgments are based solely on terminal performance, it is often impossible to track down exactly which part of instruction is deficient. Thus, the instructional plan should provide for evaluation while instruction is in progress. Prior to the implementation phase, the teacher can design items to test for the performances that demonstrate, at each stage of progress through the unit, successful completion of the learning prerequisites for the terminal performance. For instruction in Archimedes' principle, the implementation phase would test that the student not only mastered the principle of floating bodies, but also mastered the concept of length and the rules for area and volume. Thus, when the teacher makes revisions, they can be aimed at demonstrably deficient parts of the instructional plan.

These, then, are the major phases of instruction: planning, implementing, and evaluation. Taken together, and repeated often enough, they should result in learning that systematically enhances the intellectual development of students.

Until this point in the chapter we have focused on ways of helping the student acquire the skills to accomplish new performances. We will now concentrate on ways of modifying previously learned capabilities.

BEHAVIOR MODIFICATION

Behavior modification, a visible application of S-R theory to real life, refers to systematic reinforcement to change behavior. Behavioral change can occur in many ways: New behavior can be induced. Current behavior can be maintained, increased, and extended or generalized. Current behavior can also be reduced. When so defined, it is clear we have discussed instances of behavior modification in previous chapters. In the Gagné framework, the principles of behavior modification are best exemplified in learning Types 2 and 3, that is, learning connections and chains. Our discussion of ways to gain and maintain attention obviously relies heavily on principles of behavior modification.

We now consider another aspect of behavior modification, the *reduction* of undesirable behavior—also known, in a school setting, as *maintaining discipline* or *classroom management.* [9] This topic is important for the teacher, for it is nearly impossible for a teacher to complete the various steps of instruction if he must constantly deal with behavior that interferes with those steps. The topic is important for the student because instances of undesirable behavior (his own or other students') obstruct his accomplishing the learning he needs to meet the objectives of schooling—an attainment that may affect his future options.

Many behavior-modification procedures are available for reducing behavior: *extinction, differential reinforcement, punishment,* and *reinforcement of substitute behaviors.*

Before the teacher selects and implements any behavior-modification procedures, he should identify the responses the procedure will reduce. Consistent with the S-R approach, such identification must be in concrete behavioral terms—it is not enough to say Daryl often disrupts the class; we must describe particular ways Daryl is disruptive, such as to say that when other students are working or reciting, or when the teacher is talking, Daryl often makes disparaging remarks that make other students laugh. In another example, when we say Harold persistently teases Tim, his nearby classmate, we need to specify "teasing" in behavioral terms—Harold throws paper wads at Tim, makes faces at him, and whispers to him while Tim is listening to the teacher, reciting, or working on an assignment. As these examples illustrate, to reduce behavior, we must first describe the behavior specifically.

A second step is to identify the events that reinforce the problem behavior: for Daryl, it is probably the laughter of his classmates that reinforces his disruptive remarks; for Harold, the reinforcing event seems to be the disruption of Tim's ongoing activity and Tim's resulting annoyance.

A related step is to identify other events that do or do not reinforce student behavior the instructor wishes to modify. Common events are praise from the teacher and other students, the option to participate in special activities such as being a messenger or reading sports magazines in class, and earning tokens that can be exchanged for toys, books, and the like. The important thing is for the teacher to determine what particular events are reinforcing for a particular student and select ones that the teacher can deliver at will.

A final step is to decide clearly how much reduction in behavior is desirable. Some behavior is disruptive only under specific circumstances, but other behavior is generally disrupting in a school setting. Talking aloud in class, for example, is not disruptive when it occurs as part of a discussion, but throwing paper wads in class nearly always is. Such considerations will dictate the kinds of provisions that a teacher must make to generalize the behavior reduction or confine it to particular classroom conditions.

Once these preliminary steps are taken, the teacher must decide which of several available procedures can achieve behavior modification. An obvious procedure is *extinction,* the termination of reinforcement for the responses to be reduced. If it is possible to stop delivery of reinforcers, the result should be gradual and relatively long-lasting reduction in the behavior concerned. However, one significant restriction is that the reinforcing events must be controlled by the instructor. If the teacher's own activity is serving as a reinforcer, as when his proximity to a student is the reinforcer, then the extinction procedure is indicated, since he can systematically avoid moving near the student when he makes disruptive responses. (With Daryl, though, it is his classmates' laughter that is reinforcing, and so it would be difficult for the teacher to terminate these events.)

Differential reinforcement is particularly useful when the behavior to be reduced is desirable under some conditions but not others. For instance, talking aloud in class during a classroom discussion may be desirable, but when it interrupts others, it is not. Here, the instructor must reinforce the behavior when he deems it appropriate and withdraw reinforcement (extinction procedure) for it when it is inappropriate. One other facet of differential reinforcement is important for its effectiveness, namely, that distinctive stimuli be present when the behavior is appropriate and absent when it is inappropriate. Such stimuli might consist of the teacher's verbal statements, such as in "Make your comments now, Daryl" or other signals that can be associated with contexts where the given behavior will be reinforced.

The procedure of *punishment* is well known and has a long history of use, but there is considerable controversy about it, centering on two kinds of issues—its effectiveness in reducing behavior, and its side effects. The procedure itself, of course, is relatively straightforward: immediately after a student makes an undesirable response, the instructor delivers an *aversive* stimulus, one the student would avoid if it were possible to do so. The choice of aversive stimuli should depend on the individual student. Most persons will react to aversive stimuli such as spanking that result in physical pain. Sometimes the *threat* of physical pain is aversive, as are many forms of criticism such as verbal statements that include shaming or degrading assertions about a person.

Whatever the aversive stimulus, several conditions are believed to enhance its effectiveness. (Because of the considerable controversy about the effectiveness of punishment, the following statements should be regarded as hypotheses rather than hard fact.) First, the aversive stimulus should be delivered immediately after an undesirable response is made and it should be applied consistently, that is, every time the response is made. Second, precautions should be taken to prevent the student from avoiding or escaping the stimulus. Third, the stimulus should be applied with maximum intensity, whenever it is delivered. Finally, punishment should be combined with reinforcement of alternative behaviors.

When effective, punishment works rapidly. But it frequently has undesirable side effects. It may, for example, produce aggressive behavior in the person punished; he may learn to punish others. It may promote the behavior of avoiding or escaping from the situation in which punishment occurs; in the school setting, this side effect is illustrated by absenteeism, and dropping out. It may diminish the self-esteem of the person punished, so that he frequently makes negative statements about himself. In view of these potential side effects, great caution should be used in selecting punishment as a way of modifying behavior.

An appealing thing about *reinforcement of substitute behaviors* is that it not only reduces undesirable responses but strengthens and maintains desirable ones. Essentially, the procedure selects substitute behavior, and extinguishes undesirable behavior. Two behaviors are incompatible if they are mutually exclusive; if one behavior occurs, the other cannot. For example, those traits of Harold's behavior that are involved in "teasing" Tim are incompatible with attentiveness to instruction and diligent work on assignments. Accordingly, to reduce Harold's teasing behavior, the teacher might (1) move Harold's seat so that Tim, the initiating stimulus for his behavior, is at a distance, thereby extinguishing the teasing behavior; and (2) reinforce the substitute behavior of attentiveness to instruction and work on assignments.

In general, when the procedure of reinforcing substitute behavior is used, the following rules should be observed. (1) The behavior to be reinforced should be antithetical to the behavior to be reduced, otherwise both may occur at the same time and reinforcement will strengthen, rather than weaken, the undesirable behavior. (2) The substitute behavior should be chosen from among those performances the student already exhibits, so the instructor can take advantage of the learning the student has previously accomplished, and not have to induce entirely new learning to compete with the undesirable behavior. (3) The substitute behavior should consist of performances that will be reinforced in settings outside the initial setting in which the modification procedure is introduced; this will add to its strength in comparison with the undesirable behavior. Otherwise, the substitute behavior may well extinguish between the occasions when it is possible for the teacher to reinforce it. For example, it would be unwise to select some behavior that the student's friends or parents will not reinforce outside the classroom. If these rules are followed, the procedure of reinforcing substitute behavior will usually, though gradually, produce relatively enduring reductions in undesirable behavior.

These five procedures for reducing undesirable behavior are representative of several techniques developed in the field of behavior modification. The description offered here has been abbreviated, but more comprehensive discussion may be found in other sources.[10]

SUMMARY

In this chapter we explored how an S-R approach might facilitate intellectual development, though we emphasized it cannot select the objectives of development. This is consistent with what we presented in preceding chapters—that development results from learning and from the generalization and transfer of learning. Accordingly, the way to facilitate development is to establish internal and external conditions that bring about learning.

Turning to the school setting, we distinguished three phases of instruction: planning, implementation, and evaluation. In the planning phase, terminal instructional objectives are set, analyzed into performance objectives that are further analyzed in terms of the learning necessary to produce them; these types of learning are then arranged into a hierarchy, and the conditions needed to accomplish prerequisite learning are specified. The implementation phase consists of nine parts, from gaining attention to increasing the memorability of learning. In the evaluation phase—which aims to improve instruction, not judge the relative achievements of individual students—the success of instruction is evaluated by how well students perform according to the objectives developed in the planning phase. If instruction does not help students accomplish the planned objectives, revision is called for; if well designed, the evaluation will indicate what parts need revising.

The chapter also described some ways of reducing undesirable behavior, techniques related to the principles of learning connections and chains. We proposed that, properly applied, these techniques could help students develop intellectually by diminishing behavior that interferes with their learning in the nine parts of the implementation phase of instruction. As throughout this part, we repeatedly emphasized this fundamental dictum of S-R psychology: intellectual development results from learning.

Part 2

The COGNITIVE Approach to Intellectual Development

8

THE COGNITIVE POINT OF VIEW

Preview

Cognitive theory assumes a person behaves according to an act of thinking about a situation; his behavior is not determined by the situation itself. The environment and inner maturation affect a child's intellectual development only insofar as they affect his cognitive *activity* in relation to the environment.

In this chapter, we show that the cognitive theorist, especially as represented by Jean Piaget, is not an empiricist or nativist but a constructivist, because he believes the child creates new ways of thinking.

We also discuss four methods by which cognitive theorists make inferences about the way children think, and finally we show how biol-

ogy and computer science provide frames of
reference for looking at intellectual development.

Children and adults have different ways of thinking, and so do young
children and older children. Not only does a young child know *less* than he
will know later on, but what he does know already is organized differently in
his head. The "facts" of his experience are related to each other by a different
kind of mental structure.[1] From this point of view, intellectual development
is a process of restructuring, not just an accumulation of knowledge and skills.
Each new type of structure, each new way of thinking that develops, is better
than the last in the sense that it makes the child more capable of dealing
intelligently with his environment. However, new structures also build on old
ones, preserving what is useful in them. The process of restructuring, that is,
development, comes about as the child uses his present structures long enough
to realize their strengths and discover their limitations. From a practical
standpoint, the teacher should be aware of the kind of structure that the child
is likely to impose on what he is being taught, because that will determine what
he actually learns. And if the goal is to promote intellectual development, the
child must be given ample opportunity to use his present ways of thinking,
particularly in situations that will help him discover their limitations and guide
him in the process of restructuring.

In a nutshell, those are the basic ideas of the approach to intellectual
development that we call *cognitive theory*. The problem of selecting a name for
this approach has been vexing but instructive. According to the dictionary,
cognition refers to the act or process of knowing. Thus, it is hard to imagine
a theory of intellectual development that would *not* be concerned with cognition. Consequently, the term *cognitive* seems to lack distinction as a name for
one particular type of theory. This problem becomes especially acute when the
phrase cognitive development is treated as a synonym for intellectual development, as it often is. We then have to talk about "the cognitive approach to
cognitive development." There are other names for this approach ("cognitive-
developmental," "cognitive-structural"), but they are not very distinctive and
are a good deal more awkward. So *cognitive theory* it is, largely for the sake
of simplicity.

It really is not such a bad name after all, because it does suggest a
special emphasis on how children *think*—their ways of knowing or their
"cognitive structures"—as opposed to what they *do* or what they *feel*. In other
words, the name cognitive theory does set the present approach apart from S-R
theory, with its focus on behavior, and from psychoanalytic theory, with its
attention to "affect" or emotion. It leads one, perhaps, to expect a theory that
concentrates on what *ought* to be the central problem of intellectual development—how children think and how their thinking changes as they grow up
—because that is exactly what cognitive theory is most concerned with.

ASSUMPTIONS ABOUT BEHAVIOR AND DEVELOPMENT

The most basic assumption of cognitive theory is that human behavior is not determined in any direct way by the immediate situation in which it occurs. Intervening between the situation and behavior is cognition, the act or process of knowing. A person usually does not respond in a reflexive, knee-jerk fashion to a direct stimulus. Rather, he *thinks* about the situation he is in and then acts according to his understanding of it.

A second basic assumption is that a person's *way* of thinking, his cognitive structure, cannot be explained solely by associations between past stimuli and responses. What a person knows cannot be reduced to how he previously behaved in particular situations; even on those earlier occasions, cognition must have intervened between the situation and behavior just as it does in the present. A person has always had a cognitive structure of some sort, so former structures cannot be ignored in any explanation of the development of present structures. Later structures depend to some extent on earlier structures.[2]

These two assumptions show that cognitive theory gives a person a significant degree of autonomy from the environment, both in his behavior on a particular occasion and in the origins of his knowledge or ways of thinking. This notion of partial autonomy has important implications for theory and for practice.

Its theoretical importance is that it would be impossible to explain man's ability to deal with a great variety of new situations if we did *not* allow for such autonomy. People are not so tied to the past or present that they can adapt to novelty only through blind trial and error. They can generalize from their previous experience or transfer it to a new situation. The ability to do this is part of practically everyone's definition of intelligence. But "generalize" and "transfer" are just names for something that humans do all the time. To explain them, we must delve into the nature and development of cognitive structures, the ways of thinking that make intelligent behavior possible.

The practical implication of man's partial autonomy from the environment is that we are more likely to succeed in predicting or influencing a person's behavior if we take his cognition into account, along with the nature of the situation he is in. Similarly, we are more likely to be able to influence a person's way of thinking if we consider his present way of thinking, as well as the new way of thinking that is to be acquired. In both cases, we must assess the person's cognitive structure.

The cognitive theorist's basic assumptions about how cognition affects behavior and development have roots both in our everyday thinking about human nature and in formal philosophy. An example of the common assumption that behavior is not determined simply by the situation at hand is that most of us succeed occasionally in planning ahead: instead of responding to the sight of a TV set by turning it on, we manage to tear ourselves away from this diversion in order to work on a project due the next day. An observer probably would not attribute our behavior to anything inherently unpleasant about the TV set or to a past history of "avoidance conditioning." He would be more inclined to assume that we knew we were dealing with a finite period of time in which it would be impossible to watch TV and finish the project too. The point is that people are quite accustomed to explaining behavior in terms of cognitive processes that go beyond the immediate situation.

Philosophers generally agree with our everyday assumption that behavior is influenced by thoughts or "ideas," but there have been some major disagreements as to the origins of these ideas. This is the philosophical question of *epistemology*. Some *empiricist* philosophers believe that ideas such as a finite unit of time are entirely the products of our experience with the environment, that concepts of time are "impressed" upon the mind by a variety of specific experiences in which time is a salient factor. One problem with a wholly empiricist approach is that it provides no satisfactory way of accounting for conceptual differences between species—and it does seem clear that the concept of time is much more highly developed in men than in apes, for example.

An opposing point of view, *nativism,* holds that many ideas are innate and specific to a given species—for instance, the basic notions of time, space, and causality in man. Although this epistemology is a convenient way of explaining conceptual differences between species, it presents some problems for interpreting the behavior of young children: If a certain understanding of time is involved in planning ahead, and if time is an innate idea in man, then why do children seem unable to plan ahead very well? One could argue that children simply lack the will power to stick with long-range plans, but other evidence suggests that children really do not understand time in the same way that adults do. Perhaps the child does have the notion of time in some latent form, but he has not "matured" enough for this concept to become functional. This explanation would reconcile the notion of innateness with the observed differences between children and adults, but it still leaves something to be desired. "Maturation" usually refers to the passage of time—time in which a more or less spontaneous growth process can occur. However, the mere passage of time is probably not enough to cause the development of those ideas that are basic to human intelligence.

A synthesis of nativism and empiricism leads to the suggestion that basic human concepts emerge from the *interaction* of innate capacities with environmental opportunities. According to this synthesis, both maturation and experience are important in intellectual development. A certain amount of maturation may be necessary before innate capacities can be activated, but then the environment must provide opportunities for experiences that activate the capacities and determine their further development.

Nearly all developmental psychologists subscribe to an interactionist position on epistemology, although with different emphases on maturation or experience. The interactionist position most closely associated with cognitive theory is *constructivism*.[3] This point of view states that the child actively constructs his own ways of thinking and his own ideas about the nature of reality. Innate and environmental factors influence development through their effect on the child's everyday activity as he moves about and acts upon his environment. In effect, the child gradually builds a "theory" of what the world is all about, based on "experiments" he performs in his daily life. The results of one experiment lead to another and then another, and the child keeps revising his theory in light of the data he has collected. Maturation and experience may determine the kinds of experiments the child can perform at a given time, but the theory will not move forward unless the child actually performs the necessary experiments.

The chief proponent of constructivism is Swiss scholar Jean Piaget, who has investigated children's thinking for more than half a century. To a large extent, the cognitive approach to intellectual development *is* Piaget's theory, and thus many theoretical ideas, technical terms, and research observations in the chapters that follow come from him and his collaborators.

METHODS OF STUDYING COGNITION

An eminent psychologist once remarked that "methodology, the bread and butter of a scientist working in any given field, is usually spinach to those outside."[4] Most "outsiders" are more interested in *what* the scientist found than in *how* he found it, and of course the scientist himself is ultimately more concerned with the what too. But he also realizes that what he finds may depend on how he looks for it. He wants to use methods that will enhance his chances of answering the questions of interest to him. As we have seen, the cognitive theorist is most interested in learning about how children think and how their thinking changes in the course of development. The question, then, is how to go about doing this.

Making Inferences about Cognition from Behavior and Situation

The cognitive point of view poses a knotty problem in methodology. How can the scientific psychologist study cognition and cognitive structures when these are *mental* phenomena and therefore are not directly observable? In the past, some psychologists believed that a person could at least observe his *own* cognitive processes. After all, people do have the subjective experience of seeing, hearing, reasoning, planning, and so on. Given some training in the observation of subjective experience, a person might collect useful data on the working of his own mind. During one period in the history of psychology, such introspection was the principal method of psychological research. The subjects in a typical experiment were called observers and were asked to reflect on what they experienced when the experimenter put them in various situations, to analyze their experiences carefully, and to report their findings in detail.

One obvious problem with this method is that it cannot be used to study cognition in young children—and not just preverbal children. Even several years after they acquire language, children still seem unable to reflect very well upon their own thoughts. Adults too apparently cannot become aware of all that is involved in their own cognition. This is not necessarily because of the repression of disturbing thoughts, as described in psychoanalytic theory. Try to introspect on the mental processes involved in reading this sentence. What you experience is a sentence, or perhaps just a "meaning." You can analyze the sentence further into words, letters, or even dark contours on a light background, but what process enabled you to interpret those contours as a sentence in the first place? You really cannot become aware of the process, only the results. Finally—the most fundamental problem—introspection does not allow for external verification of its data; it lacks a basic feature of modern science, namely, *objectivity*.

As discussed in Chapter 2, the desire for scientific objectivity in psychology led eventually to a rejection of introspection in favor of the approach known as *behaviorism*. Mental processes may not be publicly observable, but behavior is observable, and so is the situation in which it occurs. Consequently, behaviorists defined psychology as the science concerned with laws governing the relationships between observable stimuli in the situation and observable responses to them. According to this definition, a psychological explanation of behavior should include no reference to mental processes (unless one thinks of those processes as connections between observable stimuli and observable responses). Out of behaviorism evolved the tradition of S-R learning theory. However, cognitive theorists find behaviorism overly restrictive in confining itself to what is directly observable. The *method* of behaviorism is scientifically more satisfactory than is introspection, but behavioristic *theory,* in trying to ignore the autonomy of cognition, renders itself incapable of accounting for intelligent human behavior.

Today's cognitive psychologist uses methods similar to the behaviorist's to study mental processes: he observes overt behavior and the situation it occurs in and makes *inferences* about cognition, which is, of course, an internal, unobservable phenomenon. Thus, the approach of cognitive psychology is similar to that of contemporary S-R psychology, although it has an important difference, as we shall mention presently. The general strategy for building a cognitive theory of intellectual development works like this: First, the scientist observes individuals similar in age or experience in particular situations; from their behavior, he makes inferences about their thinking in or understanding of each situation (that is, their cognition). Second, he notes regularities in cognition that occur in a variety of situations and makes further inferences about the individual's *ways* of thinking (that is, his cognitive structures). Finally, he compares individuals who are *different* in their ages or experience to ascertain possible differences in their ways of thinking, and he makes inferences about the character and causes of *change* in cognitive structures (that is, their intellectual development).

This formula is oversimplified, for the three steps are likely to interact rather than follow each other in a simple sequence. For instance, some ideas about the nature of intellectual development may influence the theorist's inferences about cognitive structures, which in turn may affect his inferences about cognition in a particular situation. However, the point is that the whole enterprise rests upon inferences from observed behavior in particular situations. An important question, then, concerns the kinds of situations in which to observe behavior for the purpose of making such inferences.

Situations in Which to Observe Behavior

Cognitive theorists have based their inferences about intellectual development on four different kinds of observations or research methods: *experiments, naturalistic observation, comparative testing,* and the *clinical method.* Each method involves a different kind of situation in which to make inferences about cognition.

Experiments. The experimental method was discussed at some length in Chapter 2, so we will briefly review its essential features and advantages, and then consider some of its disadvantages. In its classic form, an experiment involves the manipulation of one variable while all other variables are held constant or otherwise controlled. For example, two groups of children that are alike in all other respects may be treated differently in one particular way— say, one watching television, the other not—in order to see what effect this has on their behavior. The advantage of this method is that it enables the investigator to draw some relatively strong conclusions about cause- and-effect relationships between the treatment and observed group differences in behavior.

Cognitive theorists have used the experimental method productively in their research, but they have also found limitations. For instance, for ethical or practical reasons, some variables cannot be manipulated experimentally. If you wanted to study the effect on children's development of the lack of exposure to spoken language while growing up, you could not put several newborn infants in two groups, and then deprive one group of language by deafening them or by refusing to talk to them. Yet that is what is required in a true experiment. You could try isolating the experimental children from language for short periods of time, but then the experiment would not represent the conditions you were most interested in studying.

To the cognitive theorist, one basic aspect of intellectual development is ignored in an experiment that simply investigates the relationship between environmental conditions (as manipulated by the experimenter) and subsequent behavior. Behavior cannot be explained solely by environmental conditions, past or present; cognition always intervenes between the situation and behavior, and cognition always presupposes some sort of cognitive structure. Thus it follows that intellectual development cannot be simulated "in the laboratory" simply by manipulating environmental conditions in an experiment and observing their effects on behavior. What is needed is a description of the subject's cognitive structure—that is, his way of thinking about the conditions manipulated.

Naturalistic Observation. One way to make inferences about cognitive structure is to observe children in their normal daily activities to see how they behave in various natural situations, and then draw some tentative conclusions about their ways of thinking, as in the following example: A four-year-old who has been told he lives in San Francisco, California, is on his way home with his family from a vacation trip. As they cross the state line, one parent points out they are back in California. Immediately the child asks, "Are we back in San Francisco now?", apparently thinking that San Francisco and California begin and end at the same place. This suggests that he may not understand the idea of a smaller geographical unit being included within a larger one.

Naturalistic observation can be approached informally, perhaps in the form of a diary of anecdotes kept by an adult who is occasionally intrigued by something a child has said or done. Or it can be done more systematically, with the researcher staking out a situation to observe with note pad or tape recorder in hand. The method can be applied *longitudinally,* to the same child as he grows older, or *cross-sectionally,* to different children at different ages. In any case, the hallmark of this method is that the observer does not manipulate the situation but takes it as it occurs "in nature."

Naturalistic observation has been important in the development of cognitive theory. It is a rich source of hypotheses because it offers the researcher a chance to see how children "really are" and to find more than he is looking for (if he is prepared to see it). It is also useful with young children, who may not cooperate in more structured situations. A major disadvantage, however, is that the most revealing situations—those most useful for making inferences about a child's thinking—may be few and far between, and the observer may be tempted to intrude, to contrive a new situation that would follow up on an interesting observation.

Comparative Testing. The idea of contriving a special situation in which to observe behavior sounds like what most people would call a test. A test is simply a situation arranged so as to reveal what a person knows, or how he thinks. It would seem, then, that tests could be constructed for assessing cognitive structures within a particular group and for making comparisons between groups.

In the study of intellectual development, the testing method has generally been used to compare different age groups (cross-sectional comparisons) or the same children at different ages (longitudinal comparisons). For example, children at ages 2, 3, 4, and 5 might be asked to count a standard array of objects so that the investigator can see at what age children generally begin to understand that each object is counted once and only once. Aside from age differences, tests can also be used to compare groups that are different in some other respect. Recall the impossibility of doing a truly experimental study on the intellectual effects of language deprivation. An obvious alternative is to compare deaf and hearing children on tests that might reveal differences in their ways of thinking.

A problem with comparative testing is that of deciding what *caused* observed differences. Are differences between age levels caused primarily by experience? Is maturation an important factor? Are differences between deaf and hearing children caused by language deprivation or by other inherited or acquired characteristics? There is no way to answer such questions on the basis of a single comparison. But comparisons that are only descriptive can still be useful, and many comparisons between the same groups in different situations may permit one to deduce the probable causes of observed differences.

Notice that the comparative testing method is quite similar to the experimental method. In both cases, there is fairly rigid control over the situation in which behavior is observed. In an experiment, one aspect of the situation, either past or present, is varied systematically and everything else, including the nature of the subjects, is held constant. But with the comparative testing method, the nature of the subjects is what varies, according to age or membership in a particular group, and all subjects are tested in the same situation. To put it another way, an experiment examines systematic differences among situations with the same subjects, whereas comparative testing examines systematic differences among subjects in the same situations.

An important limitation of comparative testing revolves around the question of what it means to say that different subjects are tested in the "same" situation. Suppose we want to find out whether children ages 5 and 9 differ in the extent to which they understand that a pound is a standard unit of weight regardless of the material being weighed. As a simple test, we might ask, "Which is heavier—a pound of lead or a pound of feathers?" If more five-year-olds than nine-year-olds say a pound of lead is heavier, we could conclude that the standard-unit-of-weight concept is less well understood at age 5. But could we really be sure? Perhaps more children at age 5 interpreted our question to mean, "Which *feels* heavier—a pound of lead or a pound of feathers?" If our question can be interpreted differently by the two groups, they are not really being tested in the same situation. To make sure our question is understood in the same way by all, we could ask each child some additional questions that, depending on his answer, would give us a check on the meaning of his response. But such ad hoc questioning is generally not permitted with the comparative testing method, because it introduces an element of subjectivity on the part of the tester.

The Clinical Method. Jean Piaget has made extensive use of a technique which he calls the clinical method because it resembles medical diagnostic procedures: the psychologist tries to "diagnose" the subject's way of thinking from his behavioral "symptoms." He runs tests and asks questions until he is satisfied he understands what the subject has in mind. Piaget did not develop the clinical method in order to study abnormalities in intellectual development; on the contrary, his goal has been to explain development in normal children.

The following excerpt from a conversation with a child about dreams will demonstrate how Piaget actively probes for symptoms in order to diagnose the child's thinking. The dream concept is of interest because it reveals how the child makes a distinction between subjective experience and objective reality.

> (*Piaget*) Where does the dream come from? (*Child, 5 yrs. 9 mos.*) I think you sleep so well that you dream.—Does it come from us or from outside?—From outside.—What do we dream with?—I don't know.— With the hands? ... With nothing?—Yes, with nothing.—When you are in bed and you dream, where is the dream?—In my bed, under the blanket. I don't really know. If it was in my stomach the bones would be in the way and I shouldn't see it.—Is the dream there when you sleep?—Yes, it is in bed beside me.— ... Is the dream in your head? —It is I that am in the dream: it isn't in my head(!).[5]

Conversations like this one led Piaget to postulate a stage of development in which children do not distinguish between mental events and physical reality.

Sometimes Piaget's clinical method involves the manipulation of objects in addition to questions and answers. In one study, for example, children were given assorted objects and a tank of water and were asked to "experiment" with the objects and then explain why some would float and others would not. The investigator observed the children's experiments, listened to their explanations, asked questions, and suggested further experiments. Actually, the clinical method does not require any verbal interaction at all. For example, Piaget spent many hours hiding objects from his own children during their infancy in order to observe how the children went about searching for the missing objects. An infant's response to one situation would suggest a new one for Piaget to try, and the game would go on like this until the child grew tired of it. From this sort of "play," Piaget was able to see how well an infant understands the permanence of objects and their locations in space.

The distinctive thing about the clinical method is that each new step in the interaction between the investigator and the subject depends upon the preceding steps. It is improvised rather than planned entirely ahead of time. The investigator is constantly formulating new hypotheses about the subject's thinking and then rearranging the situation to test his hypotheses. One can see elements of the other three methods in the clinical method. First, the investigator's manipulation of the situation as he goes along is similar to the experimental method (in fact, Piaget refers to his studies as "experiments"). Second, the investigator's inclination to follow the subject wherever he might go in his thinking resembles naturalistic observation. And third, the clinical method closely resembles the comparative testing method in that it has most often been used to compare children of different ages, both cross-sectionally and longitudinally. When used in this way, the clinical method is actually a "liberalized" version of comparative testing.

From a scientific viewpoint, the clinical method has been criticized on the grounds that, by varying his procedure from one child to the next, the investigator has precluded the possibility of making generalizations about whole groups of children. It is obvious, too, that the investigator must beware of putting words in the subject's mouth. However, Piaget feels that the flexibility of the clinical method permits a deeper understanding of the individual subject and therefore of children in general. Consequently, he is willing to rely on the investigator's skill and judgment in determining what a child really thinks. Of course, it is always possible, in principle, for the investigator to report the details of a large number of interactions with his subjects, and then to let the reader decide for himself whether or not the investigator's conclusions seem justified. Piaget's own books are full of such details.

We have had to discuss methodology at length because cognitive theorists have not relied on any one research method to make inferences about children's thinking. Each type of method has advantages and disadvantages, but all four can be used to complement one another—indeed, two or more methods may be combined in the same investigation. However, of the methods we have discussed, the clinical method has been the most prominent in research on intellectual development from the cognitive point of view.

TWO FRAMES OF REFERENCE: BIOLOGY AND THE COMPUTER

The cognitive theorist approaches the study of intellectual development with more than just the assumptions and methods we have discussed. He has some ideas about the phenomenon he is studying and the kind of theory he will end up with. Usually such ideas derive from analogies drawn between the phenomenon being studied and another better known phenomenon. Two analogies in particular are relevant to cognitive theory—first, that the human mind is like a biological organ; second, that it operates like a sophisticated computer program. In other words, biology and computer science have provided frames of reference for thinking about intellectual development from the cognitive point of view.

One frame of reference should be mentioned that has *not* influenced cognitive theory. As explained in Chapter 2, contemporary S-R theory is similar to cognitive theory in its attention to internal as well as external conditions of behavior. However, S-R theorists define internal conditions as the persisting effects of past learning, that is, connections between specific stimuli and responses. Cognitive theorists, on the other hand, usually think of a person as being a "black box" and ask what kind of system inside the box could account for behavior in a particular situation. As we have said, cognitive theorists have some ideas about the contents of the box and how they change in the course of development. We will turn now to some of those general ideas.

The Biological Frame of Reference

It might seem that the principal contribution of biology to the study of intellectual development would be information about the anatomy and physiology of the human brain. Such is not the case. A good deal is known about various *parts* of the brain and how they work, right down to single cells or even molecules, but knowledge about the parts does not add up to knowledge about the system as a *whole*. Yet the cognitive theorist is asking questions about the system as a whole. He wants to know how it works to produce intelligent behavior and how it changes so that behavior becomes more intelligent as a result of development. If these questions cannot be answered by a study of isolated parts, they must be answered by a study of the whole system in operation, that is, by observing behavior and the situation in which it occurs. In other words, intellectual development is a problem in the field of psychology, not anatomy or physiology.

Still, there are ways in which biology has influenced the cognitive approach to intellectual development. The "system" we spoke of controls how the organism interacts with its environment. In studying other systems of the same type, biologists have discovered general properties that probably apply to the human mind as well. Consider how a house plant deals with an important part of its environment, the sun. A significant feature of this system is the coordination of give and take between the organism and the environment. The plant takes in sunlight and converts it to other forms of energy in order to satisfy its own needs. At the same time, some of the energy is expended in bending the plant toward the sun so that it can take in more light. Viewed in a similar fashion, the human mind is a system that takes in information from the situation and converts it to a usable form through the process of cognition, which then controls the individual's behavior in relation to the environment, including searches for additional information. Just as the plant has certain anatomical structures that function as converters of energy, the person has certain cognitive structures that function as converters of information. Both kinds of structure enable the organism to adapt to its environment.

Piaget has proposed that we think of a cognitive structure as an organ of adaptation, albeit an abstract one.[6] This analogy between biological and psychological organs suggests a way of accounting for changes in cognitive structures during the course of development. Intellectual development may be seen as an extension of *embryogenesis,* the process by which a single cell is transformed into an increasingly complex being, with differentiated organs that perform various functions for the organism as a whole. Embryologists know that the developing embryo does not grow by new cells coming from the environment and somehow being tacked onto the cells already there. Nor do new cells somehow spring miraculously from the genetic material of existing cells. Rather, new cells come about through the functioning of existing cells in the context of their environment. It is easy to see in embryogenesis the biological source of Piaget's idea that the child constructs his own way of thinking from his interactions with the environment.

Besides providing theoretical ideas, the biological frame of reference has influenced the methodology of the cognitive approach. There is a good deal of emphasis on careful description of the way children are "in nature." This emphasis is evident not only in the use of naturalistic observation. Even when the child is brought into the laboratory for observation under more structured conditions, the aim most often is to find out what sort of thinking the child has brought with him from the outside world, not what he can learn during an experiment.

The Computer Frame of Reference

Many cognitive theorists have been influenced by the idea that the mind processes information in much the same way as a computer. Computers can not only process vast quantities of information in absurdly short times but also can perform certain jobs that only human beings could do before, such as keeping a vehicle on course toward a desired destination (without benefit of a physical track of some sort). Computers not only save time in getting jobs done but also increase our knowledge about *how* the jobs get done. Having programmed a machine to perform a certain task, we know how the machine utilizes information to do it. And how the machine does this may be similar to how the mind works when performing the same task. Thus, in learning how to program machines so that they will perform tasks like humans, we may also be learning something about human intelligence.[7]

Consider the computerized guidance system on board a spacecraft. Basically the way it works is by detecting discrepancies between the desired course and the actual course. When a discrepancy is detected, some sort of corrective action is taken to eliminate it. When the discrepancy has been eliminated, the corrective action is stopped, at least until a new discrepancy appears. Notice that the system reacts to the effects of its own actions; it stops correcting when it can "see" that correction is no longer needed. In other words, the system gets feedback as to the results of its own behavior and then behaves accordingly. In cybernetics, the science of information and control, such a system is known as a *servomechanism*.

The helmsman at the wheel of a ship operates in essentially the same way as this servomechanism, and indeed all sorts of human behavior seem to involve a similar use of feedback (for another example, see p. 143). Not so obvious is the role of feedback in the process of intellectual development. If we recall the idea of a child gradually constructing a "theory" of the world on the basis of experimental results, then the results are feedback from the child's actions in performing his experiments. If the child detects a discrepancy between his present theory and the latest experimental results, this may lead to a revision of the theory. Thus the cybernetic model applies to the process by which the child changes, as well as the process by which he behaves.

Because a computer has no mind of its own, it must be told exactly what to do in order to perform a particular task. It must be given a "cognitive structure," a way of interpreting the information fed into it. This can be done by writing a program that gives the computer a number of specific *rules*—rules for deciding when a deviation off course has occurred, rules for prescribing an appropriate corrective action, and so on. Now if the cognitive structure of a machine can be represented as a set of rules, then so can the cognitive structures that we attribute to people. Even if people cannot state the rules by which they operate, they behave as if they have certain rules for processing information.

Because a computer has no inherent faculty of judgment, the rules given to it must be absolutely explicit, so that nothing is left unclear. For this reason, the rules are stated in languages designed especially for computers. In a similar fashion, cognitive theorists have attempted to use the special languages of mathematics, logic, and linguistics to write the rules that represent human cognitive structures. These special languages are too technical for us to use in describing cognitive structures for our present purposes, but it is important to realize that they have shaped the ideas that we will discuss in the chapters that lie ahead. The use of special languages in cognitive theory reflects a general desire to be as precise as possible in describing a child's "way of thinking."

SUMMARY

The cognitive approach to intellectual development concentrates on how children think and how their thinking changes with age. The fundamental assumption of cognitive theory is that a person's behavior is always based on cognition, an act of knowing or thinking about the situation in which behavior occurs, and not on the situation itself. It is also assumed that the person's *way* of thinking, his cognitive structure, is not determined simply by the situations he has been in before. Both experience with the environment and the maturation of innate potential influence development only insofar as they affect the child's *activity* in relation to the environment. The cognitive theorist is neither an empiricist nor a nativist in his views on knowledge, but a constructivist, because he believes that the child creates new ways of thinking in the course of using his old ways of thinking. The chief spokesman for this point of view is Jean Piaget.

The general research strategy of the cognitive approach is to make inferences about children's ways of thinking by observing their behavior in a variety of situations. There are four specific methods for making such inferences: experimentation, naturalistic observation, comparative testing, and the clinical method. The clinical method, developed principally by Piaget, has been especially useful in producing the data on which cognitive theory is based.

Two fields, biology and computer science, have provided important frames of reference for thinking about cognition and intellectual development. From the biological frame of reference, cognitive structures are viewed as being organs of adaptation that regulate the individual's interactions with his environment. The development of cognitive structures is seen as an extension of the process of embryogenesis. The computer frame of reference suggests that a cognitive structure can be represented as a set of rules for processing information from the environment and for interpreting feedback from the individual's own actions.

9

BASIC CONCEPTS AND PRINCIPLES IN COGNITIVE THEORY

Preview

In this chapter we discuss cognition as mental representation, which is determined by the content of cognition, the information channel, and the mode of representation. Cognition both transforms information and is the product of such transformations.

Cognitive structures are like sets of rules that govern these mental transformations. A structure can be described according to what it can do (competence) or how it works in processing information (process).

Intellectual development is a series of changes in cognitive structures, and the child's thinking progresses from the egocentric to the objective. Development is caused by equili-

bration, the process by which the child constructs new and better ways of thinking.

In this chapter we will examine some basic notions of the cognitive
approach in a more systematic fashion than we did in Chapter 8. Because the
focus of cognitive theory is on how children think and how their thinking
changes with age, the concepts and principles to be discussed in this chapter
fall under two major headings: *cognition* (thinking) and *development* (change
with age). A thorough understanding of this material is essential if one is to
understand the remaining chapters on the cognitive approach to intellectual
development.

Since we are in effect getting down to business at this point, let us look
ahead at the present chapter and the next four, to see what they are about and
how they are related to each other. Figure 9.1 presents a chart for this over-
view. As we have already said, the present chapter is concerned with basic
notions about cognition and development. Chapter 10 expands on the topic of
cognition by discussing the role of cognition in the process of behavior, along
with the relationship between cognition and motivation. Chapter 11 returns
to the topic of development, discussing first the *character* of development, or
the kinds of stages children go through, and then the *causes* of development,
or what makes children progress from one stage to the next. These two topics
lead, respectively, to Chapters 12 and 13. In Chapter 12, different areas of

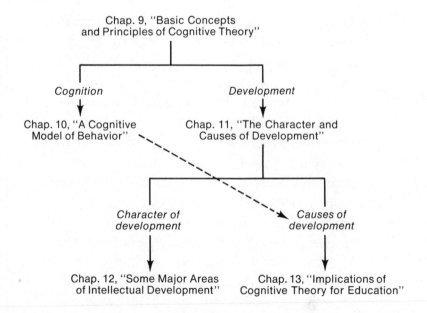

Figure 9.1

intellectual development are discussed in terms of the stages that children go through in each area. Chapter 13, dealing with the educational implications of cognitive theory, shifts the focus again to the causes of intellectual development, but discusses educational issues with reference to the specific areas discussed in Chapter 12.

Figure 9.1 seems to imply that the topic of cognition reaches a dead end in Chapter 10, but we must point out that Chapters 11, 12, and 13 pursue the topic of development specifically with reference to changes with age in cognition. In addition, we have drawn a dotted line in the figure from Chapter 10 to the second part of Chapter 11: this is to show that the model of behavior is especially relevant to the question of what causes development.

So much for preliminaries. Let us now discuss some basic concepts and principles of cognition and development.

COGNITION

In Chapter 8 we made a distinction between *cognition*, which we temporarily defined as a person's thinking about a particular situation, and *cognitive structure*, which we defined as the person's *way* of thinking about a variety of situations. Each concept needs to be examined in depth before we can proceed further.

Cognition as Mental Representation

When a person perceives or thinks about objects and events, his mental representation of these things is known as *cognition*. It is tempting to think of cognition as the person's "picture" of the situation he is in. The picture analogy has a number of limitations, but we will discuss these limitations so that we can define the concept of cognition more precisely.

First, consider the variety of things that may be the *content* of a person's cognition. We often perceive and think about our immediate physical surroundings—that which we might easily make a mental picture of. But the content of cognition may also include less tangible phenomena, such as the emotions and intentions of another person. The statement "I know that George is sympathetic toward me and would like to help me" indicates that the speaker has some mental representation of the way George feels. Furthermore, whether the content of cognition is potentially visible or not, it may extend well beyond the immediate situation. Thus, we can think about places that we have been to before or that we anticipate going to for the first time. We can even think about situations that are purely hypothetical, that have no counterparts in the real world.

A second limitation of the picture analogy becomes apparent when we realize that not all content enters into cognition through the visual *channel*. Other input channels are available, too, such as hearing or touching. A person can check to see if he is wearing his watch either by looking at his wrist or by feeling for the watch with his hand. In addition, the information coming into cognition through a given channel can be more or less abstract or symbolic. The visual channel can transmit information that is not at all picture-like. For example, we might *read* about aardvarks instead of actually seeing them. Similarly, we might hear someone describe a bird call, instead of actually hearing it ourselves. Thus, essentially the same content can enter cognition through different input channels and at different levels of abstractness within a given channel.

Finally, we all know that a mental picture is only one *mode* of cognitive representation. The same content can be "thought of" in different ways. If someone asks you to think about starting a car, how do you do it? Do you picture a key being turned in an ignition switch? Do you internally go through the motion of inserting and turning the key? Or do you say to yourself, "Put in the key and turn it to the right" (or words to that effect)? All of these are possibilities, yet only the first involves a picture. Bruner has called these three modes of representation iconic, enactive, and symbolic, respectively.[1] Representation in the *iconic* mode is the closest thing to a mental picture, in the literal sense. The *enactive* mode involves the use of actions, either overt or covert, to represent objects and events. It is the mode in which most people represent the act of tying a shoe. The *symbolic* mode is not tied to pictures or actions, because it makes use of arbitrary symbols, such as words, which need not resemble the objects and events they represent. When a person talks to himself, even silently, he is using the symbolic mode of representation.

To summarize briefly, all sorts of content can enter into cognition; it may do so through a number of input channels; and the mode of representation is yet another dimension to be considered. It should be clear that the various dimensions of cognition are not necessarily correlated with one another. Visible content does not have to enter cognition through the visual channel, nor does it have to be represented in the iconic mode. For instance, someone might describe to us orally (auditory channel) a large suitcase (pictureable content), after which we imagine ourselves trying to lift it (enactive mode of representation). For present purposes, we simply wish to stress that the concept of cognition is not limited to any particular type of content, input channel, or mode of representation.

The analogy between mental representations and pictures raises an additional question about the concept of cognition. Are we to think of cognition as the act of painting a picture or as the picture itself? In other words, is cognition a process or a product? It seems to us it is both. Consider our everyday use of the word "thinking." At one moment we might say, "I am thinking about George," in which case we are referring to a process or activity. At the next moment, we might say, "This is my thinking about George," in which case we are referring to a product, the conclusions we have reached about George as a result of our mental activity. There are times when it is useful to think of cognition as a person's "picture" of a particular situation, but it is important to bear in mind that the person has played an active role in the process of putting together whatever picture he has. The idea of cognition being an activity deserves further amplification.

Cognition as an Active Process

The fact that the feelings and intentions of others can be represented in cognition illustrates especially well the principle that cognition is an *active* process. Consider how we know what another person feels or what he intends to do. Since we cannot perceive feelings directly, we must *infer* them from the person's actions and words in the context of a particular situation. We may not be aware of our own "rules of inference," but somehow we interpret the available evidence to mean that the other person has certain feelings or intentions. Sometimes there is a misunderstanding and our interpretation does not correspond to what is really there in the other person. Misunderstandings can occur because our rules of inference are inadequate, or because they have not been applied properly, or because the evidence itself is inadequate or misleading in some way.

Even when we perceive things that seem directly observable, we are engaged in an active process. The mind does not passively record patterns of stimulation from the environment as if it were the film inside a camera. Instead, the mind actively *transforms* raw data into some meaningful representation of what is "out there." (Both the biological and the computer frames of reference come to mind here.) We can gain some appreciation for the active nature of perception by noting that different people may perceive the same situation in very different ways. This happens quite often in school, when a teacher and a student have trouble communicating about something that each sees differently. The child who perceives 5 X 2 as 5 + 2 may be puzzled as to why the correct answer is 10 according to the teacher. The role of transformations in cognition becomes especially obvious when we consider the kind of cognitive content that goes beyond reality as we know it. We have the ability to think about conditions that are contrary to fact—a world populated by two-headed people, for example. How could we conceive of such a thing, if not by mentally transforming our knowledge about the way things are?

At this point, there might be some confusion over the terms *cognition* and *perception*, that is, as to whether there is a clear-cut distinction between the two. For our purposes, it suffices to say that perception is a part of cognition—that part which is most closely related to the person's immediate surroundings. We need not attempt to draw a more distinct boundary around perception as a particular type of cognitive process.

Whenever the active nature of cognition is pointed out, there is a great tendency to assume that the individual's contribution to his own cognitive activity is the cumulative record of his past experience. It is assumed that each person has *learned* to interpret the stimuli around him in particular ways. Since different people have had different experiences, it follows that they will perform different transformations on the raw information they receive. We often refer to a child's *lack* of experience in our attempts to explain why he sees things differently from us. This emphasis on the role of learning from past experience corresponds to the empiricist philosophy discussed earlier (Chapters 2 and 8). While it seems self-evident that past experience does affect cognition, it also seems obvious that not all aspects of cognition are learned (the ability to perceive colors being a relatively clear, if elementary, example). The exact role of experience in intellectual development is a difficult question and it is discussed more fully in the section of Chapter 11 on the causes of developmental change. The important point here is that we can simply attribute a person's cognition to the type of system he has at his disposal for transforming information, without making the further assumption that the system is based entirely on past experience. In fact, as we have already seen, the cognitive theorist assumes that past experience is *not* sufficient to explain a person's system for processing information.

Cognitive Structure

We introduced the term *cognitive structure* in Chapter 8 as a name for a person's way of thinking, or his system for processing information. The word "structure" has a couple of meanings that may help to make the concept of cognitive structure clearer than it has been up until now.

The notion of structure first of all implies an organization of parts into a *whole*, such that the whole has properties unlike any or all of the parts taken separately. The "parts" of a cognitive structure are mental actions or transformations. The organization of these actions into a particular structure permits a kind of cognition that would not be possible if the component actions were to remain separate and uncoordinated. To take an example from Piaget, the cognitive structure required for understanding elementary arithmetic includes the actions of mentally combining and separating sets of objects.[2] These actions must be coordinated in a particular way for a person to see the logical necessity that, if $4 + 3 = 7$, then $7 - 4 = 3$.

The idea that a structural whole is greater than the sum of its parts is fundamental in biology. All living organisms, because they are organized, have properties or capabilities that cannot be found in any of their parts. The same can be said with regard to the subsystems and organs that make up a total organism—the skeleton, circulatory system, and so on. Piaget has argued that man's intellect is no exception to this general rule in biology. Thus, cognition always manifests some sort of structure, although the complexity of this structure may vary with age and with other factors.

Usually when we speak of a structure, we also envision something that is relatively stable. This second meaning of structure is quite appropriate in connection with cognitive structures. Unlike cognition—a process that changes from moment to moment—cognitive structures are systems that a person carries around in his head, as it were, from one situation to another. In other words, a cognitive structure is a general framework or *form* of thinking that can be applied to a variety of cognitive *contents*, depending on the situation. Thus, a mathematical structure may be used for all sorts of things, from keeping score in a game to plotting the course of a spacecraft. Cognitive structures are not so stable that they never change, but they are slower to change than cognition itself.

Cognitive Structures as Rules

As we noted earlier in discussing the computer frame of reference for cognitive theory, it sometimes is useful to describe cognitive structures as sets of *rules*—rules that govern cognition. Consider the rules of a game, such as baseball. They have much in common with cognitive structures as we have characterized them so far. The rules of baseball are relatively stable and they apply to a variety of situations. Furthermore, the rules are organized or interrelated: three strikes make an out; each team is allowed three outs in an inning; there are nine innings in a game. We usually say that the rules of baseball govern the play of the game, but it is equally true that the rules govern the individual player's cognition. In fact, the rules govern the play of the game precisely *because* they govern the player's cognition, which, in turn, guides the behavior of playing the game. The player must know the rules of the game in order to plan a winning strategy, to interpret the behavior of other players, and to have other thoughts that are involved in playing the game. Thus, in a sense, the rules of baseball are themselves a cognitive structure, or—more precisely —they describe a cognitive structure.

The rules that govern cognition are generally not as conscious or explicit as the rules of baseball. Without formal training in grammar, for example, a speaker of English nonetheless has an implicit knowledge of many rules for interpreting combinations of words in sentences. He knows, for instance, that "The dog chased the cat" means that the *dog* did the chasing, whereas "The dog was chased by the cat" means that the *cat* did the chasing. This knowledge must be in the form of general rules rather than specific facts, because most speakers of English would agree that (1) and (2) below are more similar in meaning than either is to (3), even without knowing the meanings of *glyx, wub,* and *toop.*

> (1) The glyx wubbed the toop.
> (2) The toop was wubbed by the glyx.
> (3) The toop wubbed the glyx.

Some linguists believe that the goal of their field is to discover the implicit rules that a language user knows.[3] When conceived in this way, linguistics seems very much like cognitive psychology.

Competence, Performance, and Process

Cognitive structures can be described on two different levels of abstraction. The difference between them is not easy to explain, but it is important for understanding cognitive theories of intellectual development. In our everyday thinking about behavior, we often make a three-way distinction between what a person *can* do, what he actually *does* do in a particular situation, and *how* he does it. We will call the first of these *competence*, the second *performance*, and the third *process*.[4] The point we wish to make here is that cognitive structures can be described either with reference to competence or with reference to process. Perhaps a computer analogy will illustrate the difference.

Suppose we have been given the job of watching a preprogrammed computer at work in order to determine the nature of its system for processing information—its cognitive structure, if you will. We do not have access to the program that controls the computer, nor can we learn much from looking at the insides of the machine, so all we can do is observe what goes into the computer and what comes out of it, that is, its performance. We might begin by listing all the inputs and outputs in two parallel columns. Eventually we could describe the computer's structure by deriving a general rule that relates the inputs to their corresponding outputs. For example, we might say "Given a set of N scores, the computer will calculate the mean, or average, for the set of scores." In other words, we will have discovered that the computer's internal activity is so organized that it will coordinate the operations of addition and division in order to produce a particular type of result. Thus, we are able to describe the computer's structure in terms of its *competence*. Notice that we can do this without having the slightest understanding of the *process* by which this competence is manifested in performance. That is, we do not need to know *how* the computer carries out the addition and division operations that are involved in calculating a mean.

At this point, a fair question is whether or not cognitive psychologists ought to be satisfied with a description of cognitive structures in terms of competence. If a goal of psychology is to predict behavior, a competence theory would appear to provide an adequate basis for making such predictions. After all, the performance of our computer could be predicted quite nicely, once its competence had been identified. However, the minds of human beings are not so simple. People do not always do what they *can* do, because of distractions or momentary lapses in memory, or because they simply do not *want* to do what they are able to do. In these cases, a prediction of performance based on knowledge of a person's competence would fail by being too optimistic.

To complicate matters more, there are times when performance is in some sense *better* than one would predict from a knowledge of competence. The person performs "over his head" or at a higher level than he can maintain, due to fortuitous circumstances that the prediction based on competence does not take into account. Suppose we observe that a child of five can tell us the names of written numbers up to three digits in length. We also observe that he is vaguely aware of such mathematical operations as addition and multi-plication, but has no real competence to perform these operations reliably. Suddenly the same child announces that he has multiplied 10 X 10 and gotten 100. This performance would not have been predicted on the basis of the child's assessed competence. However, the reason for the discrepancy becomes apparent when the child goes on to say that 20 X 20 = 200, 30 X 30 = 300, and so on. It is evident that the child does have a system, but it is not the kind of competence on which we would have based our prediction of his perfor-mance in multiplication.

The last example illustrates a general problem with the kinds of compe-tence theories that exist in cognitive psychology. In general, such theories deal with a restricted domain of cognition, such as logical thinking or moral reason-ing. But a particular performance may be based on several different kinds of competence, as in the example of the five-year-old "multiplying" 10 X 10. Consequently, predictions of behavior based only on one area of competence may miss the mark, because the possible contribution of other kinds of compe-tence has not been taken into account. Moreover, although we have so far been assuming that our competence theories are essentially correct, other failures to predict performance might actually reflect an incorrect description of com-petence. It might be difficult, in such a case, to distinguish between problems with the specific competence theory in question and limitations of competence theories in general.

All of these complications in the relationship between competence and performance indicate the desirability of trying to describe cognitive structures in terms of *process*. If one has a description of process—if one knows *how* competence is realized in performance—then one should have a better chance of predicting whether or not performance will be a true reflection of compe-tence at a particular time. Going back to our hypothetical computer, we could get a good understanding of process if someone would tell us about the pro-gram that controls it. But we said at the outset that the program was not available, just as no program for the human mind is available to the cognitive psychologist. Thus, we would only be able to make some educated guesses as to the nature of the computer program. Our guesses would be guided by our knowledge of the competence of the computer, and perhaps by some knowl-edge about the apparatus that the computer has for processing information. For the psychologist studying human cognition, the major problem is still that of describing competence. This was not a difficult task when we were observing the hypothetical computer, but it is a difficult task when one is observing people. Then it is a question of interpreting the meaning of observed perfor-mance in terms of an underlying competence that is only revealed through a smokescreen of complications.

Current theories about human cognitive structures are best regarded as attempts to describe competence. In general, cognitive psychologists are in a better position to characterize a given mental system in terms of what it can do, under ideal conditions, rather than to specify the procedures by which the system operates. Certainly this is true of the theories that will be discussed in subsequent chapters of Part 2. Thus, the theories cannot make exact predictions of behavior on particular occasions without hedging bets. Nevertheless, competence theories have contributed greatly already to our understanding of intellectual development, and they represent a first step toward more powerful theories that take process into account.

DEVELOPMENT

The preceding concepts and principles on cognition provide a foundation for understanding a second set of concepts and principles concerned with the relationship between cognitive structures and developmental stages, the general direction of intellectual development, and the basic cause of development in the process of equilibration.

Structures and Stages

The central principle of cognitive theory is that *intellectual development consists of a series of changes in a child's cognitive structures.* The chain of reasoning behind this principle is as follows: A child's behavior changes as he grows older. Since behavior is determined, in part, by cognition, some of the behavioral changes with age may be attributed to changes in cognition. In other words, an older child has different ways of thinking about or looking at things than a younger child, which amounts to saying that there are changes with age in the structures that determine cognition.

It is important to remember now that a cognitive structure is an organized whole, because to say that development consists of changes in cognitive structures is to say that *development proceeds through a series of qualitatively different stages.* A stage is a period during which a child's cognition is governed by one particular kind of cognitive structure. When the structure changes, there is a qualitative change in the child's thinking and he is said to be at a more advanced stage of development. From this point of view, intellectual development is not just the gradual accretion of more and more pieces of knowledge or skills. To be sure, an older child "knows more," in some sense, than a younger child, but what he knows is also structured differently. When a child acquires a new cognitive structure, he thinks according to a new set of rules, and therefore he is able to know things that he could not know before. Each developmental stage can be identified with a particular kind of cognitive structure, a particular way of thinking.

A number of stages have been identified in different areas of intellectual development, and several of these stages will be examined in Chapters 11 and 12. For the time being, we will give just one example of qualitatively different stages in the area of moral judgment.[5] There is an early stage in the development of moral judgment when a child's conception of good and bad behavior is based entirely on the immediate consequences of a particular act. If the act is punished, it is bad. If the act is rewarded, it is good. At the next stage of development, judgments of good and bad behavior are no longer based entirely on immediate consequences. It is good to do something nice for someone else so that he will pay you back later. It is also good to pay back a favor that has been done earlier for you. In fact, it may even be necessary to endure some negative consequences in the immediate situation in order to fulfill such an obligation to another person. These two stages are qualitatively different in the sense that different factors enter into the child's thinking in each case. As a result, the same act may be judged as bad in the first stage but good in the second (or vice versa). Similar stages have been found in the child's thinking about objects and events in the physical world and in his use of logic.

A person who understands what sort of cognitive structure a child has at each stage of development will be able to predict and explain much of the child's behavior. Even if this understanding is only in terms of competence (in the sense that we have just discussed), it will become apparent why some school learning tasks, for example, are much more difficult for the child than others. An understanding of the child's cognitive structures may also suggest ways to modify learning tasks so that they are more compatible with the child's own system (see Chapter 13).

Direction of Development

Developmental changes in cognitive structure do not occur haphazardly. As the child moves through a series of developmental stages, one can discern a general direction in his progress. It is as if we were to say, "As the child grows older, he becomes more and more _____." With regard to intellectual development, the word "intelligent" seems an obvious one to write in the blank. But although everyone knows intuitively what it means to say that a child becomes more and more intelligent as he grows older, this is not very helpful in clarifying the general direction development takes. It is like saying that older children are usually "smarter" than younger children. We need to be more explicit about the specific qualities that define what is "more intelligent." Accordingly, we will consider three specific trends that cognitive psychologists have used to characterize the general direction of development: the loss of egocentrism, the attainment of objectivity, and the broadening field of equilibrium.

Loss of Egocentrism. Sometimes a young child thinks that by covering his own eyes he can hide from someone else. The child's cognition seems to be governed by a rule that says that if *he* cannot see, then no one else can either. The inability to distinguish one's own point of view from other points of view is known as *egocentrism*. One general trend in intellectual development is the progressive loss of egocentrism throughout childhood and adolescence.

Infants are so completely egocentric during the first few months of life that they behave as if physical objects actually cease to exist when they lose visual or tactile contact with them. At this early stage of development, a baby will make no effort to retrieve a favorite toy that he watches someone hide under a blanket, even when the blanket is within his reach and he has the motor skills to remove it.[6] The rule here seems literally to be "out of sight, out of mind." Children soon outgrow this primitive sort of cognition, but egocentrism is lost only gradually, through a series of stages. An advanced form of egocentrism is evident in the adolescent who understands that not everyone else (for example, his parents) shares his own point of view on what is important in life, but he cannot understand why not.

Egocentrism, in the present context, should not be confused with egotism or selfishness. It is true that a child's egocentrism will sometimes cause him to behave in a manner that seems selfish or egotistical, as when he refuses to let another child take a turn at play. But the child may behave in this way, not because he is willful or arrogant, but because his thinking is determined by a cognitive structure that leaves him no choice but to see himself at the center of things.

Attainment of Objectivity. As a child becomes less egocentric, his cognition of the world around him becomes more *objective*.[7] The child's ability to imagine vantage points other than his own frees him from the distortions of reality inherent in a momentary subjective impression. After infancy, the child no longer behaves as if the very existence of an object depends upon his seeing it. This realization that objects are permanent and exist independent of perception is a type of cognition that corresponds more closely to reality, that is, is more objective than before. A more advanced level of objectivity is evident when the child understands that a pound of lead is really no heavier than a pound of feathers, even though it seems as if it ought to be heavier. By adulthood, the individual can entertain more or less objective thoughts about realities that can only be apprehended very indirectly, such as subatomic particles or remote galaxies—or even cognitive structures!

Broadening Field of Equilibrium. Another way of characterizing the general direction of intellectual development combines the biological concept of adaptation with the cybernetic concept of a control system that corrects deviations from a desired state of affairs. To say that an organism has "adapted" to its environment is to say that it has achieved some sort of self-sustaining balance or *equilibrium* with respect to the conditions it lives under. The notion of equilibrium in this case does not imply a static or resting state, but rather a dynamic system that can adjust to changes in the environment, much as a bicycle rider maintains his balance in spite of bumps and curves in the road. Piaget has taken the position that a child's cognitive structures change in such a way that their "field of equilibrium" expands in the course of development.[8] What this means is that the child can adapt his behavior to an ever-widening range of variations in the environment. The attainment of a more advanced cognitive structure does not guarantee successful adaptation, because the individual may still encounter situations that lie outside the expanded field of equilibrium. But each time the field of equilibrium expands, it makes adaptation more probable than it was before.

The idea of a broadening field of equilibrium is related to the child's loss of egocentrism and his attainment of objectivity. Children who think they cannot be seen when their own eyes are covered do not play games like hide and seek very well. They cannot maintain the type of equilibrium that is required in a situation that involves hiding oneself. Conversely, a person whose cognition is relatively free of egocentric distortions of reality is better able to adjust to the objective situation he is in when he is required to hide himself.

The statement that children become more intelligent as they grow older has now, we hope, taken on some meanings it did not have before. Specifically, more intelligent forms of cognition have the qualities of being less egocentric and more objective and of covering a broader field of equilibrium. It is interesting to note how different this view of intelligence is from the one associated with conventional intelligence tests. In such IQ tests, a person is said to be "more intelligent" when he shows evidence of being smarter than other people his own age. Furthermore, it has generally been assumed that he who is "more intelligent" at an early age will still be more intelligent later on. Naturally, the corollary of this assumption is that someone who is *less* intelligent now will continue to be less intelligent in the future. From the cognitive point of view, such a proposition is impossible (barring some sort of abnormality) because the normal direction of intellectual development, for every child, is toward more intelligence. (The issue of testing intellectual ability is discussed more fully in Chapter 13.)

Equilibration as the Basic Cause of Development

According to Piaget, the concept of equilibrium holds the key to understanding why children progress from stage to stage in the general direction of more intelligent forms of cognition.[9] Unlike the principles of decreasing egocentrism and increasing objectivity, which simply *describe* the direction of development, the notion of a broadening field of equilibrium also suggests a way to *explain* development. The process by which the field of equilibrium expands is called *equilibration*. Thus, if we can understand the process of equilibration, we will be able to explain how the child gets from one developmental stage to the next. In other words, equilibration is viewed as the basic cause of intellectual development.

Piaget's concept of equilibration is probably the most difficult concept in cognitive theory, so we will only attempt to introduce it here by means of an example. By the end of Chapter 11, we will have built up enough background in cognitive theory to discuss the process of equilibration more thoroughly.

For the moment, we can approach the concept of equilibration by asking what happens when a child encounters a situation in which his present cognitive structures do not enable him to maintain equilibrium. Returning to the hide-and-seek example, what happens to the child who thinks that other people will not be able to see him if he cannot see them? In some situations, this child's strategy for playing the game actually works. If he blocks his own view of the seeker by getting behind a large enough object, then the seeker is not able to see him either. At other times, however, the same strategy leads the child to choose a hiding place that is inadequate, in that some part of his body is still visible to the seeker. Sooner or later the child begins to realize that his strategy is unreliable, but the reasons for its unreliability are not yet clear to him. At the same time, the child also begins to notice that when *he* plays the role of seeker he often finds the hider by detecting only a small part of the hider's body, for example, his foot.

Eventually the child perceives the discrepancy between his strategy for hiding (covering his own eyes) and his strategy for seeking (looking for such clues as an exposed foot). At this point, he begins to "put 2 and 2 together" by applying his own seeking strategy to himself when he is choosing a hiding place. At first he is not very good at this, but at least he has gotten the idea that hiding involves more than covering his own eyes. With more experience in hiding and seeking he becomes a better hider, and as he becomes a better hider, he also becomes a better seeker, because he is aware of the tricks that people can use to hide themselves. In sum, the child attains a broader field of equilibrium in his thinking about hide and seek, and the steps through which he goes in doing this illustrate the process of equilibration.

It may seem curious that we have used an example as trivial as the game of hide and seek to illustrate a concept as important as equilibration, but such is the stuff from which new cognitive structures are made, especially in early childhood. There is really much more than just hide and seek involved here, too, including the child's understanding of spatial relations and his ability to take the role of another person. Moreover, the example highlights a few aspects of the equilibration process that link equilibration to the constructivist epistemology that was discussed in Chapter 8.

Notice that in our example the child himself *constructs* a more adequate strategy for hiding; it is not given to him. The new strategy arises out of the child's own *activity* in applying his old strategies for hiding and seeking. Finally, although the child needs to encounter certain hiding and seeking situations in order to discover the limitations of his old strategies, these situations would not have the same effects on the child's way of thinking if he were not already pursuing certain strategies to begin with. In other words, the effects of the environment depend on the child's use of his old cognitive structures. This is one sense in which development is, to some extent, *autonomous* from the environment.

SUMMARY

In general, we have defined cognition as mental representation, and we have noted that cognition has three dimensions: the content of cognition, the channel by which information enters cognition, and the mode of representation. Cognition may be thought of both as an active process that transforms information and as the product of such a process.

Cognitive structures are organized wholes that coordinate the mental transformations performed on information. As such, they are relatively stable ways of thinking that apply to a variety of cognitive contents. It is often convenient to describe cognitive structures as sets of rules that govern cognition. In principle, a structure can be described either in terms of competence (what it can do) or in terms of process (how it works in processing information). Although there are distinct advantages to having descriptions in terms of process, such descriptions generally presuppose a description of structure in terms of competence. At present, most cognitive theories of development are competence theories, but they are nonetheless useful.

Intellectual development consists of a series of changes in a child's cognitive structures. Each new structure defines a qualitatively different stage of development. As the child progresses from stage to stage, his thinking becomes less egocentric and more objective, and it covers a broader field of equilibrium. Equilibration, the process by which the child attains a broader field of equilibrium, is the basic cause of development. In the process of equilibration, the child constructs new and more adequate ways of thinking by applying his old ways of thinking.

10

A COGNITIVE MODEL OF BEHAVIOR

Preview

According to the cognitive model, a person's behavior is determined by the cognition that results when his cognitive structures, through the processes of assimilation and accommodation, take in and transform information from the situation around him. The person gets feedback from his behavior by perceiving its effects on the situation and so is able to judge whether his actions have brought him closer to the goal he has in mind. Behavior is generally controlled by plans for attaining particular goals. Plans consist of elementary feedback units called TOTEs. The goals themselves are selected according to the person's motives, which influence behavior through their effects

on cognition. In turn, the motives themselves
are determined by a mixture of cognition,
needs, and interests. Some behavior is intrinsically motivated by developing cognitive structures.

In this chapter, we will take a closer look at the relationship between
cognition, the situation, and behavior, using a model of behavior—a schematic
representation of the process by which behavior occurs. The model incorporates not only cognition but also *motivation,* another psychological process
that intervenes between the situation and behavior. By including motivation,
we can make our model more complete and can explore the relationship
between cognition and motivation.

There are at least three reasons why such a model of behavior is
important. First, because cognition and cognitive structures can only be inferred from observations of behavior and the situation in which the behavior
occurs, the observer should be aware of the possible relationships between
what he is observing and what he is trying to infer. Second, the same relationships should also be taken into account if the observer has already made some
inferences about an individual's cognitive structure and is using these inferences to predict the individual's behavior in new situations. Third, as we will
see in Chapter 11, the model of behavior helps to clarify the role of a child's
activity in the process of equilibration, which we earlier identified as the basic
cause of development. Thus, the model of behavior can be used in making
inferences about cognitive structures and predictions about behavior, and in
explaining the process by which development occurs.

Figure 10.1 represents a model of goal-directed behavior as seen from
the cognitive point of view.[1] This figure is essentially a flow chart in which the
arrows indicate the flow of information—or energy or control—from one
component of the model to another. We need not concern ourselves with the
question of exactly what it is that flows through the present model; an arrow
simply shows that the working of one component has some effect on another.

As for the components themselves, two of them have already been
discussed at length—namely, *cognition* and *cognitive structures.* As we have
seen, cognition is a person's mental representation of the situation that he is
in, and a cognitive structure is an organized system of mental transformations
or a set of rules for processing information. Two other components, the *situation* and *behavior,* have also been mentioned often previously. The situation
refers to the person's environment and his position in it. It includes the
environment that the person is in direct sensory contact with, through one
input channel or another, and the environment that he can only think about,
without perceiving it directly, such as an object hidden from view. Behavior
is any overt activity of the person that is directed toward a goal of some sort.[2]

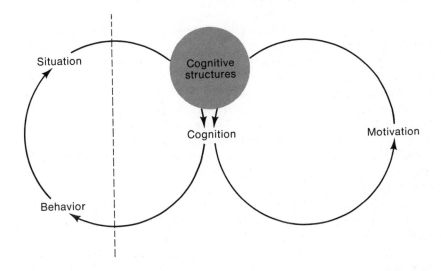

Figure 10.1

It includes not only gross motor activity but also such activities as speaking and looking. The situation and behavior are the only components of the model that an outsider can observe more or less directly, and that is why they are set apart from the rest of the model by a vertical dotted line. They correspond to the input and output of the hypothetical computer, or the "black box" that appeared in earlier discussions. The fifth component, *motivation*, refers to the fact that the person is trying to attain certain goals through his behavior. Motivation is included in the model because a person's behavior is determined not only by his understanding of the situation he is in but also by what he is trying to achieve.

In the rest of this chapter, we will use the model in Figure 10.1 to discuss first the cognitive aspects of behavior and then the motivational aspects of behavior as they relate to cognition.

COGNITIVE ASPECTS OF BEHAVIOR

The circular chain of arrows on the left side of Figure 10.1 should be familiar by now. We have seen that information from the situation is taken in and transformed by cognitive structures, and that the resulting cognition has an effect on behavior. This chain is brought full circle by the arrow from behavior back to the situation, which indicates that the person's behavior changes the situation in some way, thereby starting a new cycle through the same chain. Each link in this circular chain deserves closer examination. As we go along, we will introduce new concepts and principles that help clarify the relationships among the various components of the model.

Assimilation and Accommodation

Let us begin with the arrow from the situation to cognition. Notice that this arrow runs *through* cognitive structures, to show that information taken in from the situation is transformed by cognitive structures in the process of entering cognition. Piaget uses the term *assimilation* for this intake and transformation of information from the environment. It is a good name for this process because it emphasizes the fact that information must, in a sense, be "digested" before it is passed on in the system; it cannot be used in its raw form. Cognitive assimilation is just one case of a more general process that occurs in all living systems. People have cognitive structures for assimilating information in the process of cognition, just as plants have physiological structures for assimilating sunlight in the process of photosynthesis. The type of input to be assimilated and the transformations performed on it depend upon the particular structures that are functioning in the organism at a given time.

According to Piaget, assimilation is generally accompanied by a complementary process called *accommodation*. Cognitive structures accommodate or adjust to the input being assimilated. What a person sees—his cognition— depends not only on the structure of his visual system but also on the pattern of light entering his eyes. The transformations performed on the input are determined to some extent by the input itself. While a plant is assimilating sunlight, it is also bending toward the sun.

Although assimilation and accommodation are conceptually distinct processes, they are inseparable aspects of the relationship between the situation and cognition. The information taken in must be made to fit the structures present in the individual (assimilation). At the same time, the structures must be made to fit the incoming information (accommodation). If the structures were so rigid that they could not bend in this way, then the individual would be able to assimilate only situations that already fit easily into his present structures. He would not be able to handle new situations and therefore he would not be able to change. In other words, the process of accommodation is the agent of change in cognitive structures.

As we saw in Chapter 9, changes in cognitive structure are the essence of intellectual development, from the cognitive point of view. It follows, then, that accommodation would play an important role in a cognitive theory of development, and indeed this is the case. However, we are concerned in the present chapter with behavior at a given point in time, and not with the process of development. Consequently, we will concentrate on the process of assimilation here and discuss accommodation later, in Chapter 11. The point we want to make now is that information from the situation affects behavior only in some assimilated form—that is, cognition—and that the way information is assimilated depends on the individual's cognitive structures.

From Cognition to Behavior

The next arrow in the large circular chain indicates that cognition somehow affects behavior. The rather indefinite "somehow" reflects an old criticism of cognitive theory. E. C. Tolman, a psychologist who believed that a cognitive theory would be necessary even to explain the behavior of the lowly white rat, was once criticized for propounding a theory that left the rat "buried in thought." Tolman's critic, Guthrie, also remarked that "in his concern with what goes on in the rat's mind, Tolman has neglected to predict what the rat will do."[3] As this remark suggests, cognitive psychologists have tended to gloss over the problem of specifying the mechanisms that translate cognition into overt action. In cognitive theory, as in everyday psychology, it is generally assumed that an individual will adjust his behavior to the situation as he sees it.

The assumption of a direct link from cognition to behavior is justified in many instances, but sometimes behavioral adjustments to cognition cannot be taken for granted. A child trying to draw a straight line freehand may *know* that his attempts are something less than successful, but he may also lack the motor skill necessary to do anything about it. We might say that the child has the *competence* to draw a straight line—in the sense that he knows what a straight line is and can produce one with the help of a ruler—but that he does not have the performance mechanism for producing a straight line freehand. On the other hand, there is some evidence, as we will discuss in Chapter 12, that young children at an earlier stage of development do not even have competence with regard to the concept of straightness. Another complicating factor is motivation: on a given occasion, a child simply might not be *trying* to draw a straight line, or at least he might not be trying very hard. In any case, the arrow from cognition to behavior does not necessarily represent an automatic process, and it is wise to remember this when making inferences about a child's cognitive competence on the basis of his performance.

Feedback

The previous example is also a good one for explaining the arrow from behavior back to the situation. When the child draws a line, he is changing the situation, literally by leaving his mark on the environment. Not all changes in the situation involve a change in the environment; sometimes behavior just changes the person's orientation toward the environment. For instance, the child in our example might shift his gaze from left to right along a line that he has already drawn. The important point is that the input to the child is no longer the same as it was before.

Whether behavior changes the environment itself or only the person's orientation, it can have an effect on subsequent behavior when the changes in the situation enter cognition through the processes of assimilation and accommodation. In other words, the child in our example can monitor his behavior simply by watching what he is doing—that is, by getting *feedback* from actions. If he sees that his line has not yet reached its desired end point, then he knows that he should keep drawing and he knows which direction to take. Thus, the arrow from behavior to situation is like a feedback loop in a cybernetic mechanism, such as the guidance system in a spacecraft. It permits corrections in a course of action by indicating discrepancies between the actual situation and the goal situation.

Borrowing the basic notion of feedback from cybernetic science, Miller, Galanter, and Pribram have suggested that goal-directed behavior can be analyzed into units that they call TOTES.[4] The acronym TOTE stands for the four phases within each unit: *Test, Operate, Test,* and *Exit.* Test 1 occurs when the individual takes note of discrepancies between the actual situation and some desired state of affairs or goal; then he "operates" by changing the actual situation so as to bring it closer to the goal situation. At Test 2, he assesses the effects of his operations; that is, he gets feedback from his actions. If there is a match between the new situation and the desired state of affairs, he "exits" from the present unit of behavior and goes on to something else. On the other hand, if there is not a match, the individual may perform additional operations before exiting.

In terms of the cognitive model in Figure 10.1, the phases of the TOTE unit refer respectively to cognition of the situation at time 1, behavior that changes the situation, subsequent cognition of the new situation at time 2, and behavior directed toward a new goal situation. Thus, in the example of drawing a line, the child first sees that there is no line between points *A* and *B*. He then begins to draw and, when he sees that the desired line now extends from *A* to *B*, he turns to something else.

Plans

An important thing about TOTE units is that they typically occur in hierarchies rather than in simple chainlike sequences. The "operate" phase in a larger unit may itself be composed of one or more smaller TOTES, which in turn may contain still other TOTES, and so on. Even the example of drawing a line can be analyzed in this fashion, as Figure 10.2 shows. The hierarchical arrangement of TOTE units will be easier to see if we imagine that the line to be drawn consists of a series of dashes. The major "test" involved in drawing such a line is an assessment of whether or not the desired line extends from point *A* to point *B*. If this test is failed, the "operation" of drawing the line must be performed. However, the operation of drawing the line requires two additional tests and their respective operations: the pencil must be positioned properly on the paper, and then the next dash in the line must be completed. These two units are repeated in a cyclical fashion until the entire line is complete.

Miller, *et al.* call a hierarchy of TOTE units a *plan*. Plans vary in complexity and duration, from the relatively simple routine of drawing a line

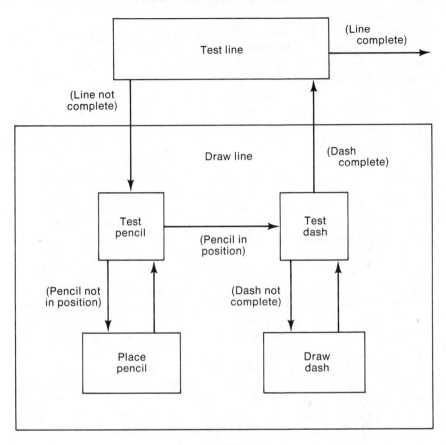

Figure 10.2.

in a few seconds to the complicated development of a scientific investigation, or the writing of a book, over a period of several years. With some plans, the lower-level units in the hierarchy are pretty well determined in advance, as when an experienced cook bakes a cake from a tried and true recipe. In other cases, the details of a plan may have to be filled in as one goes along, and a certain amount of trial and error may be necessary. Plans also vary in the extent to which their subunits must occur in a fixed order. But in spite of these variations, all plans have in common the basic organization of a hierarchy, with smaller units nested inside larger ones.

Just as plans vary along a number of dimensions, so do people in the kinds of plans they construct and use. In the study of intellectual development, we are most interested in those individual differences associated with age or developmental level. Some plans appear to be too difficult for children at a given age, and we would like to know why. In Chapter 8, it was mentioned that young children generally do not follow long-range plans. During free play in a nursery school, for example, the children often seem to bounce quickly from one activity to another, their behavior being determined by whatever attracts their attention at the moment rather than some overall plan. Teachers usually attribute this kind of behavior to the child's limited "span of attention." But the concept of a short attention span deserves closer scrutiny before it is adopted as a sufficient explanation of child behavior.

It seems reasonable to define the attention span as the amount of time a child can concentrate on one activity. If we accept this definition, the use of the attention span as an explanatory concept leads to the following statement: Children *don't* concentrate on one activity very long because they *can't* concentrate on one activity very long (that is, because they have short attention spans). This statement will suffice as an explanation only if we think of the attention span as being a basic capacity that grows with age, much like the length of a child's arm. There may be something to this view of the attention span, but it clearly is not the whole story.[5] If it were, how could we account for the curious fact that the same children who are supposed to have short attention spans will sit in front of a television set for hours? Apparently the attention span varies from one situation to another. If the span of attention has this sort of elasticity, we ought to identify those situations that cause it to expand and those that cause it to contract. Notice that we have begun now to think of the size of the attention span as an *effect* that is caused by something else.

According to our model of behavior, it is not the situation per se that affects behavior but rather the person's *cognition* of the situation. And cognition is always determined by the functioning of particular cognitive structures. So we again say that something at least partly depends on a child's cognitive structures—in this case, the child's span of attention. That is, the child's ability to stick with an extended activity depends in part on whether he has the mental systems the activity requires. In general, a cognitively complex activity will take longer than a simple one, but some extended activities—such as watching certain television programs—make relatively few cognitive demands on the child. As long as a series of cognitively simple events occurs on the TV screen in fairly rapid succession, at least one requirement for holding the child's attention will be met.

By suggesting that the dimension of *time* is not necessarily the critical one in determining whether a child can follow a particular plan of action, the cognitive approach provides a more complicated but also a more productive explanation of child behavior than the common notion of attention span. To illustrate this point further, consider the game of 20 questions. The object of the game is to identify something that one person is thinking of by asking him no more than 20 yes-no questions. The best strategy is to ask questions that progressively narrow down the possibilities; for example, "Is it a person?" "Alive?" "Male?" "Over 30?" Anyone who has attempted to play this game with younger children knows that they are not very good at it. The child's behavior in playing the game can tell us something about his cognitive structures. In fact, the 20 questions game has actually been used in research on intellectual development.[6] Younger children tend to ask specific questions too soon in the game: "Is it a person?" (Yes), "Is it the President?" (No), "Is it my teacher?" (No). When they do ask a more general question, they sometimes are unable to profit fully from the feedback in a no answer and consequently waste a question: "Is the person alive?" (No), "Is he dead?" In both cases, there is a failure to integrate a series of questions over time, but time does not seem to be the crucial factor. Instead, it is the ability of the child to think of a hierarchy of classes, subclasses, and so on, along with the ability to see that "not alive" necessarily implies "dead." These abilities depend in turn upon the development of certain cognitive structures around the age of seven, plus or minus a couple of years. Because these structures underlie many kinds of behavior, including instructional activities in school, we shall examine them in detail in the chapters that follow.

MOTIVATIONAL ASPECTS OF BEHAVIOR

Our discussion of feedback and plans has emphasized the goal-directed nature of behavior, and therefore it leads us to consider more directly the concept of motivation. We have been assuming that the person whose behavior is modeled in Figure 10.1 wants to attain a particular goal and wants it enough to do something about it. In other words, we have been assuming that the person is motivated. In the sections that follow, we will first consider the effects of motivation on behavior, and then we will discuss the question of where a person's motives come from. Finally, we will see how motivation and cognition are united in the concept of intrinsic motivation.

Effects of Motivation

In the present model of behavior, motivation accounts for both the direction and the intensity of behavior—the selection of goals and the vigor with which they are pursued. All sorts of goals are possible; we are not concerned just with the motivation to learn (but see the discussion of intrinsic motivation below). From an observer's point of view, motivation—like cognition—must be inferred from behavior, and sometimes such inferences go awry. A child who breaks the rules in a game might be accused by his classmates of cheating, when in truth he simply does not know the rules. In this case, the classmates would be making a wrong inference about motivation. An important clue to motivation is the persistence of a person's behavior. If the child in our example were to continue breaking rules, even after they were explained to him, then the other children would have a better basis from which to infer the motivation to cheat (assuming that the child was capable of understanding the rules). Sometimes a person's motives are inferred from expressions of emotion or "affect." As he approaches his goal, the individual may evidence the joy of anticipation. Signs of disappointment or anger may be seen if the anticipated goal is not attained.

To initiate a discussion of the effects of motivation on behavior, let us consider a case in which two people see the objective properties of the same situation in essentially the same way and yet behave very differently. Suppose two men are walking west on 42nd Street. As they approach a particular intersection, both men correctly recognize it as the corner of 42nd Street and 5th Avenue. Yet one man turns left and the other man turns right. Evidently the difference in behavior reflects a difference in motivation. The two men were headed toward different goals.

It could be argued that this difference in behavior actually reflects a difference in cognition. Even though both men recognized the intersection of 42nd and 5th, one man "saw" it as the place where he had to turn left and the other man saw it as the place where he had to turn right. This is not an unreasonable position to take, in light of what we said earlier about feedback. In order for cognition to guide behavior, the person must in some sense have his goal in mind. Otherwise he could not use the feedback from his own behavior to see whether or not he was getting any closer to the goal. However, to the extent that the two men had different cognitions, the difference was strictly in terms of the goals they had in mind, and the selection of goals is an aspect of motivation. Thus, there is an arrow in Figure 10.1 from motivation to cognition. This arrow passes through cognitive structures because the only way anything can influence cognition is by having some effect on the functioning of cognitive structures.

The same arrow from motivation to cognition also represents another way in which motivation can affect behavior. Instead of just determining the goal that a person has in mind, motivation can also influence the person's objectivity in apprehending the situation he is in. Suppose one of the two men had really intended to turn left at 7th Avenue rather than 5th, but he was preoccupied with other thoughts (his mind was on other goals), or perhaps he was very anxious to arrive at 7th Avenue, so he mistook 5th Avenue for 7th. Assuming that he would not have made the same mistake under more favorable circumstances, we cannot interpret the man's behavior on this particular situation as a reflection of his cognitive competence, but rather as an instance of motivation distorting the objectivity of cognition. Such effects of motivation on cognition are of much less interest to cognitive theorists than they are to psychoanalytic theorists (see Part 3). As we shall see shortly, cognitive theorists generally have confined their interest to the motivational consequences of cognition rather than to the cognitive consequences of motivation.

Sources of Motivation

Now that we have discussed the *effects* of motivation, let us consider the question of where a person's motives come from. That is, why does a person select a particular goal at a particular time? The only arrow in Figure 10.1 going *to* motivation comes from cognition. This does not mean that cognition is the only determinant of motivation but rather that cognition is *one* source of motives. Consider, for instance, what often happens when a stranger enters a classroom to observe. Some of the students are motivated by this event to show off in front of the stranger. Their cognition of the stranger's presence makes the children want to attract his attention. But clearly there must be other sources of this motive beside cognition. Otherwise we could not explain why some children, who are perfectly well aware of the stranger's presence, are not the least bit motivated to show off. In other words, there must be something in some of the children that makes them more likely than others to have the motive to show off.

The noncognitive sources of motivation go by various names, both in psychology and in everyday usage. Needs, values, interests, attitudes—all these terms refer to some disposition of a person to be motivated toward certain kinds of goals. A student with a strong need to achieve, for example, is disposed toward setting high academic standards for himself and working hard to comply with them. A given disposition (need, interest, and so on) may give rise to a variety of specific motives, depending on the situation. We need not attempt to distinguish precisely among the various kinds of dispositions for present purposes. Indeed, motivational dispositions are not even represented by a separate component of the cognitive model in Figure 10.1; their existence is only implied by the component called motivation. It is not that motivational dispositions are unimportant in understanding behavior, but rather that we have streamlined the present model in order to maintain a focus on cognition.

In general, motivational dispositions are of interest to the cognitive psychologist only insofar as they provide information about an individual's cognitive structures. That is, certain cognitive structures may facilitate the development of some interests and values; therefore, the presence of such interests and values would suggest the presence of the required cognitive structures. It is unlikely, for instance, that a child would develop much interest in magic tricks until he understood reality well enough to know that what *appears* to have happened in a particular trick could not *actually* have happened in reality.

Having acknowledged the existence of noncognitive motivational dispositions, we will continue to focus on the influence of cognition on motivation. We have already seen that cognition is one source of motives. In the simplest sort of case, the sight of a goal object may elicit some sort of approach behavior, as when an infant reaches for a brightly colored toy. But given the hierarchical organization of behavior into plans, the relationship between cognition and motivation generally is not so simple. An older child, for example, might remember a toy that he has played with before and then go to another room to find the toy again. When he gets up and starts walking, his immediate goal is to get to the other room. But this motive exists only because it is part of the overall plan for finding the toy. Thus, a plan can be a source of motives, too—the motives to attain certain *sub*goals that are necessary steps in attaining the ultimate goal for which the plan is designed.

Many of the motivational differences between children and adults probably stem from cognitive constraints on the kinds of plans children can construct or execute. In school, a child might not be motivated to attain a subgoal of the curriculum unless he can see how it fits into a plan for attaining some other goal of value to him. In a similar vein, we cannot very well expect a young child to work today for something that will happen tomorrow if "tomorrow" to him simply means "not now."

Intrinsic Motivation and Cognitive Structures

A lot of human behavior is directed toward goals that have no inherent connection with the behavior itself. A home owner calls a plumber, for instance, not because he wants to have a telephone conversation but because he wants to have something fixed. The behavior involved in phoning is a means to an extrinsic end. On the other hand, everyone does engage in some activities because the activities themselves are pleasurable. A person might play bridge simply because he is fascinated with the game, not because it satisfies his affiliative or competitive needs by helping him meet people with whom he can socialize or compete (though bridge may serve these needs, too). In other words, the behavior of playing bridge is, for some people, *intrinsically* motivated.

We will focus here on the proposition that intrinsically motivated behavior can often be attributed to an individual's cognitive structures. It might be said that a cognitive structure sometimes performs the function of a motivational disposition; the presence of the structure increases the likelihood that a certain kind of motive will be aroused. According to Piaget, cognitive structures in the process of developing have a built-in need to function.[7] They are disposed to assimilate appropriate objects or events. The material being assimilated is like food for the structures to grow on. Piaget actually uses the term *aliment* (food) for the content that is assimilated.

Around the middle of his first year, an infant is developing a sensorimotor structure that enables him to coordinate looking and grasping when he reaches out and takes hold of something that he sees. Practically any graspable object eventually becomes aliment for this structure, including the noses and eyeglasses of adults who come within range. The infant does not grasp these things in order to do something with them; the pleasure is in the grasping itself. It is intrinsically motivated behavior, and the underlying disposition is the developing sensorimotor structure. Objects are perceived as things to be grasped, and the sight of a nearby object is sufficient to arouse a motive to grasp it. Thus, there are times when cognition is virtually the only source of motivation.

Throughout childhood, and even in the adult years, it is possible to find many examples of behavior motivated by cognitive structures. One characteristic of such behavior is that it may be very repetitive. A child who is developing the cognitive sophistication needed to see the humor in a particular joke may delight in telling the joke over and over again, much to the chagrin of his family. In the early stages of language development, young children have been known to deliver long soliloquies in which they play with words or sounds by exploring the possibilities for combining and recombining them. The following example of a two-year-old's bedtime chatter was reported by Ruth Weir in a book called *Language in the Crib*.[8]

go for glasses
go for them
go to the top
go throw
go for blouse
pants
go for shoes

Although it is not clear what caused this sequence to begin, it seems quite likely that when the child assimilated the sound of his initial utterance, he was motivated to produce more variations on the same theme, simply because he was in the process of acquiring some rules for combining words in English (or because he was in the process of acquiring a general meaning for the word "go").

Intrinsic motivation is often attributed to such general dispositions as "curiosity" or "playfulness." But the role of cognitive structures must be considered, too, in order to explain why an individual is curious or playful in some ways but not in others. Following Piaget's lead, it seems more parsimonious to attribute intrinsic motivation to the structures themselves. This is not to say that all intrinsically motivated behavior reflects the development or modification of a cognitive structure. But a good deal of child behavior does seem to be motivated in the way that Piaget suggests.

THE MODEL OF BEHAVIOR IN ACTION

We can see the entire cognitive model of behavior in action by traveling step by step through the model once again, only this time we will do it in reverse, so as to convey a somewhat different perspective. To make this "backwards" journey concrete, we will use one example of behavior throughout.

A small boy is observed floating a flat board in a large puddle. As the board floats, the boy puts some stones on it one by one until the board sinks, at which point he removes the stones and—having allowed the board to float once more—he starts the procedure all over again, putting the same stones on the board in a different order.

Let us begin with the behavior involved in removing the stones from the sunken board. This *behavior* is jointly determined by *cognition* and *motivation*. The immediate motive is, let us say, to refloat the wood, or perhaps to see whether or not the wood *will* float again. We cannot fully understand the child's motivation without also considering his cognition, because cognition is one determinant of motivation.[9] Thus, we must ask how the child represents to himself mentally the physical *situation* in which a piece of board is held under water by some stones. There are a number of possibilities here, but to mention just a few, the boy may think the board is held under by the last stone —the one that precipitated the sinking—or he may think that *all* of the stones are needed to keep the wood under water; he may believe that the board will *stay* at the bottom of the puddle, even with the stones removed (in which case the stones are seen as important in making the board go to the bottom, but not in keeping it there). Whatever the boy's cognition—whatever his understanding of the situation—it depends on his *cognitive structures;* different cognitions result from different structures. The functioning of a structure depends, in part, on the child's motivation, but also on the objective properties of the situation. In other words, the child's way of looking at the situation is influenced by what he is looking *for* and by what there *is* to be seen. Finally, what there is to be seen, the present situation, depends in part on the child's previous behavior. In this case, the board was sunk by the child's placing the last stone on it.

In tracing the situation back to the boy's behavior, we have returned to the starting point for our reverse trip through the cognitive model, except that the behavior we have come to now occurred one step earlier than the behavior we started with. Thus, we are reminded that behavior is part of an ongoing, cyclical process, involving all components of the model at all times. Notice also the difficulty of making inferences about the child's cognition and motivation on the basis of just one behavioral "cycle." In order to select the most probable cognition and motivation from among the alternatives suggested above, it would be necessary to observe the boy's behavior over a number of cycles (including "expressive" behavior as well as goal-directed activity). For example, if the boy expressed concern or surprise at the feedback he got when the board floated again after the stones had been removed, we could infer that he thought the board might perhaps remain under water, even without the stones. Furthermore, we could infer that his motive in removing the stones was specifically to test this possibility. But the boy in our example did not pause when the board floated again; instead, he immediately began placing stones on it once more. From this observation, it seems more likely that the boy *expected* the board to float again (cognition), and that he removed the stones only because he wanted to try a new method of placing the stones (motivation). In other words, the removal of the stones was just one step in a larger *plan* for exploring the phenomenon of sinking. The motive involved in this one step (to refloat the board) was derived from the larger plan.

Finally, we may ask what disposed the boy to carry out his plan of action in the first place. It is conceivable that the boy's behavior is directed toward some external goal, but—more likely—the boy is simply satisfying his "curiosity." Thus, we have an example of intrinsic motivation. Certain aspects of the floating and sinking can only be assimilated to the boy's cognitive structures with great difficulty, requiring much accommodation and spurring the boy on to further attempts at assimilation. Such repeated attempts will eventually lead to changes in the cognitive structures themselves, so that the phenomenon is understood in a different way than it was before. By referring to *changes* in cognitive structures, we have broached the whole subject of *development,* to which we turn in the next chapter.

SUMMARY

In this chapter, we have examined a model of goal-directed behavior as seen from the cognitive point of view. According to the model, a person's cognitive structures take in and transform information from the situation through the processes of assimilation and accommodation. The cognition resulting from these processes determines the person's behavior. By perceiving the effects of his behavior on the situation, the person gets feedback on the extent to which his actions have brought him closer to a particular goal. Thus, the basic unit of behavior includes a test of the initial situation, behavioral operations to modify the situation as desired, and additional tests to see whether the desired goal has been attained. Such units generally occur in hierarchical arrangements called plans.

A person's goals are determined by his motives. Motivation influences behavior through its effects on cognition. At the same time, cognition is one source of motivation, along with noncognitive dispositions such as needs and interests. However, some behavior is intrinsically motivated by a developing cognitive structure.

11

THE CHARACTER AND CAUSES OF DEVELOPMENT

Preview

Following the theory of Jean Piaget, in this chapter we discuss the character of development in four stages, each with a different type of cognitive structure.

(1) The *sensorimotor* period of infancy is characterized by the development of a "practical intelligence" to deal with the environment.

(2) In the *preoperational* period of early childhood, the child acquires implicit rules that form the basis for intuitive thought.

(3) In the period of *concrete operations* beginning at about age seven, the child learns logical thinking applicable to concrete situations.

(4) The period of *formal operations,* which begins about age 12, is characterized by the

adolescent's ability to reason about hypothetical possibilities.

We will also discuss what causes the child to move from one stage to the next. Besides being shaped by maturation, experience, and the social environment, such progress is principally caused by the child's attempt to escape disequilibrium, brought about when he attempts to assimilate new situations to old cognitive structures. This leads to the creation of new structures and new equilibrium.

The model of behavior we discussed in the last chapter is intended to be used to analyze human behavior; however, before we can do so, we must consider some additional questions—namely: What cognitive structures are present at particular stages of development? and, What causes the structures to change from one stage to the next? These questions are about development rather than behavior, because they refer to how an individual changes over time rather than how he functions at a given point in time. The model we described does not by itself provide answers; what we need is a description of the character and causes of development.

The question of what causes development is, of course, the concern of parents and others responsible for bringing up children, but in dealing with children, adults tend to vacillate between two assumptions about development: One is the optimistic view that the adult has considerable influence in shaping the child's development, that what the child learns and when depends almost entirely on what the adult does with him. The other is the pessimistic view that development is a kind of inexorable force largely beyond anyone's control, that the child will learn what he is going to learn when development makes him ready for it. As usual, the truth is somewhere between: in important ways, development is independent of the environment and can also be influenced by it. Indeed, as we will try to show later, the impact of instruction may vary according to how well the givens of intellectual development—the concepts and principles that convey its character and causes—have been taken into account.

In this chapter, we will take several terms introduced in Chapter 9 and elaborate on them under the general headings of structures and stages, the direction of development, and the process of equilibration. Our discussion is based entirely on the theory of Jean Piaget,[1] but we will emphasize those basic ideas about development that extend beyond Piaget to other cognitive theories as well.

THE CHARACTER OF DEVELOPMENT: PIAGET'S STAGES

To recapitulate a basic principle of the cognitive approach, development proceeds through a series of qualitatively different stages, each characterized by a different type of cognitive structure. Piaget has identified four major stages or periods. By giving a brief over-view of each period, we can explain the general concept of a developmental stage and discuss the sequence in which stages occur.

First Stage: The Sensorimotor Period

During infancy, from birth to one and a half or two years, the child is in what Piaget calls the sensorimotor period. Perhaps it would be more appropriate to say that the infant "passes through" the sensorimotor period, because we do not wish to imply that children change only when they move from one period to the next but not while they are in a particular period. Anyone who watches a child grow up will observe continual changes in his behavior throughout the course of development. Within the sensorimotor period these changes are quite remarkable.

The newborn infant seems generally to be out of touch with the world around him. His behavior consists mainly of seemingly random movements of the arms, head, and legs or else of reflexive responses to particular kinds of body contact—a nipple in the mouth stimulates sucking, pressure on the palm causes grasping, and so on. By the middle of his second year, the same child will exhibit many kinds of behavior that seem well adapted to the immediate environment. For instance, he can find his way around a house and then return to a starting point, or he can retrieve a toy from behind a piece of furniture. Such advanced infant behavior would seem to depend entirely on development of the musculature needed to move about and manipulate the environment; however, actually it is changes in the infant's *cognition* of objects and spatial relations that have made the most important contribution.

Let us consider some examples of infant behavior that illustrate these changes in cognition during the sensorimotor period. As we mentioned in Chapter 9, a young infant will stop trying to grasp an attractive object as soon as it is hidden from his view, even though it may still be well within his reach; in other words, the infant has not yet acquired the notion of *object permanence*.[2] An object is not represented in cognition unless the infant has some immediate sensory contact with it. Therefore, the object is only a transitory phenomenon, lasting just as long as the sight or sound or touch of it. A few weeks later, the child may demonstrate a rudimentary awareness that objects have permanence beyond his immediate perception of them, but this new understanding still has some limitations. For example, with the child watching, an object can be hidden under a blanket at point A, and the child will understand object permanence well enough to reach under the blanket and retrieve it. But if the same object is then hidden under a pillow at point B, the child, instead of reaching under the pillow this time, will return to the blanket at point A, apparently expecting the object to be there once again. By the end of the sensorimotor period, this and other problems in locating hidden objects will give the child no trouble at all.

These observations suggest that a child may understand the permanence of objects before he understands the *space* that contains those objects. Apparently, objects can disappear at point B and mysteriously reappear at point A without an intervening displacement from B to A. This hypothesis about the infant's limited understanding of space is supported further by another type of observation. Suppose we place an object in such a way that the child can see it but cannot reach it directly to pick it up, because of a barrier of some sort. Even around the middle of the sensorimotor period a child may be unable to cope with this problem. Instead of making the necessary detour to circumvent the obstacle that is in his way, the child may simply appear to be stymied or he may make some futile attempts to go directly through the barrier. The reason for this failure again seems to be cognitive rather than motoric; the child has the physical ability to make a detour, but he does not see the possibility of arriving at the same point by a variety of routes, some of them less direct than others. Before the end of the sensorimotor period, a child understands space well enough to become quite adept at making detours and, for a while, he may even regard it as great fun to solve "barrier problems" that have been set up for him by an older child or adult. This pleasure in the use of a developing cognitive structure is an example of intrinsic motivation.

A variation on this problem of retrieving a desired object shows other facets of the sensorimotor period. If an object is placed out of reach on top of a large pillow that the infant can grasp at the end nearest him, toward the end of his first year, the child will develop the ability to retrieve the object by pulling the pillow close enough to bring the object within reach. He will do this without a lot of trial and error, as if he knows that one can move an object by moving the thing supporting it. This "behavior of the support," as Piaget calls it, not only illustrates the child's growing awareness of relations between objects in space, but also draws attention to a basic property of intelligent problem solving—the separation of means from ends.[3] Grasping, pulling, and releasing the pillow are all means to the end of grasping the object itself. We can check the child's ability to separate means from ends by seeing whether or not he persists in pulling the pillow when we put the object within reach for him, or by giving him a new problem that requires different means to achieve the same end. The separation of means from ends gives the child much more flexibility in adapting to his environment. The different kinds of behavior in his repertoire can be recombined in various ways, depending on the situation. Even a modest repertoire permits a large number of different combinations for the solving of problems.

Analyzing the behavior of the support into its subcomponents brings to mind the notion of a plan. Young infants cannot conceive hierarchically organized plans like the one we have just seen. Sometimes they seem to start executing such a plan, only to get hung up on the first step. For instance, in reaching for the object on the pillow, the child might grasp the near edge of the pillow, but then become preoccupied with further manipulating the pillow and not go on to grasp the object. As we discussed, we cannot explain such behavior by attributing it simply to the child's distractability or short attention span. The younger infant is more easily distracted from his original goal because he lacks the cognitive structures needed to devise and execute a plan for attaining it. We shall see how later developments in cognition greatly increase the possible complexity of problem-solving plans, both in the ends that can be conceived and in the means to their attainment.

In describing the sensorimotor period, we have emphasized the child's cognition of objects and space, but the same period can also be viewed from other perspectives, including the child's understanding of causality, or the development of play and imitation. Piaget has studied each of these areas in minute detail, largely through extensive observation and experimentation with his own three children.[4]

Piaget captures the essence of the sensorimotor period when he says that a "Copernican revolution" occurs in the child's cognition.[5] It was Copernicus who first proposed the theory that the earth and other planets revolve around the sun—a truly revolutionary idea in the sixteenth century, when scholars commonly accepted the Ptolemaic theory that the earth was a fixed point at the center of the universe. Obviously, Piaget cannot mean that the young infant literally starts out with a theory that he is the center of his world, because initially the infant is totally unaware of himself as a separate being in a world that contains other people and objects. But because he lacks this awareness, the infant *behaves* as if he is at the center of a universe that revolves around and even depends on him; he is a kind of unknowing solipsist. As we have seen, the infant later behaves as if he understands the independent existence of objects, including himself, within a general and somewhat extended spatial field. Thus, in going from an initial preoccupation with his own body to a lively interest in other objects and their positions and movements in space, the infant has in fact experienced a mini–Copernican revolution.

As a result of this revolution, the child acquires what Piaget calls "practical intelligence," which means that the child can do the kinds of things we have discussed—making detours, keeping track of an object's location, and so on. But the child's understanding of objects and space is still very much on the plane of overt action. It will be some time before he can deal with space in terms of road maps or verbal instructions on how to get somewhere. His knowledge about the *properties* of objects, such as weight or volume, is still far from complete. Of the three modes of cognitive representation mentioned in Chapter 9, the infant's cognition seems limited for the most part to the enactive mode. This is the mode in which things are represented in terms of actions that can be performed with them. It might actually be too soon to speak of "representation" at this stage of development; only later can the child "represent" to himself past experiences that he has had. In the sensorimotor period, the content of the infant's cognition seems restricted to objects and events with which he has direct contact through one sensory channel or another, either presently or in the very recent past. Moreover, there is not a clear differentiation between cognition and behavior: to "think about" something is to act on it, quite overtly. It is evident, then, why Piaget chose the name "sensorimotor" for this first period.

Second Stage: The Preoperational Period

According to Piaget's theory, the next developmental period covers roughly the years from two to seven.[6] As with the sensorimotor period, this time span includes some very noticeable changes, but it also has some constant qualities that set it apart from the preceding and following periods. The name, *pre*operational, suggests that this period is defined with reference to something that the child still does not have, and so it is. But let us begin on a more positive note by citing a new acquisition—something that the child did not have before.

The primary achievement of the preoperational period is the emergence of what Piaget calls the *semiotic function.*[7] Semiotic refers to the general phenomenon of signification—the business of making one thing stand for, or signify, another. In Piaget's terminology, the first of these two things is a *signifier,* the second a *significate.* The key development in the preoperational period is the child's ability to differentiate between signifiers and significates, to recognize and use signifiers with the understanding that they are not identical with their significates. An early manifestation of the semiotic function can be found in the phenomenon of symbolic play. We would not be at all surprised to observe a two- or three-year-old child pretending to eat a rounded pebble, as if it were a piece of candy. Young children spend a great deal of time engaged in exactly this kind of play. Usually it is clear that the child is only pretending, because he laughs or gives some other indication of his awareness that the pebble is not really candy; for instance, he does not actually bite the pebble but only holds it near his mouth as he bites. Thus, the child differentiates between signifier and significate. The pebble represents the kind of signifier that Piaget calls a *symbol,* because it bears some resemblance to the significate.

As trivial and commonplace as symbolic play might seem, it marks an important advance beyond the practical intelligence of the sensorimotor period. An infant might be observed putting a pebble to his mouth, but only because mouthing is a way for him to explore the properties of an object (or because he actually is attempting to eat the pebble!). So this case involves no signification. There are times when the semiotic function does appear to be operative in the sensorimotor period, as when an infant smiles upon hearing his mother's voice in the next room. But the mother's voice is only an *index* or indicator, which is not differentiated from its significate. When the mother's voice indicates her presence, the child responds in much the same way as he would to the sight of her walking into the room. Thus, the infant is still functioning on a sensorimotor level—still tied to the here and now—even in responding to an index. On the other hand, the semiotic function enables the preoperational child to bring the past and the future into the present, by symbolically recreating events that are remote in time and space, or by imagining things that have yet to occur.

The child in our example of symbolic play might also use another kind of signifier, by saying "Candy" as he pretends to eat the pebble. The word "candy" is a *sign* rather than a symbol, because there is no intrinsic correspondence between signifier and significate.[8] Natural languages provide the most common instances of signs, but there are other kinds, too, such as mathematical notation (+, =, and so on). The fact that signs are based on social conventions rather than inherent resemblances is important because it means that a child can only learn about signs from his elders. Having done so, however, he is in a position to profit from the experience of others in ways that would be practically impossible without signs.

We can see in the preoperational child's use of verbal signs that his cognition is still quite limited, even after the semiotic function has developed. The toddler's initial use of a word may seem rather quaint and idiosyncratic to an adult. For example, one child is reported to have used the word "maiama" (mailman) to signify a great many things: "the mailman, the door bell ringing, a noise on the front porch leading to an excited excursion to the front door, a letter or any piece of white paper, and a newspaper or magazine."[9] This collection is not entirely haphazard—one can see connections between the various items—but it certainly does not correspond to the class of significates for which an adult would use the sign "mailman" (or any other single sign, for that matter). In fact the whole idea of a class, or category, of objects is still well beyond the child's understanding when he first begins naming things with verbal signs.

As the child passes through the preoperational period, his use of language becomes less and less idiosyncratic and more and more conventional. The child can relate his experiences to others in a reasonably intelligible fashion, giving one the impression that his words mean just about the same thing to him as they do to an adult. But sometimes communication between child and adult breaks down; it seems as if the child still has some peculiar meanings for particular words. Piaget has made a great contribution in showing us that a child's use of words actually reveals something about the structure of his thinking. It has also been shown that, near the end of the preoperational period, the gap between child and adult thinking can still be quite startling, as the following example will demonstrate.

In a replication of one of Piaget's classic experiments[10]—perhaps the most famous of all—suppose we ask a five-year-old to pour the same amount of water into two identical jars, *A* and *B* (see Figure 11.1). After allowing him to make sure that the water reaches exactly the same level in both jars, we pour all of the water from jar *A* into a third jar, *C*, which has a smaller diameter than the first two. (We do this pouring with the child watching us the whole

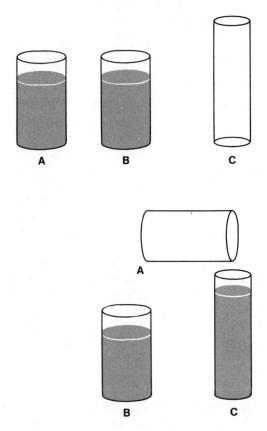

Figure 11.1. Conservation of liquid amount

time.) Now we ask the child if both jars *B* and *C* contain exactly the same amount of water, or if one has more. Typically the child will answer that the two amounts are not the same. He may say that *C* has more, pointing to the higher water level in *C*, or—less often—he may notice that jar *C* has a smaller diameter and claim, therefore, that *C* holds *less* water than *B*. In Piaget's terms, the child does not seem to understand that the amount of a substance is "conserved" despite changes in its dimensions, so long as nothing is added or taken away.

When first confronted with such an observation, many adults believe that a simple misunderstanding has occurred. The child, they argue, is just answering the wrong question: he thinks the experimenter is asking which water level is higher, or which quantity of water *looks* greater. It is true that sometimes, by rephrasing the question, one will find out that a child understands the "conservation" of amount perfectly well.[11] But in most cases, no matter how many different ways the problem is posed, children from four to seven will persist in their failure to conserve. The basic conservation problem permits endless variations. In the present example, the water from jar *A* might also be poured into a wide, shallow pan, or into several small glasses. Or we could follow a similar procedure with two lumps of clay, molding one of them into various shapes and asking questions about equality of amounts. It is advisable to try several of these variations with a given child before concluding that he is or is not a "conserver." In other words, one must have an adequate sampling of performances before inferring something about the child's competence. However, as the evidence piles up, it becomes difficult to escape the conclusion that many children really believe in the inequality of two amounts that are "obviously" equal—that their performance in answering questions reflects accurately their competence in thinking about quantity.

The limitations of preoperational thought extend beyond the area of conservation per se, but the specific conservation problem we have before us will suffice to introduce a general characteristic of the preoperational period. Notice that in the preceding example, the child is not simply wrong: he is wrong for a particular reason. He focuses his attention on just one aspect of the situation that he is responding to—either the level of water in a jar or the width of the jar, but not both. It is not hard to understand why such aspects of the situation are the targets of a child's "centrations," as Piaget calls them. In the child's experience, the levels of liquids in containers do *tend* to indicate their relative amounts. In fact, the levels are completely reliable indicators of amount as long as identical containers are being used. But with different sizes or shapes of containers, the relationship between level and amount becomes much more tenuous—a fact that the preoperational child fails to grasp. It is as if the child has used the semiotic function to draw upon his past experience and has come up with an implicit rule of thumb for dealing with amounts: the higher the level, the greater the amount. In other words, the child has certain intuitions about amount without really understanding it. His intuitions sometimes cause him to leap to erroneous conclusions. Piaget has actually referred to the latter part of the preoperational period as the "intuitive" stage in children's thinking.

The preoperational child's view of the world may differ not only from that of older children and adults, but also from the views of other children who are likewise in the preoperational period. Suppose we have two brothers, Tom and Harry, ages four and five. We ask Harry how many brothers he has, and he tells us that he has one. Now we ask Tom to tell us how many brothers Harry has. To our amazement, he says "None." In general, a preoperational child finds it difficult to take another person's point of view. Tom cannot put himself in Harry's place and then see himself as a brother. Needless to say, this centration on his own point of view can have important consequences for the child's relationships with other people.

To summarize, the emergence of the semiotic function at the beginning of the preoperational period represents a giant step toward higher forms of intelligence. As the child becomes more proficient in the use of symbols and signs, he develops intuitions that make his thinking seem more and more like that of an adult. But there is still something missing, and it is not just information—not just some miscellaneous facts that the child will pick up sooner or later. It is a whole new way of thinking, a kind of logic that older children and adults take for granted.

Third Stage: The Period of Concrete Operations

Between the ages of seven and twelve (again, these are only approximations), children pass through the period of concrete operations. At this point we are dealing with children who respond to the conservation problem with the kind of logic that was missing in the preoperational period. This advance in thinking is made possible by a newly acquired ability to perform cognitive *operations.* An operation, in Piaget's theory, is an internal, mental action that fits into a particular kind of system or structure, such that the operations in a given structure balance each other in order to produce equilibrium. The actions that Piaget has in mind are the mental equivalents of such behaviors as combining and separating, or adding and subtracting. When these actions are coordinated in a balanced way, the child can consider two aspects of a situation simultaneously and see the systematic relationship between them.

Let us use one version of the conservation problem to illustrate what is meant by "operational" thinking. Suppose a child understands that the amount of clay in a ball remains the same when the ball is rolled into the shape of a sausage. According to Piaget, this understanding is based on the child's ability to see that each increase in the length of the sausage is balanced by a compensating decrease in its diameter (or vice versa). It is as if the child mentally adds to the length and, at the same time, subtracts from the diameter, thereby maintaining equilibrium with regard to the amount of clay. Notice that the child now is attending to the *transformations* performed on the clay ball, whereas earlier he had attended only to the end *state* (the sausage), and to just one dimension of the sausage at that. To put it another way, the child's thought has become "decentered" with regard to the dimension of length (or width). The ability to decenter in this way represents a major difference between concrete operations and preoperational thinking.

Another basic property of operational thought is revealed especially well by the "class inclusion" problem. In Piaget's original experiment, children were shown a set of wooden beads, most of them brown but a few of them white.[12] Then each child was asked, "Are there more brown beads or more wooden ones?" At the preoperational level, children tended to say there were more *brown* beads, as if the experimenter had asked, "Are there more brown beads or more *white* ones?" (In a recent repetition of this experiment, one child explicitly informed the experimenter that the question being asked was incorrect, because one could only compare the brown beads to the white ones, not to the wooden ones.) Piaget found that children in the period of concrete operations answered correctly that there were more wooden beads than brown ones. What made the difference, according to Piaget, was that the older children, having mentally separated the class of brown beads from the class of white beads, could then mentally recombine these classes to form the overall class of wooden beads. This enabled them to make a quantitative comparison between the subclass (brown beads) and the higher-order class (wooden beads) in which it was included. As Piaget puts it, the mental actions of the older children were "reversible." The younger children could separate brown beads from white beads, but then they were unable to get back to the starting point and consider the larger class as a whole. Thus, there was nothing left with which to compare the brown beads, except for the white ones. (For more on the child's understanding of classes, see Chapter 12.)

Reversibility is a characteristic of all operational thought. It can be seen in the conservation problem, as well as in class inclusion. When a clay sausage is made longer, a decrease in diameter compensates for the increase in length, so that total amount is held constant. Unlike the class inclusion problem, the reversibility here is not accomplished through a simple "undoing" or *negation* of the original action but rather through a kind of *reciprocity.* That is, the effect of an increase in length is reversed by a reciprocal decrease in diameter, so that the amount of clay stays the same, even though it is not returned to its original shape. All instances of concrete operational thinking involve reversibility, either by negation or by reciprocity.

A moment's thought will make it clear that reversibility is closely related to the process of decentering, which also occurs in the period of concrete operations. A child who can mentally separate two classes of beads while simultaneously combining them can also attend to both attributes of the beads at the same time—both color (brown or white) and material (wood). This is not to say that reversibility *causes* decentering, or vice versa. The two terms simply help us look at operational thought from two different angles.

If the word "operations" represents the major achievement of this developmental period, the word "concrete" points to its major limitation. Operational structures do not appear in fully developed form at about age seven. Initially, the child can assimilate only a narrow range of content to these structures, that is, the field of equilibrium is still relatively restricted. Gradually, more and more different situations are assimilated and understood by means of the same logic. Thus, for example, children attain the conservation of amount early in the period of concrete operations, then the conservation of weight, and eventually the conservation of volume (as indicated by the displacement of water when a solid object is submerged in it). But even at the end of the period, the child's operations apply only to "concrete" situations, that is, to actual situations rather than to hypothetical ones.

To illustrate both the power and the limits of concrete operations, consider a 10-year-old who can reason that if she is a little shorter than Gladys, and Gladys is a little shorter than Blanche, then she (herself) *must* be shorter than Blanche, too. She sees no need to make a direct comparison between herself and Blanche in order to find out who is taller. In Piaget's terminology, the 10-year-old's reasoning shows that she understands the principle of "transitivity" as it applies to a series of concrete objects ordered by size. However, it may be much harder for the same child to use transitive reasoning with regard to a *hypothetical* series, especially one that is contrary to fact. We might say to her, "Suppose Gladys was shorter than you, and Blanche was shorter than Gladys. Who would be shorter, you or Blanche?" The answer in this case might very well be, "But I'm shorter than Gladys, and Blanche is the tallest of all."

This limitation of concrete operations precludes the possibility of "hypothetico-deductive" thinking, a kind of thinking fundamental to all scientific investigation. The scientist often engages in chains of reasoning that have the general form "If *A* were true and *B* were true, then it would follow that *C* is true; therefore, if I can establish that *A* and *B* both *are* true, then I will have proved that *C* is true too." Many of the propositions that enter into such a chain of reasoning have no basis in established fact, at least not when the inquiry begins. The propositions are hypothetical and therefore beyond the competence of children in the period of concrete operations.

Fourth Stage: The Period of Formal Operations

Beginning at about age 12, children enter what Piaget calls the period of formal operations. It is difficult to assign an upper age boundary to this period. The structures of formal thought seem well developed in some individuals by age 15 or 16, but other individuals pass on into adulthood with their competence at this level still very uncertain. Since we are talking here about man's thinking in its most highly developed form, it should not be surprising to find that many people achieve only a partial equilibrium at this level. In any case, the type of thinking that emerges during the period of formal operations was implied by our discussion of the limitations of concrete operations. When children can apply their logic to more than the givens of experience, when they can reason about the possible and not just the actual, then they have arrived at the level of formal operations. To clarify the nature of formal operations, let us examine the thinking involved in understanding a principle of elementary physics.

Suppose we are studying the way older children and adolescents think about the causes of floating and sinking. Our materials are a large tank of water and a diverse set of objects, including some that will float and some that will not. We ask our subjects, aged 10 to 16, to predict which objects will float and which will sink. Then we invite them to test their predictions and to perform further experiments with the objects and the water so that they can explain to us what it is that determines whether an object will float. By observing how our subjects manipulate the materials, by asking them questions, and by listening to what they say, we will try to infer the nature of their thinking about the causes of buoyancy.

In following this procedure, we may find that it takes time before the subjects begin to show us just how advanced their thinking is. Many of them may start out by basing their predictions and explanations on the type of substance from which an object is made: wooden things float and metal things sink, for instance. Notice that such generalizations require nothing more than the "intuitive" thinking characteristic of the late preoperational period. If we were to stop at this point, we might grossly underestimate the cognitive competence of some of our subjects. We need to push them a little further to see whether or not their performance will change. Having anticipated some explanations based on substance, we have been clever enough to bring along two similar plastic objects, one of which floats while the other sinks. When a subject encounters these objects, he will realize he cannot say that one floats because it is plastic and that the other sinks for exactly the same reason. (Actually, preoperational children often do engage in such blatant contradictions, but our present subjects are older and more sophisticated than that.)

When it becomes apparent that naming the type of substance does not provide a sufficient explanation of buoyancy, many subjects will focus on *weight* as the crucial variable. They tell us that the type of plastic that sinks is *heavier* than the type that floats. But, we say, how about a large block of wood, an object that floats very nicely? Isn't the wood block still heavier than the plastic object that sinks? Some of our subjects counter by saying that weight is not the only thing that counts; one must consider the size of the object as well. To demonstrate how this works, some children may even try to cross-classify the objects by size and weight, sorting them into groups that are large–heavy, small–heavy, large–light, and small–light. This kind of classification shows the availability of concrete operations that enable the subject to consider two dimensions—size and weight—simultaneously. Unfortunately, though, it does not result in very accurate predictions of floating and sinking, because some small–light objects (for example, a wooden toothpick) will float, but others (a steel sewing needle) will sink. At best it can be said that large–light objects generally float and heavy–small ones generally sink. It is important to note that the success or failure of this strategy in making predictions depends entirely upon the particular objects in the array that has been classified. In other words, the strategy is limited by its concreteness.

Some of our subjects—those still in the period of concrete operations —will get no further than the two-way classification in their attempts to explain buoyancy. Others will hit upon a more adequate way of relating size and weight, by suggesting something like the notion of density or weight per unit of volume. What really counts, they say, is the weight of an object *relative* to its size—not the absolute weight and size, but the ratio of one to the other. It is doubtful that many children will spontaneously use exactly these words, but some of them will get the idea across, one way or another.

An understanding of density marks the transition from concrete to formal operations, but one important question remains in solving the problem at hand. If density is the crucial variable, just how dense must an object be before it will sink? To answer this question, a subject will have to consider the density of an object in relation to the density of water. He might get at this by suggesting that we imagine a "piece" of water exactly the same size as a particular object. If the object weighs more than the piece of water, it will sink, because it is heavy enough to push the water out of its way. If the object weighs less than the water, the water will hold it up and make it float. A person trained in elementary physics would speak about "specific gravity" (the ratio of an object's density to the density of water) and about the "displacement" of water by an object, but at the moment we are less interested in technical terminology than in the basic idea. For reasons that we will get into shortly, our subject's explanation involving a hypothetical piece of water is a good indication that he is able to think at the level of formal operations.

The imaginary study we have been conducting derives from some very real observations reported by Inhelder and Piaget.[13] Their procedure is a good example of the "clinical method" described in Chapter 8, because the experimenter can gear his questioning to what the subject has already said and done in trying to solve the problem. In reality, the problem of floating and sinking objects reveals much more about the development of operational thought than we have shown here, and it is only one of several tasks that have been used to shed light on the period of formal operations in particular. But even the study we have outlined above illustrates some central characteristics of cognition at the formal level. For one thing, a subject who talks about hypothetical pieces of water with certain precise specifications clearly has gone beyond the concrete givens of experience. But this example allows us to characterize formal thinking in somewhat more detail now, too.

An important property of formal operations is captured in the formula *density = weight ÷ volume.* According to this formula, the density of an object can be increased by adding weight while holding volume constant. It follows that this increase in density can be nullified either by the removal of weight (simple negation) or by a compensating increase in volume (reciprocity)—or by certain combinations of both. To draw a rough analogy, if a lifeboat begins to sink as more and more people climb aboard, one can reverse this state of affairs by ordering people out of the boat or by getting a larger boat. We saw earlier that the cognitive structures that develop during the period of concrete operations involve reversibility either by negation *or* by reciprocity, but not by both at the same time. Now we see a structure at the formal level that coordinates both kinds of reversibility in a single system. As this structure develops, the individual begins to understand more fully a great variety of situations in which one variable can be expressed as a ratio or proportion involving two other variables. A common example is represented by the formula *rate of speed = distance ÷ time.*

Another aspect of formal operations becomes especially clear when we consider yet another formula: *specific gravity = density of a substance ÷ density of water.* We have already established that the concept of density—when expressed as a relationship between two variables—requires the use of reversible operations. Now, in specific gravity, we have a variable that is expressed as a relationship between two densities. An understanding of specific gravity must therefore require the use of *operations upon operations!* This last phrase makes a good definition of formal operations in general: they are operations performed on other operations, as opposed to concrete operations, which are performed directly on real objects and events (or, more precisely, on the mental representations of objects and events).

Hopefully, it is a bit clearer now how the attainment of formal operations enables a person to project beyond his actual experience. By performing operations on operations, he can systematically generate a set of possibilities or hypotheses. For instance, he might consider as possibilities the hypothesis that the sinking of an object is caused by its weight, or by its size, or by its weight in relation to its size, or by none of these. He can then devise a plan for testing his hypotheses in a way that will prove conclusively the truth or falsity of each one. The classic strategy for this type of experimentation is to vary one thing at a time (for example, try out different weights) while holding everything else constant. Thus, Piaget identifies the strategy of "all other things being equal" as one indicator of formal operations.

The period of formal operations is the final stage in Piaget's theory. But even when the structures of formal thinking are well developed by late adolescence, this does not mean that intellectual development has come to an end. The individual may still extend his formal operations over new areas of content, or become more facile in the kind of reasoning that formal operations make possible. However, there are no more major qualitative changes in the nature of his cognition, such as those that occurred during childhood.

Much more could be said about the period of formal operations, and about the earlier periods as well. Additional developments occur within each of the four major periods, and we will discuss some of these with respect to specific areas of development in Chapter 12.

Summary of Piaget's Stages with Respect to Cognitive Structure

Developmental stages are qualitatively different because each one reflects a different kind of cognitive structure. Therefore, we can summarize Piaget's theory of stages by reviewing the type of structure that characterizes each of the major periods.

The Sensorimotor Stage. Here there is little differentiation between cognition and behavior. Thus, Piaget refers to the cognitive structures of this period as "action schemes"—patterns of overt behavior that are repeated in similar situations.[14] Grasping, pulling, pushing, and looking are all examples of actions for which the infant has schemes. Moreover, through a process of "mutual assimilation," these elementary schemes combine to form more complicated structures. One structure of this sort is manifested in the "behavior of the support," where schemes for looking, grasping, and pulling are brought together in a hierarchical plan for obtaining a goal object. Whether they are simple or complex, however, the distinguishing feature of sensorimotor structures is their close identity with overt behavior.

The Preoperational Stage. In this period a greater differentiation of cognition from behavior is achieved through development of the semiotic function. The child can now represent past (and future) objects and events by means of internal, mental actions, without engaging in overt behavior. But these internal actions are not yet combined in structures that have the property of reversibility; therefore, they are not yet true "operations." The intuitive structures of the preoperational period correspond to implicit rules that work in just one direction: adding water to a container raises the water level, but raising the water level (for example, by transfer to a different container) does not necessarily mean that there is more water than before. Such rules tend to determine the child's cognition one at a time instead of being coordinated with each other. The same child may think that, in general, "longer is more" and "thinner is less," yet he fails to consider both rules when confronted with a conservation problem, basing his response on just one or the other.

The Concrete Operations Stage. This period is characterized by structures in which internal actions are coordinated to produce reversibility, either by negation or by reciprocity. The presence of these new structures is reflected in the child's logical responses to problems involving conservation or class inclusion. However, the operational schemes in the child's repertoire at this stage can only assimilate what is concrete or actual, not the abstract or hypothetical. In addition, the two kinds of reversibility are not yet coordinated with each other in a single structure.

The Formal Operations Stage. Here the child (or adolescent or adult) possesses a kind of cognitive structure that enables him to conceive of hypothetical possibilities and to reason about them with completely coordinated reversibility by performing operations on other operations. The individual can now utilize certain basic strategies of scientific thinking, such as the scheme of "all other things being equal." Notice that it is no less appropriate to use the term "scheme" with regard to a structure at the formal level than at the sensorimotor level, since we are still talking about an action pattern that can be repeated and generalized to new situations. The difference, of course, is that formal schemes represent a much more complex type of cognitive structure and are not tied to particular forms of overt behavior.

Piaget's Stages and the Direction of Development

In order to keep sight of the continuities in development, and not just the differences between stages, let us briefly reconsider the general trends or directions of development discussed in Chapter 9. One of these was the progressive loss of egocentrism, which can be seen at several levels in the developmental periods described by Piaget. Certainly the "Copernican revolution" in the sensorimotor period represents a major step in this direction. Further progress occurs when the attainment of concrete operations enables the child to see things accurately from another person's point of view. At a still higher level, formal operations free the child from his own actual experience so that he can think logically about hypothetical situations. Even within the period of formal operations, some changes occur that indicate further losses of egocentrism. For example, the ability to envision possibilities other than the status quo, and to think about them systematically, may lead initially to "adolescent idealism," a kind of centration on one's own ideas about the way things could and should be, without sufficient regard for the way things are. Later on, personal ideals are tempered by certain realities, including the different beliefs held by others, so that the individual develops a more balanced perspective.

Closely related to the loss of egocentrism is the attainment of greater objectivity. The notion of objectivity can be defined either with reference to the degree of correspondence between cognitive representation and reality as it exists "out there," or in terms of the extent to which a person's cognition facilitates his adaptation to the environment. From a cognitive point of view, these two definitions of objectivity amount to pretty much the same thing. In any case, an infant who understands object permanence has a more objective type of cognition than one who does not. Likewise, a child who understands the conservation of properties such as amount and weight is able to be more objective than a nonconserver. Finally, the ability to conceive of hypothetical possibilities and to reason about them in a logical fashion brings with it a new objectivity in the individual's interpretation of what he has actually experienced, as illustrated in the problem of floating and sinking objects.

Another general direction of development is seen in the child's progress toward broader fields of equilibrium. An infant of three or four months has achieved a certain degree of equilibrium with respect to visible objects when it can follow the movements of an object with its eyes. The direction and focus of the infant's gaze are adjusted to changes in the object's location, so that perceptual contact with the object is maintained. But before the attainment of object permanence, this field of equilibrium does not include situations in which an object disappears behind a screen. When that happens, the infant does not look for the object because he does not know that it is there. Later on, the field of equilibrium expands to the point where the child knows that a disappearing object is still there, but he only expects to find the object where it first disappeared. Thus, the field of equilibrium is broader but still restricted in scope until a further change occurs in the child's cognitive structure. A similar sequence of expansions in the field of equilibrium may be seen when a child attains the ability to reason about transitive relations among items in an ordered series of concrete objects but only later can apply the same reasoning to a hypothetical series.

GENERAL CHARACTERISTICS OF
DEVELOPMENTAL STAGES

We have seen how Piaget breaks down the general trends of development into qualitatively different stages, and we have discussed the particulars that define each stage. Let us now consider some further principles regarding stages in general, drawing on Piaget's theory for examples. These principles apply not only to Piaget's theory but also to other cognitive-developmental theories, such as the theory of moral development discussed in the next chapter.

The Reality of Stages

It is important to understand that, in reality, the boundaries between developmental stages are neither as distinct nor as closely related to chronological age as our preceding discussion might have implied. Children do not universally wake up on their seventh birthdays, for instance, to find that they have arrived at the period of concrete operations. For one thing, the age of transition between stages seems to vary from child to child over a range that may be several months for early transitions or several years for later ones. Thus, within a group of children who are the same age, one is likely to find a mixture of stages. The ages given for Piaget's developmental periods are, therefore, rough averages, based on the children who have been studied.

A second complication arises from the fact that the transitions themselves take time. We might even say that the transition into concrete operations, for example, is complete only at the *end* of that period (about age 12). Before that time, there are still situations that the child cannot assimilate in terms of concrete operations—problems that he can respond to on only an intuitive basis. At the same time, however, there may be other situations in which the child is already beginning to show signs of formal operations. Thus, stage mixture occurs even within individual children.

Piaget is aware of this mixture, and he notes that, as a general rule, new forms of cognition do not appear suddenly and completely but rather emerge through a series of gradual steps. Piaget uses the French word *décalage* when this stepwise process results in a situation where the child seems to have acquired a new form of cognition in some respects but not yet in others. Perhaps the best translation of *décalage* in this context is "time lag." If the time lag occurs within a single stage, that is, on just one level of development, Piaget calls it *horizontal décalage*. In the period of concrete operations, for example, children typically acquire the conservation of amount before the conservation of weight. Other instances of horizontal *décalage* appear to be more individually or culturally determined, so that one child first develops operational thought in area *A*, while another begins with area *B*. Piaget speaks also of *vertical décalage* in those cases where the child's cognition has developed only partially because it has yet to go through higher stages. Thus, the child loses his egocentrism first on the level of overt action, then with regard to concrete thought, and finally at the level of abstract or formal thought. Obviously, it is horizontal *décalage* that, by definition, accounts for the kind of mixture of stages within the child that we have been discussing.

The reality of stages is complicated further by the fact that people do not always perform at the highest level within their competence. For one thing, some situations simply do not require the most advanced type of thinking possible in order for adaptive behavior to occur. A man with a Ph.D. in mathematics can do simple arithmetic in counting his change (concrete operations) without reflecting on the abstract properties of number systems (formal operations), even though he is perfectly capable of doing the latter. On the other hand, there are times when people fail to manifest a relatively advanced type of thinking even though the situation calls for it and it is well within their competence. Consider the following anecdote:

> A man driving across the desert was flagged down by a woman who had run out of gas. The woman was quite distressed at the prospect of being stranded, and so was greatly relieved when the man came to her rescue with a gallon can of gasoline that he kept in his car for emergencies. But as the man was pouring the extra gas into the dry gas tank, the woman suddenly said, "Stop! You'd better not put *all* of it in right now, because I might run out of gas *again,* before I get to a gas station!"

For a moment, at least, the woman's thinking is logically indistinguishable from that of the preoperational child who fails to conserve a quantity of liquid as it is poured out of a single container and distributed among several other containers. The difference, of course, is that the woman really knows better. Most of the time she would be more logical, and even when she is not, she can easily be shown the error in her thinking. The preoperational child, however, persists in his nonconservation, and no amount of explanation will change his mind. The point is that adults are perfectly capable of behaving on occasion like preoperational children.

The woman above might seem to provide an example of what psychoanalytic theorists call *regression,* that is, reversion to an earlier mode of behavior. However, we would argue that the woman did not literally go back to an earlier stage of development, because there were certain differences between her behavior and that of a preoperational child. There is another phenomenon in development for which the label of regression seems even more questionable—namely, the occurrence of *growth errors,* instances in which a child's performance appears to get worse (more immature) before it gets better. Sometimes, in the conservation problem, a child who has consistently centered on water level in the past will begin to vacillate between water level and container width as a basis for judging relative amounts. This inconsistent behavior bears at least a superficial resemblance to the haphazard behavior of much younger children and might therefore be called regression. In this case, however, the child's inconsistency is probably a sign of developmental progress toward a consideration of two dimensions at once, rather than a step back-wards. Such behavior may well be necessary in the transition from one stage to the next.

It should be clear by now that we face some serious problems if we wish to determine precisely which stage a particular child is in at a particular time. Surely we cannot make this determination on the basis of chronological age, at least not with much certainty of being correct. Nor can we decide by giving the child a quick test of some sort—a conservation problem, for example. Because of horizontal *décalages,* the child may seem to have operations on the test, but not in another, logically equivalent situation (or vice versa). If we expand the test to include a variety of problems, we will reduce our chances of being dead wrong in assessing the child's level of cognition, but we will also increase the chances of obtaining a rather mixed picture as to where he is developmentally. Thus, we would have to qualify our statements about the child by saying things like "he *tends* to function at the level of concrete operations," or "concrete operations seem to be well established with respect to problems in area *A* but not area *B.*"

The difficulties encountered in trying to apply a stage theory to real children remind us that the notion of a stage is, after all, an abstraction. It is nonetheless a useful abstraction, because it allows us to summarize the domi-nant features of cognition during a particular part of childhood, or to specify more precisely a child's way of dealing with a particular situation. The stages in Piaget's theory seem to serve these purposes rather well, as numerous confirmatory studies have shown.[15] Any description of stages must, of course, face the test of further data on the way children really are.

So much for the reality of stages. Let us return to the general theory of stages, bearing in mind the complexities involved in moving from theory to reality.

The Sequence of Stages and the Progressive Integration of Structures

We have seen that the rate of progress through stages is not fixed. One aspect of development *is* fixed, however, and that is the *sequence* in which stages occur. In Piaget's theory, a child must go through the sensorimotor period before arriving at the preoperational period, then through the preopera-tional period before attaining concrete operations, and so on. Some children, for various reasons,[16] might not go through all of the stages, but as far as they go, they must take the stages in the order specified by the theory.

The sequence of stages in a theory like Piaget's is not arbitrary. It is determined by the fact that each stage depends upon, or is made possible by, those stages that precede it. Such dependencies between stages become espe-cially clear if we start with a relatively advanced type of cognition and work backwards in tracing its origins. For example, we saw how the understanding of density, as a proportional relationship between weight and volume, requires formal operations. But this understanding presupposes the conservation of weight, which requires concrete operations. Furthermore, since operations are defined as covert actions, or mental equivalents of actions, they must depend in turn on the semiotic function, which emerges in the preoperational period. And the semiotic function grows out of the child's overt actions during the sensorimotor period.

By shifting now into a forward gear and passing through the stages once more, we can arrive at the essential reason for the sequential dependencies that exist between stages. The action schemes of infancy become internalized in the preoperational period. Then with the attainment of concrete operations, the internal actions coalesce into structures that have the property of reversibility, either by negation or by reciprocity. Finally, the two kinds of reversibility are brought together within a single system in the period of formal operations. In other words, the cognitive structures of later stages are built from those structures that have already developed in preceding stages: earlier structures are *integrated* into later ones.

Let us pause here to consider an apparent paradox. We have just said that earlier structures become integrated into later ones. It sounds, therefore, as if an earlier structure becomes inaccessible—or at least loses its independent identity—when the child moves on to a higher stage of development. Such an implication is supported by the observation that we suffer a kind of "amnesia" for earlier forms of cognition. An eight-year-old, for example, may find it very hard to believe that a year or so ago he was a consistent nonconserver. He cannot remember what it was like to think on a preoperational level. On the other hand, we said before that earlier forms of cognition can be found alongside of later ones, because of horizontal *décalages* or momentary lapses or because the earlier forms are adequate for certain tasks. Thus, we are left with a question: How can an early structure continue to function on its own, once it has been integrated into a more advanced structure?

Perhaps a physical analogy will help resolve this apparent dilemma. Despite warnings to the contrary, some amateur electricians will attempt to replace a blown-out fuse with a penny. Suppose we think of the penny as an elementary structure that is integrated into a higher-level structure, an electrical circuit. In performing its new function as a conductor of electricity, the penny no longer is available to perform its original monetary function. Of course, one *could* take the penny out of the fuse box again and spend it, but then the electrical circuit would be broken. Similarly, a person cannot simultaneously apply intuitive thought and concrete operations to the same problem, although he might fluctuate between these two ways of thinking about the same problem over time. Recall now that cognitive structures, in Piaget's theory, are not static objects but ways of characterizing the regularities in an individual's activity, be it in the form of overt behavior or mental operations. Therefore, what changes with development is the range of possibilities for organizing actions in different ways. Within a particular range, the individual's actions will sometimes be organized in a relatively advanced way and sometimes not. Thus, when we speak of the progressive integration of structures, we mean that a more advanced organization builds upon and includes the features of a simpler organization, without eliminating the possibility that the simpler organization may still occur on certain occasions.

The progressive integration of cognitive structures is a central principle of intellectual development, but it does not suffice as an explanation of what *causes* development. One cannot say that a child goes through the period of concrete operations, for example, because he must do so in order to reach formal operations. Such an argument would assume some sort of teleology or directing purpose in development. It seems most unlikely that the young child "knows" where he is headed developmentally and what he must do to get there. Likewise, it cannot be argued that formal operations follow automatically from concrete operations because all of the structural prerequisites are available by that time. This would be tantamount to saying that a cake will somehow materialize as soon as the baker has obtained the essential ingredients. Thus, we must search further for a causal mechanism, for some means by which the child is impelled to move from one developmental stage to the next.

THE CAUSES OF DEVELOPMENT

While it is true that a description of development—even a very detailed description—does not constitute an explanation, a good description does nevertheless provide a foundation on which to build the kind of explanation we are seeking. If we know what a child acquires in the course of intellectual development, and what steps he goes through in the process of acquisition, then we can begin to infer the cause or causes involved. This is the approach favored by Piaget and other cognitive psychologists who have studied development. There is a distinct contrast between this approach and the one used in S-R psychology, where the fundamental cause of development, that is, learning, is assumed to be known a priori, and is then used to interpret and predict changes in child behavior. Cognitive psychology, with its inclination to start from a careful description of how the child changes with age, has arrived at a rather different explanation of what causes development, as we shall see presently.

The Classical Factors in Development

Let us follow Piaget's lead by first reviewing the "classical factors" in development—those causes that have been considered in one way or another in all attempts to explain psychological development.

Maturation. Certain aspects of development occur more or less automatically, regardless of environmental conditions, so long as the environment provides basic sustenance for the individual organism. Growth in physical stature is an obvious example; children generally grow taller as they get older, without any special help from the environment. To be sure, nutrition and other environmental factors can affect the rate and extent of increases in a child's height. But by and large such organic growth results from an innate process of maturation; such growth is preprogrammed, as it were, in the individual's genes. Given sufficient time, along with basic sustenance, maturation runs its course.

Other maturational changes, though less noticeable than growth in physical height, are no doubt more directly relevant to intellectual development. It is known that the structure of the brain undergoes continued change throughout the course of development, even on the level of single cells or neurons. However, very little is known about the relationship between these neuro-anatomical changes and intellectual development. One thing that can be said with certainty is that maturational processes provide only the *possibility* for subsequent changes in behavior; they do not guarantee such changes. To return to the example of growth in height, a boy who reaches a height of six feet has the possibility of being a better basketball player than he could have been when he was only five feet, but he can capitalize on this increased potential only if the environment provides opportunities for his playing basketball.

The fact that maturation contributes to development cannot be denied but neither can the uncertainty over its relative importance in intellectual development. Cognitive theorists tend to avoid the extremes on this issue, but it is hard to discern any agreement on a position in between, perhaps because we simply know so little about it. It is also possible that the importance of maturation varies with the aspect of intellectual development that one chooses to study.

Experience.   We shall use Piaget's terminology here in restricting the word "experience" to the child's encounters with the physical environment. The developmental importance of experience, in this sense, is at least as obvious as the role of maturation. We have already intimated that experience in handling a basketball, shooting baskets, and so on, is essential to the development of skill in playing basketball. On the other hand, no amount of experience will make the five-foot boy as effective on the basketball court as he can be upon reaching six feet. It is evident, then, that experience is not sufficient by itself, any more than maturation is.

Piaget distinguishes two aspects of interaction with the physical environment, as it relates to intellectual development. One is simply called *physical experience,* because it is a means by which an individual acquires knowledge about the physical properties of objects (weight, hardness, roughness, and the like) or about their relations in space. A child's understanding of weight, for example, derives (in part) from the experience he has had in lifting, pushing, throwing, and acting upon objects in all sorts of other ways. As a result of such actions, the child learns something about the objects themselves. Physical objects also present opportunities for a second kind of experience, which Piaget calls *logicomathematical experience*. In playing with a collection of pebbles, for instance, a child may discover that the number of pebbles remains the same regardless of the order in which they are counted.[17] What he discovers here is not a property of the pebbles themselves; he discovers something about the *actions* that can be performed on a set of pebbles, or on a set of any other objects. The pebbles merely serve as pawns for mathematical or logical operations, or at least for the overt actions that correspond to such operations. Piaget is perhaps unique in emphasizing the contribution of logicomathematical experience to intellectual development. It is not simply a matter of "learning by doing" but rather of "learning *about* doing." That is, the child learns which actions produce equivalent results, which actions reverse other actions, and so on. When these actions are internalized in reversible systems, they become operations in the Piagetian sense. Logicomathematical experience contributes not only to the development of logic and mathematics per se, but also to the child's understanding of the real world (see Chapter 12).

Social Environment. The third classical factor in development is found in the social environment, that is, the overall culture that surrounds the child, especially as transmitted to him by his parents and other people with whom he interacts. Prominent in this area are interactions involving verbal communication (or communication by some other system of signs) and deliberate attempts at instruction. However, the social environment can exert its influence in other ways, too—for example, by providing models of behavior that the child imitates without explicitly being instructed to do so.

As with maturation and experience, the importance of the social environment becomes quite clear if one tries to imagine what development would be like without it. Suppose a child were isolated from all contact with the social environment, virtually from birth on. Even if adequate food and shelter were available, along with opportunities for experience with the physical world, it is hard to imagine that the child's intellectual development would not be seriously impaired. In fact, we have a little more than just imagination to go on here, because the hypothetical conditions of this nightmarish experiment actually have been approximated in a number of known cases in which children have been abandoned in the wilderness or locked up for long periods of time. Probably the most famous is the case of Victor, the wild boy of Aveyron, whose story was first reported around 1800 by Itard and was recently dramatized in Truffaut's movie *The Wild Child.*[18] The most obvious deficit in such cases is in the area of language, but other aspects of human intelligence seem to be impaired too. (For more on the importance of the social environment from the psychoanalytic perspective, see Chapter 19.)

As necessary as the social environment is for normal development, it clearly cannot account for development all by itself. It just is not possible to explain trigonometry to an average four-year-old, even with hundreds of hours of explanation and an unusually attentive child. But the same child, with further maturation and experience behind him, not to mention formal instruction, can be taught trigonometry with relative ease in high school.

Each of the classical factors—maturation, experience, and the social environment—has been emphasized in one developmental theory or another. But virtually every theorist has had to admit that no single factor provides a sufficient explanation of development by itself. All three factors are necessary. All three interact with each other, the effects of each one depending on the effects of the other two. We know very little about the details of these interactions in the development of cognitive structures. However, it seems safe to assume that the interactions among the various factors in development are not haphazard; there must be some general law, a more fundamental factor, that governs the ways in which specific factors interact. It is the nature of this fundamental factor that Piaget has chosen to emphasize in his own explanation of development.

Equilibration: The Fundamental Factor in Development

From Piaget's biological frame of reference, all developmental change —whatever the specific factors are that might contribute to it—involves progress toward a broader field of equilibrium in the individual's encounters with his environment. As we saw in Chapter 9, the field of equilibrium is defined with regard to the individual's ability to maintain an adaptive state of affairs within a particular range of environmental variation. The maintenance of body temperature by homeostasis is a good example from biology. Within a certain range of external temperatures, homeostatic mechanisms adjust the body's physiological activity so as to maintain a constant internal temperature. The body actively compensates for changes in the environment.

In Piaget's theory, cognitive structures are essentially systems that permit equilibrium with regard to the individual's understanding of reality, or his reasoning about hypothetical possibilities. In a conservation experiment, for example, the child who has a certain structure of concrete operations can maintain his cognitive equilibrium despite changes in the appearance of a particular quantity. The intuitive structures of a younger, preoperational child permit only a more limited kind of equilibrium. The rule that "higher water level equals greater amount" works perfectly well in those situations where water level is the only variable. But when changes in water level are accompanied by compensating changes in other dimensions, the intuitive structure proves inadequate. And when the child begins to *sense* the inadequacy of his present structure, he is in a state of *dis*equilibrium.

A state of disequilibrium is not one that an organism wants to stay in for very long. All living systems have an inherent tendency to avoid states of disequilibrium and, consequently, they will take steps to establish a new level of equilibrium whenever disequilibrium occurs. The process of establishing equilibrium on a new level (that is, over a broader field) is what Piaget calls *equilibration.*

We just said that an organism will "take steps" to achieve equilibrium. From Piaget's point of view, this is an apt way of putting it. He insists that, above all, equilibration—and therefore the development of new cognitive structures—results from a child's *own activity* in regulating his exchanges with the environment, that is, from *self-regulation.* In taking steps toward a broader field of equilibrium, the child may be assisted by such factors as maturation, experience, and the social environment, but these factors can influence development only through their effects on the child's self-regulatory activity. This is the sense in which equilibration may be said to subsume the three classical factors and to govern the way in which they interact.

The role of self-regulation in the process of equilibration is even greater than we have indicated so far. Not only is the child's own activity essential in *eliminating* disequilibrium, it also is instrumental in *creating* a state of disequilibrium in the first place! It may seem paradoxical to say that a child first gets himself into trouble and then gets himself out of it again, but that is exactly what Piaget has in mind. In order to see exactly how the child's self-regulatory activity can perform such contradictory functions in the process of equilibration, it will be helpful to have a concrete example before us.

Equilibration in the Attainment of Conservation

Since we referred to the conservation problem earlier in connection with the concepts of equilibrium and disequilibrium, let us continue using it to illustrate the entire process of equilibration. To begin again at the beginning, a child acquiring the ability to conserve amounts of water generally will pass through a stage in which he is most likely to center his attention only on the height of the water in various containers when judging relative amounts. At other times, in the same stage, he may center only on the widths of the containers, if they are especially salient. These preoperational schemes can be applied successfully in many situations without the occurrence of disequilibrium, because height and width do indicate relative amounts when other dimensions are held constant.

Sooner or later, however, the child will encounter a situation in which a larger discrepancy in height is accompanied by a reciprocal discrepancy in width. The child wants to say that quantity *A,* due to its height, is greater than quantity *B;* but the much narrower width of *A* is so glaringly obvious that it presents a problem. Other things being equal, the narrowness of *A* would lead the child to say that quantity *B* is greater than *A.* Thus, there is a conflict and the child, because he feels the conflict, is in a state of disequilibrium. At this point, he is likely to begin oscillating back and forth between height and width as a basis for making judgments of relative amount. At one moment, the higher amount of water seems larger, but at the next moment, the wider one seems larger. Eventually, rapid oscillations like this give way to the simultaneous consideration of both dimensions, and to simultaneous consideration of the *transformations* in both dimensions, when the water is poured from one container to another. Finally, the child is able to coordinate changes in height *and* width by a scheme of reversible concrete operations, thereby achieving equilibrium over a broader field than before.

This example from the conservation problem can be used to highlight several facets of the equilibration process. For one thing, we can see how the child's own activity first gets him into a state of disequilibrium. It might be argued that the conflict situation arose because of a fortuitous set of circumstances provided by the environment (that is, the occurrence of reciprocal discrepancies between height and width) and that the initial impetus for disequilibrium and for the subsequent process of equilibration must therefore have come from the environment. However, the child in our example would not have experienced the conflict if he had not been attempting to assimilate a new situation to some old cognitive structures—the schemes that entailed centering on height *or* width (but not both). A younger child, without these preoperational schemes, could encounter the same objective situation and feel no sense of disequilibrium at all. Thus, the state of disequilibrium presupposed the right sort of assimilatory activity on the part of the child, just as much as it presupposed the right sort of situation in the environment.

Now, how does the child's own activity help him go on to establish equilibrium at a higher level? Notice that the child's "oscillating" behavior involves continued use of the old structures but in somewhat modified form. The child is now trying to assimilate new situations to *both* structures at the same time, whereas the same situations would previously have been assimilated either to the height scheme or to the width scheme. It follows that at least one of the schemes or (more likely) both of them must no longer be exactly the same as before. In other words, *accommodation* of the old schemes has occurred. The continued use of these accommodated schemes leads to still further accommodations and, eventually, to their complete coordination in a new operational structure. Thus, the child's own activity brings him out of disequilibrium to equilibrium at a new level.

What we have just said, in so many words, is that the operational structure for conservation results from the *integration* of two previous structures, thus exemplifying one of the general characteristics of development discussed earlier. We have also seen that the components of the new structure are not literally the same structures as before, but rather accommodated versions of them. In fact, the bringing together of the two schemes is itself a kind of accommodation. At the same time, it is reminiscent of the "mutual assimilation" of sensorimotor structures, which we discussed in connection with the "behavior of the support." This serves as a reminder that assimilation and accommodation must be viewed as opposite sides of the same coin.

The conservation example also can be used to show how the classical factors of development enter into the process of equilibration. The role of experience is obvious; the child must have exposure to various quantities of liquid in various types of containers (or at least to materials that lend themselves to similar cognitive activities). A social influence might enter in if an older person directs the child's attention to certain discrepancies between relative heights and widths. Such interventions might or might not make a difference, depending on the child's readiness to assimilate what the other person has told him. Finally, the child's ability to shift his centration from one dimension to the other in rapid succession may depend on the maturation of some basic capacity of the nervous system. But none of these classical factors would be sufficient by itself to produce conservation. The effect of each depends on the others, and all of them depend upon the process of equilibration to have some effect on development. Most important of all, equilibration necessarily involves some activity on the part of the child—the activity of attempting to assimilate new situations to old cognitive structures.

The conservation example illustrates one other important facet of development that emerges from the notion of equilibration. Each time a child solves a developmental "problem," he opens the door to a whole set of new problems that were not possible before. Just when the young child has mastered the preconservation strategy based on height (which is better than no strategy at all), he is plunged into the sort of cognitive conflict that we saw above. Similarly, an infant who stands upright on his own two feet for the first time may solve the problem of reaching objects on table tops, but he also experiences some new and very physical states of disequilibrium, which will eventually lead to further refinements in the scheme for standing. In a very real sense, then, the child creates new "problems to grow on" by virtue of his success in solving old problems.

Equilibration and the Cognitive Model of Behavior

In presenting the cognitive model of behavior, back in Chapter 10, we simply assumed that one factor affecting behavior was a cognitive structure of some sort that the individual "had" at a particular point in time. On the other hand, our description of the character of development, in the first part of the present chapter, concentrated on the kind of structure found at each stage of development. The question remained, then, what causes the restructuring that takes place over time in the course of development? Piaget's equilibration theory is an attempt to show how the individual's activity at time 1 leads to a new structure at time 2. Thus, the concept of equilibration provides a bridge between the cognitive model of behavior and the cognitive description of development in terms of structurally defined stages. Let us look at this connection more closely.

First, it should not be inferred from the above remarks that *behavior* and *activity* are synonymous terms, although they are closely related. We have restricted the term behavior to overt, observable activities such as manipulating, looking, and speaking. But activity may also be covert, or mental, especially after the sensorimotor period. (Recall that we initially described cognition itself as an active process.) Thus, activity is the broader term, and behavior is a special case of activity—that which is observable. But even when activity is not the observable kind, it still retains an important feature of the model of behavior, namely, the feedback loop by which behavior affects the situation, which in turn affects behavior (through cognition), which then affects behavior, and so on. Similarly, we can think of mental activity affecting a mental situation, which affects further mental activity, and so on. It is this "cybernetic" aspect of activity that is crucial in the process of equilibration, not the form in which the activity occurs. In other words, activity is essential for developmental progress, but it need not be in the form of overt behavior (at least not after the sensorimotor period).

Another important link between behavior and development resides in the terms *assimilation* and *accommodation,* which were first introduced in connection with the model of behavior and which, more recently, played a prominent role in our discussion of equilibration. Whereas assimilation refers to the process of bending a situation to fit one's present cognitive structure, accommodation refers to the bending of a structure to fit novel elements in the situation. Thus, accommodation is the immediate agent of change in cognitive structures. We mentioned earlier that situations containing novel elements and leading to accommodation might be provided by the environment. However, another source of novelty is the child's own activity, to the extent that it changes the situation into one that has not been assimilated before. The example of the child counting pebbles in different orders and getting the same result comes to mind here. In any case, the model of behavior again helps to clarify the relationship of the child's activity to developmental change.

It might seem as if the phenomenon of accommodation opens up a Pandora's box of possibilities for environmental influence on development. Would it not be possible to accelerate the rate of development greatly, or to steer development in various directions, by inducing massive accommodation through careful management of the situations that a child is in? According to cognitive theory, there is one major reason why such manipulation of development on a grand scale is not possible: accommodation can occur only if a particular situation can already be assimilated to a large extent. And, as we have said so many times, the possibility of assimilating the situation depends on the individual's present cognitive structures. For this reason, Piaget has said that learning (that is, changes induced by the environment) depends on development, which results from equilibration, which in turn results from the child's attempts to assimilate new situations to old structures. One can see, then, why Piaget has called assimilation a "basic fact" of mental life.

One more important link between development and the cognitive model of behavior remains to be discussed. Recall the notion of intrinsically motivated behavior—a kind of behavior that sometimes has the repetitive character of "practice," except that there is pleasure in the activity itself, and not just in a payoff or a final performance that the practice anticipates. We said (in Chapter 10) that intrinsic motivation can often be traced to the individual's cognitive structures. Now that the concept of equilibration has been examined closely, the dynamics of this relationship can be seen more clearly. That is, the individual will engage in certain activities in order to resolve the disequilibrium resulting from the inadequacies of his present cognitive structure. The motivation to engage in such activities is an inherent feature of the equilibration process and is therefore a natural part of development. Indeed, it would appear that Piaget sees development as an intrinsically motivated process of change. In a generally supportive environment, the child needs only sufficient opportunities to experience disequilibrium in order to make intellectual progress. This is one of the ideas that will be pursued further in Chapter 13, on the educational implications of cognitive theory.

SUMMARY

The general character and causes of development have been discussed in this chapter with particular reference to the theory of Jean Piaget. As we have seen, Piaget divides development into four periods, each characterized by a different type of cognitive structure:

(1) In the sensorimotor period (infancy), cognition is organized in terms of elementary action schemes tied rather directly to overt behavior. These sensorimotor schemes combine to give the infant a "practical intelligence" for coping with his immediate environment.

(2) The preoperational period (early childhood) begins with the emergence of the semiotic function, which frees cognition from overt behavior in response to the immediate environment. By the end of this period, the child has acquired a number of implicit rules that reflect regularities in the child's experience. These rules, although still not coordinated with each other, form the basis of "intuitive" thought.

(3) The period of concrete operations (middle to late childhood) is characterized by the development of structures consisting of coordinated mental actions that permit reversibility and decentration in the child's thinking, as evidenced by the child's logical responses to problems involving conservation and class inclusion. However, the logical thinking of this period applies only to concrete actualities, not to hypothetical possibilities.

(4) With the attainment of formal operations (adolescence and beyond), logical thinking is freed from the concrete and actual since the individual can perform operations on operations. The ability to conceive of and reason about hypothetical possibilities provides a basis for true scientific thinking in the formal period.

Each succeeding stage of development involves a kind of thinking that covers a broader field of equilibrium than before and is therefore less egocentric and more objective. A number of issues were discussed with regard to the reality of stages and the problem of determining which stage a particular child is in. Special emphasis was placed on the sequence in which stages occur and on the principle that earlier structures are integrated into later ones.

With regard to the causes of development, the classical factors—maturation, experience, and the social environment—are all necessary but not sufficient to account for the child's progress from one stage to the next. The fundamental cause of development is equilibration through self-regulatory activity on the part of the child. In attempting to assimilate new situations to old structures, the child experiences disequilibrium. Through further attempts at assimilation, with accommodated structures, the child creates a new structure and arrives at a new level of equilibrium. This process was illustrated by means of an example from a conservation problem. Finally, it was shown that the equilibration process provides a link between the way a child behaves at a given stage of development and the way he changes from one stage to the next.

12

SOME MAJOR AREAS OF INTELLECTUAL DEVELOPMENT

Preview

Here we will discuss four areas of intellectual development.

(1) The *physical world* concerns the child's knowledge of objects, space, time, and causality.

(2) *Logicomathematical thinking* deals with classes, relations, number, propositional logic, and double reversibility.

(3) The *social world* is concerned with moral judgment and expectations regarding interpersonal behavior.

(4) The area of *language* includes the development of word meanings and the learning of grammatical rules.

The cognitive approach has been applied to several different areas of intellectual development. From the cognitive point of view, an "area" of development is any domain of knowledge that people acquire through a series of changes in cognitive structure. In other words, an area is defined by the *content* of cognition, and development within an area is described in terms of changes in the *form* of the child's knowledge and thought regarding a particular type of content.

This chapter surveys the highlights of development in four major areas: the physical world, logic and mathematics, the social world, and language. We have given examples from these areas earlier in this part, but so far we have not traced the development of the child's thinking from infancy to adulthood in any one area. By carefully describing developmental changes in cognition, cognitive psychologists have generated large quantities of data on the changes that occur in some of these areas.

UNDERSTANDING THE PHYSICAL WORLD

By physical world, we mean four things: objects, space, time, and causality. Piaget has done the most work on these topics, and so we shall use his theory as a framework. In Chapter 11, we were concerned with the four major periods of development—sensorimotor, preoperational, concrete operations, and formal operations—and we gave examples from several areas of development to characterize the general nature of each period. We will now trace the development of intellectual functioning with regard to objects, space, time, and causality for each of the periods. Not surprisingly, some by now familiar examples of child behavior will appear once again, but we shall organize them differently here and add more examples.

Causality

Nearly everyone must have been driven to distraction at some time by an endless stream of "why" questions from a four-year-old. And anyone who has tried to answer such questions must sooner or later have begun to wonder whether young children are really looking for the kind of explanation that adults are inclined to give. The specific questions the child asks and the way he responds to our answers suggest that his conception of cause and effect may be quite different from our own.

Some of Piaget's earliest research was concerned with the child's conception of causality.[1] An obvious way to conduct such research is to turn the tables on the child by asking *him* a lot of "why" questions. Indeed, this is the principal method that Piaget used, but he did so with a great deal of caution. As Piaget points out, a child may very well respond with a totally whimsical explanation, simply because the adult's question is not very meaningful to him, but nonetheless seems to require some kind of answer to keep the adult entertained. To reduce this danger, Piaget patterned his own questions after the ones he had heard children ask spontaneously: "Why does the sun set at night?" "Why do we have mountains?" "Where do they come from?" "Why do the clouds move?" And so on. Even when children are serious about answering such questions, Piaget does not believe that their answers represent ideas that the children have thought about beforehand. The interesting question is what *kind* of answer does the child try to come up with at the time the question is asked.

Young (preoperational) children give some revealing answers to the kinds of questions Piaget asked. The sun sets "because it wants to" or "because it must go to bed" or "so that *we* will go to bed." These explanations reflect a type of "precausal" thinking that Piaget has called *animism.* Objects such as the sun or stones are endowed with minds of their own, as if they were animate. Another type of precausal thought, *artificialism,* is revealed when children suggest, for instance, that people made the mountains long ago for their children to slide on with skis and sleds. It seems odd that children might regard objects as both animate and manufactured, but such is the way of preoperational thinking.[2]

Further insight into the child's understanding of causality comes from some of the Piagetian experiments described earlier. Recall the experiment in which subjects were asked to predict which objects would float on water and which would sink. Some of the original subjects (four- and five-year-olds) predicted incorrectly that certain objects, for example, a large piece of wood, would sink. When their predictions were disconfirmed, these children sometimes pushed the objects below the surface of the water, apparently expecting that the objects might stay sunk when released, thereby confirming their predictions after all. One child even ordered a wood plank to remain under water after pushing it there: "You want to stay down, silly."[3]

It is not easy to interpret such behavior. One is tempted to dismiss it as a bit of wishful thinking or a childish denial of reality. But adults certainly engage in wishful thinking, too, when solving problems. Yet an adult probably would not behave like the children we have been talking about, because he really *knows* that such a ploy cannot work. With a child, however, one suspects that his attempt to make a floating object sink is not entirely capricious; he is not sure whether it will work or not. According to Piaget's interpretation, the child is not sure because he has not differentiated between the set of forces inherent in a physical situation (wood floating on water) and the forces introduced by his own intrusion into the situation (pushing the wood beneath the surface).

The inability to distinguish external from personal forces is a good example of the young child's egocentrism. Animism and artificialism are also manifestations of egocentric thought. The child has plenty of experience in "willing" himself to move about in the environment, so it is an easy step to assimilate the movements of objects to the same cognitive scheme (animism). The child also has experience in making things—sand castles and so on—so it is easy for him to think that objects in nature have similar origins (artificialism).

The egocentrism of causality is still more extreme earlier, in the sensorimotor period. Infants learn that they can reproduce interesting events through their own efforts. A kicking of the legs leads reliably to some movement of a doll suspended from the crib. The "feeling of efficacy" that results from such experiences promotes a primitive belief in the infant that he himself is the prime mover of the universe, with the magical power to make things appear and disappear, occur and reoccur. Later in the sensorimotor period, the infant begins to look around for causes that are external to himself, as when he looks at the far end of a stick that resists his efforts to pick it up, as if he expects to discover there the cause of the problem. But this externalization of causality is still on the plane of action. The semiotic function must develop before the child can represent external causes on a conceptual level, and then —as we have seen in the phenomena of animism and artificialism—this representation is highly subjective and personalized at first.

Once the structures of concrete operations are well established, a child can conceive of causes that are both external to himself and inanimate. But there are still limitations in his thinking about causality. In particular, he may be unable to isolate the true causes of a phenomenon from among several variables that might possibly account for the effect. Inhelder and Piaget report an experiment in which children were given the task of determining which rods in a large collection of rods would bend more than others.[4] The rods varied in several ways, including length, material (brass, steel), and cross section (round, square, hexagonal). An apparatus was supplied for the child to test the flexibility of whichever rods he chose. Under these circumstances, a child might discover that a long, round, steel rod bends more than a short, square, brass one. At the level of concrete operations, this discovery might easily lead to the conclusion that differences in all three variables—length, material, and cross section—cause differences in flexibility. It does not occur to the child that one or two of these variables might make no difference at all. If such a hypothesis is suggested to the child, he has a hard time deciding how to test additional rods in a way that will establish the truth or falsity of the hypothesis. In other words, the concrete operational child is still likely to interpret the co-occurrence of two facts to mean that one has caused the other. Adults often make the same mistake, but they generally have competence to understand that co-occurrence is not necessarily evidence of a cause-effect relationship.

Much of our foregoing discussion suggests that the development of causal thinking is closely linked to developmental changes in the properties attributed to objects—that objects are conceived differently by younger and older children. We turn now to a further consideration of changes in the child's conception of objects.

The Nature of Objects

We have seen before that a major achievement of the sensorimotor period is the understanding of object permanence. This understanding is first evidenced when the infant attempts to pursue an object that has left his sight or grasp, as if he knows that the object is still there, somewhere, to be seen or grasped again. The permanence of objects is just one property among many that a child must eventually understand. Other object properties are not well understood until much later in development, as shown, for example, by the "conservation" experiments.

Remember that conservation refers to the child's understanding that some property (for example, weight) remains constant despite changes in appearance (for example, shape). One of the earlier properties to be conserved is the amount of some substance—water, clay, and so on. The conservation of amount (at about seven years) is one of the major indicators that a child has entered the period of concrete operations. The conservation of weight often takes another couple of years, while certain problems involving the conservation of volume may not be mastered until early adolescence.

In one experiment on volume conservation, identical balls of clay were submerged in identical jars of water to show that the water level would rise the same amount in each case.[5] After one ball was removed from the water and broken into several pieces, the subjects were asked to predict how high the water would rise when all the pieces were again submerged in the same container of water. Interestingly, some older children (10 to 11 years) realized that the amount and weight of clay were unchanged by breaking it into pieces, yet they predicted that the water level would be higher (or lower) than before. In Piaget's terminology, these children failed to conserve "exterior volume," that is, the volume of clay as measured by its displacement of water.

It will be recalled that the experiment on floating and sinking objects involved the concept of *density,* another property that is not well understood until early adolescence. One way in which older children begin to approach an understanding of density is by thinking of objects as composed of minute particles that may be packed more or less closely together, thus giving each object greater or lesser density. Obviously, this "atomistic" notion indicates a certain amount of sophistication in the child's thinking about objects. The simultaneous consideration of a whole object along with its elemental parts reminds one of the class inclusion problem discussed earlier. But while the atomistic explanation of density has great intuitive appeal, as well as some basis in fact, it is less useful for most purposes than the definition of density as a precise relationship between weight and volume. To understand density on this level, the individual must think in terms of proportions, or "relations between relations," an ability that requires the structures of formal operations. We shall return to this theme below, in the section on logicomathematical development.

Space[6]

As the child's understanding of objects develops, so does his understanding of the space that contains them. Adults are accustomed to thinking of space in terms of certain axes or imaginary lines—north-south and east-west, or left-right, front-back, and up-down. The location of any object can be specified with reference to these axes, and its relationship to some other point in space can be expressed as a quantitative distance. This conception of space is embodied in a variety of descriptive statements: "The town of Orinda is five miles east of Berkeley." "The treasure is buried seven paces to the left of the tree and three paces in front of the large rock." The set of axes adopted and the units used to express distance may vary (Orinda is also about 38 degrees North and 122 degrees West), but the basic idea is still that of a grid whose coordinates can be used to identify any point in space.

As we shall see, such refinements as coordinate axes and scales for measuring distance are not present in the young child's understanding of space. But let us go back to the beginning. Just as objects have no independent existence early in the sensorimotor period, space, too, is not differentiated from the infant's own bodily activities. Furthermore, the infant's activities seem divided into several separate spheres, each connected with a different modality of action. There is the world of seeing, the world of touching, and so on—all quite independent of one another. In the course of sensorimotor development, these initially separate spheres of activity are integrated, so that seeing and touching eventually go on in one and the same world. Something seen can (usually) be touched, and vice versa. Moreover, this unified space no longer depends on any one activity; it is there regardless of the child's particular behavior.

This new objectivity with regard to space manifests itself near the end of the sensorimotor period in the child's ability to solve detour problems. When a child realizes that the same goal object can be approached over several different routes, this is tantamount to a realization that the goal's location is independent of the particular route taken to reach it, that is, independent of particular actions. In Figure 12.1, the goal at C can be reached by routes AC, ABC, or ADC. If one of these routes is blocked, the others will suffice because point C is just a place in a stable space that happens to contain an obstacle in one area. The presence or absence of an obstacle does not change the objective location of C.

Even with his ability to solve detour problems, the preoperational child's understanding of space is quite limited. We will cite just a few experiments to illustrate these limitations. One experiment concerns the child's ability to construct a projective straight line. When an adult says "Orinda is between Berkeley and Walnut Creek," he is saying that Orinda lies somewhere on an imaginary straight line that runs from Berkeley to Walnut Creek. Theoretically, if one looked through a telescope from Berkeley toward Walnut Creek, Orinda would appear somewhere in the foreground. The experiment described below takes place on a much smaller scale, but the same principle is involved.

The subjects in the experiment are asked to build a miniature fence between two posts by planting sticks in the "ground," which is made of

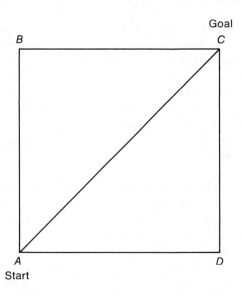

Figure 12.1 Sensorimotor space: alternate routes to a goal

modeling clay. The fence is to go straight from one post to the other. This turns out to be a surprisingly difficult task for a majority of children below the age of five or six years.[7] Without special guidance, younger children produce fences that start out in the right direction but then meander off course considerably. These children seem content to plant each stick next to the last, without reference to the imaginary axis running between the end posts. They do not realize the possibility of getting a perfectly straight fence by sighting from one post to the other until, ideally, the far post and all of the intervening sticks are hidden behind the near post. The idea of projecting a straight line in this fashion simply is not part of the younger child's stock in trade. He lacks the necessary cognitive structure.

Another experiment in this area involves the task of building a tower that is just as tall as a model provided by the experimenter.[8] The problem is complicated by the fact that the new tower cannot be built alongside the model, so that a simple visual comparison of heights (having the towers stand back to back, as it were) is not possible. Obviously, the key to success under these circumstances is some sort of measuring instrument that can be applied to both towers. But younger children do not make use of this "obvious" strategy— apparently not out of sheer ignorance (since most children have seen someone using a ruler), but because the basic idea of measurement lies beyond their comprehension.

What *is* the basic idea behind spatial measurement? Essentially, we imagine that the thing to be measured consists of a number of standard units laid end to end. This amounts to the same thing as taking a single unit and placing it successively in adjacent positions from one end point to the other (the way one measures the dimensions of a room with a yardstick). Experiments like the tower-building task indicate that children approach this conception of spatial measurement through a series of steps that extends well into the period of concrete operations.

Notice that the height (or width or depth) of an object need not be measured in conventional units like inches or feet. One can measure in "hands," or "pencil lengths," or any other object with a convenient size for the measurement job to be done. The really important consideration—one that must be understood—is that the unit of measurement is a constant quantity; it does not change as it is moved around and applied first to one object and then another. But before the attainment of concrete operations, children do not find it at all obvious that the length of an object remains the same regardless of its position. Here we have yet another kind of conservation problem, as illustrated by the following experiment.

Place two identical pencils before a preschool child as shown in the top part of Figure 12.2. Ask the child if one pencil is just as long as the other. (The child almost always agrees that the pencils are equal in length.) Then slide one pencil to the side, as shown in the bottom part of the figure, and ask if the two pencils are still the same length. Many preschoolers will say that they are *not*. If you ask which pencil is longer, they will point to the one that "sticks out" (the one you moved), completely ignoring the fact that the other pencil also sticks out but in the opposite direction.

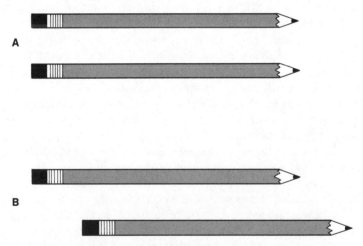

Figure 12.2 The conservation of length task

Intuition tells us that a child who fails to conserve length in this way would be unable to perform measurement operations with any degree of understanding. Piaget's work in this area suggests that our intuition is well founded. The preoperational child must be as confused about measurement as we would be if we were using an elastic ruler!

Time and Speed[9]

Just as adults think of space as an ultimately boundless "container" of objects, so time can be seen as an endless container of events. And just as different objects exist in one overall space, different events can be charted on a common time line. This point seems self-evident; it is a basic assumption that permeates much of our thinking. To cite just one example, the idea of a common time line is crucial for establishing an alibi. The suspect in a criminal investigation is exonerated if he can establish that he was somewhere else at the *same time* the crime was committed. The phrase "same time" indicates that one time line is applied to the crime *and* to the suspect's activities, regardless of how far apart they were in space.

Once again, Piaget and his associates have performed experiments that show that this basic concept is not basic at all in the thinking of young children. One experiment goes something like this. The child observes that two cars, on parallel roads, leave the same starting line at exactly the same time, run for a while, and then stop at exactly the same time. However, one of them (X) has gone faster than the other (Y), and therefore stops farther down the road (see the top part of Figure 12.3). Even very young children will say (correctly) that car X went faster and farther than car Y. However, when asked whether or not one car took more *time* than the other, they will again choose X. This observation, along with others, led Piaget to suggest that the preoperational child thinks each event has its own time—"localized time," as Piaget calls it. As we saw above, the localized time associated with a particular event is confounded with the space or distance over which the event took place. This confusion of time with space distorts not only judgments of duration (time taken), but also judgments of succession (the order in which events occur). Thus, some children will deny that cars X and Y stopped at the same time, claiming that Y stopped first.

As always, it is easy to overemphasize what is *wrong* with preoperational thinking, so let us take a moment to see what is *right* about the child's conception of time in the preoperational period, as opposed to the sensorimotor period. At the beginning of the sensorimotor period, the child's sense of time is as profoundly egocentric as his sense of space, objects, and causality. Indeed, the infant really has no sense of time independent of his own immediate activity. An activity such as sucking or grasping simply begins, has duration, and then ends. There is no anticipation of future activities nor memory for past activities. Later, when the infant can solve problems that involve the separation of means from ends, time has become objectified to some extent. The infant can anticipate a future goal activity (picking up a desired object) before engaging in a means activity (pulling on a pillow that supports the goal object). At this point, the infant has some idea of temporal succession independent of his own immediate activity. However, he still has only a sensorimotor understanding of time, because the temporal successions that he can think about do not extend very far beyond the immediate situation.

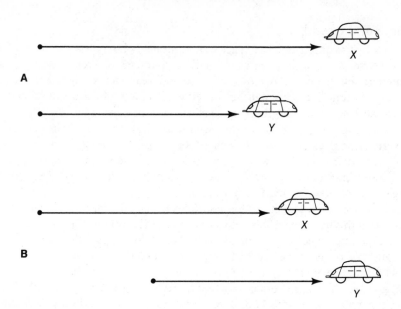

Figure 12.3. The "two-car" experiment: both cars start and stop simultaneously in [*A*] and [*B*].

In contrast, the preoperational child has a much more extended sense of time, due to the development of the semiotic function. At this point, the child can mentally reconstruct events that happened a day or two earlier, with the feeling that the earlier events had a particular location in time, and he can anticipate future events in a similar fashion. However, the preoperational child still has a sense of time that is not yet objective in many respects, as we shall continue to see.

The young child's understanding of the two-car experiment (Figure 12.3) becomes even more curious when further variations are tried. Suppose the cars again start and stop simultaneously and that *X* again moves faster than *Y*. But this time *X* starts at a point behind *Y* (Figure 12.3, bottom). When the cars come to a stop, *Y* is still ahead, but *X* has narrowed the gap considerably. Now some children will say that *Y*, not *X*, went farther and faster. The fact that both speed and distance are misunderstood in this second situation suggests that the children who appeared to understand them in the first situation actually answered correctly for the wrong reasons. We have already seen, in the conservation of length experiment, that preoperational children tend to center on the discrepancy between the ends of two equal lengths when one is pushed ahead of the other. In Figure 12.2, the pencil that extends farther to the right is seen as longer. Thus, the child's intuitive rule is to equate greater length with greater extension in the direction of movement. This rule would account for preoperational responses in both versions of the two-car experiment. In the first situation (top), the rule produces a "correct" response (distance X is greater than Y), but in the second situation (bottom), it leads to an error (distance Y is greater than X).

Piaget has proposed that a similar rule explains the preoperational child's conception of speed: one object is said to move faster than another only if it is observed to pass or pull away from another object moving in the same direction. Again, the rule produces a correct response in the top situation (speed X is greater than Y) but not in the bottom situation (speed Y is greater than X). In the latter case, no passing or pulling away occurs, so the child must base his judgment of relative speed on some other aspect of the situation— perhaps the relative stopping positions of the cars (Y ahead of X). Notice that the child is unable to anticipate that X would pass Y if the cars simply continued at the same rate as before.

The rule of passing is related to the notion of localized time. When one object passes another, two separate events with their "own" times become fused in the single event of passing. Thus, for an instant, the child seems to plot both events (each object moving) on a common time line. But this is hardly the same as coordinating two distinct events within a single, unified time.

No discussion of time concepts would be complete without some mention of a child's learning to use a clock or watch. The interesting thing, of course, is not simply the child's ability to say "three o'clock" when the hour hand is on the three and the minute hand is on the 12, but rather his understanding that "three o'clock" represents one point on a time scale that can be used to measure the durations of and the temporal distances between particular events. The measurement of time is, initially, at least as mysterious to the young child as the measurement of space. As with spatial measurement, the basic idea is that of a standard unit—a second, minute, and so on—that can be applied repeatedly to any event or sequence of events. The number of repeated applications constitutes a measure of duration. This quantification of time becomes necessary if one is comparing durations that are successive rather than simultaneous. Suppose we modify the two-car problem such that car X completes its movement before car Y even starts. To compare the durations of the two movements with any precision, we would need a stopwatch or some other instrument that counts up standard units of time. Notice that this version of the car task is analogous to the tower-building task in which quantitative measurements of height were necessitated by the fact that two towers could not be compared side by side.

We have seen that spatial measurement presupposes conservation of the unit of measurement and that preoperational children do not evidence this conservation. A similar failure to conserve affects the measurement of time. In one of Piaget's investigations, children watched the rotation of a clock hand while performing a simple task (for example, tapping on a table). The children were instructed to perform the task at varying speeds and were asked whether or not a rotation of the hand took just as long during a slow performance as during a fast one. The younger subjects (ages five to seven) tended to report that a rotation took more (or less) time when they performed quickly. In other words, a clock can speed up or slow down, depending on what one is doing! Needless to say, adults also have the illusion that time passes more or less quickly depending on what is happening. But adults know this is only an egocentric illusion, whereas young children—unaware of their egocentrism—believe it is the truth.

From all of this, we can see that "10 o'clock," for example, must have a very different meaning for the young child. He may know that "going to bed at 10 o'clock" means "staying up late"—later than eight o'clock or even nine o'clock—but what escapes him is the idea that the time from eight to nine is equal to the time from nine to 10, and that these durations are the same day after day, regardless of the events that occur within them. The older child, with concrete operations, understands the conservation of hours and minutes, and he understands the idea that these units apply to all sorts of events plotted on a single time line. With this understanding, the child can see that, if John paints a fence from 8:00 A.M. to noon and Bill paints it from 11:00 A.M. to 2:00 P.M., then the whole job took six hours and John worked an hour longer than Bill. But only with the advent of formal operations is there a complete understanding of time as a proportional relationship between speed and distance; that is, "time equals distance divided by speed."

Summary

The child's conception of the physical world becomes more objective and less egocentric on a number of specific fronts. The causes of natural phenomena are eventually seen as residing in external physical systems, instead of being assimilated to the child's own feelings and actions. Ideas about objects, space, and time are liberated from subjective distortions owing to the momentary appearances of things from the child's point of view.

We have so far emphasized the kind of objectivity that comes with the attainment of concrete operations. Although it is true that a concrete-operational understanding of the physical world will suffice for a great many daily activities, it is also true that a more formal understanding is the very basis of advanced technology in a society like ours. We shall give more attention to the level of formal operations presently; it has been postponed until now for reasons that can be seen in two trends that begin to emerge during the period of concrete operations and that are carried on into the period of formal operations.

First, as the child's understanding of the physical world approaches higher levels, it becomes increasingly *quantitative:* time and distance are measured in standard units; eventually, "speed equals distance divided by time," "density equals weight divided by volume," and so on. This is not to say that each person, during adolescence, spontaneously invents explicit mathematical formulas for defining such concepts as speed and density. But children do construct cognitive schemes that enable them to understand the mathematical formulas when they are taught in school.

Along with quantification, the role of *logic* becomes more and more central in the child's attempts to understand the physical world. An eight-year-old, for example, reasons that the amount of clay in a lump is conserved regardless of changes in shape, because nothing is added or taken away. However, it is easy to overlook the logic involved in some apparently simple operations on the physical world. Consider measurement: not only must a child conserve the unit of measurement, as we have seen, but he must also know that, if tower *A* equals 27 inches and tower *B* equals 27 inches, then tower *A* equals tower *B*. That is, two things equal to a third thing are equal to each other. This is just another instance of the logical transitivity that exceeds the cognitive grasp of preoperational children. As we shall see, logic becomes especially important in establishing cause-effect relationships among physical phenomena by means of scientific experimentation.

It is clear, then, that formal understanding of the physical world involves logic and quantitative thinking. Actually, the two areas—physical reality and logicomathematical thought—are interrelated throughout development. Thus, we must delve into logical and mathematical development in order to complete our discussion of physical concepts.

LOGICOMATHEMATICAL THINKING

In surveying the development of logical and mathematical thought, we shall continue to concentrate on the work of Jean Piaget, owing to his preeminence in the field. Specifically, we shall look into Piaget's studies of how children think about classes, relations, and number, along with the development of propositional logic and double reversibility. To investigate these areas, Piaget and his associates have used methods that may seem hard to distinguish from the studies just cited in the section on physical concepts, because the experiments involve much manipulation of physical objects and questioning about physical phenomena. In some cases, the same experiment may be used to shed light on both logical thought and conceptions of physical reality. Consequently, we need to consider what is different about observing the child's behavior with an eye toward logicomathematical development in particular.

In this regard, it is useful to recall Piaget's distinction between "physical experience" and "logicomathematical experience" as factors causing development. Physical experience refers to the kind of interaction with objects that contributes to the child's knowledge about properties inherent in the objects themselves—their weight, shape, texture, and the like. Logicomathematical experience, on the other hand, refers to *actions* performed on objects, such as grouping them together, ordering them in a sequence, or counting them. From actions like these, the child learns about classes, relations, and number. Both kinds of experience—physical and logicomathematical—may occur more or less simultaneously. In playing with a set of pebbles, for example, the young child may discover that pebbles with flat sides are hard to roll (physical experience) and also that counting the pebbles produces the same result regardless of the order in which they are counted (logicomathematical experience). Thus, in the sections that follow, we will concentrate on the actions performed on objects, not on the objects themselves or their physical properties. As we shall see, the "actions" of interest may be purely mental ones and the "objects" acted upon may be other mental actions. But we shall come to these complications soon enough.

Thinking about Classes[10]

A "class" consists of a set of objects sharing a common attribute, or combination of attributes, that distinguishes the objects in the class from all other objects. In other words, a class is a category. The members of a particular class need not be identical to one another, so long as they each have the attribute or attributes required for class membership. Thus, the class of books, for example, might be defined in such a way that it contained all sorts of variations in color, size, and content. But all books would share the attributes of (1) having pages that are (2) bound together in a certain way (3) inside a relatively stiff cover. If the class of books were defined in this way, it would include *all* objects having the necessary attributes, regardless of their locations in space and time. Even if all existing books were suddenly destroyed, the category would continue to exist, at least as a possibility. What this suggests is that classes actually exist in someone's mind, not "out there" in the world. Perhaps a better way of saying this is that we are concerned here with the mental activity of classification—of constructing categories.

The idea of a class is one more example of a basic concept that develops gradually in children, through a series of stages. Classification is basic not only in the sense that it seems obvious to adults, but also because it forms the basis of ordinary reasoning and of the real understanding of number. Thus, it is an important part of cognitive development—a part that touches on several other areas, as we shall see. But first we must trace briefly the development of classification itself.

One can begin to investigate the child's understanding of classes by means of a relatively straightforward method. Simply give the child an assortment of objects (see Figure 12.4A) and tell him to "put together the things that are alike—those which are the same as each other but different from the rest." Then observe the child's behavior in grouping the objects together. This method enables us to make some inferences about the child's mental activity regarding classifiable objects. Notice, also, that the similarities and differences among objects in Figure 12.4A are easy to see. That is because we are not interested in the child's perception of the object properties per se but rather in his use of this information in manipulating the objects according to our instructions.

Piaget has identified two general stages in the child's performance of this object-sorting task. The first stage corresponds to the early part of the preoperational period (roughly from two to five years). At this time, children

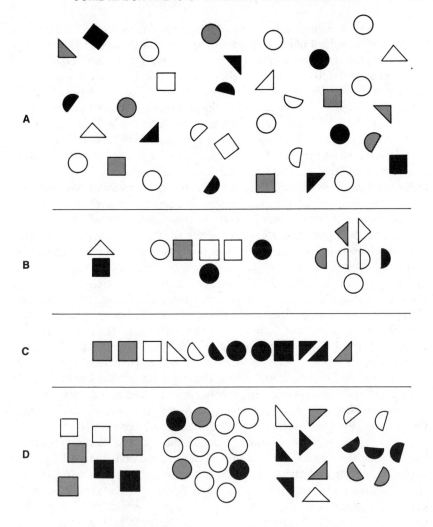

Figure 12.4 The free classification task

tend to produce "graphic collections" of objects. That is, the objects are often grouped in a way that turns out to have some pictorial or representational meaning. Thus, the first collection in Figure 12.4B might be called a house; in other cases, the collection is more like a nonrepresentational design. But generally in creating collections of this sort, children do not appear to have the finished product in mind when they begin. Instead, they seem to juxtapose objects one at a time until the overall shape of the collection is pleasing to the eye or looks like something familiar.

Although there appears to be no overall plan behind a graphic collection, the child's behavior at this stage is not entirely insensitive to the similarities among objects either. Young children often construct rows of objects like the one shown in Figure 12.4C. Assume that the child has started with the gray square and has added objects one at a time from left to right. The absence of an overall plan is evident in that there is no attribute (color or shape) shared by all members of the set. But the adjacent items do share attributes—sometimes color, sometimes shape, and sometimes both. Thus, the basis of classification has shifted from one moment to the next during the child's construction of the row. Vygotsky has called this kind of collection a "chain complex" because each object in the row is linked somehow to the one before it.[11]

As children progress from preoperational thought into the period of concrete operations, their sorting behavior changes noticeably. Now they can apply one basis of classification consistently, rather than shifting from moment to moment, and they do it in such a way that no objects are left unclassified (for one possibility, see Figure 12.4D). At this point, it would appear that a real understanding of classes has been achieved. Piaget has argued, however, that there is still one more important step in the development of thinking about classes. A child can sort the objects as shown in Figure 12.4D without necessarily seeing that the individual classes are part of a hierarchy. That is, the classes of squares and circles might be combined, for example, to form the class of "whole" objects, as opposed to the triangles and semicircles, which together comprise the class of "half" objects. On the other hand, the class of squares could be further subdivided into those which are black, white, or gray. Similar hierarchies are common in our thinking about natural objects. The class of dogs, for instance, is included in the larger class of household pets, and the class of dogs also includes the subclasses of beagles and collies. Without an understanding of the logic of class hierarchies, the child still has not reached the final stage in the development of classification, according to Piaget.

How can we assess a child's understanding of class hierarchies simply by observing the way he sorts objects? Even if a child constructs a large class of objects and then subdivides it, we cannot infer that he actually sees the two smaller classes as subsets of the larger one. Perhaps he just noticed a distinguishing attribute that he had not noticed before. A similar problem of inference arises if a child joins together two small classes to form a larger one. In neither case is it clear that a child "sees" more than one level in the hierarchy at the same time. We can circumvent this limitation of the sorting task by asking the child questions about class hierarchies. One type of question was discussed earlier with reference to the "class inclusion" problem. Suppose all the objects pictured in Figure 12.4D are made of plastic. We might simply ask "Are there more white circles or more plastic circles?" To answer this type of question consistently, the child must consider simultaneously the larger class (plastic circles) and its subclasses (white circles and so on). Notice that this involves a reversible relationship between two operations—separating and joining the subclasses of circles. Notice also that these are *mental* operations and that their physical counterparts cannot be performed simultaneously (one cannot put all the white circles on one side of a table and all the plastic circles on the other side at the same time).[12]

Questions involving the word "all" can also be used to assess the same operations on classes within a hierarchy. For example, we might ask "Are all the white circles plastic?" Before they understand class hierarchies, children are likely to say "No, because the black and gray circles are plastic too." In other words, they interpret the question to mean "Are all the white circles *all* the plastic circles?" Once again, the misinterpretation stems from an inability to think simultaneously about a subclass and the larger class that includes it.

Now what has all this to do with a child's way of reasoning? To cite just one example, "the child may reason: wooden objects float, chairs are wooden, chairs float, metal chairs . . . will float likewise."[13] There are several ways to interpret this reasoning in light of our preceding discussion. First, the child's argument is reminiscent of a "chain complex"; the first two assertions are linked by the property of woodenness, whereas the last two are linked by the property of "chairness"—that is, the basis of classification has shifted in midstream. Second, the child is failing to distinguish between a property that is shared only by members of one subclass (wooden chairs) and properties of the larger class (chairs in general, including metal chairs). Finally, the child makes the mistake of assuming that all the wooden chairs are all the chairs. In sum, it is clear that such reasoning involves only a prelogical understanding of classes.

Aside from logical reasoning, the notion of a class hierarchy is related to the development of the concept of number. Before looking into this relationship, we will discuss briefly a second basic component of the number concept —namely, the understanding of relations among objects in a series.

Thinking about Relations[14]

For the sake of brevity, we will consider just one example of Piaget's work on the child's thinking about relations, and even this example will be simplified somewhat for our present purposes. Suppose a child is shown a series of 10 sticks ordered by length, from the shortest to the longest (Figure 12.5, top). The set of sticks is then mixed up in a random heap and the child is invited to reconstruct the series in the same order as before. As is so often the case in Piaget's experiments, this "simple" task proves to be remarkably difficult for younger (preoperational) children. Typically they will construct a series that contains some semblance of the required order but that also contains deviations from a perfect ordering by size (see Figure 12.5, bottom, for example).

According to Piaget's analysis, the way the young child performs this "seriation" task indicates an important limitation in his ability to think about relations among objects. The relations in this case are "longer than" and "shorter than." Moving from left to right in the top of Figure 12.5, each succeeding stick is longer than the one before it; moving from right to left, each

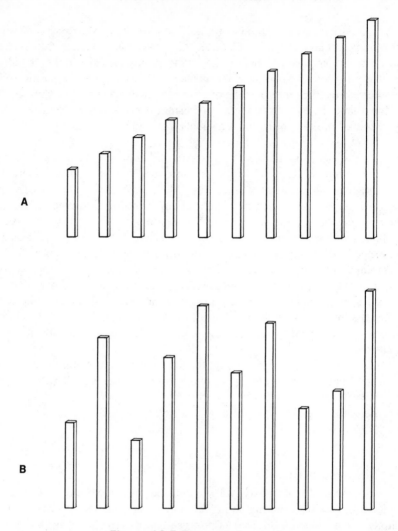

Figure 12.5 The seriation task

stick is shorter than its predecessor. Why is it so difficult for young children to use this idea in constructing a series? First, it is clear that children do understand the basic relations involved here quite early; if we were to select any two sticks from the series and ask a three-year-old which was longer and which was shorter (or "smaller" or "littler"), he would have no trouble telling us. However, the seriation task requires the child to *coordinate* both kinds of relation, "longer" and "shorter," at the same time, and this is the crux of the problem. In order to reconstruct the series in the top of Figure 12.5, the child must place each stick so that it is longer than the stick to its left *and* shorter than the stick to its right. If the child begins placing sticks with only one of these relations in mind—without considering both at the same time—he might end up with a series something like the one in the bottom of Figure 12.5. Thus, the coordination of relations is the key to successful seriation.

It is important to notice both a similarity and a difference between the seriation problem and the class inclusion problem. The similarity lies in the fact that both problems involve a kind of reversibility. That is, the child must coordinate operations that, in some sense, are opposites of each other—either the separating and joining of classes, or the relating of objects in terms of "greater than" and "less than." The difference lies in the type of reversibility involved. In the class-inclusion problem, reversibility is attained through the simple negation of one operation by another. Seriation, on the other hand, provides an example of reversibility through reciprocity: in order to insert stick X in the middle of a series, one operation (for example, finding a stick that is short in relation to X) must be compensated by another operation (finding a stick that is long in relation to X). In the period of concrete operations, these two kinds of reversibility are present but are still not coordinated with each other.

As with classes, an understanding of relations is basic to certain kinds of reasoning. The "transitivity" problem mentioned earlier is a good example. That is, if stick 2 is longer than stick 1, and stick 3 is longer than stick 2, then 3 must be longer than 1. As for the connection of both classes and relations with number, that is the next item on our agenda.

Thinking about Number[15]

We have seen, in previous sections, that preoperational children generally do not conserve such object properties as length or amount of substance when a superficial change of appearance has occurred. In a similar fashion, young children often fail to conserve the *number* of objects in a set. For example, if white and black checkers are lined up one-to-one in two parallel rows (Figure 12.6, top), most young children will affirm that there are just as many white checkers as black ones. However, if one row is then spread out (say the black row, as shown in Figure 12.6, bottom), the same children will claim that there are now more black checkers than white. Especially interesting is the fact that some children will even count, correctly, the eight objects in each row but still maintain that the black checkers outnumber the white ones. It is evident, then, that the ability to count is not the same thing as the understanding of number. If number is more than just counting, what else is involved, and how does a child attain it?

Piaget's answer to this question is complex and it is based on several different kinds of evidence. We will briefly review just two additional experiments that demonstrate the inadequacies of preoperational thinking about number. Then we will summarize Piaget's explanation of what is involved in understanding number on an operational level.

In one experiment, children are presented with a problem in which eight identical pieces of candy are to be eaten on each of two successive days.

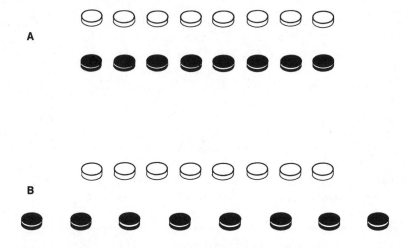

Figure 12.6 The conservation of number task.

On the first day, four pieces will be eaten in the morning and four in the afternoon. On the second day, however, only one piece will be eaten in the morning, with the remaining seven to be eaten in the afternoon. The question is whether or not there would be more candy to eat on one day than on the other. Younger children have been observed to argue that there would be more to eat on the second day, because seven is such a large number!

The second experiment can be illustrated by means of the bottom part of Figure 12.6. Basically, the purpose of the experiment is to find out if a child can maintain the "ordinal correspondence" between specific black checkers and white checkers, even after the black row has been spread out. Thus, the experimenter might point to the fourth black checker from the left and ask the child to show him the white checker that "goes with" that one. There is a stage in the development of number concepts when children use a strategy that almost works—but not quite. Beginning with the black checker to the left of the one that the experimenter has chosen, they count back to the end of the row, "one, two, three." Then, beginning at the left end of the white row, they again count off three checkers, at which point they *stop*, indicating that the *third* white checker corresponds to the fourth black one.

These findings reveal the difficulties that young children have with both cardinal numbers (one, two, three, and so on) and ordinal numbers (first, second, third, and so on). According to Piaget, these problems arise precisely because the same children have difficulty understanding classes and relations. In other words, the concept of number includes basic elements of classification and seriation. Let us see what Piaget has in mind in making this claim.

When we use numbers, in speaking of eight objects, for example, we are referring to a set or class in which each member is, in a certain sense, equivalent to every other member. But unlike other classes, the equivalence in this case may have nothing to do with the attributes of the objects themselves. Rather, the objects may be equivalent only in the sense that each was counted once—each constitutes a "unit." In a similar fashion, any set of eight things is equivalent to any other set of eight, no matter what the things might be or where they might be located relative to one another. Furthermore, just as the class of dogs can be broken down into beagles plus other dogs—or, alternatively, into collies plus other dogs, and so on—so too can a set of eight be broken down into four plus four, seven plus one, and so on. In neither case is the size of the class altered by the particular way in which it is divided. Finally, the number series can be seen as a class hierarchy such that the set of one is included in the set of two, which in turn is included in the set of three, and so on, ad infinitum. All of these points demonstrate the parallels between number and classification.

With respect to relations, there are again several connections with number. Notice, first of all, that in counting a set of objects, each is counted once and only once. (Very young children often fail to meet this requirement of counting.) Although the objects need not be counted in any particular order, the act of counting nonetheless imposes an ordered series on the set of objects. The object assigned number 3, for instance, is counted *after* the object assigned number 2 and *before* the object assigned number 4. If the object assigned number 4 has already been counted once before, then something is wrong; the count will end on too high a number (unless, of course, another object is left uncounted). Secondly, the ordinal correspondence problem outlined above entails the coordination of relations in two series: if there are three objects to the *left* of the fourth object in one series, then the corresponding object in another series must be to the *right* of the first three objects in that series. Finally, it is obvious that the set of whole numbers constitutes an ordered series, such that 1 is less than 2, which is less than 3, and so forth.

The cognitive structures underlying the logic of classes, relations, and number are attained during the period of concrete operations. The development of understanding in these areas paves the way for two further logicomathematical achievements in the period of formal operations—the logic of propositions and a system with double reversibility.

Propositional Logic[16]

To illustrate what is meant by propositional logic, let us consider a hypothetical problem. The owner of a watch company has been receiving complaints that some of his watches have been stopping after a few months of use. To make matters worse, the newspapers have run an article about the malfunctioning watches, and he has been flooded with inquiries about whether or not customers can expect their watches to go bad. Consequently, he has hired an investigator to track down the source of the problem. The investigator soon issues a progress report: "So far, I have discovered that unquestionably all watches made in the month of May are defective." With this information in mind, the company's owner wonders if he can answer some of the questions that have come up about the watches. The customers' questions can be summarized as follows:

    1. "I bought a watch which was made in May. Is it defective?"
    2. "My watch was not made in May. Is there a chance it is defective?"
The owner also wants to know:
    3. If a watch proves defective, was it definitely made in May?
    4. If a watch is not defective, does that mean it was not made in May?

    In order to answer these four questions, he conceptualizes a truth table made up of two basic propositions along with the negation of each: (1) either a particular watch was made in May, or it was not; and (2) either the watch is defective, or it is not (see Table 12.1, top). The investigator's report gives him some information as to which of the four pairings actually exist. Because the investigator reports that all watches made in May are defective, the owner can fill in the left-hand cells of the tables as shown in the middle part of Table 12.1. (A plus sign means that there exist watches about which a particular pair of propositions is true; a zero means that there are no such watches.) That is,

Table 12.1. Truth Tables for the Problem of the Defective Watches.

Was the watch made in May?

		Yes	No
Is the watch defective?	Yes		
	No		

		Yes	No
Is the watch defective?	Yes	+	
	No	0	

		Yes	No
Is the watch defective?	Yes	+	
	No	0	+

on the basis of the information available from the investigator, the owner can be safe in assuming that any and all watches dated in May will be defective and that there will be no watches made in May free from defect.

However, with just this much information and with only two cells of the table filled in, there are still four possible ways the table may be completed. Thus, the possible relationships between the two variables being considered (month of year manufactured and presence of defect) have been narrowed to four.[7] However, going back to the questions posed earlier, it appears that only the first one may be answered so far. Another piece of information that is needed for the solution of the puzzle is whether or not *any* watches have been found to be without the defect. When this question is forwarded to the special investigator, he reports back that he has indeed found watches that are not defective but has not yet determined when they were made. Now the owner can fill in a plus sign in the lower right-hand cell of his mental table (see the bottom part of Table 12.2).

Table 12.2. Hypothetical Mean Scores on a Social Studies Test According to Ability Grouping and Volunteer Status.

	VOLUNTEER STATUS	
ABILITY GROUPING	YES	NO
Heterogeneous	80	60
Homogeneous	60	40

But the owner still cannot answer questions 2 through 4, since with one cell in the table unknown, there are two possibilities for the way that the month of manufacture can be related to watch defects. That is, if a watch was found that *was* defective, the owner could not yet conclude that it was made in May, since it might be a watch that belongs in the upper right-hand cell of the table. Similarly, he could not conclude that all watches not made in May will *not* be defective. In other words, just because "made in May" implies "defective," it does not automatically follow that "defective" implies "made in May," nor does it follow that "not made in May" implies "not defective." It all depends on whether or not there exist defective watches that were not made in May—a fact still unknown. Thus, the owner now knows the one last piece of information he must get if he is to determine the relationship between month of manufacture and presence of defect in his watches.

The essence of propositional logic will become clear if we review the procedure by which we traced the owner's reasoning in the problem of the defective watches. One key step was to consider a *hypothetical possibility*—for example, that there might be defective watches that were not made in May. Moreover, we "constructed" this possibility by mentally combining two propositions about watches. This is quite different from classifying actual watches on the basis of two attributes at the same time. In the latter case, the existence of an abstract class is suggested by a concrete instance; hence, only concrete operations are required. In the defective watch problem, the class of defective watches not made in May must be "thought of" before it is known whether or not any concrete instances of such a class exist. Furthermore, in thinking of this hypothetical possibility, we also considered it in relation to the information that we already had, and we understood the implications of finding out whether the hypothetical case did or did not exist in actuality. That is, we realized that the owner's final conclusions would depend on whether or not there really were some defective watches that were not made in the month of May.

Virtually any attempt to establish cause-effect relationships in a scientific fashion involves the kind of logical reasoning illustrated by the defective watch problem. For example, a team of educational researchers once wished to study the effects of heterogeneous ability grouping on the achievement of eighth-grade students in social studies.[18] Because the heterogeneous groups would represent a departure from the homogeneous "tracking" system in the school district, only students who volunteered, with the consent of their parents, could be included in the experimental program. Now suppose the researchers had simply compared the volunteers in heterogeneous classes with the nonvolunteers in homogeneous classes, and suppose they found a higher level of achievement in the first group. Could they have concluded that the higher achievement was caused by the heterogeneous ability grouping? The conclusion would not necessarily be valid, for reasons that again illustrate the logic of propositions.

The problem includes three propositions: (1) that students are in heterogeneous classes; (2) that they achieve at a higher level; and (3) that they are volunteers. By mentally manipulating these propositions in various combinations, the researchers were able to envision the hypothetical possibility that volunteer students might outperform nonvolunteers, even within homogeneous classes, perhaps because of differences in motivation, home background, or the like. This possibility would cast doubt on the simple conclusion suggested above. Consequently, the researchers created a third group of students by assigning some of the volunteers to homogeneous rather than heterogeneous classes. When this group was compared to the group of volunteers actually attending heterogeneous classes, the possible effect of being a volunteer was "controlled" by being held constant. The researchers were then able to conclude that group differences in achievement were caused (at least in part) by the type of ability grouping. This method of controlling variables in an experiment involves a cognitive structure that Piaget has called "the scheme of all other things being equal." It is one very important manifestation of the propositional logic that develops during the period of formal operations.

Double Reversibility[19]

A second major achievement of logicomathematical development in the period of formal operations is the coordination of the two forms of reversibility—negation and reciprocity—within a single cognitive structure. By extending our discussion of the experiment on heterogeneous ability grouping, we can see an example of a system with double reversibility in action.

For the sake of the argument, let us assume that the experiment actually included a fourth group, nonvolunteers in heterogeneous classes, and that the hypothetical results shown in Table 12.2 were obtained. Now suppose that (for some reason) we wish to select a group of students with an average achievement score of 60, no more and no less. If we choose a group attending heterogeneous classes, we must compensate for this fact by making sure that they are not volunteers. Similarly, if we choose a group of volunteers, we must compensate for this fact by making sure that they are attending homogeneous classes. Thus, the two variables have a reciprocal relationship with one another; a difference in one compensates for (reverses) a difference in the other. Reversibility by negation could be seen if we selected volunteers in heterogeneous classes and consequently overshot our target mean of 60. We could reverse this error by negating the advantage gained on either one of the two variables, that is, by sticking with heterogeneous groupings but selecting nonvolunteers, or by sticking with volunteers but selecting students from homogeneous classes.

The coordination of reciprocity and negation becomes quite precise when a doubly reversible system involves continuous variables. Consider the example of a balance beam that has been thrown out of equilibrium by the addition of some extra weights to its left arm (Figure 12.7A and B). One way to restore equilibrium is simply to remove the weights that have just been added (reversibility by negation). An alternate method (C) is to move all the weights along the left arm to a point nearer the fulcrum (reversibility by reciprocity). Finally, it is possible to use a combination of negation and reciprocity (D), by removing some of the extra weights and moving the rest of the weights closer to the fulcrum. The placement of these remaining weights is not arbitrary; the relationship between amount of weight and distance from the fulcrum can be expressed in precise quantitative terms. Thus, if equilibrium is achieved when 1 pound is placed at a distance of 4 feet, then it will also be achieved with 4 pounds at 1 feet, or 2 pounds at 2 feet, or 3 pounds at 1⅓ feet. Given any amount of weight, it is possible to determine precisely the corresponding distance, and vice versa, because the product of weight x distance is a constant, in this case equal to 4. Another way of expressing the same relationship is to say that, for any pair of weights and distances in equilibrium, the ratio of the weights is inversely proportional to the ratio of their respective distances. It is for this reason that Piaget refers to the system of double reversibility as the "proportionality scheme."

Logicomathematical Thinking and the Physical World

With the example of equilibrium on a balance beam, we have come full circle to the development of thinking about the physical world. During the period of concrete operations, at the same time that the child is mastering the

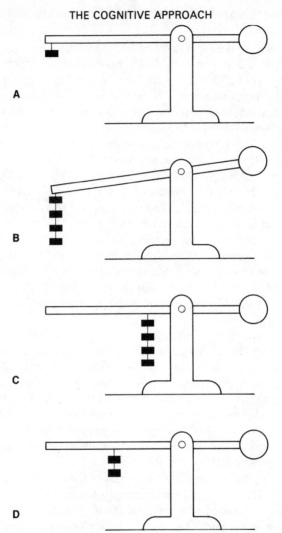

Figure 12.7. Relationship between weight and distance on a balance beam.

logic of classes, relations, and number, his understanding of physical phenomena takes on a new kind of stability and rationality. This synchrony between the two areas of development is not just a coincidence, according to Piaget. The attainment of operational reversibility in each area is facilitated by similar attainments in the other area. What we wish to emphasize here, however, is the added understanding of the physical world that results from the development of logicomathematical thought at the formal level. To quote Piaget, "the combinatorial systems [of propositional logic] and double reversibility affect the conquest of reality as well as the capacity for clear formulation."[20] In order to demonstrate the application of formal thought to physical phenomena, we will touch briefly on each of the topics discussed earlier with regard to the child's understanding of the physical world.

In the balance problem, formal logic permits an individual to understand the exact relationship between an *object property* (weight) and a *spatial dimension* (distance) in a doubly reversible system. There is a similar type of thinking involved when the object property of density is defined as a relationship between weight and volume. With regard to space, formal thought also permits one to conceive of hypothetical "hyperspaces"—spaces that involve more than three dimensions, in the sense that the location of an object is defined with reference to more than three coordinates. The idea of a hyperspace is a good example of the difference between concrete and formal thought, since there is no adequate way to visualize a space with more than three dimensions. The relationships between *distance, time,* and *speed* provide yet another example of a physical area in which formal thought can be applied. To understand that two men are walking at the same speed if the first covers four miles in one hour and the other covers six miles in an hour and a half, one must think in terms of proportions in a doubly reversible system. As for *causality,* propositional logic holds the key to establishing unambiguous cause-effect relationships by enabling an individual to conceive of hypothetical possibilities and their implications, and to construct tests that will indicate whether or not the co-occurrence of two facts is evidence that one has actually caused the other. This way of thinking is useful not only in psychological or educational research (for example, establishing the effect of heterogeneous ability grouping) but also in attempts to explain physical phenomena (for example, establishing what causes some rods to bend more than others).

With this brief discussion of formal thought as it applies to physical phenomena, we have brought to a belated conclusion our examination of intellectual development with regard to causality, objects, space, and time. As a summary of development in each of these areas, let us look at Table 12.3. We wish to emphasize that this table contains only some highlights of the process by which children come to understand the physical world. In particular, we have seen just a few examples of formal thought as it applies to the physical world. The number of possible applications is actually infinite because, at the formal level, we are dealing with cognitive structures that are independent of any particular content. They are structures for thinking about propositions and transformations, and in principle the propositions and transformations can be concerned with anything under the sun. (The caveat, "in principle," simply acknowledges the fact that an individual might use formal logic in some areas of content without using it in others—that is, that horizontal *décalages* occur in the period of formal operations, as well as in earlier periods.) In fact, the possibilities for applying formal operations extend beyond the physical world. Another realm of possible application is the social world, and it is to this realm that we turn next.

UNDERSTANDING THE SOCIAL WORLD

Throughout the course of development, along with changes in the child's thinking about the physical world, there are changes in his thinking about the social world. The growing child gains a greater understanding of

Table 12.3. Examples of Development in Understanding the Physical World.

PERIODS OF DEVELOPMENT	AREAS OF DEVELOPMENT			
	OBJECTS	SPACE	TIME AND SPEED	CAUSALITY
Sensorimotor	Object permanence	Unified space, independent of particular actions; detour behavior	Immediate temporal successions independent of actions	Initial externalization of causes
Preoperational	Intuitive rules regarding amount, weight, etc.	Intuitive rules regarding length, height, distance	Localized time; rule of passing; extended time series	Animism; artificialism
Concrete operations	Conservation of amount, weight, etc.	Conservation of length, etc.; projection of straight line; measurement of space; use of coordinates	Unified time; measurement of time	Inanimate external causality; noncontradictory causal explanations
Formal	Conservation of exterior volume; understanding of density	Proportionality with regard to space; ability to conceive of hyperspace	Proportionality with regard to time, speed	Isolation of causes through scheme of "all other things being equal"

"human nature" as it is manifested in the individual people with whom the child comes in contact, either in person or through the media. At the same time, the child acquires and revises his conceptions of the various social, political, and religious institutions in his culture. All of this belongs in the realm of intellectual development, too.

There are a great many possibilities for applying the cognitive approach to the child's understanding of the social world. While most of the possibilities have yet to be explored, enough work has been done in some areas for us to consider them here. To be specific, we will discuss a cognitive theory of moral judgment and some interesting work which has been done on the child's "naïve theory" of human nature.

Moral Judgment

In addition to his work on the child's conception of physical reality, some of Piaget's earliest research was concerned with the child's "moral judgment," his way of thinking about questions of right and wrong, his understanding of social rules, and so on. Although Piaget did not pursue this line of research in later years, his work on moral judgment deserves mention as the predecessor of a theory of moral development set forth recently by Lawrence Kohlberg.

Piaget's Findings. [21] Two of Piaget's findings with regard to moral judgment are of particular interest. One of them concerns the basis on which children make judgments about the relative "naughtiness" of various acts that are described in little stories. In one story, for example, a boy tries to get some jam from the cupboard without his mother's permission. The jam is on a high shelf and, in the process of reaching for it, the boy knocks over a cup and the cup breaks. In a second story, another boy comes in to dinner when he is called, but in opening the door to the dining room, he accidentally smashes a whole tray full of cups that had been left on a chair behind the door. After telling this pair of stories, Piaget asked children to say which of the boys was naughtier, and to explain why. Younger children (up to about age 10) sometimes said the second boy was naughtier because he did more damage. Older children were much more consistent in agreeing that the first boy was naughtier because he had *intended* to be disobedient. Either intentions do not seem very important to younger children or else younger children do not always see the intention as something separate from the deed itself. In any case, Piaget produced some evidence of a qualitative change in children's conceptions of "naughtiness."

We will mention just one more of Piaget's observations on moral thinking, but it is an especially charming one because, in order to obtain the data, Piaget got down on his hands and knees and played marbles with boys of various ages in the city of Geneva, Switzerland. Among other things, Piaget wanted to find out what his fellow marble players thought about the rules of the game—particularly where the rules came from and whether or not a group of children could decide to change the rules in one way or another. Again, Piaget found age differences. The younger children (below age seven) generally saw the rules of marbles as fixed laws that had always been the same and always would be, forever. (Interestingly, the same children were observed to violate the rules continually while playing, with little awareness or concern as to what they were doing.) Older children understood the rules as social conventions that were passed on to them from other children and that could be changed if a particular group of children decided that some changes were in order. Thus, Piaget also found evidence of a qualitative change in the way children conceive of rules.

Piaget's early work on moral judgment suggested that this area would be fertile ground for cognitive theory, but it remained for Kohlberg and his colleagues to construct a more detailed theory of the particular stages and cognitive structures involved in the development of moral thought. As we shall see, Kohlberg has gone well beyond the leads that Piaget provided, but Kohlberg is also concerned with the individual's conception of rules and his use of information about intentions and consequences in judging the rightness or wrongness of a particular act.

Kohlberg's Theory. [22]   The basic method that Kohlberg has used to study moral judgment is similar to Piaget's story-telling technique described above. The method consists of an interview in which a series of short stories is presented. In each story, the central character is faced with a moral dilemma of some sort, as in this story:

> In Europe, a woman was near death from cancer. One drug might save her, a form of radium that a druggist in the same town had recently discovered. The druggist was charging $2000, 10 times what the drug cost him to make. The sick woman's husband, Heinz, went to everyone he knew to borrow the money, but he could only get together about half of what it cost. He told the druggist that his wife was dying and asked him to sell it cheaper or let him pay later. But the druggist said no. The husband got desperate and broke into the man's store to steal the drug for his wife. Should the husband have done that? Why?

The important question is not whether the subject agrees or disagrees with what Heinz did. Rather, what is important is the *reasoning* that the subject uses to support his position pro or con Heinz's behavior. In order to ensure that he understands the subject's reasoning, the interviewer can ask whatever additional questions are necessary. In this regard, Kohlberg's interview resembles Piaget's clinical method.

Both longitudinal and cross-sectional data have been collected from the Kohlberg interview in a variety of cultures. According to Kohlberg's analysis, the data indicate that moral judgment develops through a series of six stages, which are grouped into three major levels of development. The stages in Kohlberg's theory are defined in summary form in Table 12.4. The stages are distinguished from one another by several aspects of the subjects' responses to the moral dilemmas they are given to discuss. For example, stage 4 thinking is oriented toward fixed laws, whereas stage 5 thinking emphasizes the possibility of changing laws. Stage 1 judgments of goodness and badness are based on the physical consequences of a particular act, while stage 2 judgments reflect a concern with the instrumental value of an act in satisfying personal needs.

Table 12.4   Kohlberg's Stages of Moral Judgment. [*]

I. PRECONVENTIONAL LEVEL

At this level the child is responsive to cultural rules and labels of good and bad, right or wrong, but interprets these labels in terms of either the physical or the hedonistic consequences of action (punishment, reward, exchange of favors) or in terms of the physical power of those who enunciate the rules and labels. The level is divided into the following two stages:

Stage 1: *The punishment and obedience orientation.* The physical consequences of action determine its goodness or badness regardless of the human meaning or value of these consequences. Avoidance of punishment and unquestioning deference to power are valued in their own right, not in terms of respect for an underlying moral order supported by punishment and authority (the latter being Stage 4).

Stage 2: *The instrumental relativist orientation.* Right action consists of that which instrumentally satisfies one's own needs and occasionally the needs of others. Human relations are viewed in terms like those of the market place. Elements of fairness, of reciprocity and equal sharing are present, but they are always interpreted in a physical pragmatic way. Reciprocity is a matter of "you scratch my back and I'll scratch yours," not of loyalty, gratitude, or justice.

II. CONVENTIONAL LEVEL

At this level, maintaining the expectations of the individual's family, group, or nation is perceived as valuable in its own right, regardless of immediate and obvious consequences. The attitude is not only one of *conformity* to personal expectations and social order, but of loyalty to it, of actively *maintaining*, supporting, and justifying the order and of identifying with the persons or group involved in it. At this level, there are the following two stages:

Stage 3: *The interpersonal concordance or "good boy–nice girl" orientation.* Good behavior is that which pleases or helps others and is approved by them. There is much conformity to stereotypical images of what is majority or "natural" behavior. Behavior is frequently judged by intention—"he means well" becomes important for the first time. One earns approval by being "nice."

Stage 4: *The "law and order" orientation.* There is orientation toward authority, fixed rules, and the maintenance of the social order. Right behavior consists of doing one's duty, showing respect for authority and maintaining the given social order for its own sake.

*Reprinted with permission from L. Kohlberg, *Educational Psychologists* 10 (Winter 1973), 7-8. Copyright © Division of Educational Psychology, American Psychological Association.

Table 12.4. (cont.)

III. POSTCONVENTIONAL, AUTONOMOUS, OR PRINCIPLED LEVEL

At this level, there is a clear effort to define moral values and principles which have validity and application apart from the authority of the groups or persons holding these principles and apart from the individual's own identification with these groups. This level again has two stages:

Stage 5: *The social-contract legalistic orientation generally with utilitarian overtones.* Right action tends to be defined in terms of general individual rights and in terms of standards which have been critically examined and agreed upon by the whole society. There is a clear awareness of the relativism of personal values and opinions and a corresponding emphasis upon procedural rules for reaching consensus. Aside from what is constitutionally and democratically agreed upon, the right is a matter of personal "values" and "opinion." The result is an emphasis upon the "legal point of view," but with an emphasis upon the possibility of changing law in terms of rational considerations of social utility, (rather than freezing it in terms of Stage 4 "law and order"). Outside the legal realm, free agreement and contract is the binding element of obligation. This is the "official" morality of the American government and Constitution.

Stage 6: *The universal ethical principle orientation.* Right is defined by the decision of conscience in accord with self-chosen *ethical principles* appealing to logical comprehensiveness, universality, and consistency. These principles are abstract and ethical (the Golden Rule, the categorical imperative); they are not concrete moral rules like the Ten Commandments. At heart, these are universal principles of *justice*, of the *reciprocity* and *equality* of the human *rights* and of respect for the dignity of human beings as *individual persons*.

The differences between Kohlberg's stages will probably become clearer if we look at Table 12.5, which contains a set of pro and con arguments that have been constructed to represent the kinds of reasoning used by subjects at stages 1 through 6 in response to the story about Heinz and his dying wife. The arguments in the table were designed to focus on the intentions and consequences associated with Heinz's action. Notice, for example, that the pro argument at stage 2 emphasizes consequences by saying, in effect, that the end justifies the means—the end being the satisfaction of personal needs. In contrast, the pro argument at stage 3 emphasizes intention by saying that Heinz was only being a "good husband" in stealing the drug, that is, he was trying to be a nice person. A similar contrast occurs between the con arguments at stages 4 and 5. The stage 4 con argument disregards intention altogether by saying that it is just categorically wrong to steal, whereas the stage 5 argument is more sympathetic toward Heinz's intent but expresses fears about the consequences of failing to hold people responsible for acts that violate the law. Intentions and consequences are just two aspects out of 25 that distinguish between Kohlberg's stages.

There are a number of ways in which Kohlberg's moral stages exemplify the characteristics of developmental stages in general, as discussed in Chapters 9 and 11. First of all, it appears that the Kohlberg stages represent qualitatively different ways of thinking about moral issues and that they there-

Table 12.5. Arguments Regarding Consequences and Intentions at Six Stages of Moral Development.*

STAGE 1　*Pro*—He should steal the drug. It isn't really bad to take it. It isn't like he didn't ask to pay for it first. The drug he'd take is only worth $200, he's not really taking a $2000 drug.

　　　　Con—He shouldn't steal the drug, it's a big crime. He didn't get permission, he used force and broke and entered. He did a lot of damage, stealing a very expensive drug and breaking up the store, too.

STAGE 2　*Pro*—It's all right to steal the drug because she needs it and he wants her to live. It isn't that he wants to steal, but it's the way he has to use to get the drug to save her.

　　　　Con—He shouldn't steal it. The druggist isn't wrong or bad, he just wants to make a profit. That's what you're in business for, to make money.

STAGE 3　*Pro*—He should steal the drug. He was only doing something that was natural for a good husband to do. You can't blame him for doing something out of love for his wife, you'd blame him if he didn't love his wife enough to save her.

　　　　Con—He shouldn't steal. If his wife dies, he can't be blamed. It isn't because he's heartless or that he doesn't love her enough to do everything that he legally can. The druggist is the selfish or heartless one.

STAGE 4　*Pro*—You should steal it. If you did nothing you'd be letting your wife die, it's your responsibility if she does. You have to take it with the idea of paying the druggist.

　　　　Con—It is a natural thing for Heinz to want to save his wife but it's still always wrong to steal. He still knows he's stealing and taking a valuable drug from the man who made it.

STAGE 5　*Pro*—The law wasn't set up for these circumstances. Taking the drug in this situation isn't really right, but it's justified to do it.

　　　　Con—You can't completely blame someone for stealing but extreme circumstances don't really justify taking the law in your own hands. You can't have everyone stealing whenever they get desperate. The end may be good, but the ends don't justify the means.

STAGE 6　*Pro*—This is a situation which forces him to choose between stealing and letting his wife die. In a situation where the choice must be made, it is morally right to steal. He has to act in terms of the principle of preserving and respecting life.

　　　　Con—Heinz is faced with the decision of whether to consider the other people who need the drug just as badly as his wife. Heinz ought to act not according to his particular feelings toward his wife, but considering the value of all the lives involved.

*Exerpted from table in unpublished doctoral dissertation, J.R. Rest, 1968, University of Chicago, by permission of the author.

fore reflect different cognitive structures. Secondly, there are the usual complications with regard to the reality of developmental stages. A typical subject
gives a variety of responses representing different moral stages in the course
of a single interview. Usually, however, it is possible to identify a dominant
stage in the subject's moral reasoning—the kind of reasoning he uses most
frequently. In addition, the rate of progress through the moral stages seems
to vary a great deal from one individual to another. In fact, individual differences in rate of progress may be even greater for the moral stages than for
Piaget's periods of development. It is not unusual to find an early stage (for
example, stage 2) still dominating the moral judgments of adolescents, or even
adults. Because moral development appears to extend well into adulthood for
some individuals—and perhaps falls far short of completion—we have not
attempted to give age ranges for each of the stages. However, it is most unusual
to find evidence of stages 5 and 6 in a subject's responses prior to adolescence.

The most important general characteristics of developmental stages are
their invariant sequence and their hierarchical nature, with later stages inte-
grating elements of earlier stages. Kohlberg feels that these characteristics
apply to his moral stages as well as they do to the stages Piaget has described
for logicomathematical thought and for conceptions of the physical world.
According to the theory, a person must go through the six moral stages in
proper sequence. It is not possible to reverse the order of stages, or to skip a
stage altogether. Like Piaget's stages, the order of the moral stages is fixed
because later stages build on earlier ones. To give just one example of this
hierarchical integration, stage 5 combines the stage 4 notion of adherence to
a codified law with stage 3 concern for an individual's intentions: laws should
be obeyed, but sometimes laws are unfair to people who have acted with good
intentions (see the stage 5 arguments in Table 12.5).

Aside from the general characteristics of developmental stages, the
Kohlberg stages of moral judgment also follow the general trends of development discussed in Chapter 9. For the moment, let us concentrate on the loss
of egocentrism as it is manifested in moral development. In the beginning, the
child's concern with the avoidance of punishment shows that his judgments
are centered entirely on immediate physical consequences for himself (stage 1).
Later, the child begins to consider the consequences of his behavior for other
people, but only when he can anticipate some future payoff for himself (stage
2). Then the focus shifts to the feelings and expectations of family members
and other important people in the child's life; it is good to live up to these
feelings and expectations regardless of the foreseeable consequences in terms
of rewards or punishments (stage 3).

Next, moral judgments are based on conformity to the social order,
especially as codified in laws or religious dogma. Moral thought is less egocentric than before in that it transcends the specific people whom the child knows,
but it is still egocentric in the sense that it takes the institutionalized status quo
as the ultimate authority on questions of right and wrong (stage 4). At the next
stage, there is further decentration as the individual views the present social

order as just one of many possibilities and therefore as one that is subject to change by mutual agreement. However, until such change is legislated, it is right to uphold the existing code of ethics (stage 5). Finally, the idea of abiding by the law while working to improve it is seen as inadequate, because even as the law improves, it is still imperfect. Consequently it may be right sometimes to violate the letter of the law for reasons of personal conscience (stage 6).

It might seem as if the element of personal conscience at stage 6 would bring moral development full circle to a very egocentric conclusion. However, the difference between stage 6 and the earlier stages is that stage 6 moral judgments are based not on self-interest but on general principles regarding the value of human life—principles that transcend all specific people and institutions. In any case, the notion of decreasing egocentrism helps to clarify the stages of moral development, and in the present case it has provided a good way of summarizing the descriptive part of Kohlberg's theory.

Naïve Theories of Human Behavior

Back in Chapter 8 we spoke of the child gradually constructing a "theory" about how the world works in the course of intellectual development. Such a personal theory about the nature of reality has been called a "naïve" theory, because it is based on common sense and is understood only implicitly. This is unlike a formal scientific theory, with its explicit assumptions and principles based on systematic research and logic. But just as the scientist uses his formal theory to predict and explain the data he collects, so a person uses his naïve theory to interpret what he observes in the world and to guide his behavior. In other words, a naïve theory is essentially a cognitive structure. Actually, an individual has a number of naïve theories, each for dealing with a different part of reality. The particular naïve theory that concerns us here is a theory that a child might use to predict the behavior of another person in a social situation. Thus, we are concerned with a part of the child's understanding of human nature.

We will concentrate on some research conducted by Baldwin and his associates.[23] In this research, the subjects (both children and adults) were presented with a series of hypothetical situations involving a person (O) and another person (P). In each situation, O is faced with a choice between two courses of action. Each of the alternative actions will have either positive $(+)$ or negative $(-)$ consequences for both O and P. For example, one alternative would help O and harm P (symbolized as O^+P^-), whereas another alternative would harm both O and P (that is, O^-P^-). If O had to choose between these two alternatives and he chose the first over the second, his choice would be represented as O^+P^-/O^-P^-. In other words, O had a choice between either helping himself and (at the same time) harming P or harming himself and harming P; he decided to help himself and harm P, rather than harming both himself and P.

O1

O2

Figure 12.8. Rating scale for the measurement of social expectations

Given this sort of information about O's choice behavior, the subject was then asked to indicate on a scale (Figure 12.8) how many people, in general, would make the same choice as O, as opposed to choosing the other alternative that was given. If the subject thought that most people would make the same choice as O, he would place a mark toward the right end of the scale, near "Everybody." If he thought that only a slight majority would make O's choice, then he would place his mark just to the right of "Half," and so on. The same procedure was repeated for all 16 of the situations that are possible, as shown in Table 12.6. It will be noted that four of these situations involve a choice between identical alternatives (for example, O^+P^+/O^+P^+), in which case the subject logically ought to place his mark directly on "Half"; this point becomes important later on.

Table 12.6. Sixteen Situations Used to Assess Naive Theory of Choice Behavior.

O^+P^+/O^+P^+	O^+P^+/O^+P^-	O^+P^+/O^-P^+	O^+P^+/O^-P^-
O^+P^-/O^+P^+	O^+P^-/O^+P^-	O^+P^-/O^-P^+	O^+P^-/O^-P^-
O^-P^+/O^+P^+	O^-P^+/O^+P^-	O^-P^+/O^-P^+	O^-P^+/O^-P^-
O^-P^-/O^+P^+	O^-P^-/O^+P^-	O^-P^-/O^-P^+	O^-P^-/O^-P^-

What this method finds out is how well a particular choice by O accords with the subject's expectations regarding the choice behavior of people in general. The subject's own expectations are the target of interest, because they reveal the subject's naïve theory. Presumably the subject uses his theory to predict the choice behavior of others in situations that have the same basic elements as those in Table 12.6. He also uses the theory to interpret the choices that other people actually make. If an actual choice contradicts the subject's expectations, he might look for additional information that would explain what happened; or he might decide that the other person is peculiar in some way; or he might revise his own expectations, if they prove to be wrong often enough.

But what *are* these expectations, and what is the naïve theory behind them? Let us look first at the kind of theory that adult subjects seem to use. There are three factors that, taken together, seem to account quite well for the expectations of adults. In other words, an adult seems to decide what his expectations are by weighing these three factors against each other. The first factor is *benevolence*, the extent to which the subject believes that others are generally inclined to help a person (P^+), other things being equal. The second factor is *self-interest,* the extent to which the subject believes that others are generally inclined to choose actions that will help themselves (O^+), other things being equal. And the third factor is *equality of outcome,* the extent to which the subject believes that people are generally inclined to choose actions that have the same consequences for themselves as for another person (either O^+P^+ or O^-P^-). According to Baldwin's analysis, there may be individual differences in the relative weights assigned to each of these factors, but everyone's naïve theory involves the same three factors (at least at the adult level).

Now let us see how the three factors are used in deriving an expectation with regard to O's behavior in a given situation. Suppose we are told that O has a choice between O^+P^- and O^-P^+. We have a situation in which O's benevolence is pitted against his self-interest. That is, O cannot have both P^+ and O^+ at the same time. If we believed (implicitly) that self-interest is generally a much stronger factor than benevolence, then we would predict that most people (that is, most O's) would choose O^+P^- over O^-P^+. To take another example, suppose O is given a choice between O^-P^+ and O^-P^-. This situation pits benevolence against equality of outcome (because O cannot choose O^+P^+). If we believed benevolence to be slightly stronger than equality of outcome, then we would say that a slight majority of people would choose O^-P^+ over O^-P^-. The reader is invited to analyze the remaining situations in Table 12.6 in the same fashion.

With regard to intellectual development, the interesting question is whether or not children think in terms of the same naïve theory as adults. There is evidence that strongly suggests that they do not. Instead of the three-factor theory that adults use, children below the age of about seven seem to use a theory based on a single factor, the "chosen alternative" factor. According to the single-factor theory, the child's expectations are based entirely on the alternative that O actually chooses, without taking into account what the other alternative might have been. For example, if O is said to have chosen O^-P^- over O^+P^-, young children tend to respond that no one would ever really choose O^-P^-, because the consequences of that choice are all bad. Also, these children do not consider the "equality of outcome" factor; they do not imagine that O might sometimes say "If P has to be harmed, then it is only fair for me to be harmed also." In general, young children think that all O^-P^- choices are very unlikely, and all O^+P^+ choices are very likely, and all O^+P^- or O^-P^+ choices are near "Half" on the rating scale. Piaget's concept of "centration" comes to mind here, because young children attend to only one aspect of the choice situation—that is, the chosen alternative. This is especially striking in a situation such as O^-P^-/O^-P^-, where young children seem to say that nobody would choose the first alternative over the second. What they really mean is that nobody would like the chosen alternative.

Between age seven and adulthood, there is a gradual shift away from the single-factor "chosen alternative" theory and toward the three-factor theory involving benevolence, self-interest, and equality of outcome. In other words, there is a qualitative change in the child's thinking about the choice behavior of others; one cognitive structure supersedes another. It seems reasonable to say that the more advanced form of naïve theory involves greater objectivity, in the sense that it corresponds more closely to human nature and therefore is more likely to make predictions that are confirmed by the way other people actually behave. In any case, this work on naïve theory suggests that the cognitive approach can be applied to the development of the child's understanding of human nature. But neither Baldwin's work on naïve theory nor Kohlberg's theory of moral judgment is nearly as well developed at this point as Piaget's theory of cognition in the physical world and logicomathematical areas.

LANGUAGE DEVELOPMENT

It is self-evident that language generally plays an important role in intellectual development. Much of the information that a child takes in from the world around him is conveyed through language. In addition, we have seen that language may be a mode of representation in cognition. Finally, language is one means by which the child can produce effects on the environment, when other people respond to the child's own language behavior. In all of these cases, language serves as an *instrument* of knowledge, that is, as a means to the end of information transmission or cognitive representation. But in order for language to perform these instrumental functions, the child must learn the language. Thus, language can be viewed not only as an instrument of knowledge, but also as an *object* of knowledge. As such, language constitutes another major area of intellectual development.

The process by which a child acquires knowledge of his native language is far too vast an area to be covered even superficially in a few pages.[24] We will have to ignore some aspects of language acquisition altogether, including the way in which a child learns the sound system of a language and how he comes to understand that the social situation one is in determines how one says something (or whether it is said at all). In a highly selective fashion, we will concentrate on just two aspects of language acquisition: the development of word meanings and the learning of grammatical rules. Before getting into these topics, however, we will need to discuss the nature of an individual's linguistic knowledge and the methods that can be used to study it.

The Nature of Linguistic Knowledge and Its Study in Children

In the past, developmental and educational psychologists have often charted a child's progress in language acquisition by using such quantitative measures as the size of the child's vocabulary or the average number of words in the child's sentences. Although it is generally true that a growing child's vocabulary gets larger and his sentences get longer, these quantitative measures are not directly related to what a child actually knows about language at a given point in development. Consider what happens when one of these measures is applied to the language produced by adults. In his writings, Ernest Hemingway typically used sentences that were much shorter, on the average, than the sentences of William Faulkner; yet it seems absurd to say that Faulkner knew the English language much better than did Hemingway. Some literary critics may wish to argue this point, but with regard to the kind of linguistic knowledge that we will discuss here, it is highly unlikely that there was any real difference between the two authors.

Quantitative measures of language acquisition are inadequate because they neglect the fact that a language is a *system*—a set of rules that relate sounds to meanings (and vice versa). A person who knows the rules can understand what other people have said and can say things that other people will understand. When viewed from this perspective, linguistic knowledge can be seen as a cognitive structure. And if we think of linguistic knowledge as a cognitive structure, then we can make some predictions about the manner in which this structure is acquired in the course of development. For one thing, we can predict that the mature form of the structure (the structure known by a person who "speaks the language") is preceded in development by a series of simpler structures, each of which has built upon the structures before it. In other words, we can predict that there are qualitative changes in the child's knowledge of language—changes not revealed by such measures as sentence length and size of vocabulary. In order to understand how language is acquired, we must determine what sorts of structural changes occur during the process of acquisition.

At this point, we are faced with the usual methodological question of the cognitive approach: how can we make inferences about the child's linguistic knowledge? One possibility is to adopt the relatively straightforward method used by linguists when they attempt to infer what an adult informant knows about his own language. The method is not so straightforward that the linguist can simply ask the informant to tell him the rules of the language. If this were possible, there would be no point in linguistics as a field of study, because everyone capable of speaking a particular language would already know what the linguist was trying to find out. The informant does know the rules, but only implicitly; he cannot tell the linguist what the rules are. The point of linguistics, then, is to make this implicit knowledge explicit, by spelling out the rules in the form of a grammar. To do this, the linguist can still use some rather direct methods with his adult informant. For instance, he can ask the informant whether or not two different utterances mean essentially the same thing. Or he can ask which of two utterances is "better," in the sense that one is more consistent with the informant's knowledge about the way things are said in his language. (If the linguist is studying a language that he knows, he can even be his own informant!) From the informant's responses regarding a number of specific utterances, the linguist tries to infer the general rules by which the speaker of the language operates.

Now what about the study of linguistic knowledge in children? The linguist's direct approach works well with adults, but the process of language acquisition is well under way by age two, and therein lies a problem. One attempt to treat a two-year-old as a linguistic informant went as follows:[25]

> *Investigator:* Now, Adam, listen to what I say. Tell me which is better ... "some water" or "a water."
> *Adam:* Pop go weasel.

It is partly because of this methodological problem that the study of child language is usually assigned to the hybrid field of psycholinguistics rather than to linguistics per se. The psycholinguist pays heed to the linguist's description of the kind of system that a child will end up with, but he uses the methods of cognitive psychology to discover the systems that a child constructs on his way toward linguistic maturity. Indeed, all of the research methods discussed in Chapter 8, from naturalistic observation to experimentation, have contributed to the study of language acquisition. We will see examples of several methods in the sections that follow.

The Development of Word Meanings

In previous discussions, we have seen that the infant's first words tend to have highly idiosyncratic meanings and that, even in the middle part of childhood, such words as "all" do not mean the same thing to the child as they do to an adult. Let us take a closer look at the development of word meanings, with the intention of elaborating on the basic idea that word meanings become more adultlike as the child gets older.

One account of the qualitative changes that occur in children's word meanings is the *semantic feature hypothesis* described by Clark.[26] The basic assumption of this hypothesis is that the meaning of a word can be characterized as a set of semantic features that distinguish the meaning of one word from another. For example, the meanings of *man, woman, boy,* and *girl* are distinguished from each other by two features: Male-Female and Adult-Child. That is, a man is a male adult, a woman is a female adult, and so on. Since each feature involves a pair of opposites (for example, Male versus Female), it is more economical to name a feature by mentioning just one member of the pair, along with a + or − to indicate which member of the pair applies to a given meaning. Thus, the meaning of *man* would be represented as +Male, +Adult, and the meaning of *girl* would be −Male, −Adult. Although we are using words to name the features, the features themselves are not actually words but rather conceptual components of meaning. For an adult, the meanings of most words are made up of several such features. According to Clark's hypothesis, however, children generally acquire word meanings by first learning just one or two features and by then adding others until all the features of adult meaning have been attained.

Several pieces of evidence can be cited in support of the semantic feature hypothesis. For example, many parents have noticed that the errors that very young children make in naming objects show certain regularities. A child might use the name *doggie* for his family's beagle, and for the collie that lives next door, but then he also says *doggie* when he sees a horse or a cow. In other words, the meaning of *doggie* is overextended to include objects that are not included in the adult meaning of *dog*. At the same time, however, there are still some boundaries around the child's meaning of *doggie*, even though he has overextended it. He does not say *doggie* with reference to trees or birds or many other familiar objects.

According to Clark's analysis, the child's use of *doggie* indicates that he has acquired some features of the adult meaning (for example, +Four-legged) but not others (for example, –Hooved). As the child acquires additional features for *doggie* (or *dog*), its meaning will be narrowed down until it corresponds to the adult meaning.

The overextension of word meanings is observed quite often in early language acquisition—usually during the child's second year—but even a few years later there are some rather surprising instances in which word meanings are not as well differentiated for children as they are for adults. In one study of the words *more* and *less,* children who were about four years old were shown two cardbord apple trees with unequal numbers of apples on them.[27] First the children were asked whether or not one tree had more (or less) apples on it than the other. This question was almost always answered correctly with a "yes." Then, when the children were asked which tree had *more,* they almost always pointed to the correct tree (about 90 percent correct). However, when they were asked which tree had *less,* a majority of the children again pointed to the tree with more apples on it (about 70 percent incorrect). Evidently, for most of these children, *less* meant *more!* These data on *more* and *less* are consistent with the semantic feature hypothesis, as can be seen in the analysis that follows.

The words *more* and *less* both refer to an *amount* of something (rather than its color or shape, for example). Thus, it may be said that both words have the feature +Amount. However, *more* and *less* are also "polar" opposites with regard to relative amounts, *more* being the positive pole and *less* being the negative pole. Thus, the adult features for *more* are +Amount, +Polar, whereas for *less* they are +Amount, –Polar. What has to be explained, then, is why at one point in development children treat *less* as if it, too, were +Amount, +Polar.

Clark offers the following explanation as to why *less* means *more.* First, children acquire the feature +Amount for both words. At this point, *more* and *less* are both synonymous with *some,* or *an amount of.* When a mother says to her young child, "Do you want more milk?", it is as if she were saying "Do you want *some* milk?" During this period, "I have less than you" presumably would mean to the child "I have some and you have some too." Next, the idea of relative amounts is introduced, and the positive pole is used to designate the dimension along which relative amounts are compared. The use of a positive polar term to designate a dimension is a general rule in English. Thus, in talking about the *high-low* dimension, we refer to it as "height" (or we ask "How high is that?"); the *wide-narrow* dimension is called "width"; and so on. With regard to the *more-less* dimension, the child first gets the idea of using the positive pole to refer to differences in amount. Thus, *more* is +Amount, +Polar. But at this point, because the child has been treating *more* and *less* as synonyms, he now assumes that *less* is also +Amount, +Polar. Eventually the child understands that *less* is actually –Polar, at which point his meanings of *more* and *less* both correspond to those of an adult.

The case of *more* and *less* illustrates two general principles regarding the acquisition of semantic features. First, the child begins by acquiring a more general feature, +Amount, which distinguishes *more* and *less* from other words (for instance, *hot* and *cold*), but this feature does not distinguish the two words from each other. Second, when the child does acquire a feature that ultimately will distinguish *more* from *less*—namely, ± Polar—he first attaches the + form of the feature to both words. Similar overextensions of a + pole to a – pole have been found for such antonym pairs as *long-short, thick-thin,* and *high-low.* In sum, more general features are acquired before more specific ones, and the positive pole of a feature is acquired before its negative pole.

Although it is unlikely that the semantic feature hypothesis will be able to account for all the changes that occur in the development of word meanings, the hypothesis is consistent with a variety of observations, and it does provide a way to make sense out of some of the unconventional ways in which children use the words in their vocabularies.

The Learning of Grammatical Rules

Language acquisition involves a lot more than learning the conventional meanings of words. People generally have many more meanings to express than they have words in their vocabularies. Moreover, the meanings that people have to express are often unique, so that a speaker who depended on a one-to-one correspondence between words and meanings would have to coin a new word for each new meaning. Imagine a person trying to recount a day in his life by using one word to describe each of the events that occurred. The impossibility of communicating in this fashion indicates why language acquisition is not just a matter of vocabulary development, even when qualitative changes in word meaning are taken into account.

There are two fundamental ways in which to get more mileage out of words so that they can be used to express a great variety of meanings. One way is to modify or inflect the basic meaning of a word in such a way that its inflected meaning is more appropriate for the situation the speaker has in mind. Such inflections are usually signaled by changes in the sound of a word. In English, for example, a person who is speaking of events in the past may change *come* to *came,* or *walk* to *walked.* This sort of device is much more economical than having to come up with an entirely new word for the same action in the past as opposed to the present.

The second way to extend the use of vocabulary is to put words together in combinations, such that the *combinations* express the unique meanings for which there are no single words. Even a modest vocabulary of a few hundred words can be combined in various ways to produce thousands of sentences with different meanings. And, of course, the sentences themselves can be further combined in various ways, so that the number of meanings that can be expressed is virtually unlimited. Thus, the real power of language as a way of expressing meanings derives from its combinatorial possibilities.

In order to capitalize on the combinatorial possibilities of language, a language user must know how to signal the intended *relationships* among the words in a given combination. For example, suppose the words *dog, cat,* and *chased* are spoken in one combination. Without any additional information, a listener might guess—from his knowledge about cats and dogs, or from the context in which the words are uttered—that the speaker means that "the dog chased the cat." But suppose the speaker really means to say that "the cat chased the dog." To make his meaning clear, the speaker needs some way of indicating that the cat was the chas*er* and the dog was the chas*ee.* In some languages (for example, German and Russian) the speaker could do this by inflecting the words *dog* and *cat* with appropriate case endings that would distinguish the actor from the object of the action. In other languages (such as English) these relations would be signaled by the particular *order* in which the words were spoken ("the cat chased the dog") or by the addition of certain "function" words ("the dog *was* chased *by* the cat").

Just as words have conventional meanings, there are also conventions, or rules, with regard to the ways in which words can be inflected and combined in a given language. In other words, a language has not only a lexicon but also a grammar. Thus, an important part of language acquisition is the learning of grammatical rules. We will look at just two examples of such rule learning in English, one having to do with inflections of verbs and the other having to do with word combinations in negative sentences.

Past-Tense Verb Inflections.[28] Sometime between the ages of two and three, a child will begin to produce the past tense of common irregular verbs (such as *came* and *went*). This usually happens before the child produces the past tense of regular verbs (such as *walked* and *climbed*). Later, as he begins to use regular past tenses, he may also begin to use the regular -*ed* inflection on irregular verbs (for example, *comed* and *goed,* or even *camed* and *wented*). Eventually the child goes on to consistent use of *came, went,* and so on, along with instances of the regular past tense.

It would appear that the child acquires a particular verb form, then loses it, and then reacquires it. On closer inspection, however, it seems more likely that the early use of *came* and *went* does not reflect the same linguistic knowledge as later use of the same words. Initially, words like *came* and *went* are probably learned in specific contexts, so that their status as past-tense verbs is not clear to the child. They are just separate vocabulary items that may be substituted for *come* and *go*. Later, as the child begins to get the general idea of past tense, he first discovers how it is signaled for regular verbs, and then he overgeneralizes the regular -*ed* inflection to all the verbs in his vocabulary. Finally, he learns that certain verbs are exceptions to the general rule. Thus, the emergence of *comed* and *goed* actually reflects progress in language development, rather than a step backward or a step in the wrong direction.

The overgeneralization of regular verb inflections reveals two important characteristics of language acquisition in general. First, words like *comed* and *goed* are constructed by the child, rather than being imitated from the speech of others. We know this is the case because such overgeneralizations have been observed in the speech of first-born children whose parents have not provided any examples of overgeneralization for the children to imitate. Second, the phenomenon of overgeneralization indicates that children are inclined to learn general rules rather than isolated instances. Should there be any doubt about this, it can easily be demonstrated that the -*ed* inflection represents a general rule for the child, once it has become at all frequent in his spontaneous speech. Simply give the child a nonsense verb, one that he could not have heard before, and then get the child to use the verb in a context that requires a past-tense inflection. For example, one might say the following: "I know a man who likes to gling. Every day he glings. Yesterday he _____." Most four-year-olds will supply the word *glinged* without any hesitation.[29]

Negative Sentences.[30] When a child is just beginning to put two or three words together, he has a very straightforward rule for making negative statements: just add the word *no* (or *not*) to the beginning or end of the statement that is to be negated. This rule is reflected in such utterances as "no singing song" or "wear mitten no." These statements are so simple that the child's meaning is perfectly clear (assuming that the identity of the actor can be inferred from the contexts in which the statements were made). However, notice what happens when the same rule is applied to a more complex sentence of the sort that might be uttered by an older child or an adult. If someone said "I'll stay here if you turn on the television no," his meaning would be ambiguous. He could mean "I won't stay here if you turn on the television," or "I won't stay here if you don't turn on the television."

It is evident, then, that the mature rules of negation will be much more complex than the simple rule with which the child begins. The later rules will specify that the negative element must be inserted at a particular point within the sentence and that sometimes a function word must be added, too (as when "You turn on the television" becomes "You *do* not turn on the television"). As we would predict from cognitive theory, the mature rules of negation are approached through a series of steps involving intermediate rules. This developmental progression is too complex for us to go into it here, so we will mention only a couple of interesting details.

In going beyond his first simple rule of negation, the child soon begins to use such negative words as *can't* and *don't,* as in "I can't see you." At first, however, these words seem to be single vocabulary items rather than contractions of *can* or *do* with *not.* The evidence for this is that *can* and *do* are not yet used in affirmative statements. In this regard, *can't* and *don't* are similar to *came* and *went,* in that the child does not initially construct them but rather acquires them as "prefabricated" units. When words are acquired in this fashion, one must beware of overestimating the child's linguistic competence on the basis of his performance.

The intermediate rules that a child constructs during the development of negation may lead him to produce some utterances that will horrify his parents, such as "I can't do nothing with no string." Upon hearing their child produce such a multiple negative, some middle-class parents may want to know where the child "picked up *that* kind of language." The point is that he probably did not "pick it up" at all; rather he *made* it up, on the basis of his own rules for negation. Once again, an "error" may be a sign of developmental progress.

The reference to multiple negatives leads us to one last point about the acquisition of grammatical rules in general. What the child acquires is a set of *descriptive* rules rather than *prescriptive* rules. Descriptive rules simply describe the regularities in a language as it is spoken by the members of a particular community. Such rules are not "prescribed" by an authority on the proper way to talk; they are just norms of language behavior. In some languages (such as Russian) and in some dialects of English, multiple negation *is* the norm, and therefore it is not a sign of linguistic immaturity or incorrect usage. In other words, a child's progress in language acquisition must be assessed in relation to the norms of his language community.

Summary

Although no one has identified overall stages of language development analogous to the stages described by Piaget and Kohlberg in other areas of development,[31] we have nonetheless seen evidence of stagelike progressions in the development of word meanings and in the acquisition of rules for inflecting and combining words. Such phenomena as overextension and overgeneralization indicate that the child constructs his own rules for relating sounds to meanings, and that he revises his rules until they correspond to the rules shared by mature speakers of the language. Each new set of rules may be thought of as a cognitive structure that builds upon the ones that preceded it but is qualitatively different from them.

In addition, it is possible to see in language acquisition the same directional trends that occur in other areas of intellectual development. For example, the way a child acquires the rules for negation seems clearly to involve an expanding field of equilibrium. The initial rule for negation can be applied successfully only to very simple sentences, whereas later rules will work with increasingly complex sentences. Thus, language acquisition has much the same character as other areas of intellectual development, as seen from the cognitive point of view.

SUMMARY

The cognitive approach has yielded a great deal of information on what children know and how they think about all sorts of things. Consequently, this has been a very long chapter, ranging far and wide over four major areas of intellectual development. Our summary will consist only of a brief review of the main topics covered.

The child's understanding of the physical world was discussed with respect to his knowledge of objects, space, time, and causality. Development in each of these areas was followed through the four periods described by Piaget. Our discussion of logical and mathematical thinking, also based on Piaget, touched on the child's understanding of classes, relations, number, propositional logic, and double reversibility. In the area of the social world, we discussed the development of moral judgment, concentrating on Kohlberg's theory of stages, and we examined some promising work on the development of "naïve" theory with respect to interpersonal behavior. Finally, the area of language acquisition was surveyed briefly with respect to the development of word meanings and the learning of grammatical rules. Throughout the chapter, we have tried to show how each area reflects the character of intellectual development in general, as seen from the cognitive point of view.

13

IMPLICATIONS OF A COGNITIVE THEORY FOR EDUCATION

Preview

This chapter considers some parallels between current educational practices and principles of cognitive theory, along with some limitations on putting theory into practice. It then examines three major facets of education.

In *describing and selecting instructional goals,* cognitive theory provides some general guidelines as to what is possible and desirable.

With regard to *strategies of instruction,* the theory suggests ways to extend old cognitive structures to incorporate new content, and to develop new structures for old content.

As for *assessment of the learner,* the theory offers the clinical method as a way of eliciting revealing performances.

Generally, cognitive theory has two implications for education: (1) the learner develops through an ordered series of stages, which should be taken into account, and (2) the learner should be helped to construct new understandings through his own activity.

Cognitive theory has generally not been formulated for the purpose of improving education: it is a theory of *development,* not of instruction. Nevertheless, it is reasonable to expect important educational implications from an approach that focuses on how children think and how their thinking changes during development. This expectation seems to be borne out by the fact that some basic principles of the cognitive approach correspond to a number of recent innovations in educational practice.

For instance, the principle that children do not think in the same ways as adults and that they must acquire in the course of development some basic ideas adults take for granted is in many ways the foundation for the "new curricula" of the past 20 years. Various versions of the "new math," for example, have been designed to promote the development of such basic skills as classification and conservation rather than the rote learning of arithmetic. Another principle of cognitive theory—that the child must construct his own understanding of classes, number, and the other basic ideas to be acquired— seems to be a theoretical basis for "learning by discovery" and for an "individualized" approach to instruction. The theory that a child constructs new understandings out of his own activities seems to imply an activity-based instruction oriented toward "learning by doing." Finally, Piaget's theory identifying the elementary school years as the period of concrete operations provides a rationale for stressing activities involving manipulation of concrete objects, even with older children who are in the first "stages" of learning something new.

All these theoretical notions and their practical counterparts seem to be embodied in the current concept of an "open classroom." This term, like the other educational slogans we have mentioned, has come to have many different meanings, but usually it refers to a situation in which children are free to move about the classroom, or even beyond the classroom, engaging in constructive activities of their own choosing, either individually or in small groups. The open classroom seems designed for a child who is constructing his own theory of the world through active experimentation with the environment —the kind of child described by cognitive theory.

There are both historical and logical reasons for the correspondences we have noted between cognitive theory and educational practice. The decade of the 1960s saw the "rediscovery" of Piaget by American psychologists and educators and also a renewed interest in educational reform among many groups concerned with the performance of American schools.[1] During this period, many people addressed themselves both to psychological and to educational issues. For example, Piaget, who is primarily a cognitive theorist, spoke approvingly of an approach to education that sounds much like the open classroom described above.[2] This image of the open classroom does seem logically more consistent with cognitive theory than, for example, with S-R theory, which emphasizes careful management of reinforcers and diligent monitoring of specific types of learner behavior.

Despite the apparent agreement of cognitive theory and "new" approaches to education, it is important to take a closer look at the relationships between specific theoretical principles and educational practices. The road from theory to practice is hazardous, with unmarked forks and places needing bridges. In this chapter, we will consider the implications of cognitive theory with regard to three major aspects of education: the description and selection of educational goals; strategies for instruction; and the problem of assessing the learner. But first, we will discuss the advantages of deriving practical implications from a theory versus seeking recommendations from a theorist, and we will note some limitations of cognitive theory in its implications for educational practice.

THEORY VERSUS THEORIST

As we consider the relationship between cognitive theory and educational practice, it should be clear that the first party in this relationship is a *theory* and not a *theorist.* Thus, for example, we are interested in what Piaget's *theory* has to say about education and not necessarily in what *Piaget* has said about education. Let us see why this is an important distinction.

Here a theory is a set of guiding principles that provides a framework for understanding human development. To be sure, the theory must first be stated by a theorist, but once it has been set forth, a theory becomes a public tool that anyone can use in thinking about intellectual development. A theorist, however, is one who creates or subscribes to a particular theory, and who, like all of us, has personal values and intuitive hunches about human behavior that are not part of his theory. The problem is that the theorist cannot always separate his personal values and intuitions from his attempts to use the theory for practical recommendations.

Why is this problem? Certainly the theorist has as much right as anyone else to make practical recommendations that are influenced by his own values and intuitions. Some of his recommendations might even be very helpful. But suppose he simply tells us what he thinks is a good idea, not explaining his reasoning behind it and not being available for consultation later. And suppose we encounter a new classroom situation that he did not have in mind when he advised us. All we can do then is follow the same recommendations, hoping they still work, or else follow our own intuitions, hoping they will see us through. If we follow the theorist and are not pleased with the results, it may be because the new situation requires a different use of the theory, the theory itself is inadequate, the theorist's intuitions were wrong, or the theorist has different values than we have.

The theorist would be more helpful if he showed us how his recommendation was derived logically from his theory. Then we could use the theory to decide for ourselves whether the recommendation applies to a new situation, and we could begin to figure out what might have gone wrong if the recommendation did not work out. Thus, in the sections that follow, we will concentrate on the educational implications of cognitive theory, rather than on the educational recommendations of cognitive theorists.[3]

The implications to be discussed here have been drawn from theories that must be regarded as tentative in many respects. Therefore, these implications should be tested out in actual practice. Piaget has pointed to the need for an "experimental pedagogy," a field that systematically investigates the effects of various educational programs and teaching methods.[4] For reasons we will discuss, it is not possible for an educator to deduce a reliable method of teaching simply by consulting a theory of intellectual development. Even if the theory is essentially correct, the methods it implies must be tried out and evaluated on the basis of their results. Educational researchers have been trying to evaluate teaching methods for years, but their efforts generally have not had a sufficient grounding in psychological theory and thus have not been very fruitful. Consequently, we are faced with a mass of inconclusive and contradictory findings on various approaches to teaching reading, for example. Experimental pedagogy can use theories of intellectual development as guidelines for deciding which methods of instruction to try and for interpreting the results. At the same time, as more is learned about the ways instruction actually affects development, experimental pedagogy can lead to more adequate theories of intellectual development.

LIMITATIONS OF COGNITIVE THEORY FOR EDUCATIONAL PRACTICE

As we noted in Chapter 1, no theory can provide ready-made solutions to all the teaching problems that might arise in actual practice. No theory can offer teachers a guarantee that "If you do such and such, then the learner will do such and such." The reason for this limitation is that any real situation involves far more variables than a single theory can take into account. Learners differ from each other in countless ways, and so do their physical and social environments. Moreover, a teacher's actions are bound to interact with these variables, so that a method that works in one situation may not work in others. Each theory has focused on just some of the variables that affect instruction, and therefore each theory has paid less attention to other variables that might be equally important in practice. Let us first see which variables cognitive theory tends to ignore, and then take note of the variables that concern cognitive theory most.

In discussing the cognitive model of behavior (Chapter 10), we pointed out that certain aspects of behavior are more or less taken for granted in cognitive theory. For one thing, the translation of cognition into behavior is generally assumed to be automatic, so that the performance skills that make this translation possible tend to be ignored. Thus, for example, cognitive theory would be more concerned with a young child's ability to see the difference between the letters *c* and *o* than with his ability to write them legibly. Cognitive theory does not offer the teacher much help in the teaching of such performance skills as handwriting.

A second aspect of behavior that the cognitive model tends to ignore is motivation, especially with respect to its noncognitive sources. Relying on its concept of intrinsic motivation, cognitive theory might predict that a child who is in the process of acquiring concrete operations with regard to number and space might easily be motivated to engage in instructional activities that involve the measurement of spatial dimensions. Presumably the teacher would only have to make the needed materials available and perhaps suggest what might be done with them. Notice, however, that this prediction ignores the possible effects of other motives that might compete with the intrinsic appeal of the measurement activity. The child might actually be more inclined to read or to wrestle with a classmate, in which case the teacher would have to find alternate means for engaging the child in measurement activities (or alternate activities that would lead to the same instructional objectives).

Cognitive theory also cannot make guarantees or predictions about the particulars of behavior that a teacher should use or that he can expect. Instead, it is the structure that lies behind behavior that is analyzed and specified by the theory. Thus, for example, the structure of a student's reasoning on a problem like "floating and sinking objects" cannot be unambiguously deduced from a single answer or statement or manipulation of the materials. Instead it must be inferred from the total set of his experimental procedures and verbal statements. That is, there is no key phrase or critical behavior that, by itself, will tell a teacher the structure of a student's thinking. In fact, two students who utter the same statement may be classified differently depending on what else they say or how they have organized their experiments.

A fourth limitation of cognitive theory for educational practice also stems from its emphasis on the structural aspects of cognition rather than its content. Although the cognitive approach has been applied to several different areas of content (see Chapter 12), the goal of cognitive theory generally has been a structural analysis of the child's knowledge or thought within each area. Thus, so far, it has not been a major concern of cognitive theory to discover why some kinds of content are more easily assimilated to the same structures than others. For example, cognitive theorists generally have not tried in any systematic way to explain why the conservation of weight is almost always achieved later than the conservation of amount, even though both tasks involve concrete operations.[5] But an explanation of such differences in content could be useful in planning instruction, because a teacher might want to predict which kinds of content the learner will be able to assimilate easily and which kinds he will not. At present, cognitive theory cannot make very precise predictions of this sort. What is needed is an analysis of the structure of the environment, to go along with present analyses of cognitive structure.[6]

We come now to what is probably the most basic limitation of all, so far as the application of current cognitive theories to teaching is concerned. Teaching is essentially an attempt to change the learner by manipulating environmental conditions, including not only the physical environment but also the social environment with which the learner interacts. Unfortunately, because cognitive theory has not described the structure of the environment, it has not focused on the particular environmental variables that normally bring about changes in cognitive structure. Cognitive theory does not tell teachers exactly how to present materials and give instructions that will help the learner assimilate new contents to his current structures. Nor does it tell the teacher exactly how to arrange a situation in which the learner will acquire a new cognitive structure. Instead, cognitive theory has concentrated on describing the kinds of structural changes that do occur in the course of development and on making the general point that environmental variables can only bring about changes in cognitive structure through their effects on the processes of assimilation, accommodation, and equilibration.

In evaluating these limitations of the cognitive approach, it is important to try to distinguish between those that issue more from fundamental characteristics of the theory and those that may only be the result of its current level of development. Thus, it is possible that the theory will eventually try to handle the last two limitations—the lack of emphasis on the structure of particular content and on the nature of disequilibrating environmental factors. But it may never choose to deal with performance skills, noncognitive motivational factors, or the detailed specification of behavior.

Having pointed out some weaknesses of cognitive theory vis-à-vis educational practice, we will close this discussion on a more positive note by mentioning briefly some strengths of cognitive theory. There are some variables of major importance that the cognitive approach brings to the attention of an educator who is devising methods of instruction. First, cognitive theory attempts to provide descriptions of how the learner's thinking is likely to be structured at a given point in development. Second, the notion of an invariant order of stages implies that there is a fixed sequence of steps in the process by which the learner's thinking is restructured. Third, by postulating equilibration as the basic factor that accounts for developmental change, cognitive theory suggests the *general* kinds of conditions that will bring about a restructuring in the learner's thinking. Finally, cognitive theory offers a description of an "active" learner who, at any stage of development, seeks to assimilate environmental situations to his present cognitive structures and, at the same time, accommodates those structures to novel elements in the situations being assimilated. Each of these contributions from cognitive theory can influence decisions about instruction, and each of them will be discussed further in the sections that follow.

THE GOALS OF EDUCATION

The goals of education are, of course, the changes in the learner that are intended to result from instruction—what the learner is supposed to "have" after instruction that he did not have before. Cognitive theory cannot answer all questions about the goals of education, but it can help guide our thinking about what the learner is to be taught. For one thing, the theory suggests a useful way of *describing* the goals of education. It also has quite a bit to say about how they are *selected*.

Describing the Goals of Education

Assume for the moment that the general purpose of education is to contribute to a person's intellectual development (we will come back to this assumption later). Cognitive theory states that intellectual development is a series of changes in cognitive structure, and this suggests that the goals of education can be described in structural terms, too. If someone says that a child should have a basic understanding of number, cognitive theory asks what *kind* of understanding he should have, how his thinking about number will be *structured*, since a particular area of content can be structured in different ways, at different levels. In Chapter 12 we saw that to understand number at the level of concrete operations the child must understand the structures of classification and seriation. To the cognitive theorist, a description of these structural elements would state the objective more usefully than would the phrase "a basic understanding of number."

In the above example, an educational goal was described first by identifying an area of content (number) and then by adding some structural specifications (certain schemes of concrete operations). But the description of the goal might also be approached this way: if someone says a goal is the attainment of concrete operations, we could ask, with regard to what? The conservation of amounts of clay? The inclusion of classes consisting of wooden beads? Just as a given area of content may be structured at different developmental levels, so a given level of structure may be applied to different areas of content. To attain the level of concrete operations in one area does not mean the same way of thinking works in other areas, as we saw when we discussed the concept of horizontal *décalage* (Chapter 11).

An educational objective must be described both in structure and content—psychologically, it is impossible to have one without the other. Even at the level of formal operations, where some logicomathematical structures are potentially pure forms free of any particular content, a person does not automatically apply these forms to all areas of content: some areas may be more difficult to assimilate than others, simply because the person has had less experience in these areas or because they are inherently more resistant to assimilation.[7]

If we describe the goals of education as being cognitive structures within particular areas of content, and if cognitive structures are mental entities that are not observable, how will we know when a particular goal has been attained? The answer is that we must proceed as though we were a cognitive psychologist conducting research on intellectual development: the attainment of a cognitive structure must be inferred from the child's behavior in many situations involving the kind of content specified. For example, several tasks described under logicomathematical thinking in Chapter 12 might be used to assess a child's understanding of number at the level of concrete operations.

The cognitive approach will not help us describe an educational objective as a restricted set of specific performances. Such "behavioral objectives" may seem straightforward and easy to evaluate, but they can be quite misleading. For one thing, a learner can produce specific performances without having achieved the underlying ability he is supposed to have. For example, he might spew out simple facts of arithmetic without really understanding number; thus, his *performance* may lead the observer to overestimate his *competence*. But he might achieve a deeper understanding without manifesting it in every possible performance. For example, if a child makes computational errors in arithmetic, it does not necessarily mean he failed to grasp the basic concept of number; his performance might lead to an *underestimation* of his competence. In sum, there is no one-to-one correspondence between competence (cognitive structure) and performance (behavior). Therefore, it would be a mistake to define a structural objective as a specific number of performances, or to forget that performance only indirectly relates to competence.

But we must qualify what we just said. At times specific performances are worthy objectives. For example, we might decide that no matter how well a learner demonstrates he understands number, he still has not attained an important educational objective if he cannot quickly supply the correct answer to such problems as $7 + 8 = ?$ or $9 - 3 = ?$. However, most educational objectives are selected with the hope that the learner will actually be capable of an unlimited variety of performances once the objective is attained, in much the same way that a person's knowledge of grammatical rules enables him to understand and express an infinite variety of meanings. Thus, in most cases, we could more appropriately describe the goal as a cognitive structure than as a restricted set of performances. Behavioral objectives may invite "teaching to the test"—that is, teaching the outward symptoms of a structure without teaching the structure itself.

Selecting the Goals of Education

Most people would define education as an attempt to change a person for the better by helping him acquire new knowledge or skills. But not everyone would agree on what this change for the better is. This is a question of values, and different people have different values. For this reason, many psychologists have declared their theories neutral on the value questions of selecting the goals of education. From this point of view, a psychological theory only comes into play once the overall goals of education have been established. The theory is then used to describe the objectives more precisely and to design a program of instruction for attaining them. However, the position of cognitive theory on this issue is rather different, because the theory has a kind of value system built into it. Therefore, we must discuss the matter of selecting educational goals in some detail.

In cognitive theory, the notion of a change for the better has a clear meaning: it is a change that makes an individual more able to adapt to his environment—that is, it makes him more intelligent. As we saw in Chapter 9, greater intelligence is characterized by forms of cognition that are less egocentric and more objective and that cover a broader field of equilibrium. Since these qualities describe the general direction of intellectual development, it follows that the overall goal of education should be to facilitate the natural process of development.

The developmental changes that make a person more intelligent are described in cognitive theory as changes in cognitive structure. Two kinds of structural change are possible: either a new structure may be acquired with regard to old content or an old structure may be extended to include new content. The first kind of change is illustrated when a child progresses from intuitive rules to concrete operations in his thinking about quantity and is therefore able to conserve. The second kind of change would occur if a child first acquired the logic of class hierarchies with regard to the animal kingdom and then extended the same logic in learning how to classify words by parts of speech. In both cases, the child acquires a particular way of thinking about a particular kind of content.

We suggested in the preceding section that the goals of education can be described in exactly the same way—that is, as a change of structure with regard to content, or as an addition of content to a particular structure. However, a crucial question has yet to be answered. Of all the possible changes that could be described in this way, which ones should be selected as the objectives of instruction? In other words, what should the learner be taught? Before we discuss this question, we should make it clear that we will not use the terms "instruction" and "teaching" in their traditional didactic senses. Rather, they will refer to any deliberate arrangement of conditions that are intended to bring about a desired change in the learner. Some general strategies by which this might be done are discussed later in the chapter. Two questions will concern us here: Is it *possible* to produce certain changes in the learner by means of instruction? Is it *desirable* to produce such changes? Both questions must be considered in deciding what to teach a given learner at a particular point in time.

On What Is Possible.   One question that can be raised with regard to many changes in cognitive structure is whether it is even *possible* to bring about such changes by means of instruction. Many people have had the impression that the kinds of developmental changes described by Piaget, for example, cannot be influenced by teaching. This impression probably stems from two sources. First, it has been found that virtually all children in modern industrial cultures go through the same structural changes at approximately the same ages without any special instruction. Second, several early attempts to teach conservation to preoperational children by means of experimental training procedures did not succeed. Taken together, these findings have led people to conclude that the changes described by Piaget are strictly the result of maturation, and that one therefore has no choice but to stand by and wait for them to occur.

However, our discussion of the equilibration process in Chapter 11 ought to have made it clear that this interpretation of Piaget's theory is incorrect. There is no reason, in principle, to believe that conservation might not be taught before children acquire it on their own, and the same can be said with regard to other structural changes too. Moreover, there is now some evidence from more recent training experiments showing that conservation can, in fact, be taught under certain conditions. Similarly successful attempts to accelerate structural change have been reported in the areas of moral judgment and language development.[8]

On the other hand, there are undoubtedly cases in which it would *not* be possible to bring about certain structural changes in a particular learner at a particular time and place by means of instruction. One obstacle to the teaching of a new cognitive structure might be the factor of maturation. A child may just not be ready organically to acquire a certain structure at a particular time. Recall that, according to cognitive theory, maturation is necessary but not sufficient for development to occur. Cognitive theory is not, at present, in a position to say exactly what the maturational constraints on learning are, but the possibility of such constraints must always be considered. Aside from maturation, it is also conceivable that a teacher simply would not be able to arrange enough of the experiences necessary to bring about a new structure within a particular period of time. As we saw in Chapter 11, the process of development occurs gradually, through a series of small steps, and therefore it probably cannot be speeded up beyond a certain point.

Given our present ignorance about maturation and about the small steps involved in development, probably the most we can say is that (1) it *is* possible to accelerate the acquisition of a more advanced cognitive structure by teaching, and (2) there must be limits as to how early or how quickly a particular structure can be taught. The earlier a structure is taught before its normal time of emergence, or the shorter the period of instruction, the less likely it is that an attempt to accelerate development will succeed.

With regard to the acquisition of new *content,* the question of what is possible seems relatively straightforward. To justify the teaching of new content at a particular structural level, it must first be shown that it will be possible for the learner to assimilate the new material at the intended level. In other words, it must be ascertained that the learner already has the type of structure that is to be extended to the new content. Otherwise, the content will not be learned at the intended level, at least not without the prior attainment of some prerequisite objectives.

On What Is Desirable. Just because it may be possible to do something, that is generally not a sufficient reason for doing it. Even if the acquisition of a new cognitive structure can be induced by teaching, there remains the question of whether such teaching is *desirable.* Teaching a particular structure may not be worth the time and effort involved, especially if the structure will be acquired spontaneously later on. On the other hand, there may be times when such teaching is justified. Cognitive theory can provide only a limited amount of help in answering a question of this sort. We will discuss three reasons that might be given for attempting to induce a structural change by teaching, aside from the fact that it is possible to do so.

The teaching of a structure before it is acquired spontaneously might be justified on the grounds that, in the near future, the environment will make certain inevitable demands on the learner that will require the structure that is to be taught. Without the needed structure, the learner will have great difficulty in adapting to his future environment, so he must be equipped with the structure beforehand. For example, someone might argue that the learner will need the scheme of "all other things being equal" in order to conduct controlled experiments in his junior high school science classes during the next school year. Similar arguments have been made in favor of compensatory education programs for learners who are considered to be "disadvantaged" in the usual school environment because of their past experience.

It is quite consistent with cognitive theory to select educational goals with an eye toward the learner's future environment. However, the nature of the environment is generally determined by social and natural forces that have little to do with cognitive theory. Therefore, when a particular goal is selected because it will prepare the learner for the demands of his environment, the selection of this goal is based as much on practical considerations as it is on cognitive theory. On the other hand, there are ways in which cognitive theory might actually influence the environment itself. For example, one might use cognitive theory to question the wisdom of requiring junior high school students to perform controlled experiments in their science classes, perhaps on the grounds that it would be much easier for the students to learn the same things a few years later. With this particular demand removed from the junior high school environment, there might be no reason to teach the scheme of "all other things being equal" until high school. By that time, it might not even be necessary, because most students would have acquired the scheme anyway, without it being taught.

In any case, given a description of the particular demands that the learner is likely to encounter, cognitive theory can play a role in the selection of instructional goals. It can predict the kinds of structures that the learner will need in order to meet the anticipated demands, and it can also predict the stages that the learner will have to go through in order to acquire the needed structures. However, such predictions should not be accepted as facts; they can and should be tested.

There is a second way to justify the teaching of a cognitive structure instead of waiting for the learner to acquire it on his own. This justification is based on the notion of a "critical period," a time in development during which, for biological reasons, an individual is more susceptible to specific environmental influences than he is before or after. In order for certain experiences to have an optimal effect on the development of a particular structure, they must occur during the critical period for that structure. The argument for teaching, then, is that the learner's general environment might not provide enough of the experiences needed for the development of a particular structure within its critical period, so that the structure must be taught while it is still possible. There is not much evidence to prove the existence of critical periods of intellectual development, but there is not much evidence to deny their existence either. It is a question in need of further research. In the meantime, as long as cognitive theory acknowledges the possible contribution of maturational factors to development, it must also acknowledge the possibility of critical periods.[9]

Even if critical periods do not exist, one could still justify the teaching of a cognitive structure on the grounds that it would not be acquired otherwise. It could be argued that the general environment is set up in such a way that many people would never acquire a certain structure without some sort of special help in the form of instruction. This seems to be a good possibility with respect to the most advanced structures in a given area of development. Recent research suggests that perhaps a majority of American adults do not reach Piaget's period of formal operations, or Kohlberg's level of principled moral judgment.[10] Let us assume that many of these people are nonetheless capable of reaching the highest stages of development. In other words, it would still be possible, at least in principle, to teach them the most advanced structures. The question now is, would this goal be *desirable?* Is the attainment of a more advanced structure necessarily a change for the better? For reasons that we will try to outline briefly, this is actually a rather profound question.

We have been assuming all along that the ultimate goal of education is to facilitate the natural process of development so that the learner can adapt to his environment. Now we are confronted with a large number of adults who are not fully developed intellectually. It is hard to believe that all these people are not well adapted to their environments. Perhaps they have developed far enough to get along quite well; perhaps their environments do not demand higher levels of cognition than they have attained. If so, then it would appear that the goal of education has already been achieved and that the facilitation of further development by teaching is therefore unnecessary.

Let us reconsider our working definition of the goal of education. Is the goal simply to promote the individual's survival in the world as he finds it, or is there more to education than that? Man lives in an environment that is largely his own creation. Thus, he has the option of *changing* the environment, instead of simply accepting it the way it is and learning to live with it. Man is given the possibility of changing the environment in such a way that it will enhance the quality of life for the species as a whole. The goal of education might be redefined, then, as the facilitation of man's development toward that end.

Piaget's period of concrete operations and Kohlberg's level of conventional moral judgment represent forms of cognition that permit equilibrium with regard to the way things *are*. On the other hand, formal operations and principled morality permit equilibrium with regard to the way things *could be*. Since the latter forms of cognition (or something like them) could lead to the creation of a better world, it seems clear that the ultimate goal of education should be to facilitate development *to its highest stages*.[11] In this light, the promotion of more advanced cognitive structures by teaching is desirable whenever it appears that teaching is necessary to ensure that the most advanced structures will be acquired. This is not to say that adaptation to the way things are is unimportant. One must survive in the present world in order to construct a better one. Intelligence always entails a balance between accommodation (conformity to the environment) and assimilation (transformation of the environment).

Up to this point our discussion about the desirability of objectives has been slanted toward cases in which the learner is intended to acquire a new type of cognitive structure. However, similar considerations apply to the extension of an old structure to a new kind of content. There are two main reasons for thinking that a certain type of new content might be desirable. The first is that the content has some direct adaptive value in the learner's environment. For example, the learner may be led to extend his knowledge of classification to the kinds of topics on which books are written, so that he can more easily use the card catalog in a library. A certain kind of instructional content might also be considered desirable because it would provide better opportunities for the development of a more advanced type of structure. Thus, a preoperational child might be encouraged to pursue his interest in collecting rocks, not because his interest in rocks has any direct adaptive value, but because the task of identifying various rocks might help the child learn about classification.

The latter criterion for deciding which content to teach opens up a great number of possibilities. All sorts of content could be used to further a child's structural development, although some kinds of content may serve this purpose more readily than others. However, before a particular content goal is selected on this basis, it still seems reasonable to require evidence that the structure in question might not be attained in due time without special instruction. Otherwise the educator might spend his time assisting a developmental process that needs no assistance rather than teaching something that really needs to be taught.

Summary

Cognitive theory would lead one to describe the goals of education as particular ways of thinking about particular kinds of content. The attainment of such goals is inferred from different kinds of behavior in a variety of situations, not from a restricted set of specific performances.

The general goal of education is to facilitate the natural process of development. With regard to the specific objectives of instruction, virtually any cognitive structure is a *possible* objective at some point, but there are maturational and experiential limits as to how early and how quickly the development of a particular structure can be brought about by teaching. A possible objective might also be *desirable* at a given point in time because instruction is needed to prepare the learner for anticipated environmental demands, or to ensure the acquisition of a structure during its critical period, or to promote the attainment of the highest stages of development. In short, an objective is selected because it will facilitate development and because such facilitation seems necessary.

TWO STRATEGIES FOR INSTRUCTION

Once the goals of education have been selected and described, there remains the question of how to attain them. From the educator's point of view, the question is, what methods should be used to achieve these objectives? We will begin our discussion of instructional methods here by exploring two basic strategies for helping the learner attain specific objectives. However, the topic of methods will come up again when we go on to consider the problem of assessing the learner.

In discussing the goals of education, we noted that there are two means by which a person can acquire a particular way of thinking about a particular kind of content. He can either extend an old cognitive structure to new content, or he can acquire a new structure with regard to old content. These two possibilities suggest two basic strategies for instruction. The teacher can either help the learner acquire new content in terms of a familiar structure, or the teacher can help the learner develop a new structure with regard to familiar content.

Helping the Learner Acquire New Content

In this section we will explore the first of the two strategies—helping the learner extend old structures to new content. The following facets of this strategy will be considered: teaching the learner at his own level, and promoting assimilation and accommodation.

Teaching the Learner at His Own Level.   In essence, the first strategy is based on the idea that the best way to help the learner acquire new content is to teach it to him on a level he can readily understand. The learner will generally try to assimilate new content to old structures anyway, so teachers might as well set out with the idea of facilitating this process instead of fighting it. With this strategy, the learner's way of thinking becomes an ally of instruction rather than an enemy. Let us first consider the consequences of failing to teach the learner on his own level, before going on to discuss two ways to implement the basic strategy.

Trying to teach new content at too high a level for the learner can have some distinctly negative consequences. First of all, the material will most likely not be assimilated at the intended level. In fact, some of the material may not be assimilated at all; it may simply go over the learner's head. Furthermore, what the learner does assimilate may not be structured in the most productive way possible at his present stage of development. In his attempts to assimilate what is largely unassimilable, the learner may end up with an odd collection of facts, or some rote procedures for getting by, rather than a coherent understanding of the sort that might later be restructured at a more advanced level. Even worse, the learner may misconstrue the content altogether. It is important to note that these negative consequences actually result from the selection of an instructional objective that is not *possible* for the learner in question. To make these points clear, we have constructed a rather exaggerated example of a poor fit between the level of instruction and the learner's stage of development. However, it is not entirely unrepresentative of the way in which young children are sometimes taught.

Suppose that for some reason it seems desirable to teach the concept of "parallel" to children who are in the intuitive phase of the preoperational period (roughly ages five to six). Suppose also that the concept is presented to them at the formal level, by means of a definition: "Two straight lines are parallel if they are on the same plane and would never meet even if extended in length to infinity." Now consider the kinds of structures a preoperational child would and would not have for assimilating this bit of content. Because the concept of infinity requires hypothetical thinking, it seems unlikely that it could mean much more than "very long" to preoperational learners, even if explained to them in great detail. In addition, we saw in Chapter 12 that children generally do not have the notion of a projective straight line at this stage of development. On the other hand, the learners probably would have had many concrete experiences corresponding to the words *line* (including the kind one stands in at a supermarket) and *plane* (especially the kind that flies).

Given all these conditions, it would not be surprising to find that some learners come away from the lesson with the idea that parallel refers to a long line of people waiting to board an airplane! Although it is not clear that this idea would necessarily interfere with the later learning of parallel, it is unlikely that it would be much help. Had the concept been presented at an intuitive level, the results might have been much more satisfactory. The learners probably could have understood that two objects, such as two pencils, are parallel when they are placed side by side and point in the same direction. This understanding of parallel, though not complete, is on the right track and could be refined and restructured at later stages of development.

This example relates to a question that is sometimes raised about the desirability of teaching something before the learner can really understand it. Will such teaching be a help or a hindrance later on? From what we have just said, the answer clearly seems to be that it depends on how the content is presented initially. If it is adjusted to the learner's present stage of development, there is no reason to believe that the early teaching of a particular subject will have negative consequences in the future. Moreover, it would provide an opportunity to use the second teaching strategy—that is, facilitating the formation of a new structure with regard to old content. On the other hand, if early teaching is not adjusted to the learner's level, the learning that results may very well interfere with later learning.

Promoting Assimilation and Accommodation. Instruction need not simply conform to the learner's present way of thinking; it can also try to capitalize on it. Sometimes the learner will have an appropriate structure at his disposal but will not spontaneously use it to assimilate the material being taught. The teacher's job, then, is to show the learner that he already has a structure that will enable him to understand the new material.

Suppose a high school chemistry teacher wants his students to get the idea that a given compound can be either an acid or a base in a chemical reaction, depending on the other compound in the reaction. The students are confused by this concept because they have learned to call some compounds acids and other compounds bases, regardless of the reactions they are in. For example, they are accustomed to calling ammonia a base, and so they are puzzled when the teacher shows them some reactions in which ammonia plays the role of an acid. The teacher probably could eliminate the confusion by extending an old cognitive structure to the new content. His analysis of the problem might be as follows.

The essential idea to be learned is that chemical compounds can be ordered in a series from very acidic to very basic. When two compounds react with each other, a person can identify which is the acid and which is the base by noting their relative positions in the series. Thus, though ammonia would be considered a base relative to most other compounds, it would be an acid in a reaction with a compound that was even more basic. Now the logic of relations in an ordered series is acquired by most children at about age seven (see Chapter 12). Therefore, high school students are very likely to have a cognitive structure that could be extended to the new content in chemistry. The extension of this structure might be facilitated by means of an analogy. The students probably would agree that a person who is six feet is tall relative to most other people but short compared to someone who is six feet seven. Then it could be suggested that the students think of ammonia as being analogous to the person who is six feet. In this way, the new chemistry content will be assimilated to an old structure of concrete operations.

Two additional points should be made about this example. First, the particular analogy we suggested would not be effective in teaching most children below age seven. One probably would not be teaching young children the idea that acid and base are relative terms anyway, but he might be teaching the idea that strong and weak are relative terms. In any case, the analogy to a set of people ordered by height probably would not work, because young children generally lack the kind of cognitive structure required for seriation.

Consequently, it might be necessary to facilitate the formation of a new structure in order to have young children understand that two terms can be used in a relative sense.

Second, for the high school students in our example, the extension of an old structure to new content would have had an effect on the old structure itself. In order to assimilate the new content, the old structure would also have to accommodate. As a result, the modified structure would cover a broader field of equilibrium than before. Thus, in the future, there would be a greater likelihood that the students would spontaneously assimilate new contents to the structure for seriation, without special help from an instructor. But didactic instruction is not the only way to bring about such accommodation; it also happens in the process of play.

Much of a young child's life is taken up with activities that adults refer to as play. The common view of play is that it provides a means of relaxation and a source of pleasure, but little else. However, from a biological perspective, it would be most unusual to find a species in which a large portion of an individual's behavior had no adaptive value. Accordingly, a number of people have attempted to explain the developmental significance of play in childhood. We will discuss just one of the many functions that play probably performs.

Piaget has characterized play as a kind of activity in which assimilation predominates over accommodation. When a child is engaged in play, he temporarily suspends his adjustment to certain aspects of reality (accommodation) and transforms reality into something else (assimilation). Recall our example of the young child pretending to eat pebbles (Chapter 11). The point we wish to make here is that, despite the predominance of assimilation, play still involves a certain amount of accommodation, and therefore it expands the structures that a child has at his disposal for assimilating new content. In other words, play makes a child's cognitive structures more extendable.

Imagine a group of children playing "pirates" on the porch of an old frame house. The porch is their ship and the front yard is the sea on which they are sailing. An old bed sheet has been draped between two posts on the porch to serve as a sail, and a small round table has been turned on its side to make a wheel for steering the ship.

One can see the predominance of assimilation over accommodation in many instances. For example, the immobility of the porch and its attachment to a house are all but ignored in treating it as a ship. At the same time, the children have accommodated somewhat to the real situation in which their game takes place. They have had to work out a way to put up their sail, for example—a task that required them to find a rope that was long enough and strong enough. The children also have had to accommodate to certain realities within their fantasy. For instance, one of the pirates might be criticized by his playmates for walking on the water instead of pretending to swim. In other words, the children are not simply acting out a fantasy; they are also using their intelligence. And having used their intelligence in this way, they may be better prepared to assimilate reality with the structures that were used in play.

Accordingly, there is little reason to think of play and instruction as entirely separate domains of activity. A teacher can arrange play situations that are relevant to the goals of instruction and can even participate in play with the learner.

Helping the Learner Develop New Structures

The second basic strategy for instruction is to help the learner develop a new cognitive structure with regard to his thinking about familiar content. This strategy might also be thought of as helping the learner move up to a higher stage of development. However, it must be remembered that a new stage is not attained all at once with regard to all kinds of content. The initial formation of a higher-level structure in one area of content is followed by a period of consolidation and extension to other areas of content. It is the initial development of a new structure in a particular area that will concern us here.

Having already discussed the conditions under which it might be desirable to facilitate the development of a new structure, we will concentrate now on ways of implementing such facilitation as a basic strategy for instruction. First, let us elaborate on the question of what is possible when it comes to helping the learner develop a new structure. Then we will consider the problems of inducing disequilibrium and guiding the process of equilibration.

One Stage at a Time. As we noted, there are limits as to how much the development of a new structure can be accelerated, owing to maturational factors and the gradual nature of development. And within these limits there is still another constraint: development occurs through a fixed sequence of stages. Therefore, it should be possible to move the learner only one stage beyond his present level of thinking at a particular time. Given a description of the learner's present way of thinking, cognitive theory provides a description of what the next step in the sequence ought to be (assuming that its characterization of developmental stages is correct). To put the matter another way, just as an attempt to teach new content must be adjusted to the learner's present stage of development, so too must an attempt to teach a new way of thinking. If the learner is asked to acquire a structure that is more than one stage ahead of him, he will assimilate what is being taught to his own level, and consequently no progress will be made.

For example, in one study of moral judgment, a child at stage 2 in Kohlberg's theory was told the story about Heinz and the druggist and then was given the following argument in which a friend, Karen, was supposed to have advised Heinz not to steal the drug.[12]

> You shouldn't steal the drug. Even though you are desperate, it is still always wrong to steal. The druggist is wrong—he should let you have it for less, but two wrongs don't make a right. The druggist does

have a right to the drug since he worked hard to invent it. You are going against the druggist's rights if you steal it like that.

After hearing several other arguments, both pro and con, at a variety of stages, the stage 2 subject indicated a preference for the argument that was attributed to Karen. This choice seems rather surprising in view of the fact that Karen's argument represents the kind of moral thinking that occurs at stage 4. Karen sees stealing as categorically wrong because of an owner's property rights. According to Kohlberg's theory, a stage 2 child should not be able to understand this stage 4 reasoning.

On closer examination, it becomes apparent that the stage 2 child did not really understand Karen's argument after all, as shown by his own reasons for preferring it:

> Karen gave the smartest advice because she was thinking that if Heinz would steal the drug it wouldn't help him any. If he waited, the druggist might sell it for less.

It seems clear that the stage 4 argument was actually interpreted in stage 2 terms—that is, in terms of the "instrumental relativist orientation." The stage 2 child thought that Karen had argued against stealing the drug because it might jeopardize Heinz's chances of eventually getting what he wanted. In other words, the stage 4 advice was assimilated to a stage 2 way of thinking. Similar results might be expected to occur in any attempt to move the child more than one stage at a time.

Inducing Disequilibrium. The first step in a child's progress from one stage to the next is the occurrence of disequilibrium. Thus, to facilitate the development of a new structure, it might sometimes be necessary for a teacher to set the process in motion by inducing a state of disequilibrium in the learner. As we saw in Chapter 11, disequilibrium occurs when a child experiences a cognitive conflict resulting from inconsistencies in his own thinking. However, the occurrence of an inconsistency per se is not sufficient to bring about a state of disequilibrium; the child must see it himself. When adults spot a contradiction in someone else's thinking, they are inclined to point it out simply by telling the other person that he has been inconsistent. But with younger children, it is generally necessary to find a different way of helping them see the contradictions in their thinking, as illustrated by the following example.

Suppose a teacher wants to teach the logic of class inclusion to primary grade children who have not yet attained class inclusion on their own. Before a child understands class inclusion, his thinking about class hierarchies is inconsistent in the following way: He can see perfectly well that, although most of the beads in a particular set are brown and a few are white, all of the beads are made of wood. Yet when asked if there are more brown beads or wooden beads, he answers that there are more brown ones. Now suppose that a teacher wishes to help such a child see the contradiction in his thinking. The teacher might simply verbalize the contradiction, hoping that this will draw the child's attention to his inconsistency. "You just told me that some of the beads are brown and that all of the beads are wooden, but now you are telling me that there are more brown beads than wooden ones." It seems unlikely that this would be sufficient to induce disequilibrium. The problem is that the teacher is presenting the contradiction via two *propositions,* and the task of detecting an incompatibility between propositions requires a higher level of thinking than children have, even in the period of concrete operations.

To induce disequilibrium, the teacher must cause the child to see his inconsistency *in the context of his own activity.* For example, the child might be asked to put all the wooden beads in one box and all the brown beads in another.[13] Some children might immediately see that it is physically impossible to do this, because some beads (the brown ones) would have to be in two places at the same time. Other children might simply proceed to put the brown beads in one box and the white beads in the other. The teacher might ask these children to make sure that all of the wooden beads are in the same box. In this way, a child might be led to see, as a result of his own self-regulatory activity, that his way of solving the class inclusion problem is inadequate.

At this point, it is important to be clear about what we mean by the child's self-regulatory activity. With regard to the class inclusion problem, the relevant activities are to consider all of the beads with respect to their color (brown or white) and, *at the same time,* with respect to their substance (wood). Since these are *mental* activities, it probably would not even be necessary to have the child perform the *physical* activities of putting the beads in one box or another. The teacher could perform the physical activities and the child could be asked to watch and make sure that all the brown beads were put in one place and all the wooden beads in another.

This last point raises a more general question about the role of physical activity in learning. Is it always a good idea to plan instruction in such a way that the learner will engage in as much physical activity as possible? Superficially, Piaget's theory would appear to support this idea. The theory emphasizes the role of the child's own *activity* in his intellectual development, and it refers to a large part of childhood as the period of *concrete* operations. But as we saw in Chapter 11, once the child is beyond the sensorimotor period, cognition and overt behavior are differentiated from one another. Thereafter, the most important activities for intellectual development are mental activities. Even "concrete" operations are mental activities, because an operation, by definition, is an internalized action.

School undoubtedly is more fun for most children when they can move about and manipulate the environment. Certainly it would be absurd to make children always sit with hands folded, watching and listening to their teachers. But there are times when a child's own physical activity would probably interfere with learning. A child in our class inclusion example could spend so much time retrieving beads that have rolled away from him that he would never experience the kind of disequilibrium that the situation was meant to induce. In this case, a good demonstration by the teacher (with mental and verbal participation by the learner) might be more effective. The demonstration would still involve concrete objects, and thus it would provide the kind of environmental support needed for the development and use of concrete operations.

Finally, we must note that externally induced states of disequilibrium may not always lead directly to the development of a new cognitive structure. In fact, there is some evidence that they do not.[14] Consequently, it may seem as if children would be better off if left to generate their own states of disequilibrium from their everyday activities. However, we do not know that self-induced states of disequilibrium always lead to developmental progress either. In any case, the probability that disequilibrium will have a progressive effect might be enhanced by the provision of appropriate guidance for the process of equilibration.

Guiding the Process of Equilibration. The occurrence of disequilibrium is just the first step toward the development of a new cognitive structure. It must be followed by a period of restructuring through the process of equilibration. Whether the initial state of disequilibrium has occurred spontaneously or has been induced by instruction, a teacher can try to guide the process of equilibration and thereby help the learner attain a higher level of equilibrium than before.

Unfortunately, cognitive theory does not, at present, give the teacher much to go on with respect to specific procedures for guiding equilibration. One thing that seems clear is that equilibration will not occur unless the child engages in further activity of the same sort that brought about a state of disequilibrium in the first place. The child's subsequent activity need not be simple repetition of the original task but can be variations on the same structural theme. In fact, a certain amount of variation may be necessary as a means of promoting further accommodation of the learner's present structures. Thus, what the learner needs is a variety of materials on which he can act (mentally) and ample time in which to do so. In our class inclusion example, this would mean a variety of activities requiring the simultaneous consideration of classes and subclasses.

We saw earlier that, during the process of equilibration, a child's behavior may appear to get worse (less consistent) before it gets better (more equilibrated). One example of this, in the area of language development, is the young child's use of *comed* and *goed* after he has been saying *came* and *went* for some time. A teacher who is attempting to guide the equilibration process must be aware that such apparently confused behavior often signals progress on the part of the learner. Instead of expressing disapproval of such growth errors, the teacher can at least accept them as normal and might even offer the learner moral support as he struggles to arrive at a more adequate level of understanding.

Aside from providing opportunities for relevant activities, along with general encouragement, a teacher might take some more aggressive steps toward guiding the process of equilibration. One possibility is to present examples of the kind of thinking that occurs at the stage of development immediately above the learner's present stage. We have already seen an instance in which a moral argument *two* stages above the child's own stage was simply assimilated in a *nonprogressive* way. On the other hand, there is some evidence that, by presenting arguments that are only *one* stage above the learner's, it is possible to bring about progressive changes in the learner's own reasoning about moral dilemmas.[15]

One way to facilitate the learner's exposure to examples of thinking one stage above his own is to permit him to interact with his peers in the context of a constructive activity. Any group of learners—even a relatively homogeneous group—will contain individuals who are at different levels of development in any given area of content. Those who are at lower levels can profit from examples set by their more advanced peers. At the same time, the more advanced learners are able to consolidate their own thinking in the process of communicating it to someone else. In other words, all members of a group can be led to reconsider their own points of view as a result of exposure to someone else's point of view. The loss of egocentrism in childhood and adolescence probably results to a large extent from social interaction.

It is not clear exactly *why* progressive changes in cognitive structure would result from exposure to examples of thinking at the next stage, but we can suggest a few possible reasons. For one thing, these examples stand a relatively good chance of being assimilated intact by the learner, instead of being distorted, because the kinds of thinking that occur in adjacent stages have quite a lot in common. Recall that each new stage integrates structural elements from the one before it. Once higher-level thinking has been assimilated, it may first of all have the effect of inducing disequilibrium. But it may also provide a model for revamping the old structure which no longer seems adequate.

The notion of a model suggests that the learner's initial use of next-stage thinking may at first be largely imitative. The learner simply performs in the way that he has observed someone else perform. In contrast to play, Piaget has characterized imitation as a kind of activity in which accommodation predominates over assimilation. In order to imitate, an individual must first be able to assimilate the model. But once this initial assimilation occurs, the individual's activity conforms to the model. It might seem unlikely that "mere imitation" would facilitate the development of a new cognitive structure, but as the learner begins to imitate a more advanced model, he may discover that it enables him to establish equilibrium on a new level, as new contents are assimilated to the scheme that was acquired initially by imitation. A similar phenomenon occurs when a golfer mechanically imitates another player's swing, and then discovers that his own swing has suddenly fallen into place.

When we speak of the learner making a discovery, we mean that he has arrived at a new understanding because of his own activity, even if his activity has been instigated or suggested by someone else. In this light, the examples we have discussed in connection with inducing disequilibrium and guiding equilibration may all be said to involve a discovery on the part of the learner. Thus, discovery is not something that takes place only when the teacher is not around. In fact, a good teacher can help learners make more discoveries in the course of instruction than they could on their own.

Selecting a Strategy

The two instructional strategies we discussed are not mutually exclusive. Some objectives could be approached by either one of the strategies or by a combination of both. To some extent, the choice of a particular teaching strategy will depend on what the learner brings with him into the teaching situation, and there will undoubtedly be individual differences in this regard.

If the learner has little background in a particular content area, then there will be no old content to be restructured at the desired level, in which case the new content must first be assimilated by old structures. On the other hand, if the learner *has* had previous experience in a content area, but he does not have a structure with which to assimilate the same content at a higher level, then a restructuring of the old content is in order.

If the learner has both kinds of prerequisites for the particular learning in question, then there is some choice in selecting a strategy. Intuitively, the extension of old structures to new content would appear to be easier than the restructuring of old content at a higher level. However, there are a number of variables to be considered. For example, it might be easier to facilitate the development of a new structure if the learner has an especially broad background with regard to the content of instruction. Another factor to consider might be the degree of similarity between old and new content, when an old structure is to be extended. Because cognitive theory has not yet involved much analysis of content, we can only speculate about such possibilities at this point.

In view of our present ignorance about these matters, perhaps the best thing to do is to start out with a combination of both strategies. The teacher could observe the learner for clues as to which strategy the learner is inclined to use himself. For example, the learner might discuss the content being taught in a way that shows that he is relating it to other kinds of content that are more familiar. On the other hand, the learner might evidence the kind of confusion that would suggest that he is experiencing the disequilibrium phase in the development of a new structure. In any case, the teacher's task would then be to help the learner approach the instructional objective in his own way.

Summary

Cognitive theory suggests two basic strategies for helping the learner attain a particular instructional objective. Either an old cognitive structure can be extended to incorporate new content, or a new structure can be developed for thinking about old content. In the first instance, the learner may be assisted by instructional procedures that promote the processes of assimilation and accommodation. The use of analogy and the significance of play were discussed in this regard. The second strategy is implemented by procedures that induce disequilibrium and guide the process of equilibration. In this connection, we discussed a physically impossible task that might draw the learner's attention to a contradiction in his thinking, and we noted the possible benefits of providing opportunities for the learner to imitate a model of thinking one stage above his own. A number of factors might be considered in choosing one strategy or the other, but the overriding principle is that instruction should be adjusted to the learner's current level of functioning.

ASSESSING THE LEARNER

In discussing educational goals and strategies for teaching, we have assumed that the teacher already knows where the learner is at the outset of instruction and that he can recognize any changes in the learner that might ensue once instruction is under way. In other words, we have so far bypassed the whole problem of assessing the learner. Assessment *is* a problem, because it is directed toward the learner's cognitive structures, which are not directly observable. Moreover, it is an *important* problem. In order to select goals that can be attained and methods that are likely to be effective, the teacher first needs to determine the learner's level of thinking when instruction begins. Then, in order to monitor the learner's progress and evaluate the teaching methods that are being used, the teacher needs to determine how far the learner has gone toward the goals that have been chosen.

Our discussion of assessment will deal with three topics: (1) the relationship between the learner's age and his stage of development; (2) developmental tests of ability and achievement; and (3) the use of the clinical approach to assessment as an integral part of instruction.

Age and Stage

As children progress through a series of developmental stages, they are also, of course, getting older. It is an easy matter to find the average age at which children in a given population reach a particular stage of development (according to some standard criterion as to when each stage has been reached). Such norms of development can then be used to assess individual learners. Assuming that adequate age norms for developmental stages actually existed, one could adopt a very simple procedure for assessment: find out how old a child is and then predict what stage he is in. As crude as this method of assessment might seem, there are times when it actually will suffice as a basis for making decisions about instruction. On the other hand, it clearly is inadequate for many assessment purposes. Let us first discuss some cases in which age is a useful index of the learner's level of functioning and then go on to consider its limitations.

In our earlier example of a high school teacher who might draw upon his students' understanding of seriation to teach them a principle of chemistry, we reasoned that, since the logic of seriation is acquired by virtually all children during the elementary school years, the teacher could safely assume that this cognitive structure would be available to his high school students for extension to some new content in chemistry. This assumption might be based entirely on the age of the high school students in comparison to the age norms for the attainment of seriation. To cite our other example of young children being taught the concept of parallel by means of a formal definition, a teacher who knew the age norms for the attainment of formal operations presumably would have been able to predict that six- or seven-year-olds would not profit from a formal definition.

It might be argued that anyone with an intuitive understanding of children would reach the same conclusions about teaching young children and high school students without knowing the age norms for developmental stages. However, the relationship between age and stage is sometimes more subtle than that. For instance, even though most four-year-olds can count reasonably well, it is not until a few years later that they acquire the structural basis for a true understanding of number. Thus, it is generally safe to assume that four-year-olds will not understand operations involving number, at least not without special instruction.

Notice that in all of our examples, the learner's age is used to indicate either that he has not yet reached a particular stage or that he has already passed through it. But age is a lot less useful when it comes to determining which stage the learner is presently in. In Chapter 11, we noted three main reasons why age is not a reliable index of a child's current level of thinking. First, the transition from one stage to another occurs gradually, so that age is, at best, an index of how far a child has gone *through* a particular stage. Second, there are individual differences in the overall rate of development; some children, for example, show clear signs of concrete operations at age five, whereas others do not do so until age eight. Third, there are also individual and cultural differences with respect to the particular kind of content for which a given type of structure develops first; thus, some children might conserve amounts of clay before they conserve amounts of water and vice versa.

One more limitation in using age to estimate the learner's level of understanding derives from the fact that assessment procedures are used to measure the specific effects of instruction, not just the learner's general progress toward more advanced ways of thinking. It should be obvious that the learner's age is totally inadequate as a measure of the effects of instruction; it is useful only in that it might tell us the *kinds* of effects to expect within a particular age group—but this amounts to saying that age can be used as a rough guideline for selecting the immediate goals and the methods of instruction.

For the reasons we enumerated, the learner's age provides little more than a starting point for deciding where he is in terms of his intellectual development. To get a more accurate assessment of the learner's current level of thinking, it is necessary to obtain samples of his performance from which to infer his present cognitive competence. In the rest of this section, we will consider a variety of means for obtaining samples of the learner's performance for the purposes of assessment.

Developmental Tests

Traditionally, educators have obtained samples of the learner's performance by administering tests of ability and achievement. Let us consider how the testing approach might be adapted to the task of making assessments from a cognitive point of view. It will be convenient for us to treat the testing of ability and achievement separately, even though the distinction between the two is blurred to the extent that past achievement is a good measure of ability to profit from further instruction.

Ability Tests.   The most ubiquitous ability test in education is, of course, some form of intelligence test. We noted in Chapter 9 that the term intelligence usually has not meant the same thing to a test maker as it has to a cognitive theorist. The traditional IQ score simply indicates how well a particular individual has performed on a standard set of test items relative to other people his own age. The items on an intelligence test are chosen primarily because they appear to have something to do with mental ability and because older children pass them more often than do younger children. In a sense, then, a traditional intelligence test also indicates whether an individual is relatively advanced or retarded in his mental development in comparison to others. This type of information is generally expressed as a mental age score. Thus, a 10-year-old who performs relatively well for his age level might have a mental age of 12.

From the vantage point of cognitive theory, a mental age score would be more useful than the learner's chronological age for the purpose of estimating the learner's present level of thinking. The child with a mental age of 12 should be more like an average 12-year-old than an average 10-year-old. Assuming once again that we had age norms for developmental stages, we could predict that the child with a mental age of 12 might have the cognitive structures typical of 12-year-olds.[16] In this way, we could correct our predictions for individual differences in the overall rate of development. However, mental age still has some of the same limitations as chronological age. It does not take into account the gradual nature of development, or the individual differences that exist with regard to the content of thought.

The main drawback of the conventional intelligence test is that the test items are not selected for the purpose of inferring the attainment of particular cognitive structures. Yet, as we have seen, structural information is needed to predict what a person can learn at a given time, and to decide how he should be taught. It would be more useful to know that a particular 10-year-old has the cognitive structure for understanding proportions in a variety of instances than to know that he performs like an average 12-year-old on a miscellaneous set of test items.

The implication of this last point is clear: a developmental test of ability should consist of items that reflect in a more or less clear fashion the cognitive structures that an individual has at a particular time. Throughout these last chapters we have seen numerous examples of what such test items would be like, especially in the work of Piaget. Thus, a test for children in the primary grades might consist of several problems involving conservation, classification, seriation, and so on.

Work on the construction of such tests has been under way for several years now, but the research needed to determine the validity of these tests as predictors of school learning has barely begun.[17] However, it is already apparent that developmental ability tests based on cognitive theory may face some major practical limitations. To administer even a modest number of Piaget's tasks to a single child takes a considerable amount of time. It might be possible to administer some tasks on a group basis, but group tasks may be much less reliable than those administered individually. In any case, a reasonably large number of tasks would have to be included in a test of general ability. Not only would a variety of structures have to be tested, but also a variety of contents. The problem of content would be especially important for assessing the effects of instruction, but this has generally been the purpose of achievement tests rather than ability tests. Therefore, we will turn now to a discussion of achievement testing from a cognitive perspective.

Achievement Tests. The items on a conventional test of achievement are selected to comprise a representative sample of the content domain in which the learner has been instructed. As we explained in Chapter 7, performance on such a test can be scored either on a norm-referenced or on a criterion-referenced basis. That is, an individual's performance can be evaluated with reference to the performance of other individuals, or it can be evaluated with reference to the stated objectives of instruction. From a cognitive point of view, the second approach makes more sense, so long as the test items are designed to reveal the structural aspects of the learner's knowledge within a particular domain of content.

It should be clear that an achievement test would be aimed toward the structural level, or stage, at which the learner was taught. In other words, the test should be congruent with the objectives of instruction. It would not make much sense to teach social studies, for example, on the level of concrete operations, and then present a set of test items that could only be answered reliably on the basis of formal operations. However, a good achievement test would probably have items representing more than one level of understanding, especially if instruction has been individualized to fit each learner's stage of development. It is a common practice to construct tests with both easy and hard items; cognitive theory provides one basis for deciding which items are going to be easy and which are going to be hard. However, the purpose of including items that represent different stages of development is not to "separate the sheep from the goats" but rather to determine each learner's level of understanding so that later instruction can be planned accordingly.

Limitations of the Testing Approach. Although it may be possible to modify the traditional testing approach in accordance with cognitive theory, the essential notion of testing still has some inherent drawbacks that will limit its usefulness in education. We have already mentioned the likelihood that ability tests based on cognitive theory will necessarily require a great deal of time. Cognitive achievement tests would probably require less time per administration, being more narrowly focused on a particular domain of content; but if achievement tests were given often enough to guide instruction, the total amount of time involved in testing might again become prohibitive. The problem with all this is that time devoted to testing is time taken away from instruction. It might be said that taking a test can be a learning experience, too, but we will argue below that there is a better way to combine assessment with instruction than by means of an achievement test.

There is another problem with the testing approach to assessment. From a cognitive point of view, the most important thing to assess is the reasoning behind a person's response to a question or his solution to a problem. Although it is possible to construct test items that reveal a person's reasoning, it is difficult to construct items that do this for everyone taking the test—a limitation of the testing method we discussed in Chapter 8. The remedy, we suggest, is use of the clinical method. But instead of proposing that standard tests ought to be augmented by clinical probing and questioning—since that would take still more time away from instruction—we argue in favor of a clinical approach to assessment as an integral part of instruction.

Assessment as a Part of Instruction

The thrust of our discussion has been that instruction should be geared to the individual learner and that assessment of the learner is therefore an essential part of instruction. However, it is not just a matter of giving the learner a pretest to see where he is when instruction begins and later giving him a posttest to see what he has learned after being exposed to a ready-made lesson prescribed on the basis of the pretest. To cognitive theorists, this before-and-after approach leaves a lot to be desired.

In the first place, there is always the possibility that the pretest assessment of the learner's thinking is incorrect. We have discussed in a number of places the difficulty of making inferences about cognitive structures on the basis of observed behavior. Thus, a given sample of the learner's performance at a particular time may not be an accurate reflection of his competence. If assessment occurred only before and after instruction, there would be no way of checking the validity of the pretest and therefore no way of modifying instruction, if necessary, to achieve a better fit with the learner's current level of understanding.

Furthermore, the before-and-after approach overlooks the active nature of learning and thinking. If learning were a passive, receptive process, then it might be sufficient to make sure that the learner is paying attention before giving forth the lesson that he is to receive. But learning is an active, constructive process. Consequently, a teacher would be ill-advised to ignore what the learner is doing while instruction is in progress, because the teacher's actions should be coordinated with the learner's activity.

As we said before, it is the learner's *mental* activity that should concern a teacher most. The question, then, is how to assess the learner's mental activity while teaching. In Chapter 8 we described the clinical method as an especially powerful technique for revealing a child's way of thinking. The power of the clinical method derives from its flexibility in following up the subject's initial response with additional probes or questions designed to test tentative hypotheses about the subject's thinking. In this way, each subject can eventually be understood on his own terms.

The flexibility of the clinical method has another advantage: the method can be built into the very process of instruction in a way that is not possible with more formal tests. The essential idea is for a teacher to watch and listen to the learner in order to formulate hypotheses as to the learner's understanding and then to seek additional evidence by asking questions or otherwise eliciting behavior that might reveal the learner's way of thinking. In this regard, it is interesting to note that the learner's expressive behavior can be as informative as his goal-directed behavior. Thus, for example, a look of surprise or a tentative tone of voice might be indications that the learner is in a state of disequilibrium. It is easy to see, then, how the clinical method can be a richer source of information than a conventional test.

The idea of building the clinical method into the process of instruction is not particularly radical. Most teachers plan their instruction in such a way that the learner will be called upon to answer questions, give explanations, or perform in other ways. However, both cognitive theory in general and the clinical method in particular suggest that teachers should not be satisfied upon hearing a correct answer but should probe for additional evidence that the learner really understands what he is being taught. By the same token, an *incorrect* answer is not merely an error that shows that the learner has failed to understand something. Rather, it is a clue to what the learner *does* understand, and therefore it should be followed up and interpreted instead of being met with an unexplained correction. Indeed, Piaget's theory is founded largely on his attempts to understand the "errors" in children's thinking.

The clinical approach to assessment offers several advantages. It does not take time away from instruction because it is a part of instruction. As such, it can be used on a day-to-day basis. In addition, the clinical approach solves the problem of assessing the learner's cognitive structure with regard to the kind of content that is being taught, because the method is applied to the same content. Finally, the clinical approach is, by its very nature, adjusted to individual differences.

It would hardly be consistent with the cognitive approach to suggest that the clinical method is the *only* mode of assessment for teachers to use. Just as the cognitive psychologist employs a variety of research methods, the teacher can profit from a number of assessment techniques. For example, the method of naturalistic observation is one that can easily be adapted for use in the classroom. As learners work by themselves or interact with others, their behavior may provide the teacher with additional insights into their ways of thinking. And as we mentioned before, more formal tests of ability and achievement can also supplement the kinds of assessment that a teacher is able to do on a day-to-day basis. However, the clinical method appears to be the method of choice for assessing the learner while instruction is in progress.

Summary

Given the need to adjust instruction to the learner's present stage of development, the task of assessing the learner is an important part of teaching. Equally important is the use of assessment procedures to evaluate the effects of instruction. The learner's chronological age is, at best, a very rough index of his present stage of development. Consequently, it is necessary to obtain samples of the learner's performance for the purpose of assessing his cognitive competence. Toward this end, it is possible to construct developmental tests of ability and achievement, along the lines implied by cognitive theory. However, the conventional testing approach to assessment takes time away from instruction, and it is not well suited to the task of revealing the reasoning behind each learner's performance. In contrast, the clinical approach was developed specifically to investigate an individual's reasoning, and it can be made an integral part of instruction. Thus, the clinical method appears to be the most useful assessment technique for teachers, but it can always be supplemented by data from tests and from naturalistic observation.

SUMMARY

At the outset we showed how some current educational practices apparently correspond to principles of cognitive theory. We also intimated there might be more (or perhaps less) to these correspondences than first meets the eye, because of complexities and uncertainties in the relationship between cognitive theory and education. After then discussing some general limitations in putting theory into practice, we examined three major facets of education:

the description and selection of goals; strategies of instruction; and the problem of assessing the learner.

Although children must acquire some basic ideas that adults take for granted, it does not follow that instruction should always be aimed at their acquiring these ideas. Before a particular goal is selected for teaching, one must ask whether it is possible and desirable to attain that goal by means of instruction. Cognitive theory offers some general guidelines as to what is possible and what is desirable, but they are limited by our present lack of knowledge about maturation and other factors affecting development. In the light of cognitive theory, it may be that some basic ideas being taught by the "new curricula" *cannot* be taught to some children and *need not* be taught to others. Yet we also believe that the development of basic ideas can be facilitated to some extent by instruction, and we can conceive of circumstances under which it would be desirable to do so.

Cognitive theory does not support the notion that "learning by discovery" means a learner must be left alone to muddle through on his own. It is possible to help develop a new cognitive structure by inducing disequilibrium in the learner and by guiding the process of equilibration. Similarly, it is possible to promote the processes of assimilation and accommodation that occur when an old structure is extended to new content. Even when such assistance is provided, the learner is still making "discoveries," in the sense that his cognitive structures are acquired and extended by his own activity.

Cognitive theory suggests that instruction can succeed only if it is geared to the learner's present stage of development. Since any classroom will contain learners who are at different stages in their understanding of the material being taught, cognitive theory therefore implies an individualized approach to instruction. However, the theory does not imply a kind of individualization in which the learners are, in effect, kept isolated from each other by their own work. On the contrary, interaction among learners contributes to the loss of egocentrism by exposing each learner to points of view different from his own.

According to cognitive theory, the role of the learner's activity is crucial, but so is a clear understanding of the term activity. After infancy, a child constructs his intelligence primarily by means of *mental* activity. The term concrete operations, for example, refers to reversible mental actions performed on concrete cognitive content, not to the physical manipulation of objects. Certain physical activities may be convenient for engaging the mental activities that lead to learning, but physical activity per se is not necessary and may even be a hindrance. On the other hand, it is necessary to elicit overt behavior in order to assess the learner's thinking, and some of this overt behavior may be physical manipulation, as well as verbalization. We suggested that the clinical method is the best way to elicit revealing performances on the part of the learner in the course of instruction.

The specific implications of cognitive theory for education are not simple—partly because the theory itself is not simple and partly because many areas of the theory need further development. However, two general implications are clear: First, the learner develops through an ordered series of stages, which must be taken into account if instruction is to succeed. The cognitive approach has already produced a body of data from which the stages can be inferred for some areas of intellectual development. Second, the learner actively assimilates the environment to his present level of thinking and, in the process, he constructs higher levels of thinking by his own activity. The purpose of education is to help the learner do this.

Part 3

The PSYCHOANALYTIC Approach to Intellectual Development

14

THE PSYCHOANALYTIC POINT OF VIEW

Preview

This chapter introduces psychoanalytic theory, both in its classical form developed by Freud and its newer form of ego psychology. Mental development, we will see, is more than intellectual development; it includes the development of consciousness, and the development of instinctual drives and controls over them.

The theory uses a genetic approach, trying to explain current behavior in terms of preceding problem-solving behavior, and using free association and dream interpretation to do so. Psychoanalysis takes a deterministic view of man, but it also believes in free will, for as man's consciousness increases he becomes liberated from control by unconscious drives and the environment. The theory stresses that a person's behavior results from the interplay of his innate psychological makeup with his social environment.

The name Freud and the term psychoanalysis are now familiar to most educated people. However, the popular conception of psychoanalysis is often of an emotionally disturbed patient lying on a couch, behind which sits a bearded gentleman with a heavy Viennese accent. Certainly this conception appears in a host of jokes about "shrinks" and has helped perpetuate the notion that psychoanalysis deals with the dark, murky recesses of sick individuals. Thus, to discuss psychoanalysis in a book about the intellectual development of normal children may seem surprising.

But psychoanalysis is not only a clinical theory that deals with abnormal behavior. It is also a general psychological theory that accounts for a larger range of human behavior. Psychoanalytic writings in ego psychology have scarcely appeared in popular literature, and so the public has been presented only with an early, long-abandoned version of psychoanalytic theory in which all behavior is explained by "sex" and early trauma. Moreover, it is not only the general public that holds this mistaken view—it is also held by professional critics.

To be sure, the general theory of psychoanalysis is incomplete; it is at its best in describing problems of motivation and of emotional and social development. However, psychoanalysis approaches human behavior as involving complex and interwoven psychological processes. For this reason it has been necessary to consider problems such as motivation in the context of man as a rational creature (though sometimes irrational, of course)—one who is to be distinguished from other animals by his capacity to reason, solve problems, and form abstract concepts. Thus, though psychoanalytic theory has often focused on other issues, it has consistently considered the role of intellectual processes.

This part of the book focuses on the psychoanalytic theory of mental development, which includes more than the development of intelligence or rational behavior. As we shall see, mental development is based on the modification of instinctual energy, and on the development of controls and defenses against the discharge of this energy.

Since psychoanalytic theorists consider all mental functions related, they believe it is impossible to understand intellectual development unless emotional factors, the development of drive, and controls and defenses against drives are also understood. This inclusion of motivational and emotional factors as important determinants of intellectual development critically differentiates psychoanalytic theory from cognitive or learning theories.

To distinguish the psychoanalytic from the theories previously presented, we must try to answer two questions: First, what do we have to understand in order to understand intellectual development? Second, what do we have to understand in order to understand psychoanalytic theory? The rest of this chapter will discuss these two issues.

UNDERSTANDING INTELLECTUAL DEVELOPMENT

A central tenet of the psychoanalytic theory of intellectual development is that man's capacity for *consciousness* is connected with the processes of seeing and knowing. Conscious self-awareness seems such a distinctive and important aspect of the human condition, but, surprisingly, it has been either ignored or systematically omitted by other theories of intellectual development. Yet surely the ability to reflect on one's own mental processes—to think about what one is thinking about—is a critical feature of human intellect.

To psychoanalytic theorists, the problem of consciousness is particularly important in trying to understand thinking and learning. Ordered, logical thinking depends on one's having reflective awareness to direct, select, and keep the thought processes within a given conceptual realm. Likewise, learning requires, among other things, that one be able to direct his conscious attention toward the material to be learned. In the typical learning situation, one must first be aware that there is something to be learned before learning can proceed.

When the mental function called consciousness is directed toward memories or mental processes, these memories become conscious. But psychoanalytic theorists also believe that other memories and mental processes are not so accessible to conscious reflection. These are unconscious processes, which make themselves known in dreams, in some drug states, and sometimes under conditions of fatigue or extreme physical deprivation. This emphasis on *unconscious mental processes* is the second factor that differentiates the psychoanalytic from other theories of intellectual development.

Some psychologists find the idea of unconscious mental processes logically untenable or irrelevant. They argue that if the process is unconscious, then it can never be known, so to postulate its existence is superfluous. It is not correct, however, to equate unconscious with unknowable. As is true with any mental process, we cannot observe unconscious mental processes directly, but we can observe their effects.

The concept of unconscious processes also is criticized by some investigators who state that they can study only overt behavior. Yet such a statement is clearly tied to a more philosophical question: what is the nature of reality? In everyday language, and for some psychologists, the term reality refers to those objects or events that can be seen, heard, felt, touched—that is, detected by our sensory organs. For psychoanalysis, however, there is a second kind of reality—a psychical reality. Thus, fantasies, dreams, and hallucinations are real, in the sense of being real mental activities. The fact that they do not accurately reflect the state of external reality does not make their psychological existence any less real.

Another point that psychoanalytic theorists (as well as a number of philosophers) make about reality and accuracy is that external reality is not only in large part man-made, but it is also "man-thought."[1] That is, our perceptions and understanding of external reality are only partial mental representations of what is "really" out there. To say to the psychoanalyst that we cannot "really" know the nature of unconscious mental processes—which Freud called the true psychic reality[2]—is no more discouraging to him than it is to tell him we can never know with absolute certainty the real nature of the external world. Just as our sense organs and powers of comprehension provide us with imperfect information regarding external reality, so our self-awareness —our consciousness—provides us with imperfect information regarding our inner, psychological reality. To understand behavior from the psychoanalytic point of view, one must have knowledge of both these realities. For these reasons (and others to be discussed), psychoanalysis stresses the importance of unconscious mental processes.

A third factor that will help us understand the psychoanalytic theory of intellectual development is the concept of *innate instinctual drive*. Freud believed that man is born with certain innate drives that, from time to time, build up in intensity and must be discharged in order for the person to maintain an inner equilibrium. To the psychoanalytic theorist, much of intellectual development results from the progressive control and modification of the discharge of instinctual drive energy. For such discharge to occur, the person must locate an object that will gratify the drive. Freud believed that all thinking develops in order to accomplish this goal—that is, to ensure the gratification of the basic drives of man.[3] As we shall see, as the child develops, his means for reaching this goal become increasingly successful and, at the same time, increasingly complex.

The fourth factor that is central to the understanding of intellectual development is the concept of the ego, or rather of *ego functions*. These are the mental activities that we characteristically refer to when we speak of intellectual processes—such as thought, memory, language, and voluntary control of motor behavior. The development of the ego then becomes critical in understanding the development of the intellect. As we shall see, the ego originally was considered to be a necessary "middle man," developing out of the conflict between the instinctual drives of the individual and the demands of reality. More recently, psychoanalytic theory has taken the position that the ego develops not only out of conflict between drives and reality conditions, but also as a result of the existence of inborn potentialities for ego development, which from the beginning guarantee the child's capacity to adapt to reality.[4]

In this last respect, the psychoanalytic theorist's position on intellectual development is similar to the cognitive theorist's: both assume that the potential for a particular plan of intellectual development is present at birth and is intrinsic to the human condition. Moreover, as we shall see, both theories stress the importance of *interaction* between innate and experiential factors. The difference between the two approaches lies in *which* internal and external factors are considered important. Perhaps also, psychoanalytic theory is somewhat more specific in stating the nature of the important variables.

However, lest the reader be misled, it should be pointed out that psychoanalysis does not really have a comprehensive theory of intellectual development. It contains a number of ideas that are both relevant and provocative to understanding this area, but it is the general belief of psychoanalysts that intellectual development cannot be entirely separated from understanding behavior in general. Since the theory provides a number of different levels for understanding behavior—conscious versus unconscious, drive versus ego, conflict-determined versus conflict-free, and others—to discuss the development and function of thinking, we must also consider these various levels.

UNDERSTANDING PSYCHOANALYTIC THEORY

What must one understand in order to understand the general theory of psychoanalysis? This was our second question at the beginning of the chapter, and one way to answer it is to see how psychoanalysis came to develop the concepts we discussed above. Thus, let us look at some aspects of the historical development of psychoanalytic theory.

Classical Psychoanalytic Theory

Classical psychoanalytic theory was originated by Sigmund Freud in the early 1900s as an outgrowth of his work with emotionally disturbed patients. When Freud began his work, he was an explorer in a largely uncharted territory. Little was known about the meaning of emotional symptoms or how to treat them. Initially, Freud tried to cure these patients by hypnosis, but when such cures proved transitory, he switched to a method he called "catharsis," in which the "cure" consisted in having the patient freely express all his dammed up memories and emotions. In both approaches, the patient's discomfort was largely explained as being caused by painful memories that the patient was unaware of—that is, that were unconscious.

In the patients Freud saw, the unconscious memories most often uncovered during treatment were of early sexual experiences with a parent or other adult. At first, Freud assumed these memories were of events that had actually taken place. Like today's S-R theorists, he explained the patient's problems as being caused solely by previous environmental experiences: early sexual seduction (environmental stimulus) was the cause of current pathology (observable response).

Gradually, however, Freud came to realize that the patient's memory was not altogether accurate. He found that patients' memories of their early childhood sexual experiences were not of events that had actually occurred, but rather were memories of a fantasy or a wish that they had entertained at one time. At about the same time, Freud discovered that dreams, which had seemed to be meaningless in their surface content, also could be understood by discovering the *wish* behind the dream.

These discoveries left Freud with the problem of explaining the origin of such wishes and fantasies. Since they did not correspond to events that had really occurred, Freud postulated that their origin must be entirely internal to the individual: they had provided an imaginary happening that the child *wished* would occur in reality. To account for the origin of this internal wish, Freud introduced the concept of the innate instinctual drive: it was the existence of innate drives in man that was responsible for the occurrence of certain common wishes.

We may now begin to see some connection between the way the concept of instinctual drive developed and our statement that thinking occurs as a way of gratifying innate instinctual drives. Just as Freud's patients imagined that certain wished-for events actually occurred, so it seems a child's earliest form of mental activity is a form of wish fulfillment. Initially, such wish fulfillment comes about by the young child imagining the presence of the wished-for object. Later, it is accomplished by using mental activity to acquire the wished-for object in reality. The concept of innate instinctual drive thus assumed a level of importance corresponding to that of the discovery of unconscious mental processes. It also played a crucial role in the development of the theory of infantile sexuality, which, as we shall see, is a cornerstone in the general developmental theory of psychoanalysis.

This description of the beginnings of psychoanalytic treatment of patients also indicates how the concept of unconscious mental processes came into the theory. In using both the methods of hypnosis and those of psychoanalysis—namely, free association and dream analysis, which we will discuss later in the chapter—it became apparent that under these special conditions patients were able to recall memories that had previously been unavailable to them. These empirical findings helped Freud make the important distinction between conscious and unconscious mental processes.

After the discoveries of unconscious mental processes and the innate instinctual drive, Freud shifted his emphasis from environmental events to psychological processes within the individual. Indeed, not until around 1940 did psychoanalysis begin again to focus attention on the importance of the environment in an individual's psychological development.[5]

Psychoanalytic Ego Psychology

As we implied above, classical psychoanalytic theory placed great emphasis on motivation and the fulfillment, or gratification, of instinctual drives. The development of the ego was almost entirely considered as a result of the need to obtain gratification in reality. Ego development also was assumed to occur as a result of the child's need to control the uninhibited expression of drives, such as occurs in the temper tantrums of young children, since such uncontrolled outbursts are unsuccessful, in and of themselves, in obtaining gratification. Thus, it was thought, the main function of the ego was to ensure drive gratification or drive reduction.

But recent psychoanalysts such as Hartmann, Rapaport, and Erikson have come to consider ego development in a new light.[6] No longer is the ego considered to have resulted from the impact of reality experiences on the unformed infant (this is, incidentally, the *tabula rasa* view of some S-R theories of development). Current psychoanalytic theory has abandoned the idea that *all* ego development is due to the need to solve the conflict between instinctual needs and reality conditions. Although *some* ego development is presumed to occur as a result of such conflicts, other aspects of ego development are believed to occur outside of, or independent from, conflict. The role of the ego is to maintain a balance among psychological motivations, but this does not mean that it only reduces drive; indeed, it may be an innate source of nondrive motivation and so maintains tension rather than reduces it.

Such ego functions are not present at birth. The assumption is that the infant is born with certain innate *potentialities* for ego development. Thus, though at birth his mental state is undifferentiated, he has within himself the seeds that will determine the kind of ego functions that subsequently develop.

As mentioned, psychoanalytic ego psychology also emphasizes a reconsideration of the importance of environmental stimulation—especially experiences with maternal, nurturing, or teaching adults—on psychological development. Increasingly, psychoanalytic investigations have recognized that behavior is determined not only by internal motivations but also by external causes, removing current psychoanalytic theory from the awkward earlier position of having to state that the cause of all behavior could be traced to some instinctual drive.

Psychoanalytic ego psychologists have changed the explanation for the development of thinking: it is no longer believed to have developed solely to ensure wish fulfillment; it is due also to innate ego potentialities, which impose some realistic organization of experiences on mental processes. For example, we seem to have an innate tendency to record and recall experiences in terms of their co-occurrence in time and space. The fact that memory processes operate according to principles of temporal and spatial contiguity rather than, for example, recording every other experience, or every third experience, results in our having a particular mental conception of reality. That is, the innate tendency of memory to function in this particular way imposes on our experiences an organization based on contiguity.

The emphasis by current theorists on ego functions has implications for man's capacity for self-determination, for it means that man may have some autonomy from his drives. Drive tension may increase, but the individual need not be directly dominated by the need to satisfy this impulse, since the ego can control and restrain the drives. Thus, unlike some lower animals, man is not at the mercy of his drives.

Such development of ego functions also gives man some independence from his environment. His behavior is due not only to the immediate environmental stimulus but also to accumulated past experiences, including the ego functions of memory, learning, and capacity for logical thinking. Thus, man is not simply a robotlike, reflexive respondent to whatever environmental stimulus is present. Also, some of this autonomy is guaranteed by the existence of drives within the individual, although, as psychological development proceeds, these are expressed more and more indirectly. Thus, the development of the ego means that man is relatively independent from being dominated by internal drives and from being under the control of external stimuli—a point that leads us into another issue important for understanding psychoanalysis, the issue of free will versus determinism.

Free Will versus Determinism

The question of free will versus determinism in human behavior is an old one, and it appears more often in philosophical than in psychological discussions. Psychoanalytic theorists continue to believe in a "thorough-going psychological determinism":[7] all human behavior is determined by previous experience with external or internal reality plus present drives, their defenses or controls, and innate ego potentialities. Although it is exceedingly difficult to specify all the relevant antecedent conditions, the theorists assume that all behavior results from potentially specifiable causes, so that if all relevant causes were known, behavior would be totally predictable.

Such determinism also is present in the psychoanalytic theory of thought processes. Freud asserted that the association between one thought and the next is never arbitrary but is always determined by a "purposive idea." There was no such thing as a truly "random thought," he believed; whatever a person's momentary thought, it was connected to the immediately preceding thought (which might be unconscious).[8]

The psychoanalyst's conception of human development is also deterministic. There is the belief in an innate plan that, before birth, controls the way all organic factors of the embryo develop and that, after birth, governs the development of the person's emotional and social potentialities.[9] There is the assumption of an inborn coordination between the developing psychological functions of the child and his physical and social environment. Finally, there is the idea that in each phase of development a specific task must be solved. This conception of innately determined modes, sequence, and ascendancy of behavior for social interaction results in a thoroughly deterministic theory of emotional and social development.[10]

But as we have seen, it is a person's ego that insures his autonomy. It may save him from being dominated by drives or from responding automatically to "conditioned stimuli." To psychoanalytic theorists, the individual is far from being a driven robot. In fact, compared to S-R or cognitive theory, psychoanalytic theory provides more chance for individual freedom. As compared to the focus of S-R theory on environmental stimulation, psychoanalysis focuses more attention on the importance of the person's internal nature in determining the actions he will take. Cognitive theory likewise focuses on the importance of one's inner nature, but psychoanalytic theorists believe they have designated more internal variables as important in determining behavior, including the influence of individual attitudes, values, and personal motivations. Thus, psychoanalytic theorists focus on both the greater complexity of man's behavioral determinants and his potential freedom to choose among them to determine his course of development.

Although some will object to the theory on just this basis—that there are too many explanatory concepts—others will welcome a conception of man that attempts to reflect something of his obvious complexity and inability to be explained by a simple set of conditioning principles.

Three Methods Used in Psychoanalysis

The assumptions of psychological determinism, of unconscious mental processes, and of the importance of the genetic approach (that is, tracing current kinds of behavior to their developmental origins) have influenced and been influenced by certain psychoanalytic methods. Like the cognitive theorists, psychoanalytic theorists have made more use of the clinical method than of the experimental method of S-R theorists, although in recent years there has been an increasing effort to put psychoanalytic concepts to experimental test.[11] But the clinical method of psychoanalysis also differs from that of the cognitive approach in its use of three features: free association, dream interpretation, and the genetic approach. Let us look at these one at a time.

Free Association.   The use of free association as a method to discover the thoughts and feelings of central importance to the individual comes directly from the assumption of psychological determinism. If one believes that any succession of thoughts has a meaningful connection and direction, and that this direction is being determined by the needs, wishes, or interests important to the individual at that moment, then by examining the uninterrupted flow of thoughts it should be possible to determine this central motivation or purpose. The method of free association asks the individual to try to verbalize any and all thoughts that come to mind, as they occur, regardless of how silly, meaningless, or embarrassing they might seem. The patient need not be as concerned with being logical, coherent, and socially appropriate as he usually is during ordinary discourse. This capacity to verbalize inner thoughts in the absence of self-criticism usually takes considerable practice. When it is possible to eliminate such inner censorship, the use of free association often leads the individual to recover unconscious memories, which had not been previously available.

Dream Interpretation. This is another method used to discover unconscious memories and wishes. Freud said that dreams were "the royal road to the unconscious";[12] that is, they provide the best means we have for discovering what is going on at that level of mental functioning. Psychoanalytic theory assumes that the earliest thought processes are illogical, magical, and without understanding of causal relationships or the intrinsic qualities of objects. This earlier, more primitive form of mental functioning does not disappear but continues to exist throughout life. Mostly, however, we are unaware of its existence and become aware of it only under conditions of extreme relaxation, fatigue, illness, or some drug-induced state. The occurrence of dreams in sleep is perhaps the best evidence we have for the continuing existence of the early illogical form of mental functioning. As with the mental activity of the infant, the motive behind the dream is one of wish fulfillment —that is, drive gratification. It is partly due to this relationship to the earliest form of mental activity that the occurrence of dreams is considered a significant mental event.

Some popularizations of psychoanalytic theory have led to the erroneous idea that dream analysis involves a stereotyped translation of dream symbols—for example, a tower always represents a phallus, a ship always represents a woman. This is an unfortunate misconception, for it completely misses the point that the interpretation of a dream depends in large part on the person's unique associations to the dream. Although it is true that, as humans, we may tend to use some common symbols to represent a common feeling or thought—for example, the cartoonist uses a light bulb to represent a "bright idea"—dream interpretation would never assume that a particular symbol must always have a single, stereotyped meaning. On the contrary, after the dreamer reports the night's dream, the next step in the process is for him to free-associate to the dream, thereby continuing the mental processes begun in the dream. It is these unique associations that make clear the meaning of the dream and of its individual elements. In other words, the process that is begun in the dream is continued in the process of free association.

The Genetic Approach. By "genetic," we are referring not to genes and chromosomes, but to the idea that any current behavior has a genesis, a historical beginning. Thus, the genetic approach consists in beginning with a current behavioral situation and tracing backwards in time the series of previous kinds of behavior that led up to it. The genetic approach assumes that the current psychological functioning of the individual can always be traced to previous experiences in his life. This method differs from the approach of the S-R theorist in that it is not only the previous external experiences in a person's life that are considered important. Rather it seeks to explain current behavior by tracing back to those previous kinds of behavior that were attempts to solve the same problem that the current behavior attempts to solve —that is, the problem that is created by increasing tension from instinctual drives. The ways in which this problem was resolved in different previous situations and at different stages of development constitute the behavioral antecedents, the "experiences," on which the present behavior is based. The further back in a person's life history one goes, the less important are the external situations or conditions and the more important are the stage of development and instinctual factors in determining the behavior. The genetic approach to the explanation of behavior, then, focuses on tracing the development of a complex unit of behavior—behavior as a problem solution—rather than attempting to explain the development of isolated functions or abilities.

In the early days of psychoanalysis, the data for this genetic approach were obtained from the introspections of adults regarding their memories of childhood experiences. The developmental theory thus was based on retrospective reconstruction of the previous behavioral solutions that were antecedents of the current behavior. In more recent years, this kind of information has been supplemented substantially by empirical studies of infant and child behavior.[13]

IMAGE OF MAN

The psychoanalytic conception of the nature of man—his most important characteristics—is rather different from those theories which view development primarily as a function of the individual's conditioning history or of other nonmotivational factors. To the psychoanalytic theorist, the general trend of human development is a result of the continuous interaction between the innate factors of drive and developmental plan, on the one hand, and environmental influences, on the other. Development is seen as a progression from a passive, helpless, stimulus-dominated state to a condition of self-determined activity. This progress does not come about automatically but, as will be discussed below, comes about as a result of the interplay of innate and experiential factors. Nor is such development seen as being entirely equivalent to the development of man's intellectual or rational functions. Although the development of logical or rational thinking is obviously helpful in facilitating man's interaction with the environment and with himself, psychoanalytic theory does not consider the development of intellectual functions by themselves to guarantee the optimum level of mental functioning available to man.

Nature and Nurture

When we consider the image of man, we must ask what is the source of the strongest determiners of man's development, for one's view of the nature of man will depend on whether he thinks innate factors (nature) or experiences after birth (nurture) are primarily responsible for the way man develops. Here we will consider the position of psychoanalytic theory.

As discussed above, the theory assumes the existence of innate instinctual drives and ego potentialities. D. Rapaport has suggested that the central achievement of psychoanalysis as a developmental psychology was to separate out these innate maturational factors from the complexity of developmental changes apparently brought about by experience.[14] That is, in the concept of instinctual drive, Freud postulated an innate factor that progressively changes or matures *independent* of the individual's particular experience. Behavior, as a problem solution, comes to be organized around this intrinsic drive. The particular form that behavior takes at any point in development will be determined in part by past problem solutions with that intrinsic drive. Thus, the concept of an unfolding, progressively maturing innate drive is the independent contribution of "nature" to development, and past experiences, along with present environmental conditions, are the role played by "nurture."

Nature: The Innate Givens

Let us look at the factors that the theory postulates are innately given at birth. These factors can be divided into those dealing with motivation and emotion and those dealing with psychological structures.

It is the presence of innate instinctual drives that causes certain kinds of behavior to occur. The aim of the drive is always to discharge accumulated energy—that is, to strive for drive gratification. When this occurs, we say the drive has been satisfied.

A related factor is affect (emotion). If, despite mounting tension, a drive remains ungratified, it may discharge *within* the organism and will be experienced as affect. Affect, then, is the inborn safety valve for the discharge of drive tension.

Inborn factors are also important in the development of certain of a person's psychological structures. Three innate factors are especially important in this regard: (1) ego potentialities, which, once they are activated, help in the development of drive restraints and ensure that the infant can respond to the environment; (2) laws of maturation; and (3) innate coordination between instinctual drives and the objects that gratify them. Innate ego potentialities are seen as the result of a long history of evolutionary selection. Their existence guarantees that the person can eventually adapt to an average expectable environment, that is, to those aspects of the environment that have been relatively constant over a number of generations—such as dirunal variations in light and dark—and that people have adapted to by the process of evolution.

In addition, psychoanalytic theorists believe that underlying ego development are laws of maturation, and an innate maturational plan.[15] This plan includes the emergence and predominance of different modes of behavior at different stages of development, independent of the specific environment in which the development takes place. We will discuss this in greater detail in Chapter 17.

Finally, psychoanalytic theorists assume an innate coordination between instinctual drive and objects that will gratify it[16]—a coordination that reflects the process of evolutionary selection.

Nurture: The Interchange with the Environment

Although psychoanalytic theorists assume that there are innate motivational and structural givens and that an intrinsic maturational plan determines the sequence of ego development, they also believe that the ego is always undergoing readaptations in its interaction with the social and physical environment—that is, that there is continual interchange between the individual and the environment.

For example, we mentioned that a person's internal psychological equilibrium is in part assured by the innate coordination between drive and object. In man, unlike in lower animals, this coordination is fairly flexible, and so, through experience, a variety of objects may come to serve as adequate substitutes for the original object and thereby provide drive gratification. Thus, while the maturational drive continues on its innately determined course, one's experience will determine the variability and nature of the objects that will gratify that drive.

Another way the environment interacts with the intrinsic maturational plan is to promote psychological growth. As we mentioned, psychoanalytic theorists do not assume that development progresses automatically. The child's relationship with a significant, nurturing adult and his experience of being frustrated by the environment in attempting drive gratification are two ways in which interaction with the environment is critical for psychological growth to occur. The ways in which the environment may foster such growth is discussed more fully in Chapter 19.

A third way the environment affects a person's development is that it determines the outcome, or behavioral solution, of the innately determined psychological problem characteristic of each developmental stage. Thus, just as psychoanalytic theory assumes that the sequence of developmental stages is innately determined, so it also assumes that the developmental problem or crisis associated with each stage is predetermined. What is *not* predetermined, however, is the particular behavioral solution that the individual will adopt or the modes of behavior that will predominate in that solution. How the individual solves each developmental crisis varies from society to society—another way of saying that the particular behavioral solution adopted by the individual is determined by society. The attitudes of any given society will determine which of the individual's intrinsically determined modes of behavior will predominate and which will recede. It is by influencing the *way* the child solves the innately given developmental problems, that society accomplishes its socialization of the child.[17]

SUMMARY

This chapter briefly described the history of psychoanalytic theory, both in its classical form as developed by Sigmund Freud and in its newer form as psychoanalytic ego psychology. We noted that the theory assumes that the concept of mental development involves more than intellectual development, that it also involves the development of consciousness and the differentiation of conscious and unconscious mental processes. Intellectual development also depends on the development of instinctual drive energies and of controls for discharging these drives.

As we have seen, psychoanalytic theorists have become more attentive to the interaction of the environment with the person's innately given characteristics. They have also increasingly stressed that innate potentialities for the functioning of ego structures allow the individual to develop the capacities for perception, learning, and memory, and to make his way in the world.

The predominant method that psychoanalytic theorists use to explain behavior is the genetic approach, which sees behavior as a complex unit—a problem solution—and explains current behavior in terms of preceding kinds of behavior that were attempts to solve the same problem. Whether a person's previous behavior and experiences are relevant to understanding his current behavior depends on whether they were attempts, at earlier stages of development, to solve the same kind of problem. Free association and dream interpretation are the methods used to discover these earlier modes of problem solution.

Psychoanalytic theory takes a deterministic view of man and assumes that behavior or thought is not random, but is caused by some preceding behavior or thought. Thus, if we could know all relevant preceding psychological events in a person's life, we could fully predict his behavior and thoughts —but, of course, the number of such relevant preceding psychological events would be quite extensive.

Despite this belief in determinism, psychoanalytic theorists also believe in free will, for they see the goal of development to be that man's behavior is increasingly determined by his own conscious ego functions, as opposed to being dominated by unconscious drive factors or by the environment. In fact, more than S-R or cognitive theory, psychoanalytic theory provides greater potential for man's freedom—first, because it assumes there are many more variables important in determining behavior and, second, because it believes development is the progressive freeing of man's behavior from external and internal forces. S-R theorists may see development as the increasing control of the organism's behavior by the stimulus and cognitive theorists may believe that affect (emotion) does not contribute to the development of the intellect. Psychoanalytic theorists postulate that the goal of development is that man *masters* both external and internal stimuli, thereby mastering his own destiny.

On the image of man underlying psychoanalytic theory, we discussed the issue of nature versus nurture in determining man's behavior. Psychoanalysis assumes that a person's behavior is not solely determined either by the impact of the environment or by the unfolding of innately determined patterns. Rather, it assumes that there is a complex interplay between environmental-social factors and an innately determined plan of psychological development, so that the general sequence and problems of development are innately given, but the particular solutions to each developmental problem are influenced by the attitudes of the person's society.

15

BASIC CONCEPTS AND PRINCIPLES IN PSYCHOANALYTIC THEORY

Preview

The concepts and principles of psychoanalysis will be described here from five viewpoints: (1) The *genetic* viewpoint looks at behavior according to its origin and development, and it includes the concepts of mode and zone. (2) The *dynamic* viewpoint considers motivation, and it includes the concepts of drive and of activity–passivity. (3) The *economic* viewpoint considers energy shifts, and includes affect, pleasure–pain, and anxiety. (4) The *structural* viewpoint considers the devices that regulate the discharge of energy, such as ego, superego, and defense mechanisms.

(5) The *adaptive* viewpoint considers how a person relates to his environment and includes the concepts of wish fulfillment and reality testing.

Unquestionably, psychoanalytic theory lacks the simplicity and clarity of S-R and other behavioristic theories, which can be grasped quickly and unambiguously. It is satisfying to be able to say, "If I apply this stimulus, I will get this response." Such a simple, clear system works, by and large, at the level of the white rat, and even for some higher level animals, but there is serious question whether it can explain more than the simplest forms of human behavior.

Compared to the behavior of lower animals, much more of man's behavior is determined internally and much less is determined by the immediate environment. Motivations, expectations, values, and fears that are internal to the individual are often more important in determining what he will do than are any external stimuli. It is difficult for S-R theory to account for all these important inner conditions, for man's greater complexity and capacity for self-awareness. The appeal of simplicity is lost when it becomes necessary to postulate hundreds of stimuli to predict one response. The appeal of clarity is lost when it becomes difficult to say which of this multitude of stimuli are really stimuli and which are responses. In other words, when it comes to predicting things like the cognitive behavior of human beings, the simplicity and clarity of the behavioristic approach breaks down.

Psychoanalytic theory, on the other hand, contains a number of rather complicated concepts and principles. As will become apparent, many terms overlap in describing related or even the same functions from different vantage points. This state of affairs, which complicates understanding, in part reflects a certain looseness in the theory. More important, it reflects the conviction that human behavior is extremely complex and so must be considered along several different dimensions. In fact, psychoanalytic theorists believe that, to have a full psychological understanding of a person, he must be looked at from several viewpoints, each focusing on a different aspect of the same phenomenon.

This understanding that reality consists of multiple viewpoints is well illustrated in contemporary literature (for example, Lawrence Durrell's *Alexandria Quartet*) and films (for example, Akira Kurosawa's *Rashomon*), as well as in courts of law, where it is clear that a description of "objective reality" varies according to the point of view. Only by combining the information from several viewpoints and resolving apparent inconsistencies can we begin to fully understand any phenomenon. Similarly, in psychoanalysis, we assume that the use of multiple levels for explanation will enhance the richness and depth of our understanding of human behavior.

It has been stated that to fully understand behavior within psychoanalytic theory, the behavior must be considered from five different points of view:[1] (1) The *genetic* or developmental point of view, discussed in the previous chapter, asserts that any explanation of behavior must consider its origin and development. (2) The *dynamic* point of view asserts that any explanation of behavior must include some statement about drives—that is, about the direction and magnitude of the motivational forces underlying behavior. (3) The *economic* point of view assumes that all behavior requires psychological energy—that is, that all psychological functioning involves shifts of energy within the mental apparatus. (4) The *structural* point of view states that drives exist in relation to structures that regulate their discharge; consequently, any explanation of behavior must account for these drive-related structures, as well as those drive-free structures of the ego that allow the individual to adapt to reality. (5) The *adaptive* point of view believes it is necessary to consider the relationship between the individual and his environment. To the psychoanalytic theorist, only when the variables involved in these five points of view are considered is it possible to explain man's behavior.

Table 15.1. Important Concepts and Principles of Psychoanalysis According to Five Points of View.

POINT OF VIEW	CONCEPTS	PRINCIPLES
Genetic	Mode	Innate maturational plan
	Zone	Stages of development
		Critical period of development
Dynamic	Instinctual drive	
	Activity–passivity	
Economic	Energy	Limited amount of energy
	Affect	Displaceability of energy
	Pleasure–pain	
	Anxiety	
Structural	Id, ego, superego	
	Defense mechanisms	
	Ego potentialities	
	Consciousness	
	Conscious, preconscious, unconscious[2]	
Adaptive	Primary process, secondary process	Reality principle
	Wish fulfillment	Pleasure principle
	Reality testing	

In this chapter, we will consider some important concepts and principles of psychoanalytic theory, as shown in Table 15.1, within the context of these five points of view. Some concepts are relevant to more than one of the five viewpoints, but we will discuss them in connection with the viewpoint they best exemplify. It is hoped that the reader will see that psychoanalytic theory uses different concepts to describe the same behavioral phenomenon, depending on which of the five aspects of behavior is of greatest interest.

THE GENETIC POINT OF VIEW

Psychoanalytic theory considers that the human infant at birth is largely undifferentiated, and that certain psychological functions, the potentiality for which existed at birth, gradually become more distinguishable and separate, like the progressive physical differentiation of the embryo in the womb. Just as we might describe the differentiation of the limbs, organs, or nervous system in the embryo, so we can also differentiate certain psychological structures, states, forms of thinking, or characteristic approaches to the world. The theory assumes an innate maturational plan governs the unfolding of both physiological and psychological stages of development.[3]

The idea of an innate maturational plan also assumes that development consists of different stages, each characterized by a particular *mode* and *zone*. The term *mode* refers to a particular type or style of behavior. Erikson has identified five modes of behavior that emerge in a predetermined sequence during early development: taking in (such as food or visual stimulation), taking in and clamping down (such as biting), retention (holding on), elimination (letting go), and intrusiveness (or, in the female form, receptiveness).[4] (We will discuss these modes in detail in Chapter 17.) The term *zone* refers to an area of the body that is progressively sensitized or eroticized, also in a predetermined sequence, by the application of the instinctual drives. It is assumed that for the first months of life, the mouth, or oral zone, is the most sensitized region of the body and is the region that, when stimulated, provides the baby the greatest sensual pleasure. Somewhat later, the region of greatest sensitivity shifts to the anal zone. Finally, the area of sensitivity and greatest sensual pleasure shifts to the genital zone.

Another principle important to understanding the genetic viewpoint is that of a critical period of development. This principle assumes that an inborn coordination occurs between the emergence of certain psychological functions and the maturation of certain physiological functions, and that by combining them the person is capable of a new and more complex level of psychological organization. This new level of integration marks a turning point in the development of the child. The period is termed critical because, if the appropriate psychological function does not emerge, an inadequate or deviant organization will occur. This, in turn, will result in a developmental imbalance.[5]

THE DYNAMIC POINT OF VIEW

The concept of *instinctual drive* is central to psychoanalytic theory, but it is a psychological concept and does not necessarily refer to any physical state or source of energy. Thus, it is not the same as the "instinct" of animal psychology nor the "drive" of S-R theory. The term instinctual drive refers to a mental representation of an internal excitatory state. For example, we are not directly aware of physiological or biochemical changes in our body; we experience them as mental phenomena. As you sit reading, you do not know your blood sugar concentration or hormonal level, but you may be *aware* of feeling hungry or sexy. You have translated a physiological state into a psychological one: you have a *mental representation* of the drive state. This mental representation or idea of the drive is what psychoanalysis refers to when speaking of instinctual impulses.

But an instinctual impulse does not depend on identifying an underlying physiological drive; it implies only a *psychological* need—a force that impels the individual to psychological action, which may in turn lead to overt physical action. The instinctual impulse is a mental phenomenon. Furthermore, the concept of instinctual drive is not that of a blind, driving force but rather one that has some purposive direction; it is innately coordinated with an object or set of objects that will provide gratification by reducing the tension.

Instinctual impulses are grouped together because they share three common chacteristics.[6] (1) They are innate sources of psychological energy for the organism; (2) they have the same aim, to discharge accumulating drive tension; (3) for each drive there is an object or class of objects with which the drive is innately coordinated, and the attainment of which will produce drive gratification.

Two other concepts related to drive discharge are *activity* and *passivity*. Activity does not necessarily mean physical movement, and passivity does not mean inertia. The concepts of activity and passivity do not refer to what appears to an observer to be active or passive behavior. Rather, these concepts refer to the person's relative autonomy from the domination of internal or external stimuli in determining his behavior.[7] Consider the analogy of a person swimming in the ocean who is suddenly lifted by a huge wave. He is in a sense active at that moment, in that he is moving swiftly over a long distance. But he is being carried along, or driven, by the power and direction of a force (the wave) not under his control—which means his role in the physical movement is passive. On the other hand, the boy who sticks his finger in the hole in the dike, or engages in any isometric exercise while not displaying any physical movement, is in fact actively engaged in work. Activity and passivity, then, are defined according to how much the individual is controlling and directing the course of his behavior and how much it is being determined by factors outside of his control.

THE ECONOMIC POINT OF VIEW

This point of view assumes that all psychological behavior involves the displacement of *energy*. Although not all psychoanalytic theorists agree, Freud suggested that there was a limited or fixed amount of psychological energy available to the individual.[8] This means that if energy is being used for one mental function, less is available at that moment for other mental functions. Put another way, this idea of a fixed amount of psychological energy means that there is some limit to the amount of stimulation to which a person can attend at any one moment.[9]

Since drives push for discharge of energy, it is assumed that if the drive energy is not discharged through one channel, it will be discharged through another. For example, if the drive energy is not discharged by obtaining the appropriate goal object, it may be discharged internally, which is experienced within the individual as *affect*.

If the energy is discharged in connection with attaining the goal object, it results in a reduction of psychological tension. In psychoanalytic theory, the reduction of such instinctual drive tension is the definition of *pleasure;* the increase in such drive tension is the definition of *pain.*[10]

When the individual is unable to control his own behavior, when he feels threatened that painful internal or external stimuli will overwhelm him, he experiences *anxiety*. Anxiety is probably most commonly thought of as being detrimental to psychological functioning; thus it may seem paradoxical to say that anxiety is basic to the development of cognitive functioning. But it is indeed because of the need to avoid being overwhelmed by anxiety that the individual develops cognitive processes. Such mental mechanisms that control or modify the instinctual impulses, thus protecting the individual from excessive anxiety, are called *defense mechanisms,* which we will explain in detail in Chapter 18.

THE STRUCTURAL POINT OF VIEW

When we discuss psychological mechanisms that control, delay, or otherwise modify the uninhibited expression of drives, we are beginning to discuss behavior from the structural point of view, and, in fact, defense mechanisms are examples of psychological structures. To psychoanalytic theorists, man's mental apparatus can be divided into three conceptual parts: the *id,* the *ego,* and the *superego.* These concepts refer to a differentiation of the psychological nature of man, in terms of drives (id); cognitive, motor, and other executive functions (ego); and conscience (superego). These concepts do not mean that there are such structures located anatomically in the brain, but rather that the mode of functioning, the goals, and the outcome of each are different and sometimes conflicting.

The mental activities grouped together under the term *id* are man's drives or instinctual impulses, discussed above. The *ego*—or, rather, the intellectual processes called ego functions—mediates between the instinctual impulses (id) and the external world. By means of perception, memory, searching, and problem solving the individual is actually able to obtain the object of drive gratification. Some ego functions are innate, including potentialities for memory (for example, the potentiality for memory traces to be laid down in certain predetermined patterns), for motor and perceptual functioning, and for regulating the level at which affect or accumulated drive energy will be discharged. These structural givens are not the *physical* organs of perception or the muscles controlling motor activity; rather, they are the *psychological* structures through which such activity is regulated.

According to current psychoanalytic theory, such ego functions develop from the individual's innate potentialities interacting with his experience. It is assumed he is born with certain basic potentialities for ego functioning, but they are activated by his interacting with the environment.[11] For example, the person's capacity to perceive external stimuli and to store these images as memory traces is an innate ego potentiality, but there must be some external source of stimulation in order for these potentialities to be activated. Thus, certain basic ego functions are not learned but are activated by experience. The next chapter will discuss this issue in greater detail.

It is assumed that individuals are born with innate potentialities not only for ego functions but also for other kinds of behavior such as defense mechanisms and ego modes. For example, the defense mechanism of repression—whereby a painful instinctual impulse is kept out of conscious awareness —may be an innate potentiality of the ego. Likewise, ego modes, the styles of behavior connected with specific stages of development, are also thought of as innate potentialities, so that the first mode of behavior—sucking or taking in —is a potentiality in every normal infant. An appropriate stimulus will activate this sucking and it will remain the dominant mode of behavior until the infant moves into the next stage of development, when a new mode of behavior will be activated.

A later mental structure to develop is the *supergo,* the values, ethics, and prohibitions that the child has experienced in interacting with other people (generally his parents) and that he has *internalized* as his inner watchman. Since the child has simply adopted these dictates from others and not subjected them to his own evaluation, the superego is only a primitive form of conscience. Furthermore, just as increasing drive tension may produce instinctual anxiety, so the pressure from internalized moral dictates may produce superego anxiety—as when a person feels guilty for having violated one of his own rules for behavior. Here also, the ego mediates between id and superego forces.

The mental apparatus can also be looked at in terms of how aware the individual is of his own mental functioning.[12] The memories or psychological processes (such as defenses) that he cannot become aware of under ordinary circumstances are called *unconscious* thoughts. *Conscious* thoughts or ideas are those occupying his attention at the moment. Those thoughts that he is not aware of at the moment but that are available to him to think about if he chooses are called *preconscious.*

The model of unconscious, preconscious, and conscious does not exactly correspond to the structural model of id, ego, and superego. The instinctual impulses (id) may be largely unconscious, but not entirely so and this may vary according to the individual. The ego capacities may be largely preconscious and conscious, but certain ego functions, such as defense mechanisms, may be unconscious. Finally, the superego may consist largely of prohibitions derived from external sources that the child must have been aware of, but it may also include irrational elements of which he is unconscious.

The comparison between the two models also becomes more complicated when we try to further distinguish between conscious and *consciousness*.

The concepts of unconscious, preconscious, and conscious refer to the current temporal *state* of an idea or mental mechanism, but the concept of consciousness refers to a *mental process* or *function*. [13] For example, a person's memory trace for the date of the Battle of Waterloo may be stored in a preconscious state. By the direction of consciousness to that trace, the memory may become conscious. Applying consciousness changes the state of the memory from preconscious to conscious. Thus, consciousness is an ego function— and, as we shall see, one that is critical for learning to occur.

THE ADAPTIVE POINT OF VIEW

Two other important concepts related to the distinction between unconscious and conscious are those of *primary process* and *secondary process* thinking. Primary process thinking is illustrated by dreams, which are often illogical, nonsensical, and full of inconsistencies and physical impossibilities. Primary process thinking is also closely tied to drives and is based on the mental representations of those drives. Often it serves the function of *wish fulfillment* or substitute drive gratification through fantasy. Such thinking also occurs in drug states, in conditions of extreme stress or fatigue, in certain forms of psychopathology, in some kinds of creative thought, and in the thinking of young children, for whom the difference between fantasy and reality is not well established.

Secondary process thinking is rational, orderly, and logical and has at its disposal all except unconscious memories. It is the form of thinking expected in older children and adults. It is oriented toward problem solving and is intimately connected with reality testing.

Reality testing is the ability to distinguish between what one wishes or hopes for, or fantasizes, and what really exists; it is the ability to search for the drive object by detours. Reality testing enables the individual to adapt to and survive in his environment. As we will see in the next chapter, fantasies are important in mental development, but in the long run they do not provide adequate gratification. To imagine that one is sitting at a table loaded with sizzling steaks and chocolate cakes does not, in fact, reduce one's need for food. It is only by locating such a table in the external world that hunger can be reduced. The capacity to search out the environment and locate an object that matches the memory image of what one wants is another aspect of reality testing.

Reality testing is one thought mechanism that exemplifies the reality principle. Whereas in primary process thinking a person is governed by the *pleasure principle*—by striving for immediate discharge of drive energy through any available channel and without regard for consequences—in secondary process thinking he is governed by the *reality principle*, by postponing immediate discharge of energy so as to ensure he can obtain the drive-gratifying object in reality. Uncontrolled screaming, for example, may give some temporary relief from the mounting internal tension of hunger, but only controlled, systematic investigation of reality and external surroundings is likely to produce food—the object that will in fact reduce drive tension. In this way, the reality principle serves the purpose of the pleasure principle—to obtain drive gratification.

SUMMARY

This chapter reviewed some basic concepts and principles used in psychoanalytic theory. We associated these concepts with five viewpoints, each of which describes behavior from a different perspective. The genetic viewpoint looks at behavior in terms of its origin and development and includes the concepts of mode and zone. The dynamic viewpoint considers the role of motivation and includes the concepts of drive and of activity and passivity. The economic viewpoint is concerned with shifts of energy within the individual and includes concepts of affect, pleasure–pain, and anxiety. The structural viewpoint accounts for the psychological structures that regulate the discharge of energy, such as ego, superego, and defense mechanisms. The adaptive viewpoint considers the relationship between the individual and his environment and includes such concepts as wish fulfillment and reality testing. While each of these concepts has a specific definition, they also overlap somewhat with each other insofar as they are referring to different aspects of the same behavior.

16

A PSYCHOANALYTIC MODEL OF BEHAVIOR

Preview

The model here shows that the infant's mental activity starts with the push of instinctual drives.

When the tension of a drive (such as hunger) increases and is satisfied by the right object (milk), the drive is gratified. This sequence is recorded in the infant's memory, so that later, when the object is absent, the drive tension activates the memory of the object. This is the first step in developing thinking.

When the infant searches his environment for an object to match his memory of the drive-gratifying object, it is the beginning of reality-oriented thought.

We will describe a specific example of this model and apply it to a classroom situation.

In the preceding chapters we said that instinctual drives are important to the development of cognition, but we did not explain why. Let us now look more closely at the relationship between drives and the development of thinking, and see why psychoanalytic theory places such great emphasis on the role of drive in intellectual development.

To see this relationship, consider the schematic model that appears in Figures 16.1 through 16.9. These figures do not correspond to any physical structure of the mind; rather, they represent the flow and direction of psychological processes. The model also shows how these processes are mutually determined by both internal and external conditions. Finally, the model represents the line of development of thinking from more primitive to less primitive forms.

THE GENERAL MODEL

As we stated, psychoanalytic theory assumes that every infant is born with instinctual drives that continually push for discharge. This basic condition of instinctual drive is represented in the upper right box of Figure 16.1. As drive tension increases, the unfulfilled need results in a state of discomfort for the infant. This condition of tension remains until an object that will satisfy the drive is obtained. This situation of drive leading to increased tension and need is represented in the uppermost box in the figure. The large dotted circle represents the mental functions of man. Although mental functions are drawn as being independent, in fact, the theory assumes much greater interaction and overlap than we have indicated here.

What happens as a result of increased drive tension depends partly on the external environment. The two arrows indicate two possibilities—that the object that will satisfy the drive is present (heavy black arrow) or that it is not present (double-line arrow).

Figure 16.2 shows the outcome of these two situations. Depending on whether the drive object is present or absent, the flow of psychological energy will go one way or another. (a) If the object is present, and the organism makes a motor reaction to it (for example, grabs hold of it and puts in mouth), drive tension is discharged, the impulse is gratified, and the infant experiences a feeling of pleasure and relaxation. (b) If the object is not present, however, drive tension continues to increase, and the mounting psychological energy must then be discharged in other ways, such as through an affective outburst (as crying), or through certain cognitive processes (such as imagining).

If we put these two figures together, we obtain Figure 16.3. In this first overall look at the model, we should emphasize two important features of the psychoanalytic theory of thinking. First, the theory assumes that the impetus for thought processes is *internal:* the arrows in the diagram originate *within* the circle of the individual's mental processes and are directed *out* into the external world. Thus, the flow of psychological energy is from within the individual out toward the environment. This view is in marked contrast to the

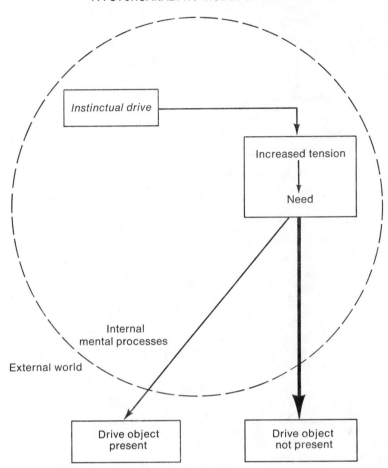

Fig. 16.1. An infant is born with instinctual drives that push for discharge.

S-R and cognitive models, which assumed that the impetus for cognitive activity begins with an *external* stimulus. (Learning theory, of course, is the more extreme in this regard.)

Second, the direction psychological processes take, after the infant experiences internal tension, depends on whether the drive object is present in his environment. If it is present, his tension is reduced, a pleasurable feeling is reinstated, and he settles back into a state of "comfortable stupor." However, if the drive object is *absent,* only then does the need for cognitive mechanisms—to search for and locate that object—become activated. For a theory of cognitive development, the implications of this aspect are enormous. It means that a child who is continually gratified, who never experiences any frustration or temporary nongratification, will have no reason to develop cognitive processes. As long as his every need is met, his every impulse satisfied, he will remain a passive, receptive, noncognitive organism. Only when needs are not immediately met, when impulses are not automatically gratified,

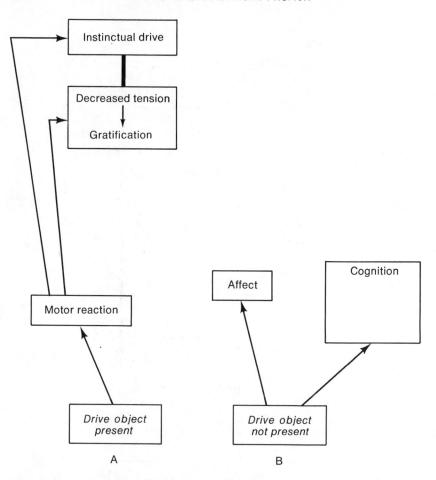

Fig. 16.2. Two external possibilities: (a) an object is present that will satisfy the drive or (b) it is not present.

does a new level of mental development occur. Thus, contrary to some misconceptions about psychoanalysis, the theory holds that moderate frustration is not only unavoidable but necessary for mental development. And besides, fortunately for the child, continual immediate gratification is impossible.

A SPECIFIC EXAMPLE OF THE MODEL

Let us now look at the model in detail. We will use a specific example from the earliest period of an infant's life which illustrates the relationship between instinctual drives and the development of cognition. Hunger is an instinctual drive of great importance to the young infant. Periodically, the strength of this hunger drive increases, accumulating drive energy and producing psychological tension, which is experienced as discomfort or pain. The infant is in a state of need—the need for food.

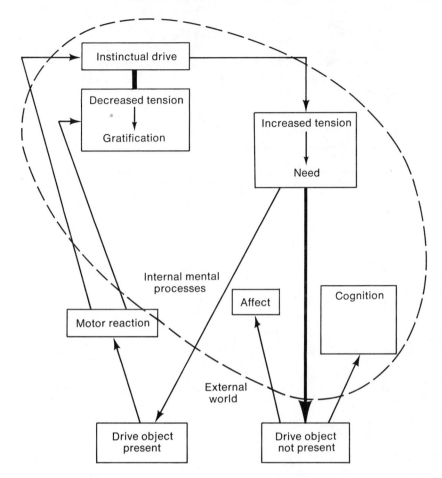

Fig. 16.3. First overall view of psychoanalytic model of intellectual development.

This is a description of the internal condition of the infant. Now let us consider the environment. The environment, in the form of the mother, can provide the object, food, that will satisfy the drive. When the nipple is placed close to the infant's mouth, a series of reflexive reactions are initiated that eventually result in the sucking response. This response obtains the milk necessary to meet the hunger need, decreasing drive tension and finally gratifying the drive.

In the life of a well-cared-for infant, the mother is alert to the signs the baby gives to indicate this state of increased tension, such as restlessness, irritability, and crying. Time after time, as she notes the signs that represent the internal state of drive tension and need, the mother intervenes to provide the drive object. As a result of the many repetitions of this sequence of associated events (drive increase—pain—drive object—drive gratification), a memory trace or image of the drive object (the breast or bottle) is laid down in the mind of the infant (see Figure 16.4). Moreover, this image is laid down in *association* with the experience of drive increase and drive gratification. This image is indicated in Figure 16.4 by the small box within the cognition box. The dotted arrows leading to the image indicate its sources—need, presence of the object, and gratification.

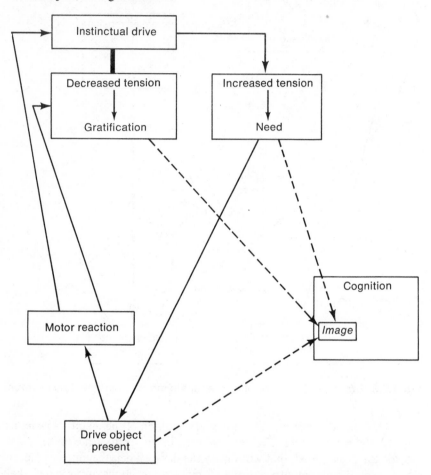

Fig. 16.4. Image of drive object laid down in mind of infant.

What we have here, then, is a paradigm for the initial development of memory. According to psychoanalytic theory, the first memory traces are laid down in connection with the experiences of drive increase and drive gratification. In other words, the mind does not passively record every event that crosses the infant's vision. Rather, the recording of memories is selective and, in the beginning, depends on the event being associated with conditions of instinctual drive increase and decrease.

WHAT HAPPENS WHEN DRIVE INCREASES

Let us turn now to the situation in which there is an increase in drive tension but no drive object present in the environment to gratify that need. As Figure 16.5 shows, this situation may have three outcomes. First, the increas-

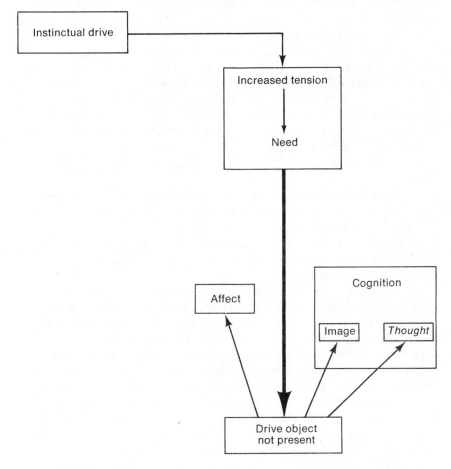

Fig. 16.5. What happens when drive object not present.

ing drive energy may be discharged within the body as *affect,* manifested in crying, moaning, fretfulness, or random thrashing about. This behavior provides some relief in that it reduces the infant's level of drive tension, but it does not bring him any closer to obtaining food—that is, it does not provide any lasting drive gratification. (It may, however, serve as a *sign* for the mother to produce some food.)

A second outcome may occur as the infant develops and as memory traces are laid down. As the infant's hunger drive increases in strength, some of its energy is transferred to the memory *image*—for example, of the breast —via the associative connections already established. When this memory of the drive object is aroused, it will provide some partial drive gratification because it has been previously associated with experiences of drive gratification. Psychoanalytic theory further assumes that this image can become so intense that it is experienced as a perception—that is, as representing an object actually present. The experience of such an hallucinatory image during infancy has neither been proven nor disproven, but we know that such experiences occur in adults in states of extreme need. Men lost in the desert without water often see a mirage, such as an oasis of palm trees, with pools and water, when no oasis exists. Such hallucinations, it is understood, reflect an extreme state of need, in which large amounts of drive energy are transferred to the memory of a gratifying object or situation. Because so much energy is invested in the image, it is so intense as to appear to be a perception rather than a memory, and hence the individual believes that it represents something external to himself.

Such hallucinatory images are abnormal for an awake adult, but they regularly occur during sleep—dreams, after all, are made up of perceptual images intense enough to assume a degree of "reality." We are often not sure, while dreaming, whether what we are seeing is "really true" or not. This is partly because during sleep we suspend certain cognitive functions that we use for reality testing during the day.

For the young child, whose reality-testing abilities are weak even when he is awake, the confusion between memory image and perceptual image is potentially quite large. That is, the young child has difficulty separating the products of his imagination from real things. Children can become genuinely frightened of their thoughts, and certainly of their dreams or nightmares. The products of dreams or fantasies seem as real to them as any others. Thus, these products can serve, at least partially, the same function as the real object.

To return to our example, this means that the image of the breast can, in part, serve the same function as does the breast itself—the function of drive reduction. Psychoanalytic theory postulates that the first forms of mental activity are closely tied up with drives and drive gratification. The earliest memory traces are laid down in conjunction with the feeding situation, and the earliest form of mental activity, primary process thinking, occurs when there is an increase in drive tension and the drive object is absent in reality.

This early form of mental activity, however, brings about only a partial and temporary reduction of drive tension. The ideational substitute—the image of the breast—brings about some temporary relief; but since it is not followed by food for the infant to ingest, it does not provide any lasting gratification. In other words, though primary process ideation brings about immediate gratification on a fantasy level, it does nothing to provide gratification in reality. To do this—to decide what object is needed and to locate this object in reality—a higher level or form of mentation is needed.

The third possible outcome in which the drive object is not present (see Figure 16.5) involves *thought.* As Figure 16.6 shows, thought serves as a guide to motor action for locating the drive object in reality, which is then followed by a reaction to that object, which in turn is followed by drive gratification.

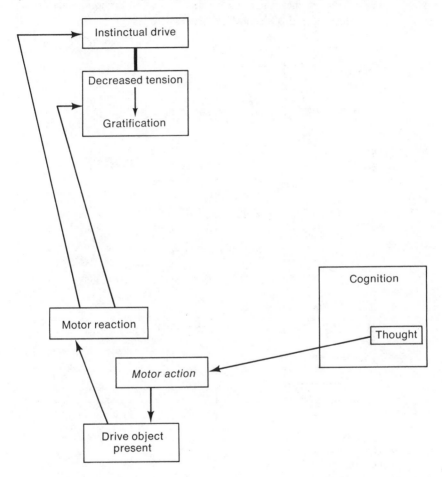

Fig. 16.6. Thought may lead to drive gratification.

Let us illustrate this process from our example, using Figure 16.7. As the drive tension associated with hunger continues to increase, an internal search process begins in order to locate the memory of the object that was previously associated with the gratification of that drive. Eventually, this search process results in the activation of the memory (image) of the breast. At this point, further mental processes are set in motion. These processes involve perceptually scanning the environment and evaluating the information thus obtained. The evaluation takes the form of comparing the various perceptions of the objects present in reality—for example, rattle, crib, blanket—with the memory image of the drive object, and then deciding whether any of these perceptions match the memory. If they do not, the perceptual search continues until the infant locates in reality some object that matches his memory. The development of this early form of judgment—of searching the environment to make a match between internal memory and external perception—is at the basis of reality testing and of secondary process thinking.

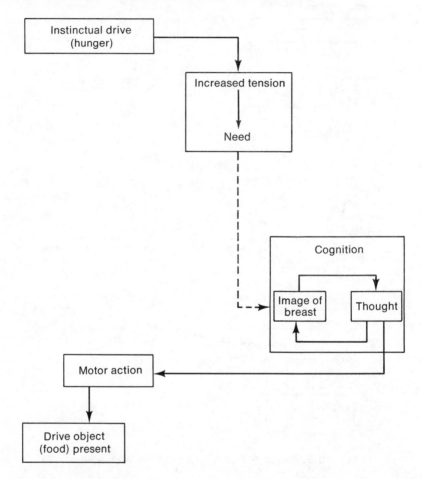

Fig. 16.7. How hunger may activate the thought process to bring about desired change in reality.

Once the infant judges that the drive object (food) is present in reality, further thought processes are initiated. These processes are concerned with how to obtain that object, and are necessarily connected with the level of development and maturation of the child. Depending on his current skills, the child may be able to crawl, or walk, or climb in order to obtain the object. Also depending on his current level of development, he may be able to *think about* crawling, walking, or climbing. The development of secondary process thought processes allows him to *think about* what actions to take to obtain the object —that is, it provides him with the possibility for experimental action in thought. He no longer is only a *re*active organism, he can now initiate purposive action. Moreover, he can now mentally try out and discard those plans of action that do not lead him to the goal object.

Several differences should be pointed out between this outcome of secondary process thinking and that of primary process thinking. First, primary process thinking stops at the point of activating the memory previously associated with drive gratification; that is, it stops at the point of arousing the fantasy or hallucinatory image of the breast. Secondary process thinking involves activating the memory of the source of gratification and *then* beginning a search in the real world for an object that will match that memory image. In other words, the mental process does not stop at the imaginal level; it is continued until an object is found in reality that corresponds to the memory of a previous source of gratification.

This continuation or prolongation of the mental process has certain other implications, which are apparent when we look at the completed model shown in Figure 16.8. In primary process thinking, the absence of the drive object in reality is followed by an *immediate discharge* of drive energy that activates the memory image. The single arrow from *drive object not present* to *Image* indicates the immediate, direct nature of this process. Secondary process thinking, on the other hand, involves a series of *detours* before any drive gratification takes place, as indicated by the several heavy arrows representing this process. This means that for some period of time the rising drive tension must be kept in check—that is, that the mental apparatus must have the capacity to control and inhibit the immediate discharge of drive energy until the object is obtained in reality. It is the development of mental mechanisms for defense and control that makes possible this *delay* of drive gratification.

We have seen so far that conditions of both drive increase and drive gratification are closely associated with the initial laying down of memory traces. We have also seen that the temporary nongratification of drives is responsible for the development of mental functioning. The first form of ideation to develop—primary process thinking—affords some immediate, but temporary drive reduction. It is only with the subsequent development of secondary process thinking that the child is able to satisfy his own needs.

As the child matures, these needs will be expanded to include more than the basic physiological necessities for life. There will be needs for achievement, for mastery, for competence, for self-esteem, and so on. Despite the fact that these needs reflect ego interests, rather than being id-determined, the same model of behavior generally applies. The arousal of the need is accompanied by a state of increased psychological tension. If the need is not immediately gratified, then one of three consequences may result: (1) an affective outburst, (2) a fantasy that the need is magically met, or (3) some realistic plan of action developed and carried out to fulfill the need.

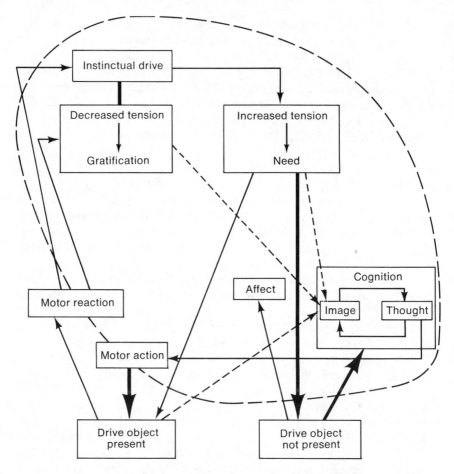

Fig. 16.8. The complete psychoanalytic model.

AN EXAMPLE FROM THE CLASSROOM

Let us translate this into a classroom situation. Suppose a fourth-grade class has been given a difficult mathematical reasoning problem to work out. Suppose also that all the children in the class are motivated to solve the problem—they have a need to demonstrate their competence and ability to master the present situation. As the problem is given to them, and as they read it over, the need for solution and mastery increases, as does the level of internal psychological tension. The overt level of squirming, gum-cracking, giggling, and other signs of tension and uneasiness increases markedly. Provided that the answer is not immediately supplied by the teacher or another student, there are three possible outcomes to the situation, as Figure 16.9 shows.

First, as the tension associated with the need to solve the problem increases, the discomfort may become too great. The child may be unable to contain the mounting psychological pressure, and all at once this tension is released in an outburst of *affect*. The frustrated young student, unable to solve

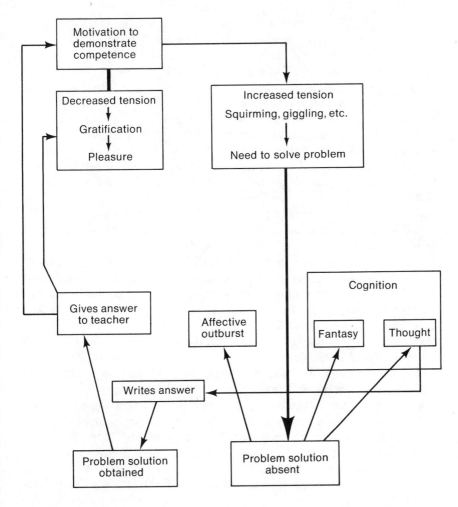

Fig. 16.9. Reactions of fourth-grade children to difficult mathematics problem.

his math problem, instead begins to kick the desk, the wall, or other students, to run around the room, to yell or sing or be otherwise "disruptive." These behaviors help reduce his level of internal discomfort, but of course they do nothing to gratify the need for mastery and competence. In the end, the original need is no closer to being fulfilled than it was at the beginning of this sequence. For this reason, because the need remains ungratified, and drive tension has been only partly reduced, we can expect this sequence of events to be continually repeated. The child's acting up is no more than a temporary relief; his real need—to be able to solve the problem given him—has not been met. When the child is able to attain that goal, the acting-up behavior will disappear, for the drive will have been discharged via other, more constructive channels.

A second outcome of this situation—in which the child is given a problem to solve for which the answer is not immediately forthcoming—is that the child will lapse into a state of daydreaming and fantasy, that is, into primary process thinking. Unable to solve the problem in reality, the child may fall into a daydream in which he has not only figured out this problem, but in fact is such a mathematical whiz that he is about to plan the first space module to fly to Venus. The elaboration of this fantasy into the child's imagining himself to be so competent in mathematics that all the great scientists in the world must come to consult with him provides some degree of drive gratification, in that it clearly fulfills the need for competence and mastery—at least on the fantasy level. But the fantasy stands in marked contrast to the reality of the situation—that he cannot figure out his fourth-grade math problem. The original need remains unfulfilled. While the fantasy provides some temporary drive reduction, the original psychological tension will continue to increase. Both the child who acts up and the child who is daydreaming (or not paying attention, or is uninterested, or however else this retreat into fantasy is labeled) remain in a condition of psychological tension and discomfort. Although their behavior provides them with some temporary and partial gratification, they do not experience any basic satisfaction. (Such unsatisfactory behaviors do continue, however; this issue is discussed further in Chapter 19.) Unfortunately, their methods for discharging painful inner tension bring them no closer to a feeling of fulfillment and pleasure.

The third possible outcome of this situation requires the use of mental mechanisms to temporarily restrain and delay the immediate discharge of accumulating psychological energy and instead to channel this energy into activating those cognitive processes that will be of use in arriving at the solution of the problem. By searching through the memory store, by the use of secondary thought processes, by trying out different approaches both in thought and action, the child may eventually reach the solution to the problem. The need for mastery and competence is then fulfilled through his own efforts and activity, and he experiences a feeling of satisfaction and pleasure. Although the satisfaction was not so immediate as with the other two examples, the basic need has been met, and in that sense the satisfaction is more genuine.

SUMMARY

This chapter presented a model illustrating how mental processes get started in the infant. We have seen that, from the psychoanalytic point of view, the push of instinctual drives causes the beginning of mental activity. When drive tension increases, and an appropriate object is present to satisfy that drive, the infant reacts to the object and the drive is gratified. The repetition of the sequence *drive increase, drive object present, drive gratification* is also recorded in the memory of the infant.

Subsequently, if the drive increases but the drive object is not present, the drive energy may be used to activate the memory image of the drive object.

This is the first step toward the development of thinking. The activation of this memory of a drive-gratifying object often produces some temporary satisfaction, but eventually the infant will have to locate the object in reality, if any true gratification is to occur. Accordingly, he begins to search the environment to try to locate an object that matches his memory of the drive-gratifying object. This is the beginning of reality-oriented thought.

After presenting the general form of this model, we looked at a specific example of how the hunger drive may initiate thought processes in the infant. Finally, the model was applied to the classroom situation.

17

THE CHARACTER AND CAUSES OF DEVELOPMENT

Preview

Here we will show how the psychoanalytic idea of change involves the concepts of an innate developmental plan and of five stages of development from birth to adolescence:

(1) *Taking in,* ranging from birth to 15 months, in which the infant learns to differentiate inside from outside, first by contact, then by visual perception.

(2) *Autonomy and will,* from 15 to 35 months, in which the infant alternates between holding on and letting go. He also begins to communicate verbally and to develop a sense of self.

(3) *Exploration and intrusion,* from three to five years, when the child gains initiative, a superego, intellectual curiosity, and a capacity for fantasy.

(4) *Industry,* from six to 10 years, when the child learns skills that enable him to complete tasks that have meaning in the real world.

(5) *Adolescence,* in which the genital drive gradually becomes predominant and new intellectual capacities develop.

THE CHARACTER OF DEVELOPMENT

Psychoanalytic theory believes development can be characterized as consisting of five stages. The nature and sequence of these stages are determined by intrinsic maturational factors. That is, there is an innate plan that governs emotional and social development, as well as organic development.

These stages are not simply the cumulative effects of growth and learning. Rather each stage is qualitatively distinct from the preceding stages; each has a different psychological configuration that results when different *modes* of behavior and *zones* of activity become predominant. The first stage, for example, is characterized by the taking-in mode and the oral zone.[1]

Because each new stage of development has a change in mode and zone, it also has a reorganized psychological structure. While this reorganization is going on, the psychological state of the individual is rather shaky and vulnerable to disruption, but at the end of each stage there is a new psychological integration, which will have a lasting effect on future development.

As we discuss developmental change, we will focus on the development of the ego. According to psychoanalytic theory, the new psychological integration that occurs at the end of a stage modifies the structure of the ego, making it possible for the child to adapt, to participate more actively, and to attain greater mastery over his environment.

When we discuss developmental change, we must also discuss the basic dimensions along which such change occurs.[2] One dimension is the change in behavior from being *involuntary* to being increasingly *voluntary*. Involuntary kinds of behavior, over which a person has no control, are more characteristic of earlier periods of development; voluntary behavior is more characteristic of later stages. To psychoanalytic theorists, involuntary behavior is due to the uncurtailed discharge of instinctual drives, whereas voluntary behavior results from the control of direct drive discharge, through the development of ego structures. This means, then, that there is *decreasing drive determination* of behavior and *increasing control by ego functions.* An example of this kind of developmental change can be seen in crying behavior. A young infant cries as an involuntary response to an increase in tension (for example, hunger), whereas an older child's cry may be a voluntary way of signifying his wishes (such as wanting a chocolate bar). In the first instance, only relief of tension will put an end to the crying; in the second, the crying can be stopped on demand from the parent.

Another dimension along which change occurs begins with simple *reflexive reaction* and ends with self-initiated *directed action*—a change that requires not only maturation of motor potentialities but also the development of judgment. An example is the reflexive grasp response during the first weeks of life, with which the infant may even support his own weight. Around six months, this reflex is replaced by a purposive, directed reaching and grasping of objects. Stated another way (see Chapter 15) change occurs from *passivity*, in which the ego is overwhelmed by drive or external forces, to *activity*, in which the ego masters those forces.

THE FIVE STAGES OF DEVELOPMENT

In the following sections, we will discuss five stages of development from birth to adolescence. Since we will emphasize intellectual development, rather than personality or emotional development, we will describe each stage according to its predominant ego mode or type of behavior, rather than according to its psychosexual zone (the oral, anal, and phallic categories). The discussion of one of the most important aspects of psychological development —the development of defense mechanisms—is postponed to Chapter 18 so as not to overburden the reader and because it is difficult to show an exact correspondence between specific stages and the development of various defenses.

In this discussion, a great deal of attention is paid to the earliest years of life—an emphasis that reflects three basic premises of psychoanalytic theory. The first is that development is connected with the need to control instinctual drives present from birth on; thus, to understand development, we must understand the early beginnings of such control. The second assumption is that the earliest modes of activity and styles of thinking do not disappear later. These early forms become less dominant, but they are not lost; they remain in the person's potential behavioral repertoire and may be activated under certain conditions. The third assumption is that we can understand current behavior only by knowing its developmental history—that is, by the genetic approach. To fully explain the child's behavior in the classroom today, we must understand what needs or drives he is trying to gratify and how he has tried to gratify them in the past. Stated another way, the modes or styles of behavior used during an early stage of development to obtain gratification continue to occur in later stages, and this is especially noticeable in situations in which the child is unable to satisfy his needs in a more mature fashion.

The First Stage of Development—Taking In

The taking-in stage is characterized by introjection or incorporation.[3] The infant responds to external objects by taking them into his mouth and swallowing them. This incorporative mode is also expressed through taking in by the hands (grasping) and by taking in through the various sense organs (for example, seeing). In all, it is a receptive mode of behavior, and it is largely at the mercy of what the environment offers. Apart from this incorporative behavior, the reactions of the infant are largely uncoordinated.

Psychoanalytic theory divides this first stage of development into three substages or *phases.* [4] The first phase is *nondifferentiation* —neither within the infant nor between the infant and the external world, nor among the various objects in the external world. As William James said, life is truly one "big, buzzing, booming confusion."[5] The second phase is marked by the infant's developing the ability to *recognize his first visual percept* (*percept* is an object recognized through the senses), to differentiate the human face from other external stimuli—as manifest in the emergence of the infant's smiling response. In the third phase, the infant is able to differentiate his mother's face from other faces; the beginning of this phase is marked by the emergence of "stranger anxiety."

First Phase—Nondifferentiation (Birth to Two Months). Psychoanalytic theory makes several assumptions about the state of the newborn. The first is that the infant at birth is largely nondifferentiated: he does not distinguish between internal and external sources of stimulation, nor does he differentiate among the perception of a thing, the internal imagining of it, and the experience of gratification derived from it. In this nondifferentiated state, everything is part of himself.

An exception to this state of nondifferentiation is that there appears to exist, from birth onward, a distinction between inner states of pleasure and lack of pleasure (unpleasure). From the beginning, the infant appears to respond to increases and decreases in inner tension, as shown in his crying, and his restless, fretful behavior. At birth, the infant operates entirely according to the Nirvana principle—he strives for reduction of physical tension. A bit later his behavior becomes regulated by the pleasure-pain principle—he strives for reduction of psychological tension.

"Strives" is not quite accurate, for the condition of the infant during this period is one of helplessness and passivity. He responds reflexively to what is given, but he lacks consciousness or awareness of the objects that reduce tension. At most, the infant is aware that such reduction has taken place. Since there is no differentiation between internal and external, the source of gratification—tension reduction—is experienced as coming about through changes in his own body. In this sense, the infant's experience is one of omnipotence; he alone provides his own grafitication.

The absence of consciousness means not only that the infant lacks awareness of objects (his world is objectless), but also that he is without available memory. In the next few weeks, however, the existence of *memory traces*—mental records of experience—will begin to be apparent.

It is clear that during this first phase there is little ego organization. This phase consists of undifferentiated psychological functions, out of which the instinctual drives and drive-control structures will be differentiated. Those few ego functions that are available are mostly reflexive, hence involuntary and passive. The potentialities for ego development are present at birth, but it will be some time until they are all activated.

However, psychoanalytic theorists do postulate that one psychological structure is present at birth to protect the infant from being overwhelmed by excessive external stimulation. This *stimulus barrier* shields him from external stimulation until internal psychological structures are well enough established to deal with it. Sleep, with its withdrawal of alertness from the sense organs and resulting nonreceptivity to external stimuli, is one example of how the stimulus barrier works. Another is the infant's relatively high threshold for sound and light stimuli. The stimulus barrier begins to diminish, theorists believe, when the infant develops the ability to withdraw from excessive external stimulation—either physically, as in moving his body, or psychologically, through the defense mechanism of denial.

Gradually, out of this passive, nondifferentiated state, the development of perception begins. Although the infant initially responds primarily to stimuli originating in his own body and very little to those coming from the outside, there is one zone in which the two sources of stimulation coincide. The oral zone is not usually thought of as an organ of perception, but psychoanalytic theorists consider it the locus of the earliest differentiated perceptual activity. This zone not only responds to both external and internal stimuli, it also is characterized by the presence, at birth, of extremely reliable reflexes. Two of these reflexes, *rooting*—the reflexive rotation of the head toward a stimulus following stimulation of the external part of the mouth—and *clinging* or *sucking* are assumed to be important in subsequent psychological development. As we shall see in Chapter 18, rooting is important because it is a behavior that eventually leads to drive gratification, but it is not directly gratifying in itself. As such, it is a form of *detour behavior,* which is considered to be an ego function. Rooting is thus an example of an innate ego potentiality.

In contrast, clinging and sucking provide *immediate* need gratification. As the basis for instinctual need gratification, this activity is seen to be critical in the development of emotional attachments to other objects that will gratify instinctual needs. Thus, the activity of sucking and the pleasure experienced following taking in food forms the very early origin for the development of later positive emotional relationships.

Three other rudimentary sources of perception, which are subordinate to the oral zone, are the hand, the middle ear, and the outer skin surface. Reaction to stimulation of any one of these areas tends not to be differentiated; rather the infant experiences it as a generalized "taking in"—the predominant mode of reaction of the entire first stage.

If the mouth is the first perceptual zone, then the first perceptual activity is *contact* between the mouth and the breast or bottle, and the first percept—a *contact percept*—is that of the breast or bottle. Perception thus begins on the contact level. Gradually, however, it shifts to visual-distance perception, with the infant paying more attention to the surrounding environment, particularly his mother's face.

Another important cognitive change that develops out of the nursing situation is *memory.* Freud wrote that when internal drive tension is reduced by a gratifying object, memory traces of this experience are laid down in the mind.[6] The repetitive experience in nursing of contact perception, need gratification, and tension reduction, is assumed to leave some sort of trace, and so begin the development of memory (see Chapter 16).

As the infant progresses through this first phase of life, two kinds of differentiation occur. The first differentiation is *between internal and external stimuli,* and is facilitated by three developments in the infant: (1) The increasing reliance on distance perception of external stimuli means that the infant begins to become more aware of his surroundings, which in turn helps him begin to differentiate between internal and external. (2) The infant begins to perceive that tension is internal, whereas the object that reduces the tension is external. (3) The motor response of withdrawal shows the infant that what he can withdraw from is external and what he cannot withdraw from is internal.

The second differentiation the infant makes is *between his own body and the rest of the world,* between "I" and "non-I." This partly results from the early experiences of contact perception, in which drive tension and the object providing drive gratification occurred jointly. The simultaneous occurrence of both types of experience within the infant helps him mark off his body as separate from the rest of the world. It is the only place in which the simultaneous experience of stimulation from two sources occurs. The development of the mental representations of this body image, or body ego, contributes to the differentiation of the I and the non-I.

The differentiation of I and non-I also results from the development of *judgment.* At this early period, judgment is of a primitive sort; it is a judgment of quality, concerned with whether a particular stimulus has certain attributes. Freud suggested that this type of judgment is first made about objects to be put in the mouth.[7] Objects judged to taste good are incorporated, those judged to taste bad are expelled. These bad objects are made alien to the ego and so belong to the external world. Thus, this early differentiation between the internal I and external non-I is made on the basis of the qualities of good and bad—that is, on the basis of the pleasure-principle. Such a good-bad distinction does not involve a moral judgment, of which the infant is incapable.

Spitz interprets this early form of judgment in the differentiation of I and non-I somewhat differently:[8] the experience of I, he believes, is based on what the infant feels inside: the differentiation of non-I is based on what the infant can only see, after having lost what he felt inside—as during nursing when the breast or bottle slips out of his mouth but remains in his vision.

Whether the theory emphasizes pleasurable–unpleasurable (Freud) or retention–loss (Spitz), it explains the development of I as directly related to the differentiation of internal and external; I is the mental representation of experience of the internal. The internal-external differentiation in turn depends on the development of an early form of judgment, the judgment of quality. As we shall see, further development in the capacity for judgment coincides with further delineation of the self.

Second Phase—Recognition of the First Visual Percept (Three to Seven Months). The shift from contact to visual perception, and the increasing reliance on the visual-distance percept of the human face, is an important event in the child's psychological development. It also underlies the transition to the second phase of development. The emergence of the infant's smiling response, which is based on the ability to distinguish the human face from all other visual stimuli, marks the beginning of this phase.

To backtrack a bit into the first phase, when the infant is about two months old, the approach of a human being when he is hungry will result in his becoming quiet and his beginning movements of the mouth or of sucking. No other visual stimulus evokes these responses. A few weeks later, the infant will follow with his eyes any human face that moves across his visual horizon. Then, in the third month, a new response appears, which is evoked only by a face: when presented with a face or facelike stimulus, the infant smiles. Clearly, the infant is now able to differentiate the face as an object different from all other "things." The face, then, is the first *visual* percept.

How is the development of this visual percept important in forming a rudimentary ego?[9] First, the fact that the infant responds to a specific visual stimulus and not to others indicates that a *memory trace* of the face has been laid down. To psychoanalytic theorists, available memories are stored in the preconscious, whereas drives are generally unconscious. Thus, the appearance of a memory trace means some differentiation has taken place in the infant's mind—there has begun a division of the mental apparatus into conscious, preconscious, and unconscious.[10]

Also important is the fact that the infant begins to be able to mentally associate two separate events, as shown when he can match his present visual percept of a face with a memory trace of a past percept of a face; this capacity is called *recognition memory.* This association also is evident when the activation of the visual memory trace serves as a "signal" for some further event, so that the infant is able to anticipate need gratification. This capacity to shift attention from one memory trace to another is the psychoanalytic definition of thinking, and thus we have the beginnings of the first thought processes.[11] The process of differentiation of internal and external, which began during the first phase, is now followed by the beginning of exploration and probing of the external world, much of it occurring in the infant's interchanges with his mother. There is an increase in active, directed, and intentional behavior, a shift from passivity to activity. Along with such expansion of activities, however, the infant begins to experience the limits of his capacities in interactions with the environment. For example, when he feels hungry, he may move about or grasp nearby objects, but these activities do not reduce his hunger. Eventually, he may learn that, by crying, he can bring his mother and then food to him. However, now that he differentiates between internal and external (in this case, his mother), he realizes that satisfying his hunger totally depends on the appearance of mother. This realization, plus his inability to independently master internal tensions, leads to a loss of his previous feelings of omnipotence.

Instead, he now considers the adults to be all-powerful, and his relationship to them accordingly becomes one of extreme dependency.

This puts the infant in a rather difficult situation. On the one hand, he is struggling to maintain the recently acquired differentiation between internal and external, but at the same time his increasing feelings of dependency on the nurturing adults produces a continual pull for regression and merging with them. The infant's struggle to maintain separateness during this period can be seen in the physical actions of stiffening, turning, and looking away from the mother, as well as pushing away from her body.

The fact that it is now possible for the infant to carry out these self-initiated actions helps him maintain the newly accomplished differentiation. The repetition of self-initiated behavior, as an attempt to maintain the difference between internal and external, is exemplified by his tendency to produce and repeat sounds and to differentiate these self-produced sounds from those emanating from the environment. Moreover, insofar as the observed repetition of sounds in fact reflects the infant's *imitation* of his own babblings, it is assumed that such imitation lays the groundwork for his imitation several months later of the sounds made by his mother. In general, however, the fact that he can produce his own stimulation is assumed to bolster up his declining sense of omnipotence, to help maintain differentiation, and to give him a certain sense of mastery over the environment.

In these many ways, then, we see how early ego functions have developed (although one important function, synthesis, has not yet appeared). Associative connections among separate memory traces are beginning to be established, as when the infant associates a pleasant emotion with a particular image, or associates a memory image with a percept. The establishment of primitive memory organizations during this second phase is also shown in the infant's withdrawal in response to particular stimuli, which indicates that memory traces of these stimuli are associated with unpleasant emotions.

With such memory systems and other rudimentary ego functions, the infant can deal with external stimulation in a new way. The role of the stimulus barrier as a protective threshold against incoming stimuli is progressively taken over by the rudimentary ego. Excitation from such incoming stimuli can now be handled either by distributing it along the various memory or associative pathways that have developed or by discharging it in directed action. For example, if an unwanted bottle appears, it may start a train of thought that begins with the memory of the presence of unwanted objects in the mouth and ends with the memory of turning the head away and clamping the lips shut. The end point of this train of thought may then lead to some active behavior to avoid the bottle. *Internal* stimulation can also be handled in a new way. Instinctual drive energy is not immediately discharged; instead, the primitive associative memory pathways provide a more circuitous route over which the drive energy will pass. In this process, the drive energy may itself become somewhat modified. This *delay of immediate drive discharge* marks the beginning of still another important ego function.

Third Phase—Differentiation of Mother's Face (Eight to 14 Months).
The third phase begins with another distinctive development: at about eight months, the infant shows that he is able to differentiate not only the human face, but also to distinguish mother's face from all others.[12] In psychoanalytic theory, this occurrence is referred to as the differentiation of the *libidinal* or love object. Here "object" does not refer to a concrete "thing" but to some-thing—in this instance, a person—that satisfies an instinctual drive. The drive in this case is a drive for self-preservation, and the object is the person (usually the mother) who takes care of the infant. Obviously, this object (the mother) cannot exist until it can be differentiated from other stimuli (other faces).

The ability to differentiate a particular (loved) face emerges along with an important kind of behavior known as *stranger anxiety.* At about eight months of age, the infant begins to respond to faces other than his mother's not with a smile but with signs of discomfort, ranging from mild apprehension (or even curiosity) to fearful withdrawal. The occurrence of this anxiety indi-cates a major change in the ego, namely, that drive and object have become integrated—the establishment of true object relations has begun.

The emergence of stranger anxiety also indicates that the infant's men-tal processes are becoming more complex. The infant's negative response to the stranger is not due to any association of that stranger with a previously unpleasant experience. Rather, what the infant does is to compare the stran-ger's face with the memory of his mother's face and discover they do not match. It is the discovery that the stranger is *not* his mother—that his mother is *absent,* rather than that the stranger is present—that produces the anxiety. In other words, the infant's anxiety is really about the temporary loss of his mother.[13]

A number of other ego developments occur during this third phase. Individual memory traces are synthesized to form stable memory organiza-tions, which in turn make it possible for the infant to carry out more complex mental operations. He also begins to show early forms of communication, of identification, and of causal thinking. Also, he shows the ability for a new type of judgment. Finally, he forms his first concrete concept (mother's face).

The organization of memory traces into associated clusters, begun in phase 2, continues during this third phase. The principal organization is the combination of many separate memory traces of the mother to form the single object *loved mother.* This shows the ability of the ego to synthesize various memory images of the mother—which differ pictorially as well as in positive and negative emotional associations—in such a way as to form a single, consis-tent representation of her.

The establishment of more memory systems also means more complex mental operations can be carried out. This development, along with the matu-ration of motor abilities, results in behavior that is increasingly directed and diversified.

During this phase the infant's interest in the outside world largely depends on his mother's presence: he is comfortable when she is present, anxious when she is not. His interest in his mother, and the development of his ability to discriminate between her and others, forms the first (and thus critically important) basis for the subsequent development of interest in the world and provides the basis for *discrimination learning*.[14] In this way, the infant's emotional attachment to the mother plays an important role for all further learning, and so, obviously, a good relationship with the mother is critical. If there is no "good" mother, there is little need to differentiate her from other people, and thus little reason to take the first step in learning about external reality.

Two other developments that occur in this relationship with the mother are the beginnings of *communication* and of *identification*. As we noted, in the second phase the infant discovers that if he expresses his internal state by producing certain cries or actions, there will be some action by his mother to relieve his discomfort. Later he learns he can use these gestures to purposely influence the environment to provide gratification. In other words, the use of gestures to indicate what he *feels* is changed so as to indicate what he *needs*. The anguished cry that originally functioned to partly discharge psychological tension is now used by the infant to call forth the mother and the drive gratification she provides. This is the beginning of communication.

The beginning of identification occurs when the child starts to adopt certain characteristics of the love object. Initially, these are immediate imitations of his mother's gestures while she is interacting with him. Later these imitations may occur even in her absence, indicating the infant has incorporated certain characteristics of the love object into his memory system. Such identification also means that a modification in the structure of the ego has taken place.

Another ego development in this phase is in early forms of thinking. With the decline of the infant's feeling of omnipotence, the increasing differentiation of internal and external, the recognition of the love object as the source of gratification, and the production of certain kinds of behavior such as sounds to influence the environment so as to relieve discomfort, the infant has his first experience with *causality*. Finally, the development of the capacity to compare the percept of the stranger's face with the memory of the mother's face requires the intellectual capacity for a new type of *judgment*—the judgment that this person is *not* his mother.

Summary. We have seen how, in the first stage of development, the mode of taking in—first through the mouth, then through the eyes—interacts with maturing physical and psychological functions to produce striking changes in the infant's mental development. We also stressed the importance of the *mother* in this process. The infant's emotional attachment to her is responsible for his interest in the external world and for his development of a variety of ego functions, such as discrimination, judgment, decision, communication, and early forms of causal thinking.

During this first stage, several abilities critical to intellectual development begin to appear. Differentiation occurs along a number of lines. First, the infant develops the capacity to differentiate between internal and external. With this differentiation goes the development of the first percept, a contact percept, which depends on the joint presence of internal and external stimuli. Later visual perception develops. This shift from contact to distance perception is critical, for it is the start of the dominant perceptual mode in the person. It also makes possible the subsequent development of discrimination learning and recognition memory.

A second line of differentiation is in the separation of the "I" from the rest of the world. This occurs when the infant recognizes his physical and psychological limits and so loses his feelings of omnipotence and assumes a position of dependency. The discovery of the ability to make self-initiated sounds and to use them as communication to obtain gratification provides the earliest beginnings for some understanding of causality.

A third line of differentiation occurs when the infant is able to recognize the human face, which indicates that a separation between conscious, preconscious, and unconscious has taken place. A differentiation also occurs between the instinctual drives and the ego. The differentiation of ego functions is shown by the development of perception, by increasing voluntary motor activity, by the laying down of memory traces, and by the association and organization of these memories—which makes it possible for the infant to engage in directed, volitional activity. The ego begins to function as a steering organization, and the infant begins to change from passivity to activity. The association of memory traces and affect also make possible the development of anticipation. The beginning of the synthetic function of the ego is seen in the integration of many different memory traces of the mother to form the image of the love object. The existence of this organization of memory traces into a higher order "concept" is also connected with the beginning of the capacity for judgment and decision-making.

The Second Stage of Development— Autonomy and Will (15 Months to Two Years)

The second stage of development is characterized by the modes of holding on and letting go.[15] The conflicting nature of these two modes indicates a predominant characteristic of this period—that of conflict and struggle. The development of increased motor skills also contributes to this struggle, for the child is now capable of going and coming, doing and undoing, making and unmaking, and, in the area of toilet behavior, retaining and eliminating. His increased mobility also bring him into more conflict with his mother—he gets into things and places she does not want him in. In all these activities, the child is beginning to exercise his will, and in so doing he experiments with many alternative and even conflicting kinds of behavior. The importance of having a choice becomes a critical issue during this stage.

In this second stage of development, the child also develops an increasing sense of autonomy, both from internal drives and from environmental demands. How does autonomy from drives develop? It depends, in part, on the development of defense mechanisms, which act as buffers against internal and external pressures. According to psychoanalytic theory, the direct discharge of drive energy is first restrained by the force of an opposing source of energy. Subsequently, mental structures develop that can control or delay drive discharge, which makes such a counterforce less necessary. This in turn results in freeing that opposing energy, which then becomes available for use in other ways, such as in exploration.[16] At the same time, the development of defense structures means that the mental representations of instinctual drives are now prevented from entering consciousness—they remain unconscious.

There is an important relationship between the beginning of exploratory behavior, the development of drive controls, and the child's belief in the constancy of the world. The child must believe in the permanence or constancy of things in order to move out into that world. Only when he feels secure in the repeatability, constancy, and certainty of his immediate environment can he begin to venture forth and search out novelty.

The concern for permanence and stability is often reflected in the child's concern, at this stage, for sameness and for rituals. He is disturbed if anything is changed, or different, from what it was on a preceding occasion, and he is pleased by repetition. Psychoanalytic theory sees this concern for constancy in the *external* world as reflecting the child's concern for lack of constancy in, or control over, his *internal* world—that is, for lack of stability of his own mental processes, as well as his inability for complete self-determination.[17] At the same time that he strives for autonomy, he must face again and again the limits of his capacities and the recognition of his relative powerlessness.

The second kind of autonomy to develop during this stage is autonomy from external demands. This is perhaps best exemplified in the further development of communication.[18] An important event in the second stage is the development of *speech*. Following the self-initiated sounds and acoustic imitation that occurred during the preceding stage, there is a transitional period in which the child uses words to express an internal need state, just as we might say "Ouch!" when experiencing pain. Gradually, such expressions of internal states become expressions of appeal. However, speech as a means for communicating meaning beyond an appeal for help does not begin until the second stage of development.

Development of Communication.   Until this point, communication depended on direct contact with or action by the infant (such as crying or various kinds of motor behavior). With the emergence of a semantic gesture, distance communication is begun. The child now can make his intention known to someone (such as his mother) that he is physically separated from. He is no longer restricted to making a motor response to a stimulus that is immediately present and physically impinging on him.

To psychoanalytic theorists, this development is a critical turning point for man as individual and as species. The first semantic symbols are thought to be the gesture of the negative headshake and the word "No," not words like "Mama" or "Dada," which are believed to express needs or wishes.[19] The headshake and "No" represent a concept, the concept of negation or refusal. The development of "No," in gesture and word, as the forerunner of semantic communication, is thus considered to be an important indicator of cognitive development, much like the smile response and stranger anxiety in the preceding stage.

The development of this verbal refusal makes it possible for the infant to shift from the passive submission to an unpleasurable situation (or, at the most, physical resistance) to a level of verbal refusal. With this capacity, the child also has a new kind of autonomy from external pressures: he no longer has to use physical action as the only way to express his likes and dislikes. With "No," he is able to express his aggression through stubborn refusal to do even those things he is known to enjoy. This alternative of verbal communication helps free the child from the predominant use of "flight or fight" responses— physical or mental—as the only way to handle unpleasant external situations. With this new ability for active negative judgment, he comes to experience himself as an individual with a will of his own.

Other Important Cognitive Developments. Besides increasing the child's autonomy, the occurrence of "No" is significant in his cognitive development. With it he can replace action by communication—which, as with all symbolic activity, helps save energy. This distance communication is also the beginning of all future verbal communication, which marks the way for mental development of much greater complexity. In addition, "No" is the first *abstract concept* in the behavioral repertoire of the child, and it signifies he has expanded his capacity for judgment. In fact, there is a kind of continuum in the movement from contact percept to visual percept to concrete concept to abstract concept. This continuum moves from a mental representation based on a concrete, sensory-bound experience to a mental representation based on a distillation and abstraction from many experiences.

Another important cognitive development that begins with the acquisition of speech is in memory organization. Freud postulated that, in the adult, memories of "things"—concrete objects or events—are stored in the unconscious and so are unavailable to normal conscious recall.[20] Memories of words, on the other hand, are stored in the preconscious. The conscious memory, Freud suggested, consists of the word-memory plus the associatively-linked thing-memory. Thus, it is possible for two different organizations of memory to exist—one on the preconscious level, involving words, and one on the unconscious level, involving things. The advent of language in the child thus provides the material for new types of memory organization to develop.[21]

If this differentiation between two types of memory seems strange, consider these examples, one from everyday life, the other from research. Until the infant has words to label his experiences, these experiences must be recorded in some perceptual form—as pictorial images, sounds, tastes, and the like. However, with the development of language, experiences can be recorded in words. Recent experimental studies indicate that as the child grows older he automatically applies verbal labels to pictures he is shown.[22] This ability to store the experience in memory in both a pictorial form and a verbal form results in the older child's memory being superior to the memory of the younger child.

Adults also show this automatic tendency to apply verbal labels, and there is evidence that much of their daily thinking is carried out in terms of words. On the other hand, most dreams occur in pictorial form; dream thought is based on images. It is rare indeed to dream only words. Now since both our daytime (word) thoughts and our dream (image) thoughts display a certain degree of organization, and since the two do not intermingle much, it seems reasonable to assume, intuitively, that the two kinds of memories are stored and organized separately.

Studies of the storage of verbal and pictorial memories have demonstrated that behavior based on memory of the word does not follow the same rules as behavior based on memory of the thing. Summarizing an investigation of this problem, one psychologist wrote, "Somehow, names are responsive to volition in a way that images are not."[23] This statement is no surprise to psychoanalysts, since volition is intimately tied to consciousness, and only memories stored within the preconscious (words) are available to consciousness.

The development of language thus marks the beginning of purposive, volitional thought. Through the increasingly active use of the various ego functions, the child comes to experience pleasure not only in attaining a goal but also in exercising the ego function itself. Psychoanalytic theory refers to this phenomenon as *pleasure in function*. It plays a critical role in the acceptance of the reality principle and as the impetus for future learning.[24]

Development of Self. The expression of volition or will by verbal communication rather than by direct drive discharge marks a change in the child's relationship with his mother, from the level of instinctual drive to that of social relations. At the same time, the child's increased ability to differentiate between his mother's will and his own leads to an increasing awareness of her and an increasing awareness of his own *self.*

The development of a sense of self is the final important occurrence in this stage. It begins, first of all, with the differentiation of "non-I" from "I" during the first stage of development. In order for this differentiation to occur, we noted that the child must be able to make the judgment as to whether the origin of a perception was internal or external. The differentiation of self from others *also* depends on a judgment; this second kind of judgment has to do with whether or not an object exists. That is, to differentiate between the self and others, the infant must have the ability to recognize that others exist. Only after the child recognizes that others exist can he begin to differentiate himself from those others. Judgment, then, contributes to the development of "self."

We also spoke of the establishment of "I" as the cognitive representation of the infant's internal experiences, and noted that this depends on the infant's developing an awareness or consciousness of these experiences. Developing a sense of self *also* depends on an awareness of experiences, but now they must be organized at a higher level of integration. In order to achieve this integration, the ego makes use of the capacity for abstraction, which has newly emerged during this second stage of development.

The development of the sense of self is also aided by the child's emerging autonomy and by his capacity to become his own observer. On the one hand, he begins to have a sense of his own independent actions. On the other, the child can now make a separation between his ego functions (such as perception) and his sense of self; once this is done, the self can be treated as an object for observation. This is sometimes seen in games children of this age play with dolls; the child makes a division between ego and self, and then acts (ego function) on the doll as if it were himself or herself.

The ability to objectify the self is also helped by the child's new capacity for negation. Previously, the use of "No" against the mother facilitated the separation of the child from the mother. Now, the ego applies this same capacity for negation to the self, as it had previously been applied to the mother. This operation facilitates a differentiation between ego and self, and by treating the self as an object the child helps to objectify it.

This new capacity to observe the self, to make judgments, and to execute wishes helps the child to learn from experience. It also helps the child to differentiate his will from the will of his mother and to attain autonomy. From these new developments, he is able to decide when to hold on and when to let go.

Summary. We have seen that the characteristic mode of this stage—of holding on and letting go—is expressed in the struggle to control inner impulses and to be freed from the domination of external stimuli. In other words, the conflict of this stage is of autonomy from internal drives and from the external environment. Both types of autonomy depend on the development of defense mechanisms and other cognitive abilities to act as a buffer between the child and the internal and external forces pressing on him.

One such cognitive ability that emerges in this stage is language and semantic communication. Language allows the child to communicate needs and react to his environment at a distance. The capacity to express himself and to communicate verbally allows the child to separate the stimulus force from his response to that force—that is, it allows him some autonomy. Language also makes it possible for him to develop a new memory organization, based on words, which in turn makes it possible for him to have conscious, volitional thought.

The struggle for autonomy is closely related to the increasing sense of self that occurs during this stage. The cognitive formulation of a self is based on the earlier differentiation between "I" and "non-I," but now the increased capacity for judgment helps the child develop the sense of self in two ways. First, it helps him differentiate between inanimate objects and people, so that he can then differentiate between his own will and the will of other people—

and recognition of his own will contributes to the child's sense of self. Second, the child's new ability to use judgment to objectify others increases his capacity for self-observation and for self-definition.

In this stage, also, the capacity for judgment is extended to include things and events not directly related to drive gratification. The development of the ability for negation contributes to this expansion of judgment.

Finally, we noted that psychoanalytic theory believes that semantic communication begins with the emergence of "No" as a meaningful gesture and that "No" is the first abstract concept.[25]

The Third Stage of Development—Exploration and Intrusion (Three to Five Years)[26]

The third stage of development is characterized by the child's increasing exploration of the world. As his motor abilities continue to develop, he is able to walk farther, run faster, and generally extend the arena of his physical activities. Moreover, as these motor skills become better established, the child attends less to their performance per se and more to the purpose for which he will use them.

This ability for increased physical activity contributes to the characteristic mode of this period, that of *intrusion*. Intrusion may be physical, as when one bursts into an already formed group, or into a room or yard, or it may be verbal, as when a child continually interrupts or shouts down a playmate. The child at this stage is expanding his environment by pushing his way into it.

The important psychological conflict of the stage is in the child's final attempt to obtain the love object as his own. For boys of this age, the fantasies are full of undisguised wishes for exclusive possession of the mother; for girls, it is of the father. There are strong feelings of jealousy and competitiveness with any rival for the attentions of the love object, whether this be the other parent or another sibling. For some time, the child continues to believe he can actually become his (her) beloved parent's exclusive lover and her (his) exclusive love object. But his attempts in this direction eventually bring him into conflict with the parent and the parent's mate. As his capacity for reality testing increases, the child cannot help but notice that he must inevitably lose out in any competition with this mate. Nevertheless, the struggle continues for some time, and is referred to in psychoanalytic theory as the *Oedipal conflict*.

While the child is trying to become the exclusive partner of his parent, some important ego developments occur. Whereas in the preceding stage the child was more likely to use his capacities for autonomous behavior in a defiant manner, he now redirects this autonomous behavior so as to attain certain ends. The little boy engages in intrusive behavior—the enjoyment of competition and attack, unrelenting insistence on getting what he wants, and pleasure in conquering. The little girl may modify the intrusive mode into the inclusive mode—teasing, being provocative, and ensnaring. In either case, whether the attempt is to obtain the goal by intruding oneself into it or by incorporating it into oneself, psychoanalytic theorists see the development of both kinds of behavior as a means for gratifying instinctual drives. That is, such behavior first occurs as a means of attaining a particular goal—possession of the love object—and it is then that the capacity for self-directed striving, or *initiative,* develops. Later, after the quest for this particular goal has been abandoned, the child will retain the sense of initiative—a quality that will be important for learning and mastering future skills.

Development of the Superego. Gaining initiative, however, depends on how the Oedipal conflict is resolved. As we noted, this try at exclusive possession of the love object is destined to meet with frustration. This failure is due both to the biological immaturity of the child (he is in every way weaker and less capable than the other parent) and to the prohibition against incest of virtually every culture. As the child adopts these prohibitions as his own, as he internalizes them, and as a result of his frustrations, he develops guilt about the prohibited impulse. The internalization of this prohibition by society, which has been occurring for some time as a part of the child's identification with his parents, is now used to control his own instinctual drives. When such prohibitions are applied to the self, and when violating these prohibitions leads to a feeling of guilt, psychoanalytic theory considers that the conscience, or the superego, of the child has developed.

The establishment of the superego can both help and hinder further development. On the one hand, by internalizing the values, mores, and traditions of society, it gives the child a frame of reference within which he may act and expect to receive gratification. Put another way, the superego makes drive gratification possible by redirecting these drives into channels of activity that are acceptable and meaningful to the society the child lives in. For example, the boy who is continually getting into fights and beating up other children he plays with may come to be considered a bully, and be shunned or disapproved of by the people of his neighborhood. The society he lives in does not accept the expression of aggression in this manner. However, if this same boy were to take up boxing at the local gym and were so adept at hitting and punching other boys that he were entered in a tournament contest, the same neighbors and parents would now come to cheer him on. In this sense, the superego serves to organize and direct instinctual drives into acceptable forms of behavior.

As the superego channels the child's instinctual energy into socially acceptable endeavors, it helps develop his initiative by indicating to him what is socially possible. However, the superego also restricts initiative, in that it delimits what is impossible within his society. For the first time, the child has an inner watchman or guide that restricts his activities to those consonant with his conscience. If he disregards this conscience, he will suffer feelings of guilt.

To resolve the Oedipal conflict, a superego must be developed that is firm enough to direct the child's drives into socially meaningful channels, yet flexible enough to leave sufficient channels open to him. If the superego is too restrictive, if too many activities arouse guilt in the child, then his initiative will be severely hampered. Such excess guilt feelings prevent the child from moving out into the world, from trying to learn and to develop the skills he will need and that will contribute to his self-esteem.

Important Intellectual Developments.   This third stage of development is also a time during which new intellectual capacities are emerging. Along with the general mode of intrusion and exploration of this period, the child develops increasing *intellectual curiosity.* He explores the world not only physically but mentally. He is filled with questions and is often intellectually intrusive. As was true for the development of initiative, this curiosity is initially motivated by the infantile sexual drive, and it is seen in the increasing concern of children of this age about the differences between boys and girls, and men and women. However, as with initiative, the form of the behavior—the curiosity and exploration—remains after the original aim is given up. That is, after the resolution of the Oedipal conflict, the child is left with the capacity for exploratory behavior that is now directed to new areas of endeavor.

A second important intellectual development of this stage is the child's increasing capacity for fantasy. In his daydreams and make-believe creations, the child of this age can imagine himself to be everything he is not in reality; whatever he wishes to be, exists in his fantasies.

Not all his fantasies, however, are pleasant. The development of this new mental capacity is also used as an outlet for his aggressive and sexual impulses, and many of his fantasies or dreams will express these drives. The child of this age is often frightened by the things he thinks up. Such fears can take rather elaborate forms, since the child may imagine committing some aggressive act against the parent, and then may fantasy that the parent will retaliate for this imagined aggression.

At the same time that the capacity for fantasy is increasing so is the ability for reality testing. The capacity to separate fantasy and reality is very important in establishing a basis for learning. That is, until the child gives up the fantasied notion that he can do everything he wishes—until he recognizes that there are some things he is unable to do—he has no real reason to try to learn. It is only when the child recognizes that there are things that he does not know and that he wishes he did know, and believes in the possibility of overcoming his current limitations, that he can begin to ally himself with the process of education.

Finally, the development of the superego contributes to the establishment of *inner goals and interests* in the child. In the process of internalizing the values, mores, and style of his parents and their society, the child is laying down in himself a set of attitudes and beliefs that will help foster his future cognitive development. These internalized values shape the child's decision as to which areas of endeavor are important and which not. In other words, the superego influences the direction in which the child will expend his initiative.

For example, a child who grows up in a family or society that stresses the importance of acquiring and keeping material goods may be expected to become a collector—at first of stamps, butterflies, or toy guns, later of money, houses, or business holdings. Such interests, in turn, would contribute to his choice of profession as banker, realtor, or businessman. Another child, however, who grows up in a milieu more concerned about interaction among people might express this later in his goal to become a social worker, minister, or clinical psychologist.

Summary. We have seen that the intrusive mode dominates this stage of development and that it contributes to the development of initiative, of self-directed striving. Moreover, although such initiative first develops in connection with drive gratification—that is, with obtaining the love object—it eventually becomes a more general style of behavior that can be used to obtain a variety of goals.

The development of intellectual curiosity during this stage also demonstrates the generalization of an ego function that first occurs in connection with an instinctual drive. Although exploration and curiosity are originally closely tied up with a concern about sexual differences, they are later extended to finding out about other aspects of people and things in the world. Still another aspect of the child's expanding mental capacities occurs in his increasing capacity for fantasy and in his increasing ability to separate fantasy and reality. All of these developments—initiative, intellectual curiosity, and better reality testing—contribute to the cognitive development of the child and help prepare him for an affiliation with the process of education.

Finally, the third stage is a time in which the internalization of societal values occurs. The development of the superego helps the child redirect his instinctual drives into channels acceptable to society. This is the beginning of the establishment of personal goals, and it helps in determining the direction for self-initiated behavior.

The Fourth Stage of Development—Industry (Six to 10 Years)

This fourth stage is a time in which the pleasure that the child has previously experienced from the *process* of play—that is, from his sense of initiative—is now modified into pleasure derived from the *outcome* of the process. Whereas in the preceding stage the child had little interest in the practical value of his goals, he now becomes concerned with being able to produce something useful. The sense of initiative from the preceding stage now comes to include a pleasure from industry—that is, from the making of a product or the completion of a task. At the same time, this new stage is characterized by a relative quiescence of the instinctual drives and hence has been referred to as the period of *latency.* The temporary decline in the strength of the instincts that occurs during this stage has an important ramification for the child's development of ego functions. Since the drives are weaker and less insistent, this means that less energy need be expended in controlling drive discharge. The energy previously so used is now available to the ego for other tasks—for example, for learning and mastering new skills.

The combination of increased pleasure from making and doing—that is, from work—and of increased energy for ego activities provides an excellent psychological setting in which learning and education may flourish. The child of this age enjoys putting things together, figuring out how they work, building his own products, and creating his own games. It is also important to him that the things he makes be functional, that they work and serve some purpose. He is no longer satisfied with just fantasying that he can build an airplane or pretending that the cardboard box he holds aloft is an airplane. He now wants to build a *real* airplane, at least on a model level. For this reason, he is ordinarily eager to acquire the information and skills that will further his capacities for production. Given the appropriate opportunities, he has seemingly endless energy to expend in such activities.

Still another contributor to the child's readiness for learning is the defense mechanism of *sublimation,* which develops in the preceding stage during resolution of the Oedipal conflict. Sublimation redirects the weakened instinctual energies into areas of endeavor that are socially valued and produces a sense of satisfaction from working in those areas. Impulses are now gratified on a social level rather than on a purely physical basis. The impulse to obtain physical possession of the mother is modified into producing attractive objects that she will praise. The need to incorporate more and more food so as to ensure survival is changed into an interest in acquiring the information, techniques, and means by which man provides for himself. The new capacity for delay, for redirection of energy, and for pleasure through work adds to the child's growing sense of industry.

Changes in Intellectual Functioning.   Considering this new eagerness and readiness for learning, and the fact that this occurs at approximately the point that the child is entering school and being provided with the opportunity to learn, it is somewhat ironic that there may in fact be a decline in intelligence during the beginning of the latency period. Psychoanalytic theory holds that this decrease is due to the temporary inhibition during the latency stage of the use or development of two aspects of intellectual functioning—curiosity and abstract thinking.[27]

In part, the reduction in intelligence reflects a general inhibition of curiosity. This inhibition begins during the preceding stage, in which the development of the superego produced prohibitions against sexual curiosity. Subsequently, this inhibition generalizes to other forms of curiosity, with the result that the child shows less exploratory behavior and less involvement in finding out about the world. In a paradoxical way, then, the sexual drive serves both to initially foster the development of curiosity and then to result in its inhibition.

The second factor that contributes to the decline in intelligence stems from the decrease in the strength of the instinctual drives characteristic of this stage. Psychoanalytic theory holds that thought develops as a way of controlling instinctual drives and facilitating their gratification through indirect means: thus, any change in the strength of the drives will produce a change in the strength of the controls required. Anna Freud[28] has suggested that abstract thought in particular, especially during adolescence (the next stage), helps control the expression of strong instinctual drives. It follows, then, that during a stage in which instinctual drives are relatively weak, there is relatively less need for abstract thinking.

In this connection, it is noteworthy that the kind of intelligence that develops during this stage is best characterized as concrete. The child acquires concrete skills and techniques and information, but the capacity for handling abstract symbols does not appear until the next stage of development.

Summary. We have seen that the fourth stage of development is a time in which the instinctual drives are fairly quiescent, so that no new drive-related mode of behavior emerges. At the same time, it is a period that is optimal for the process of formal education to begin. On the one hand, the child's interest shifts from pleasure derived simply from activity itself (such as play) to satisfaction from the outcome of the activity; fantasy becomes less rewarding and reality more so. On the other hand, the energy previously used to control and defend against the pressure of strong instinctual drives is now available for use in ego functions. Moreover, energy derived from the weakened drives can now be channeled, by the newly developed defense mechanism of sublimation, into activities that will be socially rewarded. Thus, both in the kinds of activities the child finds enjoyable and in the available energy to carry them out, the child is in an optimal period to ally himself with the goals of education.

The Fifth Stage of Development— Adolescence

At puberty, several hormonal and physiological changes occur, along with corresponding changes in the person's mental and emotional life. The term *adolescence* denotes these psychological changes and adaptations to the new physiological condition.[29] As we shall see, the psychosexual drives from earlier stages gradually become hierarchically organized, a parallel organization of existing ego functions develops, and distinctly new ego functions emerge.

Adolescence may be divided into four phases—preadolescence, early adolescence, adolescence proper, and late adolescence.[30] We will discuss each in turn.

The First Phase—Preadolescence. This marks the beginning of the stage. At this time, the relative calm that has characterized the child's instinctual life during latency comes to an end, as does the balance attained between instinctual and ego forces. The changing physiological conditions of puberty are reflected in an upsurge of the psychological instinctual drives, and once again the ego must find new ways to control these threatening forces.

The Second Phase—Early Adolescence.   Here the increase in the quantity of instinctual drive energy continues, but now a new drive *quality* appears. This results from the arrangement of the earlier pregenital drives and the current genital drive into a hierarchical organization. Lower in the hierarchy are the pregenital drives, which now give rise to the experience of sexual forepleasure; this is the new quality of adolescence.[31] At this stage of development, however, satisfaction of these drives no longer leads to a feeling of satiation. This is accomplished only by the discharge of the genital drive, which is dominant in the hierarchical organization. In other words, the erogenous zones of the preceding stages are gradually subordinated to genital primacy.

This change in the organization of drives also initiates a hierarchical organization of ego functions, with some dominant, others subordinated, although in this phase the hierarchy is unstable, with a frequent rearrangement and turnover of the dominant interests, capacities, and values. Not until adolescence proper is a more stable hierarchy of interests and skills achieved.

Finally, in this phase there is frequently an increase in close relationships with friends of the same sex. Some relationships may be very intense and highly idealized, occupying the larger part of the adolescent's life.

The Third Phase—Adolescence Proper.   This phase is marked by a greatly increased interest in heterosexual relationships outside the home, although sometimes only on the fantasy level. At the same time, the adolescent gradually dissolves his strong emotional attachment to his parents.

There are two major problems of this phase: First, because of the increased strength of the instinctual drives, the id is relatively strong and the ego relatively weak,[32] so the adolescent is constantly threatened with being overwhelmed by instinctual anxiety. To avoid this threat, he must develop new ways of controlling drive discharge. Second, the adolescent must dissolve or break parental ties, so as to be free to establish new heterosexual relationships.

There are many ways an adolescent may try to handle the threat of instinctual anxiety, but two approaches adopted by the ego are especially characteristic at this stage.[33] The first is to perform a psychological flight, such as repudiating all wishes and activities linked with instinctual needs. An excessive concern for morality, healthiness, religion, athletics—for being pure and true and honest—may be used to flee from internal threats. By such *asceticism,* the adolescent removes himself from possible temptation and tries to control inner impulses by imposing a set of prohibitions on himself. The superego, which was used to solve the earlier Oedipal conflict, is now used again with a vengeance, producing the vindictive moral righteousness so often found in adolescents. This moral outrage may be directed toward himself, but more often it is expressed against his parents. It is a time of being supercritical of the many small failings and inadequacies of human beings—including those of parents.

This ascetic repudiation of drives works by restricting the functioning of the ego. The adolescent who adopts this defense finds that the range of activities he may engage in is severely limited; furthermore, he makes little effort to communicate with or relate to the outside world. In this way, asceticism curtails development and serves as a "holding action."[34]

The second way the adolescent may cope with instinctual anxiety is through *intellectualization,* manifested by more time spent in speculating and mulling over ideas, in endless "bull sessions" in which ideas are considered and reconsidered, argued about, made the basis for starting and dissolving intense friendships. This strong involvement in thought is a means of handling disturbing intrapsychic imbalances. However, these intellectual debates and philosophizings are not genuine attempts at problem solving, for the outcome of such lengthy serious discussions is more often than not a maintaining of the status quo. Whatever idealistic, "meaningful" discoveries and conclusions are discussed, at the end, each participant returns to his previous *modus vivendi.* The rehashing of ideas, engaged in with such intensity, was not really directed to solving problems in reality. On the contrary, the problems being dealt with were internal—they arose from the pressure and threat of the instinctual drives. It is as though an inner alertness warns of the impending emergence of those drives and attempts to ward them off by linking them up with ideas that can then be dealt with by conscious mental processes.

The increased strength of instinctual drives may also be dealt with by motor expression—either indirectly, as when the energy is discharged through some substitute strenuous activity such as sports, or directly onto the environment, as in sadistic gang fights or sexual promiscuity.

Another way of coping with the drive problem is through discharging the drive within the body, which frequently results in physical upsets that have no organic basis but are nonetheless real, such as stomach aches or vomiting.

The ways the adolescent handles his drive impulses characteristically shift back and forth, so that he is often in considerable turmoil. This confusion is eventually resolved by the adoption of guiding principles, but since these principles are often derived from the parents, their adoption is impeded until the adolescent has successfully separated himself from his parents.

We mentioned that the second major problem of this phase of adolescence is of dissolving the ties to the parents so the adolescent can be free to choose a new love object. There are several characteristic attempts at solution of this problem.[35] The adolescent may suddenly withdraw his attachment to his parents and displace it onto some new person, either older or his own age. The critical feature of this new person is that he must be as different as possible from the adolescent's parents, so that, in transferring his attachment, the adolescent feels free of his parents and at the same time less anxious about acting out his impulses, since they now do not involve the original (and forbidden) love objects.

Another way the adolescent may try to dissolve ties with his parents is to *reverse* the emotions he feels toward them: love becomes hate, dependence becomes independence, admiration becomes disgust. But this maneuver is not really successful, for the adolescent remains as bound to his parents as before; his negative feelings are based on his continuing attachment to them. At the same time, he may find that his hostile feelings toward them arouse excessive anxiety; in that case, he may project the hostility onto them and then view his parents as persecuting him. Alternately, his feelings of hostility, if they arouse too much anxiety, may be turned inward against himself, with the result that he feels worthless and depressed.

Still another way the adolescent may try to dissolve parental ties is to withdraw into himself the positive emotional feelings that had been used to form the attachment to his parents. In a sense, he transfers his love from his parents to himself and so becomes excessively narcissistic. This is often accompanied by feelings of superiority, or grandiosity, of being special or chosen. Alternatively, the narcissism may result in excessive concern with his body and appearance or in hypochondriacal fears of body changes or possible physical ailments.

Although all the problems of coping discussed so far are normal in adolescent development, there is a danger that an impoverishment of the ego will occur, to such degree that the adolescent experiences a severe loss of self-identity. Such an impoverishment of the ego is the potential result of three main problems of adolescence (two already discussed). First, the ego is considerably weaker than the id; furthermore, additional ego energy is used up in trying to control instinctual drives. Second, in rejecting his parents, the adolescent must also abandon the ego-support and positive emotions they previously provided and that helped promote his self-esteem. Third, the superego, a support or authority figure that the ego could lean on, is also weakened during adolescence; since the superego is derived from the parents, it is weakened to the extent that they are rejected.

One way of dealing with the resulting ego impoverishment and threatened loss of identity is for the adolescent to adopt a strong position of *negativism*[36] or *negative identity*.[37] Here the adolescent defines himself in terms of what he is not: he is *not* like his parents, he does *not* have their values, he will *not* agree to their standards of behavior, and so on. In this way, he maintains his separation from them but manages to create a new identity for himself; that is, he is the opposite of his parents. Such a negative identity, of course, is entirely dependent on his continuing relationship with them.

Other adolescents attempt to defend themselves against a total loss of self by adopting the narcissistic position discussed earlier. By taking the feelings of love and positive emotion they formerly directed to their parents and redirecting them toward their own selves, they provide themselves with renewed self-esteem. Normally, the fantasies and daydreams that accompany such self-preoccupation are followed by a turn toward the outer world. The previous narcissism is then replaced with self-esteem derived from achievements in reality, and the fantasies of self-glorification give way to the search for a new love object.

The Fourth Phase—Late Adolescence. As the third phase ends, each adolescent has worked out a more or less unique organization of drives, defenses, and methods of handling conflict. It is not until the last phase of late adolescence, however, that this organization develops into a consistent and stabilized system. This fourth phase is thus primarily a time of consolidation. The hierarchical organization of ego functions and of predominant defenses are reflected in an increasingly clear pattern of interests and in the development of related skills. This is also the time in which the adolescent arrives at some conclusions about the meaning of life. He makes some choices regarding the possible roles, occupations, and directions he wants to explore, as well as some decisions regarding the values, goals, and philosophy he will live by. Erikson has described this process as that of acquiring an identity, of finding a place in society that makes sense to oneself and to others.[38] The failure of this kind of consolidation, on the other hand, may well lead to an identity crisis[39]—a prolongation of the loss of self and of ego impoverishment discussed above.

Cognitive Developments in Adolescence.   The two new cognitive mechanisms of asceticism and intellectualization, which emerge in adolescence as means for coping with instinctual drives, can also become the basis for further cognitive developments—specifically for ego interests and skills and for abstraction. In contrast to asceticism, intellectualization provides more positive potential for the development of the adolescent, for instead of retreating and restricting, the ego is actively engaged in trying to master the problem. The mastery occurs by the defense mechanism of *displacement*; that is, the drive energy is displaced onto abstract concepts or symbols, which are then manipulated and brought under control. This is another example of a defense mechanism that initially developed as a defense against drives but, once established, becomes separated from its initial origin. In adolescence such displacements can serve an adaptive function when they subsequently become the basis for an ego interest.

Intellectualization also helps develop the ability for abstraction. As the child leaves the latency stage, his interest in concrete, real things diminishes and is replaced by an increasing interest in abstract thoughts and symbols.[40] As psychoanalytic theorists see it, the development of the ability to think abstractly is a direct result of the increase in instinctual drive tension. As we noted, intellectualization is a means by which drives are linked up with ideas, and these ideas can then be controlled by conscious mental processes. Most often, these ideas are of a highly abstract nature—love, fidelity, responsibility, honor, and so on. The defense of intellectualization thus translates the irrational inner forces into abstract thought or symbols. These ideas can then be manipulated and controlled in ways that drives cannot be.

Another frequent development in adolescence is the enhancement of creative activity. This development comes about, first, because the adolescent's increased self-absorption and introspection brings him in closer touch with his own feelings and unique perceptions and, second, because his rejection of his parents and their representation of the world also helps free him for new and unique perceptions of what is going on around him. By being closer to inner processes but more distant from the established view of the world, the adolescent achieves an increased state of sensitivity and perceptiveness.[41] When this is accompanied by the increased use of thought to work out instinctual drive conflicts, the necessary ingredients for the activation of creative thought processes are there. Often, a tremendous capacity for creative productivity results that is not equaled again in the life of the individual. Needless to say, this dedication to the creative process often provides a needed enhancement to the adolescent's flagging self-esteem.

As with intellectualization, then, the withdrawal of psychological energy into the self, which is characteristic of many adolescents, has some positive features for the development of cognition. Not only does it promote enhanced creativity, it also makes it possible for the adolescent to engage in trial-and-error behavior in thought. Through thought, he can eventually attain a level of internal mastery[42] over problems, which will help him to cope with the outer world when he eventually refocuses his energies in that direction. Often, such a period provides a needed respite, during which the consolidation needed for the development of ego identity can occur.

For some adolescents, however, the normal development of new cognitive mechanisms is disrupted. As we noted throughout, thinking develops as a substitute for the immediate motor discharge of drive tension. During adolescence, however, there is a strong aversion to passivity and a proclivity to action.[43] In some cases, this need for activity is seized upon and used as the primary means for discharging drive tension. Such so-called acting out (the uninhibited overt discharge of drives on the environment) then interferes with the development of thinking, insofar as thinking is really a kind of trial or experimental action.

Summary. Apart from the two main problems of adolescence—the increase in drive strength and the need to separate from the parents—and the characteristic ways in which adolescents attempt to cope with these problems, probably the most general feature of this stage is its variability. It is a time of continual changes—of friends, of interests, of moods, of attitudes, of energy level, of involvement with and retreat from life; unpredictability is rampant.

Another way of describing this situation is to note that ego development proceeds unevenly. For a time, the most notable changes may be in the development of new defenses—for example, intellectualization. This may be followed by a period of intense activity, of trying out new roles and possible courses of action. This in turn may be followed by a withdrawal from contact with others and a time of intense self-preoccupation. Such a condition of continual change and variability, which contributes to the personal turmoil often associated with this stage, generally comes to an end with the close of adolescence, by which time a relatively permanent stabilization and integration of drives, interests, and defenses has taken place.

This eventual adoption of characteristic methods for coping with instinctual drives is likely to be highly idiosyncratic. Equally unique is the individual's eventual stabilization of the hierarchy of ego interests and skills. It is the idiosyncratic pattern of these ego functions that contributes to, and becomes the basis for, the eventual development of "character." Thus, we see again that the development of adaptive and cognitive ego functions originates out of the need to control or channel instinctual drives.

Summary of Stages of Development

The first five stages of development cover the years from birth through adolescence. During the first stage, the infant changes from a totally un-differentiated, passive, helpless creature, with virtually no intellectual capacities, into a child who has developed the abilities for differentiating internal from external, for recognition memory, visual discrimination and judgment—albeit all of a primitive kind. The predominant mode of this stage is that of taking in. Erikson has described the child's definition of himself at this stage as being "I am what I am given."[44]

In the second stage, the differentiation of the child from his surroundings continues, now in connection with an increasing sense of his own will, or volition, and his increased striving for autonomy. The characteristic mode of this period is that of an alternating holding on and letting go. The acquisition of language and the ability for semantic communication contributes to the child's increasing sense of self, as does his increased capacity for judgment. At this stage, his definition of himself is in terms of "I am what I will."

In the third stage, the intrusive mode contributes to the child's increasing exploration of the world and to his increasing pleasure in carrying out activities, although often these activities may involve purely fantasy behavior. At the same time, the child of this age begins to internalize the values and mores of his society, which in turn helps him to direct his activity into acceptable channels. Nevertheless, his definition of himself at this stage is "I am what I imagine myself to be."

In the fourth stage, no new drive-related mode of behavior emerges, for this is a time of relative quiescence of instinctual drives. Instead, the latency stage is characterized by the child becoming increasingly interested in the usefulness of the concrete products of his activity, and this interest facilitates his acquiring new information and skills—that is, it facilitates the process of education. The child's definition of himself in this stage changes to "I am what I learn."

In the fifth stage, adolescence, there is again an upsurge of the instinctual drives. The rearrangement of these into a hierarchical organization results in the new modality of this stage—that of sexual forepleasure. As a result of the need to gain control over potentially disrupting impulses, new cognitive mechanisms develop, including an increased capacity for abstract thought. Other new styles or patterns of behavior develop in connection with the need to dissolve strong emotional attachments to the parents. In connection with these problems, the adolescent often feels a temporary loss of self and he is increasingly concerned about the meaning and direction of his life. The question at this stage becomes, "Who am I? What is my identity?"

THE CAUSES OF DEVELOPMENT

Thus far, we have been discussing the different stages of development and have noted that certain qualitative changes distinguish one stage from the next. We have seen how developments in one stage depend on developments in preceding stages, and to that extent we have discussed how it is that change comes about. In the present section, we will look more specifically at those factors which psychoanalytic theorists believe cause developmental change.

We have already discussed the concept of an innate plan for development, unfolding over several years. This concept implies that development, including ego development, is partly based on a process of maturation. One cause thus comes from the innate factors that determine the course of ego development, independent of the effects of the environment. As different ego functions mature, qualitative changes in the behavior of the child emerge.

The idea of a maturational plan also assumes that there is an innate plan that determines how the instinctual drives are manifested. The shift of drive energy from sensitizing the oral zone, to the anal zone, to the phallic zone— each of which is manifested in qualitative changes in behavior—is due to an innate plan of development. Thus, changes in both ego development and drive development are due partly to innate factors.

Given this rather broad plan of maturation, however, interaction with the environment is necessary for normal development to occur. Environmental stimulation may act as the catalyst for the emergence of an impending ego function. For example, every infant is born in a stage of nondifferentiation, it is assumed, but his experiences of gratification derived from external objects and of successful flight from external stimuli help him differentiate internal and external. As another example, we noted that the absence of the external goal object is responsible for the development of thought processes.

Environmental conditions also may determine which of several types of behavior will predominate in the person's repertoire. For example, a child who experiences excessive gratification during the first stage of development may overly rely on the mode of taking in, which is characteristic of that stage, and so may become in temperament overly optimistic, without sufficient thought to planning for the future. Likewise, a culture or society that stresses saving, thriftiness, and acquisition will directly or indirectly reward the holding-on mode of the second stage, whereas another society without such values of accumulation might be more likely to reinforce the letting-go mode.

Thus, change is determined both by innate factors and their interaction with the environment. To psychoanalytic theorists, one specific type of interaction is especially important for development to occur—namely, from the first weeks of life, the emotional attachment of the child to the mother, which contributes the major impetus for the development of cognitive functions. As we have seen, the first contact percept, the first visual percept, recognition memory, discrimination learning, the first judgment, and the first abstract concept are all developed in connection with interactions with the mother. As the child grows older, much of his learning and acquiring of new skills is done to win the approval of his mother. Because of his positive emotional attachment to her, he learns in order to please her. But even at the earliest periods of development, the importance of this positive feeling for her is evident. For example, it is the infant's experience of the mother as "good"—as one who makes him feel good—that provides the reason for him to differentiate her face from all other faces. Throughout childhood, then, the mother plays a critical role in fostering developmental change.

However, not only *positive* emotional experiences contribute to change; anxiety, frustration, and conflict are also significant. As we noted, the threat of overwhelming anxiety promotes the development of mental defense mechanisms. Frustration following nondrive gratification promotes the differentiation of internal and external, and may foster the development of secondary process thinking, which is oriented toward finding the drive object in reality. Also we have noted that out of the conflict of wills between child and mother, the child's internalization of certain social prohibitions is based on his love for his parents *and* on his anxiety about losing them.

Psychoanalysis is quite clear in its stand that experiences of conflict and frustration, in moderate degree, are absolutely necessary for development to occur. The child who has every need anticipated and met for him will not show the normal progression in development. It is out of the need to overcome obstacles and to lessen frustration that the child learns. Without such experiences, he remains complacently immature—that is, cognitively underdeveloped.

As may be apparent, psychoanalytic theory posits a middle-of-the-road policy as optimal for normal change and development to occur; that is, the child should experience neither excessive gratification nor excessive frustration of his needs. The experience of either one of these extremes can thwart his development. By creating a situation in which undue emotion, either positive or negative, is associated with a particular stage of development, the child may be hampered in his progression to the next stage. When, as a result of excessive gratification or frustration, a child becomes stuck in this way, we say he is *fixated* at a particular stage of development. Such fixation is generally not total. What we mean is that though the child continues to mature physically and appears to try to learn new types of behavior, he is in fact trying to solve these new problems with a mode of behavior that was appropriate once but now is maladaptive. For example, a school-age child fixated in the first stage of development will try to get through his school work and playground activities by being given to—that is, by incorporating what someone else provides him, and perhaps by *insisting* that he be given to—rather than by the more appropriate behavior of initiative and striving on his own. Children themselves recognize this issue of age appropriateness in behavior and would probably call

passive taking-in behavior in a school-aged child "babyish." When physical
maturation proceeds but psychological development is fixated at an earlier
stage, we speak of a developmental imbalance.[45] The innately determined
coordination between physical and psychological, worked out through natural
selection over thousands of years, is thrown out of kilter.

To conclude, let us state again that the landmarks in ego development
and cognitive growth are associated with the increasing need to control the
discharge and gratification of instinctual drives. Anna Freud has written,
"instinctual danger makes human beings intelligent."[46] Just as external dangers have caused man to seek new ways to conquer the environment, so
internal dangers make it necessary for him to develop cognitive mechanisms.
In the absence of such dangers, men tend to become placid, indolent, and
stupid. It is the need to control instinctual as well as objective anxiety that is
responsible for the intellectual and cultural growth of man.

SUMMARY

The five stages of development have been summarized throughout this
chapter and will not be repeated here. In this chapter we tried to show that
all development, including cognitive development, is intertwined with innate
instinctual drives, on the one hand, and emotional experiences in relation to
the environment, on the other. These are the basic causes of development.

The assumption of this relationship between the strength of instinctual
drives and the development of thought is a unique contribution of psychoanalytic theory to the understanding of cognitive development. As we
discussed, the first mental processes of imagining develop in connection with
the gratification of the oral drive; recognition and visual discrimination develop in connection with the gratification of libidinal drives; the first abstract,
semantic concept is formed in connection with the expression of the aggressive
drive; the capacity for learning is developed through sublimation of the sexual
drive; and the development of abstract thought serves, in part, as a defense
against sexual drives.

The importance of both positive and negative emotional experiences
was stressed. It is in the context of positive emotional exchange with the
mother that the infant first develops any interest in finding out about the world.
Only through the mother does the world take on the quality of being "good"
and satisfying and thus worth finding out about. Only through the sense of
basic trust that the good mother provides can the child tolerate the inevitable
disappointments, failures, and frustrations he must inevitably meet and yet
maintain his interest and motivation to try again.

At the same time, we have seen how these experiences of frustration
are absolutely necessary for cognitive development to proceed. Excessive gratification may be as harmful as excessive nongratification in hampering ego
development. It is this continual alertness to and stress on motivational and
emotional factors that most differentiates psychoanalytic theory from other
theories of cognitive development.

18

SOME MAJOR AREAS OF INTELLECTUAL DEVELOPMENT

Preview

This chapter examines how specific cognitive functions develop and how the child shifts from primary process thinking to secondary process thinking.

It also describes how defense mechanisms and other new forms of thought grow out of the necessity of dealing with instinctual drives. Here we will see how drives contribute to the development of cognitive processes.

This chapter also looks at how specific forms of secondary process thinking develop—perception, judgment, semantic communication, and reality testing. Finally, we will see how psychoanalytic theorists understand the learning process and how the basic units of

learning are conceptualized as cognitive structures. To show how such structures are established, we will consider the theory of
consciousness, the development of memory
organization, and the use of neutralized drive
energy.

In many ways, the psychoanalytic approach to the development of
specific cognitive functions is similar to that of Piaget, and many psychoanalytic theorists find Piaget's concepts compatible with their way of thinking.[1] However, the *reasons* given for cognitive development are quite different
in the two approaches. For example, psychoanalytic theorists stress that the
first mental representations, or memories, will be laid down only if they are
associated with affect (pleasure or unpleasure).[2] For Piaget, affect is not important. This means that for psychoanalytic theory the first mental representations
are those of the mother, whereas for Piaget they consist of any stimuli with
which the infant has sensorimotor experience. Nevertheless, psychoanalysis
and Piaget's approach have more features in common than either does with
S-R theory.

THE SHIFT FROM PRIMARY TO
SECONDARY PROCESS THINKING

In psychoanalytic theory, the variety of abilities generally considered
to be cognitive functions are included under the general heading of *secondary
process thinking:* reality-oriented perception, visual discrimination, judgment,
learning, problem solving are all examples. On the other hand, fantasy, daydreams, night dreams, and certain aspects of creativity are examples of *primary
process thinking,* but since these activities do not occur as much in the classroom, we will not discuss them here in any detail. The shift from primary
process to secondary process thinking is critical for the development of cognition, and so it is important to understand how this change comes about.

As we indicated earlier, the shift occurs gradually. The secondary
process eventually becomes dominant, but the earlier form of thinking continues to exist throughout life. Moreover, the development of the reality principle,
as part of secondary process thought, carries out the purpose of the pleasure
principle, which governs primary process thinking. That is, the reality principle, by actually obtaining the drive object, works to ensure drive discharge, the
goal of the pleasure principle. We have also seen how early forms of primary
process ideation—that is, arousal of the memory trace of the drive object—
form the basis for the eventual development of secondary process thought.
Thus, in certain ways there is a continuity between the two types of thinking.

But secondary process thinking does not occur simply as a gradual
modification of primary process. There are potential ego functions at birth that

guarantee that the infant can adapt to his environment and that organize his experiences (or rather his memories of them) to accurately reflect reality. These autonomous ego potentialities for movement, perception, and memory make it possible for the infant to develop the capacity for reality testing and thereby develop secondary process thinking.

For primary process to shift to secondary process, ego structures must develop to make possible the delay and detour of immediate drive discharge. Structures for *delay* either prevent the child from acting on the drive demand (for example, by inhibition) or they prevent him from becoming conscious of it (for example, by repression).[3] Such structures develop partly from the internalization of experiences of *external* delay and nongratification. Structures for *detour* stave off drive discharge until an object has been located in reality that corresponds with the memory image of the drive object.[4] In other words, detour structures involve secondary process thought. As may be apparent, detour always involves some delay, but the reverse is not necessarily true.

Let us look now at some examples of ego structures and how they affect the shift from primary to secondary process. One example is in the area of intentional, directed motor behavior. At first, withdrawal from a painful external stimulus is a reflex reaction, but before long the infant is able to voluntarily remove himself from a stimulus he anticipates will be unpleasant. This capacity to withdraw is important in learning to differentiate external from internal: if it can be physically withdrawn from, it is external; if it cannot be withdrawn from, it is internal.[5] As we have seen, the differentiation between external and internal is essential for the development of reality testing and thus for the shift from primary to secondary process. In this way, ego structures that mediate voluntary physical withdrawal contribute to the development of secondary process.

The development of memory organizations is another example of ego structures that further the development of secondary process thinking. When the child is able to associate memories of the three experiences of "drive tension increase" and "presence of drive object" and "drive tension decrease," he will know which object to locate in reality in order to gratify the drive. In other words, this organization of memories makes possible secondary process problem solving.

Language is yet another ego structure that contributes to the shift to secondary process. The capacity to label experiences or memories with words makes it possible for the child to anticipate trial action—that is, to think—with greater precision.[6] This increased precision in thought, in turn, allows for better reality testing and thus for secondary process thought.

Thus, directed motor behavior, memory, and language help the child develop secondary process thinking. The activation of these capacities, then, is both a cause of and an aspect of secondary process thinking.

However, there are more important ego structures to develop that make possible the delay and detour of immediate drive discharge and so further develop secondary process thinking. These ego structures are the defense mechanisms. Whether they are innately given or caused by the instinctual drives interacting with the environment is not always clear, but one must develop them if he is to survive and adapt to reality. If he did not have structures for delay and detour, so that he could locate the drive object in reality, the human organism would soon perish. It is important to stress, then, that defense mechanisms serve an *adaptive* purpose. Only when they are used to excess, to the exclusion of other cognitive structures so that they interfere with reality testing, are they maladaptive. During infancy and childhood, the development of defense mechanisms is normal and indeed necessary, if the shift from primary process to secondary process thinking is to occur.

THE DEVELOPMENT OF DEFENSE MECHANISMS

As mentioned, defense mechanisms develop in order to prevent the infant from being overwhelmed by painful stimuli, both internal and external. At first, this protection is accomplished by the stimulus barrier, which prevents too much stimulation from reaching the infant. Later the stimulus barrier is replaced by several mental operations that protect the child from painful stimuli. One obvious way to avoid such stimuli is to move away from them, to physically flee the sources of danger. The motor abilities of the infant, however, have not developed to a point that he is able to physically remove himself from painful situations. It is only through the development of some mental operations that he will be able to protect himself from being overwhelmed with unpleasant stimulation. Such mental operations are referred to as *defense mechanisms.* Often, the child (and the adult) is not aware of these defense mechanisms, since they operate on an unconscious level, although it is possible to become aware of them.

Defense mechanisms develop partly out of some *predefenses,* which in turn are based on qualities that reside in the nature of the instincts themselves.[7] A psychological instinct can be turned on oneself instead of discharged toward an object, as when a child frustrated with his environment discharges his aggression by beating on himself rather than on some more appropriate object. An instinct—or rather the *active aim* of an instinct—also can be reversed into the *passive aim* of *having the drive discharged.*[8] This reversal may take the form of having the drive discharged on oneself, so that an angry child, rather than discharging his own aggression, instead provokes someone else to act aggressively toward him.

Psychoanalytic theory assumes that some defenses are innate, that their development does not depend on learning, and that they unfold on their own accord as the psychic apparatus becomes more differentiated. The function of the defense mechanisms is to control and regulate the discharge of instinctual drives while protecting the individual from experiencing overwhelming anxiety.

One way to understand how defense mechanisms develop is to consider the *source* of the anxiety they are defending against.[9] Some defenses develop to act as a buffer between the individual and *external* conditions that are too painful or too threatening. The source of the anxiety comes from outside of the individual, and we speak of defenses against *objective anxiety*. Other defenses develop to act as a buffer between the instinctual drives (id), on the one hand, and ego functions, on the other. At early stages of development, especially, these two segments may conflict, so that direct expression of instinctual impulses is threatening to the newly established ego functions. The source of the anxiety is thus *internal,* and we speak of defenses against *instinctual anxiety*. An example of anxiety resulting from threatening instinctual drives would be the emergence of strong wishes to act aggressively toward the mother. This impulse would arouse anxiety, because to act on it would destroy the child's much-needed source of sustenance and nurturance.

Finally, as the psychic apparatus further differentiates to include the superego, an internal conflict may develop between the forces of the id and the prohibitions of the superego, or even between some ego functions and certain superego dictates. In this case, we speak of defenses against *superego anxiety*. An example would be the child who feels hungry and wishes to eat a tantalizing chocolate-marshmallow candy but knows that he must not help himself to the candy without first asking permission from his parents. If he goes ahead and violates the internalized sanctions of his parents, he will feel guilty—that is, he will suffer from superego anxiety.

The Early Defenses

The first defense mechanisms appear during the first stage of development. They are *denial* (of painful external stimuli) and *repression* (of painful internal stimuli). Actually, since external and internal are not well differentiated, these two mechanisms are essentially one. Both involve the withdrawal of attention from an unpleasant perception. When the infant's mental apparatus becomes differentiated to the point that internal and external can be separated, denial will be used as a defense against objective anxiety, and repression will be used as a defense against instinctual anxiety.

Denial.   This earliest defense mechanism against a painful external stimulus involves a complete reversal of the real situation. Denial may occur on a purely psychological level, meaning that the psychic apparatus fails to register, or fails to recognize, external stimuli.

Our understanding of how defenses operate during the early period of development is inferred partly from retrospective evidence and partly from a theoretical understanding of how the mind develops. Later we can see more directly the continued functioning of these early defense mechanisms as, for example, when we observe a child simply "tune out" a nagging parent or overly critical teacher. It is a psychological turning off of the perceptual apparatus, like the hard-of-hearing husband with the complaining wife who simply turns off his hearing aid.

In subsequent stages of development, when increasing motor capacities allow for physical withdrawal from a painful stimulus, *denial in act* may occur.[10] In this case, the child performs an act to exclude perception. Denial in act involves a conscious and intentional behavior on the part of the child. For example, he may close his eyes to avoid seeing something unpleasant, cover his ears or his head so as to avoid hearing or seeing, or hide his face in his mother's skirts when faced with a strange situation.

With the development of language, *denial in word* may occur. The fatherless child may insist verbally that he has a Papa; the death of a favorite pet may be followed by the insistence that the pet has just gone on a trip. (Parents occasionally foster such denial, believing that it will lessen the child's discomfort.) Such behavior is often seen in young children when they want to escape from a painful situation, and it often does ease the discomfort of the child, at least temporarily.

It should be pointed out that denial involves more than simple avoidance of an unpleasant stimulus. The difference between denial and avoidance is in the outcome of the act. In denial, the child subsequently behaves as if the unpleasant stimulus no longer exists. Such behavior clearly involves some magical thinking: it is as if when the child denies the presence of the stimulus by refusing to let it register in his mind, it will somehow cease to exist.[11] Although this primitive defense is more characteristic of young children, it is sometimes seen in adults in severe forms of pathology, and even in the normal adult who uses sleep to blot out the necessity to perform some unpleasant task. Sleeping through an exam or an important appointment is one way of shutting out, or denying, the demands of reality. This mechanism has been caricatured in the three monkeys who see no evil, hear no evil, speak no evil.

Denial in word or act, however, is likely to encounter difficulties when it conflicts with the perceptions of the child's parents or peers. If the stories he tells them or ways he behaves do not coincide with their perception of reality, his behavior may exceed their limits of tolerance and they may refuse to accept his acts or words. Social pressure, then, may be one way to impel the child to give up this defense.

The defense mechanism of *denial in fantasy,* however, need not encounter this difficulty of social nonacceptance. As the mental apparatus becomes more differentiated, and more memory traces are laid down, the child may develop private, internal fantasies to be used as a protection against painful external stimuli. The little boy who finds his small size and relative weakness too painful may imagine himself to be the biggest, bravest, strongest lion tamer in the world. That is, he reverses the facts of reality by use of his imagination. Although he knows at some level that this fantasy is not true, the pleasure he derives from it far outweighs the pain he feels when he perceives reality. At this stage, the inconsistency between denial and reality testing is not disturbing, probably because the ego function of reality testing is still immature and weak and thus more easily suspended, particularly when the information it brings is painful. Moreover, the synthetic function of the ego, which makes it impossible for opposites to coexist, is also relatively weak and immature. With increasing ego development, however, the mechanism of denial becomes progressively less effective as a defense. At the same time, the increasing mental capacities of the child make it possible to replace denial with other defenses against objective anxiety.

The way denial protects the child against painful external stimuli seems fairly clear cut. Whether by psychological withdrawal of attention from the external stimulus, by denial in word or act, or by denial in fantasy, the child manages to ward off stimulation that is too painful for him to deal with. We can all imagine that every child, no matter how benign or nurturant his environment, must at times encounter such painful stimuli. There will be times when needs are not immediately gratified, when anxiety-producing stimuli are present, or when the comparison of himself with another cannot help but make him aware of his current inadequacies. Unable to flee from the situation, the mental defense mechanism of denial protects him from too much objective anxiety.

Repression. This defense is against painful *internal* psychological stimuli or, more specifically, against the mental representations of instinctual drives. But how can the representation or satisfaction of these drives be painful, since, by definition, drive satisfaction always leads to pleasure, that is, to tension reduction? Freud answered this apparent contradiction by relating it to the increasing differentiation of the mental apparatus; that is, there comes a point in development where satisfaction of the drive produces pleasure in one part of the mind but pain in another.[12] Such a situation can come about once there is a separation between the id and the ego, for what brings pleasure to the former may bring pain to the latter. For example, sucking or biting may bring the id pleasure, in that it effects a drive discharge, but at the same time it will result in the mother's withdrawal, which produces ego pain. It is not that the infant "knows" that biting is "bad," which would imply some development of conscience; it is just that he comes to associate biting with ego pain, that is, with his mother's withdrawal. At a later stage of development, he may feel a certain pleasure in discharging aggressive impulses by beating up his younger brother. But again, the consequences—for example, loss of his mother's approval—may produce ego discomfort. This capacity for the same activity to produce pleasure in one part of the psyche but pain in another also may be seen as a precursor for the later development of conscience.

In such a situation, when pain outweighs pleasure, the drive representation is *repressed;* that is, it is kept out of consciousness. This does not mean that the drive disappears or even that it is not satisfied. In repression, the individual is simply not conscious of the drive or its representation. Repression is "healthy" for it successfully prevents pain and anxiety; however, if it is too

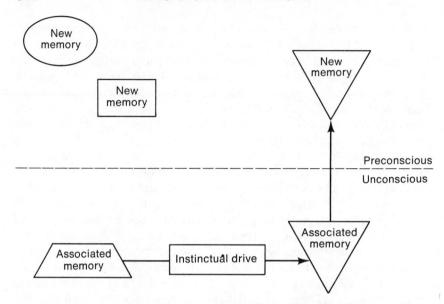

Fig. 18.1. Associative connection developed between repressed drive-related memory and new memory, owing to similarity. Transfer of drive energy to new memory.

extensive it removes too many thoughts and memories from consciousness and thus interferes with thinking and reality testing. Maintaining the repression also requires more and more energy to keep the memories out of consciousness, which in turn means that less energy is available for other mental operations.

As a way of handling painful stimuli, repression lies on a continuum somewhere between flight and the more advanced mental mechanism of condemnation or judgment.[13] As a means of avoidance, flight is limited by motor inadequacies, and in any case is ineffective in dealing with internal stimuli: a person cannot run away from himself. Condemnation, on the other hand, requires that a person be able to make a conscious judgment, to consciously recognize the drive representation and then pass a negative judgment on it. However, this capacity does not develop until later. Prior to its emergence, the mechanism of repression is used to control painful internal stimuli.

Freud identified two phases in the development of repression.[14] *Primal repression* occurs early in development. Like denial, it is a withdrawal of attention from a painful perception. The percept thus removed from consciousness remains as a memory trace in the child's unconscious. Since that memory is from then on not available to consciousness, it remains unchanged—unmodified by experience—in the unconscious and is inextricably associated with the instinctual drive.

Repression proper develops after primal repression. This defense mechanism is used not only against instinctual anxiety but also against objective and superego anxiety. It can continue to occur throughout every stage of life. Repression proper develops according to the model of the associative organiza-

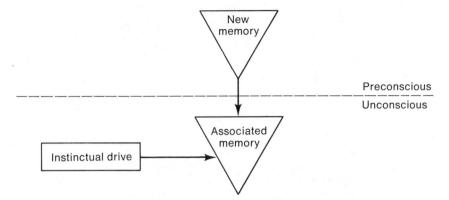

Fig. 18.2. New memory being "pushed" and "pulled" into unconscious.

tion of memories. In the course of living, the individual will have some experiences similar to those represented by the primally repressed memory. As with all experiences, a memory trace will be laid down in the preconscious and, owing to the similarity between this memory and that already repressed, an association will develop between the current memory and the primally repressed memory. Drive energy is transferred from the repressed memory through associative links to these new memories, which then become derivative drive representations (see Figure 18.1). Whether these ideas will be removed from consciousness by repression proper depends on the number of links between the present idea and the repressed idea, the amount of distortion of the current idea by mental censorship, and the amount of drive energy transferred to the idea. As Freud put it, the likelihood that any memory will be repressed depends on its "distance" from the drive.[15]

Repression proper occurs in several ways. An afterexpulsion may occur: an idea that was once conscious is now banished from consciousness, and a counterforce is from then on directed against that memory to prevent it from regaining consciousness. At the same time, memories already repressed may attract conscious memories and pull them into the unconscious. This occurs via the transfer of drive energy over the associative links discussed above (see Figure 18.2). Finally, memories that are already unconscious may be withheld from consciousness by a withdrawal of attention from them, a kind of primitive psychic flight.

One further point to be made here is that a drive representation consists of both an idea and an emotional energy charge (see Figure 18.3, next page). Repression is successful only if *both* are kept out of consciousness. However, the two may undergo different fates: the idea may be repressed, but the affective charge may not be. Instead, the energy charge may be experienced as anxiety, so that the individual may consciously feel from time to time strong feelings of anxiety but be unaware what is causing them; he experiences it as unintelligible or content-less (see Figure 18.4, next page).

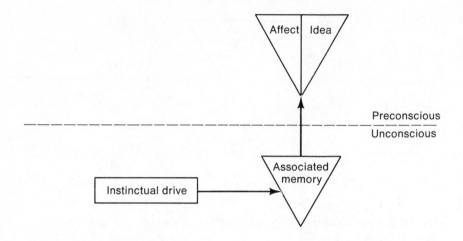

Fig. 18.3. New memory consists of two components: affect and idea.

The reverse may also occur: the idea may remain available to consciousness, but the emotion or anxiety may be repressed. In such a case, the person may be able to think and talk about the drive and its gratification, but he does not experience the emotion one would expect to find associated with such activity. For example, a young man may easily talk about a series of sexual encounters, which seem to give him neither pleasure nor pain, but which he nevertheless compulsively continues. As he describes his experience, he seems like a robot, affectless and detached from his own behavior. Such behavior is called *isolation of affect;* the affect has been split off, or isolated, from the drive representation (see Figure 18.5).

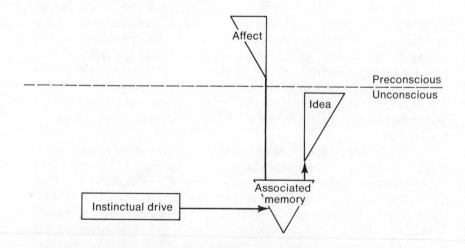

Fig. 18.4. Affect remains available to consciousness, idea repressed.

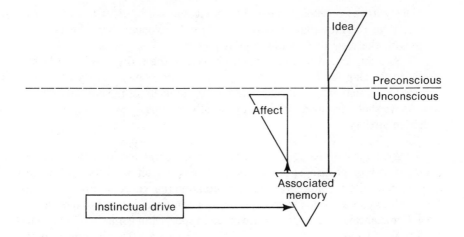

Fig. 18.5. Idea remains available to consciousness, affect repressed.

Negation. As should be clear from the above, the development of repression depends on the separation of conscious and unconscious. But as the mental apparatus continues to differentiate, a new defense mechanism, negation, develops to control the discharge of instinctual drives. Note again that control means *regulate;* it does not imply the *prevention* of drive discharge. Freud called negation the intellectual substitute for repression.[16] Whereas repression demands a constant counterforce against the repressed memory in order to avoid pain, negation uses intellectual judgment to avoid pain. In negation, the repressed idea is allowed into consciousness but then is subjected to a negative judgment. For example, "I want to return to sucking on mother's breast" is changed into "I don't want to return to sucking on mother's breast." Or, "I want the teacher to pay special attention to me" is changed into "I don't want the teacher to pay special attention to me."

Negation differs from repression, then, in that it allows the repressed idea into consciousness—for example, sucking from the breast, or enjoying an exclusive relationship—but it does so only by attaching a negative judgment to the idea. Thus, negation and repression are alike in that neither accepts the drive representation, but negation requires consciousness—that is, a conscious judgment—whereas repression occurs outside of consciousness. Because negation involves the use of judgment, it is a considerable advance in intellectual development. While the function of judgment is by no means fully developed in this early period, its use in negation furthers its growth. Moreover, negation allows for considerably more efficiency in mental functioning, for it requires considerably less psychic energy than does the continual expenditure of opposing energy required by repression. It also enriches the thinking process, for it frees a storehouse of memories that would otherwise be unavailable to consciousness. Finally, the development of judgment reinforces the ego: potential sources of pain may now be recognized and dealt with by the intellect, whereas previously it was necessary to avoid such recognition in order to avoid pain. Rather than the idea that "ignorance is bliss," psychoanalytic theory sides more with the view that "knowledge is power."

Repression and negation, then, are two of the earliest defense mechanisms to develop, and in varying degrees they continue to act as defenses against instinctual anxiety throughout the development of the normal individual. As we shall see, however, denial generally disappears as a defense against objective anxiety.

Restriction of the Ego. With increasing mental development, denial is replaced with other defense mechanisms such as restriction of the ego. In this defense, the child encounters an external situation that causes him anxiety, and he withdraws his attention from it, perhaps switching his interest to some other area. For example, he may first be involved in sports and games but then come to feel that he is inadequate in athletics. The idea of continuing athletic participation may become a source of objective anxiety for him. In defense, he withdraws his psychological involvement—his need for mastery and competence—from sports, disclaiming any interest in them, and from then on does not participate in athletics and does not acquire the usual physical skills and social knowledge children gain from such activities. He has psychologically closed off an area of ego functioning.

Restriction of the ego resembles denial in that both withdraw psychological energy from an external situation that produces anxiety. However, denial *distorts* reality, whereas in restriction of the ego the person makes a *conscious judgment.* In denial, one does not consciously perceive the threatening aspects of reality, whereas in restriction of the ego, one decides he is not interested in certain aspects of reality that he perceives.[17] But, at the same time, the individual who restricts his ego functioning may be quite unaware of the underlying psychological reasons for doing so.

Restricting the ego, although it curtails some ego functions, can be a perfectly normal aspect of development. The child may try out a variety of areas of work and play, withdraw his interest from one area and become active in another, and repeat this a number of times until he finally settles on some areas that give him pleasure and satisfaction. Moreover, restriction of the ego, as a response to objective anxiety, is closely tied to the external environment. It is a way of avoiding external experiences that might remind the child of past unpleasant experiences and thus produce negative affect or anxiety. However, if the environment were to change, this defense might disappear. If a boy experienced anxiety about sports in one neighborhood where the majority of children were older and better coordinated than he, and if his family moved to a new neighborhood, then he might change his attitude toward sports. It is not sports per se that is the source of the anxiety, but rather the pain that involvement in the activity produces, under a particular set of environmental conditions. If under different external conditions the activity does not produce pain, the ego restriction will vanish.

Inhibition. In inhibition, the child is unable to use certain ego functions that have developed and that normally are used by children his age. However, unlike ego restriction, the results of inhibition do not change with a change in environment: the child who avoids sports in one neighborhood will still avoid them in a new neighborhood. The difference is that ego restriction is a defense against objective anxiety, whereas inhibition is a defense against instinctual anxiety.[18] To defend against unacceptable inner instinctual impulses, the child develops a fixed, unchanging symptom of inhibition.

Summary of the Early Defenses. We discussed the development of defenses against objective and instinctual anxiety, from the time of earliest infancy, when no differentiation exists between conscious and unconscious, ego and id, internal and external. We have seen that certain defenses, such as denial and repression, do not depend on consciousness, although repression implies the differentiation of conscious and unconscious. Others, such as denial in word, act, or fantasy, imply the separation of internal and external, and require the participation of conscious mental processes. Negation, in addition, depends on the development of the ego function of judgment. Restriction of the ego also involves judgment and implies that a number of ego functions have developed (or would have if the defense had not prevented them). Finally, inhibition, too, implies the existence of several ego functions, as well as the earlier differentiation of conscious–unconscious, ego–id, internal–external. Thus, as differentiation progresses, ever more complex defense mechanisms are formed to deal with instinctual and objective anxiety.

We pointed out that drives may be repressed because their expression would bring too much pain to the ego. For example, the objective consequences of aggression may be that mother withdraws her attention and affection. We also noted that the child may avoid activities that he associates with pain. In each case, the child anticipates that some suffering may be inflicted on him from some external source. Anna Freud[19] calls such objective anxiety a kind of "forepain"—a warning signal that governs the behavior of the ego and prevents it from engaging in activities that might produce pain. This warning signal, in response to an objective anxiety-producing situation, is a precursor of superego anxiety.

Later Defenses

Whereas the defenses against instinctual and objective anxiety begin to develop early in the child's life, anxiety resulting from an internalized conscience—that is, superego anxiety—does not begin until the fourth or fifth year of life and is a result of maturing instinctual and ego processes and their interaction with the social environment. There are seven types of defense mechanisms that develop during this later period: identification, projection, reaction formation, undoing, sublimation, intellectualization, and rationalization.

Identification. One of the mental processes that contributes to superego development may serve a defensive function. The child may identify
with the parent, or other significant adult, in several ways.[20] At the earliest
stages of development, he may imitate the gestures or sounds made by the
mother. A little later, imitation may take the form of dressing up like the
parent, that is, of physical impersonation. Identification may also occur by the
child imitating broader forms of parental behavior—for example, aggressive
behavior, as might be seen when a little boy scolds his dog after he (the boy)
has been scolded by a parent. Imitation of nurturant behavior is common in
doll play, in which children treat the doll as mother has treated them. Identification may also occur when the child assumes the attributes of the parent—
as, for example, when a little boy assumes certain styles of behavior he perceives to represent the attribute of masculinity.

As with all defense mechanisms, identification is a normal process in
the development of the child. It helps him develop the quality of humanness
and assume the values of the society he lives in. Why, then, is identification
considered a defense? As with many defenses, identification may or may not
be used in a defensive way. In some situations, identification is used to avoid
anxiety, such as when the child feels threatened by the environment and
experiences objective anxiety. One way the child may master this anxiety is to
identify with the individual threatening him—to imitate his behavior, to assume his attributes. By becoming like the one who threatens—by identifying
with him—the child thus transforms himself from the one who is threatened
into the one who threatens. He now becomes critical of others, and he directs
threats toward the outside world. This particular form of identification is
referred to as *identification with the aggressor.*[21] As we have seen, at an earlier
stage it is important in helping the child acquire the semantic concept "No."
As a defense, it also helps him assimilate previous traumatic experiences and
ward off further objective anxiety.

Identification with the aggressor also contributes to the development of
the superego. The internalization of the criticisms, standards, and values of the
aggressor provides the material out of which the superego is formed. The
behavior the parent has criticized is now criticized by the child; the attitudes
the parent condemns are condemned by the child. In the beginning, however,
the child only directs these criticisms against others; he becomes intolerant of
their behavior, but he does not criticize himself. Later, when the superego is
fully developed (as the outcome of the Oedipal conflict), the child directs the
criticisms internalized by identification against himself. In this role as part of
the superego, identification helps the child avoid instinctual anxiety.

Projection. This defense interacts with identification with the aggressor to produce the intolerant criticism described above. Projection helps the
child avoid instinctual anxiety by displacing the representation of the instinctual drive onto the outside world. Thus, rather than recognizing the drive
representation as his own, he projects it onto someone else. For example,

rather than recognizing the feeling "I hate the teacher," the child may instead claim that "John hates the teacher" or that "The teacher hates me." When the defense of identification with the aggressor develops, the child may use this defense along with projection to handle his own unacceptable impulses. That is, he may project his impulses onto someone else and then may be sharply critical of that other person for "having" these unacceptable characteristics.

Like repression but unlike negation, projection prevents the child from becoming conscious of the drive representation within himself. Also like repression, it is not associated with any particular source of anxiety but may be used to protect the child from instinctual, objective, or superego anxiety. It differs from other defenses, however, in that it does not modify the instinctual process itself: it only prevents the individual from perceiving it within himself. Clearly, before projection can develop, the child must differentiate between internal and external. Until he knows what is inside and what is outside, he cannot displace an impulse inside of himself to someone outside of himself. Such projection of an unacceptable feeling to the outside has its forerunner in the infant's earlier spitting out, as a way of expelling the undesirable.[22] Repression, on the other hand, requires a distinction between conscious and unconscious, but not between internal and external.

Projection may also be used as a means of vicarious gratification. A person projects his instincts, wishes, or needs onto someone else and then—and only then—can he work for their gratification in the other person. That is, because the need is unacceptable to the individual, he cannot recognize its existence in himself nor work for its gratification. However, when he perceives it as somebody else's need, he can accept it and help that person satisfy it. In this roundabout vicarious manner, he manages to satisfy the need despite the prohibitions of his superego; that is, he manages to avoid superego anxiety. Projection used in this manner has been referred to by Anna Freud[23] as "altruistic surrender"—that is, surrendering up one's own needs and wishes and working only to gratify them in someone else.

Projection is closely allied with another type of thinking found in the young child. After a child learns to differentiate "I" and "non-I," he further learns to differentiate the "non-I" into animate and inanimate. This differentiation comes slowly, and for some time the child confuses the two classes, attributing feelings, intentions, or motivation to inanimate objects. This is called *animism* or *animistic thinking*. In a sense, animism is a variety of projection; that is, one's own human feelings, needs, and impulses are projected onto some other object, in this case, an inanimate one.

Reaction Formation. This defense, like projection and repression, keeps the individual from becoming aware of his impulse. Rather than expressing the impulse, the individual expresses just the opposite attitude. Rather than say, "I think that spinach tasted dreadful," he says "Of course, I'd like some more." The precursor of this defense is denial, in which the child uses his imagination to change his perception of painful external reality into something pleasurable. But in reaction formation, it is a painful *inner* impulse that is reversed into its opposite, that is, made into something acceptable to the individual.

Undoing. In this related defense, the individual actually expresses both sides of the conflict. That is, he does something and then does something else that is just the opposite. For example, he may ask for spinach, but then drop the plate it is on. Undoing may also occur by an action that is not the actual opposite of the original action; it may reverse the first action only in some magical or imagined sense. For example, children may promise to do something while secretly crossing their fingers, thereby, they think, invalidating the promise.[24]

Sublimation. This defense is of a rather different sort from those discussed above. As indicated in Chapter 17, sublimation first appears in connection with the Oedipal conflict and the ensuing superego development. It channels instinctual impulses into new directions or displaces them onto new objects, either of which is more acceptable than the unmodified expression of the impulses themselves. Sublimation is different from many of the other defenses, in that the drive impulse does find an outlet; it is not bottled up or pushed down. To be sure, the channel or outlet is a substitute, but the drive energy *is* discharged by this route. With other defenses, the drive is not fully discharged; instead, there must be a continual expenditure of counterenergy against it. For this reason, sublimation has been referred to as a "successful" defense.[25]

Sublimation is also important for the normal development of the child, for this capacity to redirect instinctual energy into socially acceptable channels provides the impetus for the child's exploration of the world. The sublimation of instinctual energy promotes learning, athletic prowess, artistic endeavors, and, as Freud put it, the development of a culture.[26] In this sense, sublimation is an optimal defense, and one that should be the goal of education and educators. The development of other defenses might be considered as stopgaps along the way: they are necessary to curtail the unimpeded expression of raw drives, but they are less successful than sublimation in promoting cognitive growth.

Intellectualization and Rationalization. These two defenses do not appear until somewhat later in development and they rely on secondary process thought to carry them out. We mentioned intellectualization in Chapter 17 as a mental mechanism used to defend against the drives that reemerge during adolescence. Rationalization is similar in that it involves secondary process thought, but the thought is used somewhat differently. In rationalization, a prohibited drive goal is pursued in the guise of some other, more acceptable ego goal. For example, a child may eat forbidden candies as part of a "scientific test" to discover whether light chocolate or dark chocolate melts more quickly in the mouth.

Developmental Reversals: Regression and Fixation

These two mechanisms handle the threat of overwhelming anxiety by reverting to some earlier developmental level, to a period when experiences were more pleasant and gratification more assured. Unlike other defenses, these mechanisms are not the result of new ego structures; rather they are caused by the passivity of the ego slipping back into some earlier established mode of behavior. The process of reverting back to an earlier developmental stage is often related to a *fixation*—that is, an experience of earlier development that has been repressed and that remains unchanged in the unconscious. Neither defense contributes to the shift from primary to secondary process thinking. However, regression is a common phenomenon among children faced with too difficult problems, too complicated environmental situations, or too extensive demands. The occurrence of thumb sucking, pants wetting, or babbling after a period of time in which the child has given up these behaviors are all examples of regressive behavior. Parents are intuitively correct when they respond by saying "Don't act like a baby"; they recognize that such behavior represents a return to the "baby" period. What they may overlook, however, is that such behavior is a *defense,* an attempt to cope with anxiety that threatens to overwhelm the child.

This last point, of course, applies to all of the defenses. Defenses function so as to protect the individual from overwhelming anxiety, either from internal or external sources. When the defenses are protecting the individual from inner anxiety, they are doing this by preventing the immediate discharge of instinctual impulses by one of a number of mental maneuvers. In this sense, defenses are adaptive, for they make possible the continued functioning of the individual without undue inner upset.

Defenses as Cognitive Styles

Defenses may take on another adaptive function. Any particular defense used for a long time may become autonomous from its drive origin and instead become a general style of thinking for the individual. As a form of thinking, it may appear not only when instinctual impulses are aroused, but also in any problem-solving situation. In other words, defenses may generalize to other motivations, that is, become controls. For example, intellectualization develops in part as a defense against the upsurge of instinctual impulses during adolescence. However, it may become a person's more general cognitive style —as when an adolescent concerned about his physical or genital adequacy discharges this concern by extensive reading of physiological data obtained in encyclopedias and medical textbooks. This adolescent is handling the problem by gaining extensive knowledge of the facts related to puberty and the associated physiological changes. Subsequently, this fact-gathering approach may be used to face any new problem—an approach that is often quite adaptive.

A mental mechanism freed from its defensive function to a more general style of thinking is an example of *change of function.* Any behavior may undergo a change of function, and defenses are no exception. Ego structures that separate from their drive origins in this way are called *structures of secondary autonomy;* ego potentialities present from birth, on the other hand, are called *structures of primary autonomy.* Both kinds of ego structures are important in making possible the shift from primary to secondary process thinking.

To psychoanalytic theorists, styles of secondary process thought established from defense mechanisms and drive-related modes of behavior show how cognitive development depends on innate drive factors interacting with experience. Mental mechanisms first developed to delay and detour drive discharge or to implement drive gratification may, through repeated use and through the influence of society, be separated from their drive origins and be maintained as more general styles of thinking. Modes of behavior developed for one zone may generalize to another, and eventually these modes may form the basis for general thought patterns. Although the form of these mechanisms is innately determined at first, their development into cognitive styles depends greatly on the influence of society.

THE DEVELOPMENT OF SECONDARY PROCESS FUNCTIONS

Throughout, we have stressed the importance of the mother in the child's cognitive development. We have seen that the earliest memory traces are laid down in connection with her presence, and that the earliest forms of discrimination learning, recognition memory, and communication develop out of interaction with her. From these developments and from continuing positive interaction with her, the child develops an interest in the world and a desire to find out about it. The positive experiences with mother cushion the inevitable disappointments the child will meet in his beginning explorations. Also, mother's love and the child's wish to keep it are powerful motivations for cognitive development: the child becomes willing to give up gratification of his infantile drives in order to please his mother and become more like her. Eventually, the child becomes pleased with himself for renouncing his drives, and he derives pleasure from identifying with the adult world. It is important to stress here that the infant would have little reason for reality testing or developing any other interest in the external world if he did not feel the environment held potential satisfaction and gratification. This belief in a basically supportive world in turn derives from the infant's earliest experiences with the first representative of that world—that is, his mother.

Let us look now at how psychoanalytic theory explains the development of several ego functions. It is important to keep in mind that the theory stresses the *development* of secondary process functions; that is, it assumes there are earlier and later forms of, for example, judgment, rather than that at some time the function appears full blown in mature form. In other words, psychoanalytic theory uses the genetic approach in trying to understand intellectual development, as well as to understand personality development. The theory has not attempted to explain in detail the development of all ego and secondary process functions; however, the following discussion of perception, judgment, concept formation, verbal communication, and reality testing shows the general approach to understanding intellectual development.

Perception

As we stated in Chapter 17, *perception* begins on the contact level, and the earliest percept is a contact percept. The mouth, or oral region, is the earliest organ of perception, and the earliest percept results from the contact between the mouth and the breast or bottle. For this first percept to develop, two factors must be present: (1) an external stimulus that the infant has associated with need gratification and (2) the internal stimulus indicating his need for food. In terms of the model (see Chapter 16), this means that for the first percept to develop the drive object (breast or bottle) must be present at the same time that there is an increase in instinctual tension (hunger).

Contact perception, however, gradually gives way to distance perception. This shift is assumed to come about as follows. While the infant is experiencing the contact percept of the nipple in his mouth, he is staring at his mother's face, so the two percepts coincide to form a single experience. During nursing, the infant occasionally loses contact with the nipple, as it slips out of his mouth, but he does not lose the visual percept at that moment. Gradually, the visual or distance percept comes to be counted on as being the more reliable and hence the more consistently rewarding. This increased reliability is assumed to be responsible for the shift to visual perception.[27]

For these reasons, supported by empirical studies,[28] psychoanalytic theorists believe the first organized and recognizable visual percept is that of the human face. This percept is eventually refined, so that the infant can distinguish between his mother's face and other human faces.

Judgment

In Chapter 17, we noted that the earliest form of judgment occurs in connection with drive satisfaction. Thus, judgment is first concerned with deciding whether something tastes good or, stated more abstractly, whether it possesses a certain quality. Besides taste, the softness, warmth, and texture of objects are additional qualities to which the primitive form of judgment is soon applied.

A second form of judgment appears later when the infant is able to differentiate his mother's face from all other faces. This form of judgment differs from the earlier form, in which the infant judged whether an experience possessed a certain *quality*, whether it provided pleasure or pain. The second kind of judgment is concerned with whether a thing exists in reality or not—

for example, whether mother is there or not. Thus, judgment has been expanded so that it evaluates not only inner psychological states but also external reality.[29]

The capacity for judgment is further expanded when the child develops the defense mechanism of negation. Whereas previously judgement was concerned with whether mother was present, it now becomes a more general mental ability that can be applied to many situations. By being able to make a negative judgment, the child can decide whether a particular object is the one he wants, or a particular action the one he wants to make, and so on. These are secondary process functions, and they add to the increasing dominance of the reality principle over the pleasure principle.

Concept Formation

As with judgment, concept formation also develops out of the early situation of oral drive gratification. Psychoanalytic theory views concept formation as occurring on a continuum: the earliest concepts are very concrete and the later concepts are more abstract. Thus, the development of the earliest contact percept of the breast or bottle can be thought of as the earliest concrete concept. Subsequently, the development of the visual percept of the human face—that is, the recognition of the distinguishing features of a particular object—represents a concept on a slightly higher level of abstraction.

Not until semantic communication begins, according to psychoanalytic theory, do abstract concepts occur. The development of "No" is the first abstract concept in the child's repertoire, since he uses this term in a more complex way than simple imitation of the meaning provided by the mother.[30] "No" is used not only to express prohibition (the mother's meaning) to *not* do something; it is also used to express the aggressive refusal *to* do something. This is a new meaning added by the child, and it changes "No" from simple imitation to a concept with several subordinate meanings—that is, to an abstract concept.

Abstraction—that is, determining the common attribute shared by different objects—is an active process and so requires energy. According to psychoanalytic theory, all abstract concept formation, since it splits off a common attribute from a larger whole, requires aggressive drive energy. The essential split-off attributes are then recombined, by the synthetic function of the ego, to form an abstract concept.

The mobilization of aggressive energy to establish "No" as the first abstract concept is facilitated by the fact that the child first experiences "No" along with frustration—that is, along with a prohibition not to do something. This frustration, in turn, arouses aggressive drive energy, which becomes associated with the memory trace of "No," so that subsequently the child uses "No" to express this aggressive drive.

Semantic Communication

We see that "No" is important in developing judgment and concept formation. It is also important in psychoanalytic theory as an example of the development of semantic communication.

Let us trace the development of the "No" *gesture*. The infant's rooting reflex of turning the head back and forth after being stimulated in the oral region (discussed in Chapter 17) is an innate pattern of motor behavior that has the same form as that used later in the "No" gesture. Rooting is an intermediary step between mounting drive tension (hunger) and attaining drive gratification. It is a type of behavior that is not immediately gratifying in itself but that leads to drive gratification. In psychoanalytic terminology, it is a *detour behavior*.[31] From this standpoint, it has been argued[32] that, since the development of verbal communication is also a kind of detour behavior, verbal communication must originate in the rooting activity.

At the earliest nondifferentiated phase of development, the rooting gesture has a positive function, in that it is used to approach the breast and initiate nursing behavior. Lacking psychological differentiation, the infant has no consciousness and thus rooting has no ideational content; it is simply a reflexive response to the joint presence of an internal need and of tactile stimulation in the oral region.

The second part of the sequence occurs when the infant turns his head away as a way of expressing refusal of food. By then, the differentiation of conscious and unconscious has occurred, and a rudimentary ego has been formed. Thus, this head-turning behavior indicates both conscious and purposive refusal. However, the infant's behavior is not yet a *communication* directed to an individual; it is an expression of his internal psychophysiological state of satiation. It is important to note that head turning has changed in function from being positive (initiate nursing) to being negative (terminate nursing).

The sequence is completed around 15 months of age, when head-rotating behavior and the use of "No" occurs not only as a refusal, but also as a semantic signal directed to another person to communicate this refusal. Thus, a type of behavior that was initially reflexive and without psychological content, through interaction with the environment, takes on new meaning. The capacity to give a gesture meaning depends on the functioning of the ego.

Psychoanalytic theory assumes that the "No" gesture, as a tool for communicating meaning, depends on more than the infant's repeatedly hearing his mother say "No" while prohibiting certain activities. It is assumed that the child is not able to understand all the reasons behind his mother's "No," that is, whether she is concerned for his safety, or is annoyed at him, or some other reason. Rather, the child experiences "No" along with prohibition as a feeling of frustration, and this unpleasurable emotion arouses an aggressive drive. Thus, while the memory trace of "No" is being laid down, it is repeatedly associated with the arousal of an aggressive drive. Eventually, through this association, "No" becomes a way of expressing aggression. Thus, the child uses "No" not only to express prohibition, in an imitation of the mother, but also to express *refusal* and aggressive anger toward the mother.

The development of the "Yes" concept occurs several months after the achievement of "No."[33] Its prototype is a motor response of the infant that occurs between three and six months. Prior to that, a forward and backward motion of the head had been associated with sucking (head forward) and swallowing (head back). Subsequently, if the nipple is withdrawn from a nursing infant, he will approach the breast with nodding movements of the head in a conscious attempt to regain it. This approach movement subsequently becomes a semantic gesture, taking on the meaning of affirmation.

Head shaking and head nodding are similar in that both arise during nursing and both are types of detour behavior and hence appropriate to later expression of communication. However, nodding is not innate and not present at birth. More importantly, its function remains affirmative, whereas head shaking changes from an approach or affirmative function to one of negation.[34]

Reality Testing

Like semantic communication, reality testing is a detour behavior. Since rooting is a prototype for detour behavior, it also contributes to the eventual development of reality testing.[35] During the early period of life, however, no reality testing occurs.

Reality testing cannot occur while the infant is still at the level of contact perception, because there is no differentiation between perception and drive gratification. That is, the behavior that is motivated by a drive (hunger) and leads to contact perception of the drive object occurs at the same time that the need is being gratified; sucking results in both perception and drive gratification.

This coincidence of perception and drive gratification makes reality testing impossible during this early period for two reasons: First, since reality testing requires that a drive-aroused internal memory be matched with an external perception, the child must be able to separate between the drive and the perception; this is not possible with contact perception. Second, reality testing involves delay and detour in drive gratification, but contact perception does not allow any delay between perception and gratification, and thus again reality testing is ruled out.

Only after distance perception and the differentiation of internal and external develop can reality testing occur. Both of these developments allow the drive to be separated from the perception and tension increase to be separated from drive gratification—equally necessary for reality testing to develop.

It is not until the smiling response occurs, according to psychoanalytic theory, that reality testing begins. Smiling results from the convergence of particular ego functions. First, an infant's smile means he has stored in memory an image of an object once present but then lost. Second, the smile occurs when the lost object can be rediscovered in reality, by matching up the stored memory image with the current perceptual image. This capacity to rediscover in reality an object once present but then lost forms the basis for reality testing.[36]

LEARNING

Despite the obvious importance of learning for understanding human behavior, psychoanalytic theory for a long time paid little attention to this area. Even now, there is no real psychoanalytic theory of learning; attempts to formulate one are incomplete. Nevertheless, psychoanalytic theory has outlined a general approach to understanding learning, emphasizing factors overlooked or purposely omitted in other learning theories.

To begin with, psychoanalytic theorists believe learning occurs as part of the interaction between the person's intrinsic maturational plan and his experience. The innate factors of development unfold independently of experience—that is, independently of learning—and, in fact, serve to organize experience. For example, in the early months of life, the oral drive organizes experience into those things that can and cannot be eaten, and memory reflects this organization. Thus, during the earlier years, the organization of memory is determined, in part, by innate factors. Psychoanalysis sees the development of such memory organizations as a foundation for a learning theory.[37]

These early memories of experiences are organized as to whether they do or do not satisfy a drive. This kind of memory organization, based on the association between the memory and a drive, is called the *drive organization of thought*[38] and is the basis for primary process thought.

When early experiences are "organized" as to whether they do or do not satisfy a drive, this is really a form of learning; the infant learns which experiences satisfy and which do not. It is for this reason that psychoanalysis bases learning theory in the development of memory organization. However, there is a difference between saying that experiences are "organized" and that they are "learned," and this difference underscores the distinction between the psychoanalytic approach to learning and that of some other theories. In psychoanalytic theory, during the first year or so of life, only experiences somehow relevant to a drive are learned; others are not. Memory organization is selective, based on the relevance of the experience to the drive. Thus, this interaction between drive and experience determines what learning will occur.

But the relevance of experience to a drive is not the only basis on which memories are organized. There are also, from the beginning, other innate factors that make possible a *conceptual organization of memory*. For example, from the beginning, the mental apparatus may organize memories according to similarity, contiguity, and perhaps other dimensions that reflect formal relationships among experiences.[39]

Thus, in the beginning, the interaction of drive and experience determines which memories are laid down and launches a drive organization of thought; later, the mind's innate potential for a conceptual organization of thought makes possible a second organization of those same experiences. For example, cookies, grapes, peas, and eggs are objects that all satisfy the oral drive, but they also are all round in shape; thus, memories of these objects can be both drive organized and conceptually organized.

The conceptual category "round" can, of course, include many other objects and, of course, it can include objects that are not drive related. Eventually, as secondary process thinking increases, the drive organization of thought gives way to the conceptual organization of thought. From then on, experience is recorded not primarily as to whether it is drive related, but rather as to whether it fits into the existing conceptual categories—for example, those of contiguity and concrete similarity.

As the strength of secondary process thought increases, experiences become useful in facilitating delay and detour mechanisms. Here the infant develops a new category—namely, what an object can be used for—which becomes another basis for the conceptual organization of thought. Again, a new kind of learning develops—learning what things are good for and what they can be used for. Psychoanalytic theory understands this kind of learning as being based on innate mental potentialities to organize experience into certain kinds of categories—in this case, the category of what things can be used for. Thus, the early categories of memory are based on innate factors rather than simply being the result of experience with the world.

From the start, the potential for the conceptual organization of thought is independent of drives, although experiences recorded as memories are initially *selected* for their relevance to drives. As primary process thinking shifts to secondary process, the organization of experience—that is, learning—proceeds increasingly according to these conceptual categories.

Interestingly, psychoanalytic theory stresses the importance of instinctual drives in development, but these drives are understood to play a decreasing role in learning as the child grows older. Here the psychoanalytic approach to learning is very different from that of certain learning theories, in which drive is a central concept. In psychoanalytic theory, the kind of learning that involves the conceptual organization of thought is based on drive-free cognitive structures, and on nondrive energy. Drive-free cognitive structures are ego functions present from the beginning (structures of primary autonomy) as well as structures split off from their original drive origin (the structures of secondary autonomy). We will discuss below the assumption that learning is based on nondrive energy. For now, let us just note that, in formulating a theory of learning, psychoanalysis wants to account for the subjective experience that learning involves work and work requires energy. Thus, a theory of learning must deal with the role of psychological energy in learning processes.

Learning as Structure Building

We said learning is based on the existence of cognitive structures. But it also consists of *forming* cognitive structures; that is, new learning is based on old learning. Since the basic unit of learning is referred to as a structure, we must ask how a process (learning) is turned into a structure—that is, how an activity state assumes a stable, somewhat permanent existence in the psyche.

Psychoanalysis has no definitive answer to this question, but the theory assumes three conditions contribute to structure building.[40] First, the process must occur several times, which, in turn, requires considerable psychological energy. Through this repetition, it is assumed, some of the energy becomes attached to the structure and helps ensure the continued existence of the structure. Second, it is assumed that the person from time to time reexperiences the stimulus situation that gave rise to the structure, and that this reexperience helps maintain the structure. Third, it is assumed that when there is a relationship between an already established structure and the material to be learned, structure building is facilitated. This might occur by psychological energy being transferred by associative bonds from the old to the new structure or the new material being assimilated to the already existing structure.

As an example, consider how a child learns to extract square roots from numbers of several digits. First the method is explained to him, and then he must practice the process on several examples. Through this repetition, a series of memory traces, representing the steps in the process, are laid down. This organization of related memory traces is called a *cognitive structure*. From the repetitive practice, a small amount of psychological energy is attached to this cognitive structure. This helps prevent the structure from disintegrating; that is, it helps prevent forgetting.

Once established, cognitive structures may be self-maintaining for years, especially for intellectual skills that were initially highly overlearned, such as multiplication tables. It may also be true for an event that occurred only once, if enough psychological energy was connected with the memory of that event, such as in seeing a highly exciting acrobatic feat or a tragic accident. But more often the continuation of a cognitive structure requires that the child periodically reexperience the process or event that gave rise to the structure. Thus, for the child to maintain the ability to extract square roots, he must practice the method occasionally.

Finally, a new structure is helped if previous cognitive structures exist that are related to it. Thus, having previously learned a cognitive structure of the Arabic number system and a cognitive structure for long division will help a child learn to do square roots. Because these structures already existed, the learner does not have to focus his energy on these aspects of the new process and may instead concentrate on those operations that are wholly new. With more energy available, building the new structure becomes easier.

In this discussion of structure building—of learning—we have not once referred to the concept of *reinforcement*. Psychoanalytic theory does not assume that for learning to occur the child must be "reinforced," in the sense of being supplied with some extrinsic reward. This does not mean, however, that learning is not motivated or that it is separate from the experience of gratification. However, psychoanalytic theory believes that little human learning is caused by conditioning, by externally aroused drives and extrinsic reward. Rather, the sources of motivation are internal, and the child's experience of satisfaction is quite different from receiving candies following a "correct" response.

As with defenses after repetitive use, a cognitive structure gradually becomes independent of its origin. When a defense mechanism is split off from its origin as a defense against instinctual drives, it can then be used also as a general approach to problem solving, becoming a cognitive style. When a cognitive structure is split off, eventually it may be aroused even when the external situation that gave rise to it is absent. In other words, a person no longer has to perceive the situation to activate the structure; he can activate it by his internal processes. When a structure has been thus split off from its origin, we say that *automatization* has occurred. For example, the child's ability to solve square-root problems no longer depends on a problem being presented by his teacher. Rather, once this cognitive structure has become autonomous, he can call it into use on his own. In fact, he may use it to solve some other, more complicated problem, just as long division once helped him learn to do square-root extraction.

The capacity to develop autonomous mental structures is one way man, unlike lower animals, is able to free himself from domination by the environment. Just as the development of defense structures provides man with some autonomy from his drives, so the development of other cognitive structures ensures some autonomy from the environment.

Learning, Consciousness, and Attention

We all know the subjective experience that learning takes effort. Put another way, learning requires energy. What is the source of this energy and how does it function?

The answer comes from the psychoanalytic theory of consciousness. Consciousness is omitted from other learning theories, which implies either that the determinants of behavior, including learning, lie outside of consciousness[41] or that the concept of consciousness is not considered useful. Psychoanalysis, on the other hand, sees in the theory of consciousness the explanation for some aspects of learning.[42]

How does man come to learn about the external and internal world? Psychoanalytic theory would answer that learning is closely related to consciousness. Although some special types of learning may occur outside of awareness, in most learning—especially the classroom type—the learner must be aware of the material. Thus, we must understand the theory of consciousness.

Consciousness is considered to be a structure of the ego and operates somewhat like a sense organ.[43] This ego function is to scan the outer and inner environments to bring certain stimuli into the individual's awareness. To do this, consciousness requires psychological energy.

This functioning of consciousness is similar to what we mean when we talk about paying attention to something: to know about something, we must direct our attention to it. In psychoanalytic theory, consciousness directs attentional energy toward those stimuli, internal or external, that the person is to become aware of.

Such an approach is consistent with the experience that not all stimulation that registers on the retina of the eye results in perception. We may entirely "overlook" some object or internal signal because we were not paying attention to it. This approach is also consistent with the experience that after steadily paying attention to environmental stimulation, one experiences a sense of fatigue—that is, of energy being used up. Since this can occur even when the entire period has been spent sitting in a chair, this energy must clearly be different from that used in physical activity.

Psychoanalytic theory postulates that such attentional energy is of a nondrive type. Its source may be either the autonomous ego structures or neutralized drive energy. About the first source, Freud wrote that originally attention functioned in the infant and young child so as "periodically to search the outer world"[44] in order to record potentially useful information. Attention, he said, was an active function that "meets sense-impressions halfway, instead of awaiting their appearance."[45] However, as development continues, attention becomes capable of actively searching the *inner* world of memories, so as to use past experience to best implement adaptive behavior.

The second source, the neutralization of drive energy, is assumed to result from the increasing differentiation, structuralization, and hierarchization of the mental apparatus.[46] Over time, a number of stable ego structures are acquired, and as it comes into contact with them, drive energy becomes neutralized—like salt water converted to fresh water, by being passed through filters and successively smaller pipes so that the *quality* of the water is changed. With development there is a successive layering, or hierarchic organization, of drives and control structures.[47] At each new level, and as a result of having passed through still another set of control structures, the *quality* of the energy is changed. What was originally entirely drive energy is increasingly changed into neutralized energy.

With the development of this capacity to change drive energy into neutralized energy, the nature of *behavior* also can change. Whereas initially the infant's behavior was dominated by the intrinsic characteristics of instinctual drives—a striving for immediate discharge by obtaining an appropriate drive object—the characteristics of neutralized energy are different, and hence behavior based on that energy can be different.

Different from drive energy, neutralized energy does not arise spontaneously and does not strive for discharge. It can, however, be used for the function of attention.[48] It is in equilibrium until it is disrupted or triggered by some internal or external stimulus. That is, attention may be directed either toward an external stimulus or toward some internal mental event, such as a memory or a wish. Attentional energy, unlike drive energy, has no specific goal or object with which it is coordinated. It is aroused by or commandeered by encounters with stimuli, either internal or external. Following such an encounter, a state of internal disequilibrium continues either until the stimulus disappears or until a cognitive structure is formed—that is, until learning occurs.

Thus, by the neutralization of drive energy, *behavior* becomes decreasingly drive determined and increasingly reality oriented. The existence of neutralized energy thus increases the capacity of the individual to attend to external reality.

The theory assumes that for any stimulus to reach the threshold of awareness, a certain amount of attentional energy must be directed toward it. The mere *presence* of a stimulus is not sufficient for a person to recognize it. Moreover, some stimuli will be more likely to attract this attention than will others, depending on their intensity and duration. When attentional energy is directed toward a stimulus, this is represented internally by the activation of a mental process—for example, the individual perceives something. When attentional energy has been directed to a stimulus over some time, a more permanent representation of that stimulus is laid down and the process becomes structuralized, either as a memory trace or as a more elaborate cognitive structure.

Such a structure is relatively resistant to change and can itself become an internal stimulus toward which attentional energy is directed. In this way, memories (cognitive structures) may be raised to consciousness. That is, the process of becoming aware of an internal stimulus is the same as in becoming aware of an external stimulus—attention is directed to the stimulus. However, just as the nature of external stimuli—that is, their intensity and duration—determines which ones are attended to, so the nature of internal stimuli determines whether attention will be directed to them. One characteristic is that the internal stimulus must possess a "quality" (as contrasted with pure quantity of excitation). In the genetically early stages of the development of thinking, the only quality connected with thought was pleasure or unpleasure. But, it turned out, activity was maladaptive when it was based on ideas whose presence in consciousness was determined solely by internal pleasure or pain. Mechanisms for delay of discharge had to be developed so that the child could act realistically and hence adaptively. Consciousness of an idea no longer could depend on the quality pleasure–unpleasure; however, *quality* remained as a necessary condition for consciousness.[49] The necessary quality was then derived from *verbal memory traces,* each of which carried within itself a small residue of quality.

A second characteristic internal stimuli must have for attention to be directed to them is that they must be memories stored in the preconscious state, in order to be available to consciousness. Such memories consist of the concrete memory of the thing and the verbal memory corresponding to the concrete thing. Unconscious memories, on the other hand, are of the concrete thing alone.[50] It is the linking up with a verbal trace, then, that distinguishes a preconscious idea from an unconscious one. The distinguishing feature of an idea that can be made conscious—that is, that can have attention directed to it—is that it is connected with the memory traces of *verbal* stimuli.

For example, a child may have stored as an unconscious memory an image of an early toy. In order for the memory to become conscious, he must also have a name for that toy stored as a preconscious memory. Finally, there must be an association between the image and the name of the toy, between the picture of a bear and the name "Teddy bear."

Given these characteristics of internal stimuli that are *available* to consciousness, the process of actually *becoming* conscious depends on the direction of attention to them. The process of memory *recall* depends on the direction of attentional energy to scan the entire storehouse of cognitive structures. The process of *recognition* memory involves directing attentional energy toward both the external stimulus and the internal memory structures, and then deciding if they are congruent.

Let us consider now the relationship between attentional energy and learning. As we have seen, psychoanalytic theory considers *learning* to be structure building. As attentional energy is repeatedly directed to a stimulus situation, it forms a cognitive structure representing that stimulus. How easily a structure is formed depends on the intensity and duration of the stimulus: the more intense the stimulus or the longer it is present, the more likely that attentional energy will be directed to it and that a structure will be formed— that is, that it will be learned.[51]

It is important to notice here that this is an interactional theory of learning. Learning depends not only on the characteristics of the stimulus to be learned and how it is presented, but also on the presence of attentional energy in the learner. If not enough such energy is available—for example, because the individual is fatigued, drugged, or asleep—learning will not occur. Thus, this theory is concerned with the nature and condition of the learner, including how much attentional energy he has at his disposal.

Such energy, it is hypothesized, is limited, which means that energy being spent in one way is not available for other purposes.[52] In a situation with two (or more) competing sources of external stimulation, we cannot attend to both at the same time—we cannot simultaneously watch television and listen to the radio and fully comprehend the message from each. Generally, we direct our attention to one source of excitation, which becomes the focal stimulus, and "ignore" (do not direct attention to) the other, which becomes the incidental stimulus. Focal and incidental are relative terms, however; a person may redirect his attention so that the incidental stimulus becomes focal and vice versa. This same principle applies to the activation of internal stimuli; that is, the availability of attentional energy determines the number of memories a person may be conscious of at any one time.[53]

Since learning—that is, structure building—requires that a person repeatedly direct his attentional energy to a stimulus for a period of time, and since the attentional energy available to him is limited, energy will not be available during that period for other structure building. This is how psychoanalytic theory explains the finding that there is a fixed limit to the amount that people can remember[54] and that learning is often more difficult when one has just learned something else, a fact documented in numerous experiments on human learning.[55]

Once a structure is established, the attentional energy that went into building it becomes available; only a small amount of the energy is tied into the structure. Accordingly, once a structure is established, there should be no interference with new learning; in fact, the existence of an old structure may mediate further structure building, as we saw in our example of the child learning square-root extraction.

An established cognitive structure is said to be autonomous; its continued existence does not depend on repeated external or internal excitations. Rather, it has "jelled," retaining only a small amount of the energy required for its formation. We must emphasize that autonomy means the structure is independent of external stimuli and internal drive stimuli; it does not mean the structure stands in isolation. On the contrary, autonomous ego structures are integrated with other ego structures, and the more autonomous the ego, the more these structures can be reenergized and maintained through their interrelationships.

We mentioned that the attentional energy necessary for structure building may be diminished in two ways, either by changes in ego states owing to fatigue, drugs, or sleep, or by competition from some other stimulus for the limited amount of energy available. A third way it may be diminished is when an inordinate amount of energy is used for defensive purposes. The more energy is required to prevent disturbing instinctual impulses from breaking through, the less energy is available for attending to external and internal stimuli and thus for structure building. Thus, unresolved conflicts between drive demands and reality or ego considerations can markedly affect an individual's capacity for learning.

The process of being attentive to stimuli is generally effortless and involuntary. If, because attentional energy is unavailable or because of the nature of the stimulus, effortless attention becomes impossible, the person may begin to purposefully apply the available attentional energies—an act called *concentration*. What is responsible for the change from attention to concentration? In general, it occurs when a stimulus is new, does not correspond to some existing cognitive structure, and must be organized into a new structure—that is, into new thought patterns. "New" means not only the subject matter is unfamiliar; it also refers to the level on which it must be dealt with. The material may be new because it synthesizes many previously known elements into a new, complex whole, so that the complexity obscures the correspondence between the old material and existing cognitive structures. Or the material may be new because it requires the individual to *create* a new whole out of well-known material, to build a new cognitive structure out of previously familiar elements. In each case, the creation of new cognitive structures and thought patterns requires concentration. Once new patterns are established and constantly used, they may become involuntary and effortless. However, if such structures fall into disuse or if there is a marked change of context, the person may have to reestablish them by concentrating on the stimulus material.

Let us now consider how attentional energy affects thought processes. As we mentioned, psychoanalysis believes that thought processes depend on the associative connections among cognitive structures and that all thought is determined by these associative pathways. Also, we stated that autonomous cognitive structures are associated with other such structures, and that whether an existing structure is activated depends on whether attentional energy is directed to it. Once it is activated, Freud believed, the attentional energy spreads along "all the associative paths that radiate from it; this energy sets the whole network of thought in a state of excitation which lasts for a certain time and then dies away."[56]

To explain the course of thought processes, then, we must know the associative connections that have developed among cognitive structures. However, often the attentional energy is directed by a *purposive idea,* which both determines where the process starts—that is, which cognitive structure the attention is initially directed to—and selects from the alternative pathways radiating from each structure.[57] A purposive idea is generally a secondary process function such as a rule, task orientation, or problem-solving attempt.

Freud provided an example that shows how associative connections and a purposive idea determine the flow of thought processes.[58] In attempting to remember the name of a town he had visited (purposive idea), Freud thought of *Piedmont, Montenegro, Montevideo,* and *Colico* (associated ideas), but none was the right name. Then he noticed that three of the recalled names bore a formal similarity, the syllable *Mon* (the basis for the association), and suddenly the forgotten name—*Monaco*—occurred to him. The three names first recalled had appeared in memory because they shared a common syllable with the desired name, and the fourth name was similar in syllabic and rhyming form (the basis for the association). But it was the purposive idea that led him on beyond these initial memories to finally arrive at the one he was looking for. All of us have probably had similar experiences in trying to remember a name or an event and coming up instead with a variety of other memories— although we perhaps have not stopped to determine the basis for the particular erroneous memories that do occur.

Sometimes, however, the course of thought—that is, the associative pathways traversed—may not be determined by a conscious purposive idea but instead by an instinctual wish or by drive energy. In that case, the succession of ideas aroused may bear little relationship to the logical, conceptual organization of secondary process thought. Although associative connections among the individual cognitive structures are still important in determining drive-organized primary process thinking, the particular connections that are traversed depend on the nature of the activating energy—that is, on its drive basis.[59]

SUMMARY

This chapter discussed how the interaction of innate and environmental factors gradually changes the child's thinking from primary process to secondary process. We saw that secondary process, since it functions according to the reality principle, actually carries out the purpose of primary process thinking and of the pleasure principle, since it obtains the drive object and thus ensures drive discharge. We saw that the shift from primary to secondary process occurs gradually, and depends on the development of ego structures for motor behavior, for memory organization, for language, and especially for defense mechanisms.

We then looked at how specific types of cognitive defense mechanisms develop to facilitate the delay and detour needed for secondary process thinking. We noted that some defenses develop to protect the person from being overwhelmed by external stimuli (objective anxiety) while others protect against discomfort from internal sources (instinctual anxiety). Denial is an example of the former type of defense; repression, and its intellectual substitute negation, are examples of the latter. Similarly, restriction of the ego is a defense against objective anxiety, while inhibition defends against instinctual anxiety. We also discussed how the development of these five early defenses depends on increasing degrees of differentiation within the psyche.

With the development of the superego comes a new possible source for anxiety. Identification is one of the defenses used to cope with this anxiety. Projection, reaction formation and undoing are other later defenses which help defend against superego anxiety, as well as against instinctual anxiety. At puberty, with the increase in drive strength, two new defenses—rationalization and intellectualization—develop to control instinctual anxiety. Finally, we discussed sublimation as a particularly successful defense.

We noted that these defense mechanisms, though originally developed to handle drive discharge and prevent overwhelming anxiety, can become the basis for new patterns of cognition. In this sense, instinctual drives promote the development of cognitive processes.

We next described how specific cognitive functions develop, noting how they originate in early emotional experiences with the mother and how later, freed from their early drive origins, they can be applied to a wide variety of new situations. In this connection, we discussed the development of perception, judgment, concept formation, semantic communication, reality testing, and learning. We described the conditions under which new cognitive structures would most likely develop, and we saw how drives may facilitate learning. First, drives form the basis for early memory organizations, and second, drives provide at least some of the energy that, once neutralized, will be used for the work of learning. We also discussed the relationship of the psychoanalytic theory of consciousness and attention to understanding the learning process. We noted the conditions under which stimuli were most likely to be attended to and thus learned, and we saw that, for psychoanalytic theorists, the ability to consciously remember what has been learned is closely connected to the development of language.

Finally, we noted that the energy available for learning is limited, and that when energy is being used for one mental operation there will be less available for another one. Since defense mechanisms require energy, if they are used excessively to control drives, this will reduce the amount of energy available and hence will interfere with the child's capacity for learning.

19

IMPLICATIONS OF PSYCHOANALYTIC THEORY FOR EDUCATION

Preview

In describing some implications of psychoanalytic theory for education, we will stress the relationship between the child's learning experience and his stage of psychological development. We will see that as the child's subjective sense of himself changes, the type of educational experiences most meaningful to him will also change.

In addition, we will discuss several emotional factors that affect the child's ability to learn. Most important is his relationship with his mother, which affects his general orientation of wanting to find out about the world. We will see that the inability to learn may be caused by developmental imbalance, deprivation, overgratification, or other factors that interfere with reality testing. We will also consider the role of frustration and conflict in learning.

LEARNING RELATED TO DEVELOPMENTAL STAGE

Development and learning, we have stressed, result from the interaction of maturation and experience. Thus, the kind of learning a child can do depends on his stage of development, as well as the experiences he encounters. To understand his learning capacity, then, we must know what developmental stage he has reached.

We must also know this if we want to understand the potential effect of any experience—including educational experiences—on him. Erikson has pointed out that what education (both formal and informal) actually accomplishes, either purposely or accidentally, is to systematically interfere with the unfolding of the maturational plan so as to accentuate some innate potentialities and inhibit others.[1] This kind of education occurs in the areas both of personality (as when different cultures produce different personality traits, such as retentiveness or industry[2]) and of intellectual processes (as when different cultures produce different ways of thinking[3]). The outcome of such environmental interference is to produce a child whose emotional and intellectual traits are congruent with his society.

Because learning, the establishment of cognitive structures, results from the interaction of developmental stage and environmental experience, it follows that the same environmental experience may have a different effect at different stages of development. Conversely, at different developmental stages, the child may be particularly affected by certain kinds of environmental experiences. In terms of educational practice, then, there are optimal periods of development for certain kinds of encounters with the environment, and the teacher should try to coordinate where the child is with what kind of educational experiences he is exposed to.

This idea of optimal periods of development has been well documented in research with animals,[4] and it is related to the idea of learning "readiness" discussed in educational theory.[5] It differs, however, in its stress on the contribution that innate tendencies make to certain forms of behavior. These tendencies are dormant until their critical time occurs in the maturational plan. If the appropriate environmental conditions are present during this period, the innate potentiality will be activated and a new cognitive structure, or mode of behavior, will develop. For example, if the infant has ample experience with people during the first weeks of life, he will begin to recognize the human face when he is about two months old. These early experiences thus activate the capacity for recognition memory. If the appropriate environmental conditions do not occur then, the structures will not develop, and so maturation will continue in a deviant manner, out of phase with psychological development. This is because psychological development depends on the range of ego functions being expanded as the number of cognitive structures is increased. For example, if the infant is deprived of contact with people during his first weeks of life, he will not learn to recognize the human face. Failure to develop this kind of recognition memory will interfere with the subsequent development of the ability to discriminate between mother's face and all other faces. That is, the basis for discrimination learning will be missing.

Coordination of Developmental Stages and Educational Experience

The educator should try to be sensitive to the kinds of behavior associated with these critical periods. He should be aware of which predominant mode the child is using to approach the environment, and he should encourage interaction with the environment, and thus learning, on that level. At the same time, he should be sensitive to where the child has been (the modes of behavior he previously depended on) and where he is going (the modes he has still to develop). Likewise, he must be sensitive to the development of defenses. As we discussed in Chapters 17 and 18, at different stages of development children have different and characteristic ways of dealing with anxiety and conflict. The educator must recognize these defense mechanisms as important if he is to understand their purpose and thus the meaning of the child's behavior.

For example, the characteristic mode of the five-year-old boy entering school is intrusiveness. His typical approach to this new situation can thus be expected to produce some disruption and to upset the classroom from time to time. This disruption is not necessarily due to his being "naughty" but rather reflects the perfectly normal and stage-predominant mode for approaching the world around him. At the same time, he is beginning to incorporate into himself social mores and expectations in the development of the superego, but this development may not yet be complete. Thus, the child may periodically disrupt classroom activities, but at the same time severely criticize other children for being disruptive. This paradox does not mean the child is "hypocritical"; to adults, the two kinds of behavior appear inconsistent, but both are fully consistent with the child's developmental stage. The aware teacher can help the child understand that the critical judgments he applies to others may also be applied to himself.

If the adult fails to consider the modes of behavior, defenses, and other cognitive structures that predominate during each stage of development, there may well be continual misunderstandings between him and the child. A child may interpret a stimulus event quite differently from an adult, for his interpretation depends relatively more on the instinctual drives, the corresponding anxieties and defenses against them, the modes of behavior, and the fantasies that predominate in his developmental stage. The younger the child, the more this is true. His interpretation is egocentric, and this is furthered by the relative weakness of secondary process thinking as compared to the strength of drives and fantasies during the early developmental stages. Further misunderstandings between adult and child can also arise because the child has limited powers of comprehension and so often misconstrues the world around him, which in turn may result in fears and anxieties that interfere with learning. The adult can help facilitate education by being sensitive to the child's need for learning and thought as a way of increasing his mastery and decreasing his anxiety. To disregard the purpose for which the *child* needs cognitive structures and thought is to lose a strong collaborator in the process of education.

Coordination of Subjective Self-Experience and Education

The child's learning experiences should be coordinated not only with the predominant modes of behavior of each stage, but also with the child's subjective sense of himself. As we saw in Chapter 17, Erikson described how, during each of the five stages of development, the child has a subjective feeling of what he is all about. The kind of learning that can go on, we suggest, must fit into that subjective sense of self.

The First Stage: "I Am What I Am Given" (Birth to 14 Months). The infant's feeling of "I am what I am given" is related to the predominant mode of taking in. The implications of this for learning are clear: The infant will learn from what is given to him, and he will not learn about what is not given to him. For example, the baby who is given blocks of various sizes and shapes to play with will learn something about form discrimination, whereas the infant who has no experience with such objects will be handicapped in the development of this ability. The infant's role during the first year is thus mostly passive, and so likewise is the learning that takes place.

The Second Stage: "I Am What I Will" (15 Months to Two Years). Because here the central conflict is a struggle for autonomy, the subjective sense of self becomes "I am what I will." The child's feeling about his relationship to the environment changes into one of active interaction, and conflict, with the world around him. He is eager to determine his own course of behavior and to encounter those aspects of the environment *he* is interested in. From these encounters, he learns something about what he can and cannot do—that is, about the limitations of his capacities. For example, he may learn how to drag a chair to the kitchen cupboard, climb up on the chair, open the cupboard, and pull out the cookie jar—only to discover that he cannot unscrew the top of the jar. In contrast to the first stage, the learning that occurs here is active.

The Third Stage: "I Am What I Imagine I Will Be" (Three to Five Years). With its central theme of intrusiveness and exploration, the child's subjective feeling about himself becomes "I am what I imagine I will be." Both in behavior and thought, his activities are centered in play and imaginative productions, which often show a striking disregard for reality. There is often a confusion between wish and actuality and a belief that anything that is thought about is possible. Although he is still learning about the environment, much of this learning is accomplished by make-believe and fantasy. Thus, the learning that occurs during this stage of development may be characterized as make-believe learning.

The Fourth Stage: "I Am What I Learn" (Six to Ten Years). This is the latency period, and the average child becomes increasingly interested in learning about the world. Since his subjective sense of self becomes "I am what I learn," the important question is what form this learning will take. It may be primarily passive and respondent, as in the first stage, or active, as in the second stage. Ideally, the child should be able to use both, when it is appropriate, and to abandon both, when it is not. Furthermore, the child must be able to advance beyond the taking in of passive learning, the desire to control the environment of active learning, and the curiosity of make-believe learning, to a desire to grow up and join the adult world. That is, he must get past problem-solving on the fantasy level and make use of all the forms of learning at a more advanced level. For example, a high school student may sometimes employ passive learning as the best approach to a problem, but it will not be passive like that of the infant, for he can *select* when to use this approach and decide *how long* to use it before switching to some other style of learning.

To give up passive learning, the child must experience *pleasure* from active ego functioning. To give up make-believe learning, he must in addition accept his limitations. This is especially difficult for some children, for they think to acknowledge their limitations means to acknowledge their inferiority. Depending on the social pressures at home and in the larger society, this may be more of a problem for boys than girls. In such cases, the child may stubbornly insist that there is nothing for him to learn, or he may actively resist any attempt to teach him. Such a state obviously interferes with any real learning at this stage.

The educator has an important role to play, for he can decide on a balance between encouraging the child to assimilate reality and encouraging his imaginative fantasy. Too great an emphasis on assimilating reality may result in a constricted, stimulus-bound, and overly conventional child—for example, one who can never embark on any new activity without first seeing how other children do it and then copying their behavior. Too great an emphasis on imaginative fantasy may produce a child with such idiosyncrasies and eccentricities that he is handicapped both in his thinking and in his relationships with other children—for example, a child so dominated by playing out his personal fantasies that others cannot make sense of them and so cannot join him in his activities. Thus, he is cut off from the benefits of social learning that children usually experience at this time, which further isolates him from his peers. For this reason, the educator needs to be cautious in forming too great an alliance with the make-believe thought of the child.[6]

The Fifth Stage: "Who Am I?" (Adolescence).   Here the subjective sense of self becomes itself the critical issue, for the central concern of the adolescent is "Who am I?" "What is my identity?" The source of this sense of identity will be all the previous ego developments—including learning—that have occurred in his life. As Erikson points out, the child who learns to walk repeats this behavior not only because of the pleasure he derives from the behavior itself, but also because of the new stature it gives him.[7] The child becomes "He who can walk," as well as whatever additional connotations this ability has in his particular culture—such as "He who will go far," "He who is upright," or even "He who will go too far." In other words, the development of an ego function contributes to a person's sense of knowing who he is, both to himself and to the larger society. It is the synthesis of these "senses of self" that eventually becomes the individual's sense of identity.

From this viewpoint, it is clear that what the child is learning all along the way, and the *way in which he is learning it,* will contribute significantly to his identity formation. At the same time, since this process also depends on the unfolding of innate potentialities, what the educator is trying to teach the child must to some degree coincide with this innate unfolding. As Erikson has put it, "whoever wants to guide, must understand, conceptualize, and use spontaneous trends of identity formation."[8] Throughout each stage of development, the child's planned learning experiences must be coordinated with the ego functions and subjective sense of self that are predominant for his stage of development.

EMOTIONAL FACTORS IN LEARNING[9]

With its emphasis on the importance of drives and affect in development, it is not surprising that psychoanalysis stresses the importance of emotional factors in learning. From this point of view, it is difficult indeed to comprehend how other theories can overlook or ignore the central and pervasive role that emotion plays in learning. From the earliest weeks of life, the development of cognitive structures occurs in intimate connection with affective experiences.

The Mother's Role

As we discussed in Chapter 16, the earliest mental structures and functions occur only in connection with experiences of tension increase and decrease. Because the mother mediates these experiences, she is an important contributor to the child's mental development. As we saw in Chapter 17, memory traces are laid down, the first recognition learning occurs, a visual concept emerges, discrimination learning and judgment develop, and the first abstract semantic concept is formed—all as the result of the emotional interaction between mother and infant. To psychoanalytic theory, these interactions with the mother are important bases for the earliest cognitive structures because they occur in connection with affect, with pleasure and pain.

However, the mother participates in the child's cognitive development on an even more basic level. It is clear that to learn about the world the infant must have an interest in external reality. This interest begins with the infant's attachment to his mother because of her capacity to provide him pleasure. Because of her importance to him, he becomes aware of her and learns about her, and this is the prototype for his learning about the world. Through her he develops ties to reality and an interest in finding out about the world. If he has found it pleasant and rewarding to learn about mother, he will be positively oriented toward learning about the world. This learning will be furthered by the emergence of his needs for activity, for autonomy, for exploration, and for mastery in the normal course of development.

The early use of the incorporative mode also affects the child's subsequent orientation toward learning. If in using the incorporative mode he has found that what he takes in produces pleasure, then he will have acquired an orientation basic to learning—that of being able to take in information. But if he has experienced excessive disappointment or inadequate gratification from his interaction with mother, he will have little reason to want to look further into the world. The tragic developmental consequences for infants who were deprived of adequate early emotional attachments have been documented in a number of clinical studies.[10] These babies lie frozen in their cribs, apathetic and withdrawn, showing no interest in the world around them, and eventually deteriorating into an unresponsive, stuporous condition.

The early attachment of the infant to his mother is important for learning in still another way. The development of an object attachment involves a process that creates a relationship between drive and object. Learning also depends on creating lasting relationships (between ideas or mental representations of events or experiences), and so it has been suggested that learning processes may be based on early object attachments.[11] Moreover, new objects may replace old drive objects, and so the coordination between drive and object may change as a result of experience. This process seems quite similar to that which we call learning—that is, change as a result of experience. For this reason, the development of object attachments may be seen as the earliest form of learning.

Thus, the infant's earliest mental functions are based on emotional experiences in which the mother is a regular participant. His growing interest in the external world is an extension of his interest in her. His ability to take in information about that world depends on the earlier success of the incorporative mode in taking in what mother provided to eat. And the process of establishing a lasting attachment to mother forms a basis for learning about other relationships. In these three ways, then, the early mother-infant relationship is important for cognitive development.

The importance of the early attachment to the mother does not end with infancy; this emotional bond continues to be important in later learning. It is through the child's introjection and identification with the parent that he is able to engage in social learning—to take over, as his own, the actions, the feelings, and subsequently the thoughts of other people. Without this kind of orientation, the child's thinking would remain egocentric.

The original mother-child relationship is also important because the early attitudes and attachments to the parent are carried over to the teacher. A child from whom too much has been expected at home, and who resents his parents for placing overly high demands on him, is likely to transfer this resentment to the teacher. A child from whom too little has been expected is likely to have difficulty in learning, not only because he lacks prerequisite skills, but also because he misses out on the shared pride between mother and child that results from learning age-relevant skills at the time they are normally acquired. He will probably eventually acquire these skills anyway, but doing so will not give him the same emotional experience of shared pride. This interferes with the child's developing a sense of ambition, of wanting to do things because of the good feeling such activity produces. Such a child, on entering school, will be passive and apathetic, with little motivation to learn. It becomes the teacher's job, then, to try to establish an environment in which the child can experience shared pride as a result of his activities, thereby enhancing his self-esteem, which in turn will provide the motivation for future initiative and ambition.

Self-Esteem

It is the need of the child to maintain his self-esteem that makes him educable. In his earliest years he experiences feelings of self-love and omnipotence, if they are supported by a nurturant and stimulating environment. If these feelings continue to be nourished by love and affection from his parents and other significant people in his life, they will provide the basis for the growth of his self-esteem. But for these more infantile feelings to become feelings of self-esteem, the child must acquire skills and abilities and then have an opportunity to employ them.

Following the infantile period but prior to the period when the child derives his own self-esteem from working and learning is a period in which he derives his self-esteem almost entirely from the approval of adults. To psychoanalytic theory, the best way to educate the child is to use this dependency on adult approval for his self-esteem. It is because of this need that the child becomes willing to give up his infantile ways and learn new skills; moreover, this also enables him to become more like those adults, and this identification also enhances his self-esteem. Such internalization of and identification with the adult world depends on emotional attachments as much as on specific learning experiences. As Ekstein and Motto so aptly phrase it, the child initially works and learns for love (that is, in order to obtain love), but later, through identification, he loves to work and learn.[12] We must qualify this statement, however, by pointing out that identifying with significant adults will enhance the child's learning only if these adults value intellectual achievement in themselves or others; otherwise, the child will have no reason to feel that academic performance will enhance his standing with his parents or himself, and so may become a pedagogical problem for his teachers. On the other hand, if parents *say* they value intellectual achievement, but the child observes their behavior is not consistent with this statement, it may create a conflict for him that later leads to problems in the classroom.

Communication of Feelings and Fantasies

As we have seen, verbal communication also develops out of the emotional attachment between mother and child. Obviously, this capacity is extremely important for the child's intellectual development. Moreover, it allows him to express his feelings and frustrations in words rather than in behavior. But, most important, it contributes to his subjective sense of being capable of learning, if he can translate his feelings into thoughts and can use his mind to figure out solutions to problems.

Most adults understand that it is important for the child to learn to communicate verbally, but they often forget that the child may not know how to ask certain questions. Because a young child is continually asking "why" about endless different situations, adults may assume that he is able to ask all the questions he wants or needs to. But the child may have things on his mind that are so vague and confusing that he does not know how to put them into words, or he may have thoughts for which he has never been provided verbal labels. For example, children may be intensely curious about the origin of life, about sex, about death, or about themselves, but they may not know how to ask questions about such concerns. Similarly, they may not know how to express verbally certain emotional states such as sadness, aggression, or elation —for although parents are concerned that children learn the names of objects and persons and places, they often do not teach children how to verbally express their inner feelings.[13] When the child does not know how to ask certain questions or to express certain feelings, what he does ask or express is often a substitute for what he would really like to say or know about. Consequently, the adult's response to the question is never satisfactory, for the real question is not being answered.

For example, the young child who asks "Why does the top keep spinning?" and "Why does the ball roll downhill?" may be less interested in the laws of motion and gravity than he is in why he is unable to stop or control his own bodily activities at certain times. The job of the sensitive adult in such a situation is to try to understand, or to translate, what the child is really talking about. Teaching the child to express his feelings verbally is of great assistance to ego development. By offering him an alternative to motor activity, it helps the child to delay action, and, as we have seen, the ability for delay and detour is a central contributor to the development of reality testing.

Again, what we are saying about the education of children is that the teacher must be aware of the child's inner mental life. In any interaction with children, there is more going on than might be discerned by paying attention only to the manifest exchange of questions and answers between adult and child. We have discussed before the need to be aware of the child's pull to deny reality, when to recognize its existence would be painful, and the need for the adult not to cooperate too fully in this defensive maneuver of the child. We have discussed also how the child's recognition of reality entails the recognition of his own limitations, and that adults should be aware that for some children recognizing limitations may mean admitting inferiority. The educator, then, has the dual role of encouraging reality testing and hence recognition of limitations, on the one hand, but not downgrading the child nor making him feel hopelessly inferior, on the other. What the educator can help him understand is that his limitations are temporary and that through learning this temporary state will change.

Conveying such a positive belief in the potentiality of the child is really part of a larger attitude needed by the educator or parent—the sense of believing in what one is doing. Beyond the particular kinds of behavior that the adult encourages and discourages in the child, and beyond the specific information that he teaches the child, it is the *way* he conveys this information to the child that is important. In his teaching, the adult must convey to the child a deep conviction that what he, the adult, is doing has meaning. It is the way the educator conveys this sense of doing something meaningful—something he believes in, is excited by, pursues, and yet maintains discipline about —that may influence the child, through his identification with the teacher, as strongly as any specific curriculum or experience of reward or punishment.

This point of view has further practical implications, especially for the early stages of learning. During these early periods, teaching machines or other mechanical devices can never be acceptable substitutes for educators. The desire to learn, to acquire skills, and to understand greatly depends on experiences of identification with, and internalization of, a sense of work and learning as leading to satisfaction and self-esteem. And these experiences come out of the interchange between human beings, not machines.

However, once the child has internalized a sense of wanting to learn and has developed a feeling of self-satisfaction or pleasure from engaging in such activity, the use of mechanical devices for instruction may be successful. Moreover, as we shall see, use of materials appropriate to the developmental stage can actually foster a sense of self-esteem in connection with learning.

Pleasure in Function

It should be clear that psychoanalytic theory sees emotional factors as potential facilitators of learning, and in fact necessary for learning to occur. Certainly, learning proceeds most easily when the task to be learned corresponds with the child's predominant wishes and needs. But most important, to facilitate learning, the child should experience a sense of *pleasure in function*. All the learning principles in the world will be of little avail if the child does not want to learn, and to want to learn he must get some personal pleasure from his activities and some feeling of self-esteem. Spitz has given a pointed example of this issue: ". . . toward the end of the first year of life, the maturation of the innervation of the lower part of the body enables a child to walk. But *the wish to walk must be there,* and if it is not, the child will not walk [emphasis added]."[14]

What is this pleasure in function and how does it develop? Most generally, it is a subjective positive feeling that derives from the functioning of one's own body or mind. In the infant, such pleasurable feelings are first experienced as bodily sensations that awaken and activate the sensory-motor apparatus. Later the child experiences such pleasure from activity and doing. Finally, this develops into a pleasure deriving from achievement and mastery.

This final concept of pleasure in function requires that the child have the ability to integrate several different kinds of effort and skill so as to produce a successful outcome. He must also have the ability to anticipate the future (at least to some degree), to orient his activities accordingly, and to coordinate his behavior to achieve the ends he wants. If this integration is successful, the exercise of these functions provides pleasure and becomes a source of motivation in itself.

The development of such pleasure in function is closely connected with the processes of imitation, identification, internalization, and the growth of self-esteem discussed above. Adults can encourage pleasure in function by providing children with play materials that allow them to experience the kind of successful outcome of integrated efforts just described. Where the *materials* provided by the environment do not encourage such experiences the pleasure derived from achievement will come less from the completion of a project and more from the self-esteem derived from the praise and approval of adults. That is, the child will continue to function as he did during the earlier period of development.

This situation will affect the child's orientation toward learning and work. His pleasure from achievement itself will then come somewhat later, and it will be more a result of the internalization of the external sources of self-esteem, rather than of pride in the development of his own inner capacities and skills. In later childhood, the motivation of these two kinds of children for learning will be quite different. For one, the reason to acquire knowledge is primarily to secure the approval and love of others. For the other, knowledge contributes to an inner sense of pride and accomplishment, which may or may not evoke some external acknowledgment. For both, learning contributes to self-esteem, but it does so in different ways.[15]

Defenses and Learning

Pleasure in function also is closely related to the process of *sublimation,* in which instinctual drive energy is discharged through channels that lead to socially accepted and sanctioned behavior. This defense mechanism helps the child give up his more infantile forms of gratification for the pleasure derived from participating in the work and attainment of goals valued by the culture he lives in. Clearly, this is a defense that the educational process should encourage. The development of sublimation is necessary if the child is to get on in school. Without it, he is bored, restless, "acts out" (discharges instinctual impulses in direct behavior), and does not like school, for he finds no gratification there and thus no reason to invest his energies in learning.

Another defense mechanism that contributes to learning is *isolation,* which develops out of the need to control affect and drive discharge. Isolation disrupts the connection between ideas and their associated affects so that the ideas remain available to consciousness without arousing disturbing emotions or anxiety. The ability to think about ideas without becoming emotionally involved in the thought process—that is, the ability to think objectively—is necessary for the exercise of logical thinking.

Actually, as we stated, *all* defense mechanisms contribute to the child's intellectual growth and his capacity for learning. They give him ways of dealing with potentially disruptive drives and emotions, thereby allowing him to get on with finding out about the world. The need to control drives thus contributes to the normal intellectual development of the child. Only when a defense mechanism is overused does it interfere with learning.

However, one defense mechanism that differs considerably from others is regression, in which no new cognitive structure develops and in which there is no activity by the ego. The role of the ego is passive: regression simply *happens* to it. When a person is faced with a new or difficult or anxiety-provoking situation, he reverts to earlier ways of behavior that gave him more pleasure and satisfaction than he is currently experiencing. He longs for "the good old days" or wishes that he could be taken care of. Because it is apparently not activated by the ego, but "set in motion by the instincts,"[16] regression indicates a weakness of the ego.

Not surprisingly, children are particularly apt to use this defense, since their ego organization is still weak; in fact, it is normal in young children. When a young child has a difficult problem or new task to master or is tired or hungry, we may expect regression, and we should understand it for what it is: the child is not being purposely naughty or difficult; unable to solve his current problem, he is returning to a level of functioning at which he *was* able to solve problems. That such functioning does not help him solve his current problem is less important to him than the feeling of security he obtains from returning to a time when he was successful.

Frustration and Conflict

Not all frustration and conflict is deleterious to a child's development; indeed, excessive gratification can be as harmful as deprivation. In fact, as we discussed in Chapter 16, it is out of the experience of nongratification that the need for reality testing develops. When the drive level increases and the drive object is not immediately forthcoming, the infant begins to search the outer world in order to locate an object that matches up with his memory of the drive-gratifying object. Thus, if the infant never experienced nongratification, there would be no need for thought processes to develop.

This early relationship between frustration and development carries over into all subsequent development of the child. To psychoanalytic theory, the child's capacity to solve problems grows out of the necessity to resolve conflict; hence, the resolution of conflict and frustration is a critical condition for growth. On this issue, psychoanalysis is often misunderstood; some people take the theory to mean that the child should never be prevented from following his own impulses because such frustration is thought to be damaging to him. But psychoanalytic theory holds that without some frustration normal development will not occur. Experiences of nongratification, plus the need for control and delay of drive discharge, produce cognitive structures and intellectual functioning.

Frustration also contributes to the child's development in a more general way. One powerful force that motivates the child to give up infantile ways and to struggle to learn more grown-up skills is his dependence on his parents and his fear of losing their love and protection. Such anxiety, in moderate amounts, facilitates development. Similarly, the child's concern with attaining his parents' values and goals so as to maintain their approval, and his anxieties about losing it, become the basis of his own self-esteem and helps develop a sense of industry. Thus, both specifically and generally, moderate frustration enhances the child's development.   •

Theoretically, a child could grow up without ever being frustrated, but it is probably fortunate that this could hardly occur. Even the most solicitous mother cannot be so omnipresent and omniscient as to anticipate the child's every need, and he will necessarily experience some frustration in his growing up. Moreover, even if there were no anxiety about violating parental codes of behavior or fears about not being gratified by the environment—that is, superego and objective anxiety—the child would still experience anxiety, for beyond these two *external* origins of anxiety is a third possible source that is internal to the child. Once a differentiation of the ego and id has occurred, there is always the possibility of antagonism between the aims of the two systems. There is a recurring threat that the ego will be overwhelmed by the discharge of instinctual drives, and this can lead to experiences of instinctual anxiety, derived totally from psychological happenings within the child.

What are the implications for the educator of this psychoanalytic view of frustration and conflict? The most general principle to keep in mind is that excessive frustration or gratification will interfere with the child's development. When the child experiences continual frustration in his encounters with the world, he is likely to withdraw from it, to give up trying, and to restrict the range of his behavior to the few activities that give him pleasure. But if the adult is sensitive to what the child might reasonably be expected to do at his stage of development and provides him the opportunity to try out such new behavior in an atmosphere of acceptance, it will help protect the child from excessive frustration.

At the same time, although it is important to be sensitive to the child's impulses and needs related to his developmental stage, allowing unrestricted or uncontrolled expression of these impulses will not help him grow. What the child needs to learn is how to channel these energies into activities that enhance his development by creating new cognitive structures, thereby enlarging the range of ego functions available to him and increasing his autonomy. To allow the unrestrained expression of impulses hampers the development of autonomy, for it keeps the child passively at the mercy of his drive impulses. Moderate frustration of direct drive discharge—that is, of conflict between the demands of external reality and internal reality—is what causes cognitive structures to develop.

There is yet another area in which frustration and conflict are important. In the latency period children characteristically want to avoid objective anxiety, and this often determines the behavior and activity they choose. When faced with a problem they cannot solve, they often take the path of least resistance—of least pain—and avoid the conflict rather than try to solve it. However, continual avoidance of such conflicts interferes with the child's development: instead of expanding his interests and his coping abilities, he sticks with what he knows, thereby restricting his potentialities. Thus, to allow the school-age child complete freedom in choosing his activities may be undesirable, for he may well choose activities because they avoid pain rather than because they allow him to channel his energies into areas in which he can develop his particular talents.[17] Unless some external requirement makes him face and attempt to resolve conflict, he may well lose valuable opportunities for expanding his abilities and interests, retreating instead to the easy and overlearned. It is too much to expect that the child of the latency period will freely choose activities that create frustration and conflict. Children left in a situation that demands too little for too long often suffer impaired ego development. The educator's task is to encourage the child to try things that are difficult, to face tasks that may produce frustration and conflict, and to find ways to solve them.

DEVELOPMENT OF EGO STRENGTH

From successive resolution of conflicts the ego continues to develop, and its capacity to deal with conflict and frustration indicates its strength. Ego strength is not only the number of cognitive structures or ego functions a person has to cope with problems, but also the independence of these structures both from the external stimuli he happens to encounter at the moment and from the demand for discharge of internal drives or the defenses against such drive discharge.

As we said in Chapter 18, the energy available for ego functions is limited. To the extent it is used for defensive purposes, it is not available for attention, perception, learning, and other functions. A child who has too much energy tied up in defending against drive discharge or who lacks sufficient autonomy from external control will be hampered in his ability for self-determined learning. The more autonomous the ego, the greater the ego strength and the more energy the child will have to enter into the learning process. Unlike some behaviorists, psychoanalytic theorists do not believe education is a process of bringing the behavior of the child under the control of the external stimulus.[18] The idea that an autonomous ego is the optimal condition for learning contradicts the conception of learning by conditioning.

INDIVIDUAL DIFFERENCES

Another popular misconception about psychoanalytic theory is that it considers all people to be helplessly driven by "sex" or other inner forces and so it overlooks their many differences. But psychoanalysis is not just a mechanistic formulation of a single "mold" of mankind and unaware of individual differences. In fact, it is quite concerned with such differences and—more than in S-R or cognitive theories—holds there are many sources that contribute to this variability. Like S-R theory, psychoanalysis stresses the importance of environmental experiences in determining the patterns of individual behavior, but unlike S-R theory it does not assume that two individuals exposed to the same environment necessarily have the same reaction. Although both theories believe the effect of any stimulus depends on the person's relevant past experiences, for psychoanalysis, the time or stage of development at which any experience occurred is as important as the experience itself in determining its effect. Thus, an eight-year-old and a twenty-year-old, despite having had a similar sequence of relevant past experiences, would not be expected to react in the same way to identical current stimuli.

Because of the *interaction* between internal and external factors, any single experience may produce a very great variety of possible outcomes. For instance, psychoanalysis stresses that the outcome of each stage is critically determined by the experiences the individual encounters at that time. Further, individual differences, both congenital and acquired, may interact with and influence the way the innate maturational plan is expressed. For example, on the side of congenital differences, empirical studies show that from the very early days of life, infants differ in drive strength as well as in their thresholds for tolerance of external (and presumably internal) stimuli.[19] It also appears that there may well be congenitally determined preferred channels for drive discharge. Moreover, psychoanalysis has pointed out that, because of certain congenital abnormalities—such as blindness, deafness, or certain forms of brain damage—some ego potentialities may not be available; since experiences based on the functioning of these potentialities is a critical ingredient for ego development to proceed according to the innate maturational plan, a developmental imbalance may result.[20,21]

Individual differences also reflect the tendency of children to move forward and backward along developmental lines—to progress and regress—in a somewhat uneven manner, so that some aspects of ego functioning may be progressing while others are temporarily regressing.[22] Each child may show a different "profile" of ego development, with some ego functions being relatively more advanced than others. Thus, according to the psychoanalytic understanding of individual differences, children are an extremely various and individualized group, and the implication for educators is that the best situation for learning is that in which each child is understood to be an individual.

The environment contributes to the development of individual differences in that it varies the opportunities for drive discharge at any stage because it varies in the availability of drive objects. The greater the opportunities for establishing a relationship between drive and object, the greater the individual variations in behavior that will occur. Acquired individual differences also occur because mothers, with their own predilections and interests, stimulate and reward the potentialities of their children differently. In addition, social environments may differ in their stress on the appropriate modes of behavior or types of controls over drive expression that are sanctioned. This leads to the cultural variations in behavioral styles we discussed earlier.

In all, then, there are many internal and external sources of variability that, in interaction, can produce many differences among individuals. Since psychoanalytic theory is concerned with both internal plans of development *and* external variables (important in S-R theory), it is much more similar to cognitive theory than to S-R theory. But cognitive theory has not paid much attention to individual differences or questions of motivation, and so psychoanalytic theory allows for many more variations among individuals than do the other theories.

WHEN THINGS GO WRONG

So far we have discussed the more optimal conditions in which learning may occur. We have assumed that the child's development is proceeding normally and that at each stage he is encountering a more or less usual environment. But this kind of developmental progress is not automatic; it requires an unhampered unfolding of the innate maturational plan in an environment that provides appropriate experiences for each stage of development. If this normal coordination between maturation and development fails to occur, a developmental imbalance will likely result.[23]

Developmental Imbalance

When some part of psychological growth is deficient, the individual will try to compensate for it by the overusing of those psychological functions that do exist. Psychological growth then proceeds askew: the deficiency continues, the overcompensation grows, the initial discrepancy is widened, and the imbalance increases. The child then will appear to have reached a certain level of maturity, but he will lack some of the most basic components of psychological development. At the same time, those areas of psychological functioning that have continued to develop are often somewhat distorted, idiosyncratic, and less adaptable. It is, in other words, an overdevelopment of one part of the system in the absence of certain basic supports.

An example of such an imbalance is a five-year-old child who develops too quickly during the second stage an apparent sense of autonomy and independence. Such a child appears to be quite self-sufficient, capable of making his way without support from others, and may often be remarked upon as being so "grown up." There is, however, one area in which he is not so grown up, for he still soils his pants. Embarrassed by the possibility of this occurrence, he tends to avoid others who might detect his "failure"; he retreats from games and any other activities that might bring him into close contact with others and thus reveal his "secret." Along with his rigid insistence on being self-sufficient, his need to avoid others produces a child who is a loner, a social isolate. The more he strives to prove his self-sufficiency, the more the discrepancy between his apparent and actual self-control, and the more his isolation from others. Such a developmental imbalance may come about in several ways.

Developmental Imbalance Due to Deprivation.   Early experiences of deprivation, especially of emotional deprivation, may stunt or disrupt the normal establishment of attachments, first to the mother and subsequently to the world in general. Without the expectation and experience of gratification from the external world, the young child has little reason to look, to investigate, to learn. He remains in, or reverts to an orientation in which the few pleasures that do exist are derived from experiences of his own bodily functions, and thus he turns away from the outside world.

Such deprivation obviously interferes with psychological development. For one thing, the resulting body-centered orientation severely limits the actual experiences of the child with objects and events in his environment. But even more devastating to the development of the child is the lack of positive or trusting expectation, and hence of motivation, for finding out about the world. In extreme cases, such children become withdrawn, unresponsive to any external stimulus, appear with blank eyes, vacant stares, and with total indifference to the world about them.[24] Their physical development may proceed for a time, but they do not show the usual accompanying psychological developments of increasing sensory-motor coordination. Eventually, in the absence of psychological development, physical development also begins to atrophy.[25]

Developmental Imbalance Due to Excessive Gratification.   As we discussed above, the young child is strongly motivated to maximize pleasure and avoid pain. Thus, if a particular mode of behavior or level of drive organization is found to be extremely rewarding—and especially if it continues to be so beyond the stage of development in which it is most appropriate—the child may continue to rely on this mode, overemphasizing its use to the exclusion of the development of new psychic functions. This result of overgratification shows up when the child fails to develop subsequent higher-level modes of psychological functioning or when he too readily reverts to the overgratified level of functioning under conditions of stress. In either case, psychological development has failed to keep pace with maturation.

An example here would be the child who has been excessively fed or otherwise given to during the first stage of development. If his mother dealt with every upset or discomfort by sticking something in his mouth or hand or by providing him with some other sensory distraction, then later he is apt to experience difficulties in delaying gratification or actively striving for it. Thus, he will have a low tolerance for learning new skills that require time and effort to acquire. Faced with the lack of immediate gratification, he is likely to regress to a helpless "do it for me" position or to a habit of relieving his sense of frustration by gorging himself on sweets or other edibles.

Regression.   Deprivation and overgratification are two different external experiences, but they may produce highly similar internal effects. In both cases the child remains at or reverts to the level of psychological functioning that gave him the greatest pleasure; that is, he *regresses* to the point of fixation. This regression is perhaps more easily understood for overgratification, as in the example just given. For deprivation, the reason for regression may be less clear, since the early situation seems to lack pleasure. In that situation, however, the infant's greatest pleasures often came from the experience of his own bodily sensations—that is, from the period prior to the beginnings of recognition of the external world. This period just prior to the experience of deprivation then becomes the basis for the fixation. In cases in which the environmental deprivation has occurred at a later stage of development, the regression will be less extreme, but it will still be determined by the principle of attempting to reinstate a condition in which pleasure outweighed pain.

In one study of regression as a result of deprivation, Spitz worked with nine-month-old infants who were early separated from their mothers and subsequently raised in institutions.[26] He noted that the approach of a stranger would often produce a reaction in the infant in which he would turn his head back and forth, from side to side. At first, it appeared as though the baby were saying "no, go away." However, since this capacity for semantic communication does not appear, even for babies raised in optimal settings, until a considerably older age, this interpretation of the head-turning behavior was ruled out. Instead, what seemed to be going on was that the infant, made anxious by the approach of the stranger, was regressing to that early period in his life when he did obtain adequate gratification, and was using that mode of behavior —rooting—that was associated with the early oral gratification.

Other Causes of Developmental Imbalance.   Developmental imbalance may also result from a congenital defect that interferes with normal maturation or from maturational level being mismatched with environmental stimuli. If experiences occur before the child is maturationally able to handle them, or if maturation proceeds without appropriate environmental stimuli—that is, if maturation is not coordinated with experience—a developmental imbalance will probably result. In that case, maturation may continue, but the psychological integration achieved will be deviant.[27] Ego functions that would normally emerge may remain dormant or appear in some distorted form. Those ego functions already established may be relied on excessively, so that the child's psychological development is out of pace chronologically with his maturational status. He becomes awkward and ineffectual, both in his dealings with the world and in his abilities to gratify his own needs. Such a child is ill at ease in the world, which in turn can find him very difficult to take.

Implications of Developmental Imbalance for Learning

Severe developmental imbalances may seriously disrupt the child's capacity for learning, but lesser degrees of regression are a normal part of the psychological life of children. Occasional reversions to infantile behavior are likely to occur when the child is tired, ill, or otherwise physically uncomfortable. For example, just prior to lunch, or toward the end of the day, or following a period of illness, children do not function at their most advanced level of development. Their capacity for new learning, for understanding higher-level concepts, and for sustained concentration will be considerably less than at other times. Both the behavior and the thought patterns are likely to be more childish, and the kind of learning they can accomplish then is less complex, developmentally, than what they can accomplish at other times.

Such regressive states may also be brought on in an individual child by psychic pain, as well as by bodily discomfort. He may respond to situations that are threatening to him, that arouse his inner fears and anxieties, with an increase in infantile behavior—by regressing to some earlier and safer developmental level.

The difficulty in these situations is that the adult observes only the increased childishness and may be quite unaware that this is a reaction to a state of physical or psychological discomfort in the child. At the same time, the child is most likely unaware of, or at least incapable of verbalizing, what has set off the regression. But these regressions are the child's way of coping with strain and stress, and as such serve an adaptive function. Because they are temporary and reversible—for instance, with a period of rest or other physical replenishment—such regressions are a normal part of the development of the child, without serious implications for the child's capacity to learn. However, it can also happen that, in reaction to psychological stress or anxiety, regression becomes a more permanent reaction of the child. In this case, the energies that would be used to further his intellectual development remain bound up in the earlier stage, and the development of new ego functions may be seriously impaired.

In either case, whether the regression is temporary or more permanent, it should be understood as a symptom, or result, of some other psychic process. If the adult recognizes the child's regressive behavior as being both defensive and adaptive—that is, as reactions to some state of discomfort—he should be able to respond in a more effective manner. If he sees that the child's infantile regression is an attempt to protect himself from feelings of overwhelming threat, then the way to undo the regression is to lessen the threat. On the other hand, if the adult's reaction increases the child's feeling of threat or anxiety, it is likely to increase the regressive behavior. For example, if a child is unable to solve arithmetic addition problems, he may instead start scribbling, sucking his thumb, or creating a store of spitballs. If the teacher insists that he do what he knows he cannot do, it will only add to his frustration and produce further regressive behavior. If the threat is that his failure will be discovered, then there are at least two possible approaches: First, the teacher can make the problems simple enough so that the child can solve them. This might be accomplished by using manipulatable objects or materials (such as candy) that are of intrinsic interest to the child. Second, the teacher can allow the child to acquire this basic skill by putting him in a situation in which he is not competing with others, so that he will not experience his attempts as being failures in comparison with the activities of others. In other words, once the teacher understands that certain types of behavior are symptoms of some other cause, he can treat the cause—whether it be physical or psychological—rather than try to eliminate the symptom per se.

Another possible outcome of developmental imbalance is that some children, instead of dealing with frustration by fixation and regression, may try a "fake progression."[28] If supporting ego functions do not develop, the child may act *as if* he has these capacities, and in fact may overplay the role. Thus, the child who feels without the necessary ego strengths to control his own body, and who thus basically feels himself to be at the mercy of other more powerful persons, may assume a role; he may act as if he is entirely self-sufficient, needs no one, and is superindependent. This stance is seen as a fake progression because the role is defensive; in fact the child feels helpless before his own sense of incompetence and before the threat of being overpowered by others.

The danger here, as in the case of regression, is that the teacher will not see this overcompensatory behavior as a defense but will treat it as reality. He assumes the child really has the overplayed capacities he pretends to have, thus placing an intolerable overload on a system already lacking basic supports —the lack of which was responsible for the fake progression in the first place. If the adult responds to a child who fears he has no control of his own functions as though he were totally self-reliant, it will only increase the child's sense of discrepancy between what he truly feels himself to be and what he senses he should be. And the intensification of this discrepancy inevitably leads to further distortions, idiosyncratic integrations, and often intolerable stresses with the psychic organization.

What we are suggesting is that many childhood disturbances that interfere with learning are symptoms of some more basic problem. Exercising these symptoms does not fully satisfy the child's underlying need, but they often give him some *partial* gratification, as, for example, when the child can demonstrate social independence even though he is not independent in his own body functions. Also, symptoms often bring the child some secondary gratifications. The child who reacts to frustration by disruptive "acting up" may gain himself some additional benefits. For instance, he may attract more attention, even though it may be critical or punitive. In fact, he may gain a reputation as the class clown, thereby occupying a special position with his classmates, and so may come to think of himself as someone special, thereby enhancing his feelings of self-esteem.

Since symptoms do provide these additional benefits, they will not be easily given up. Their removal requires a twofold attack: First, the sources of secondary gratification must be eliminated. Second, there must be a concerted effort to promote the ego function the child is deficient in, so that he will be able to master the situation that now produces his frustration. To try to remove the symptom by punishing measures, without dealing with the cause, is generally a poor idea. The symptom is serving a need, and unless that need is otherwise satisfied, the removal of one symptom will be followed by the development of another.

Other Learning Difficulties

Teachers occasionally encounter children who seem to have unusual difficulties in learning. Sometimes they are traceable to some physical disability such as poor hearing, to a poorly planned curriculum, or to ineffective teaching methods. But in other cases, they may have an emotional basis. To determine if this is so, it has been suggested[29] that it must be demonstrable that one or another of the child's ego functions is impaired. Psychoanalytic work with children has suggested that several different emotional conflicts may produce inhibitions that interfere with the child's capacity to learn.

Insufficient Energy Available. As we discussed in Chapter 18, psychoanalytic theory assumes that most intellectual functions, such as learning, memory, and judgment, require that one expend attentional energy, but only a limited amount of this energy is available. Because the same pool of energy is used in learning and in defensive functions, any situation that creates the need for increased defenses—whether instinctual, objective, or superego anxiety—will decrease the amount of energy available for other ego functions. In clinical studies, this reciprocal relationship between the amount of attentional energy available and the level of an individual's anxiety is shown by the finding that the attention span of anxious individuals is markedly restricted.[30] In other words, energy that is being used up in defensive functions is not available for use in learning.

Reflection of Parent-Child Relationship. A number of learning difficulties can be traced to the relationship between the child and his parents.[31] Parents who are themselves secretive, who suggest either directly or more subtly that there are things best not known, will contribute to the child's stifling his own curiosity. Similarly, parents who are overly restrictive, both of the child's physical mobility and of his normal aggressive impulses, can limit the child's capacity for assertiveness and for perseverance in the face of obstacles. These limitations interfere with his moving freely in the world, with normal inquisitiveness, and with a healthy self-promotion. His orientation becomes too strongly determined by the need not to disturb others and too little determined by his own needs for psychological growth and mastery.

Parents may also contribute to a child's sense of helplessness and incompetence out of their own distorted but often unrecognized need to keep the child this way. Parents who are themselves unsure of their own capacities of self-worth may unknowingly enter into a conflict with their child as to who has the stronger will. The child, being so dependent on the parent, cannot hope to win that conflict directly. What he can do, however, is to triumph through total cooperation with the parent's low estimation of himself. That is, rather than fight the battle of wills directly, he in essence says, "Yes, I *am* helpless, incompetent, and of little worth, and therefore I must fail in everything I undertake." Such a child does poorly in school, to the chagrin of his parent, who would like the child to be successful in comparison with other *children*. By means of this self-destructive cooperation with the parent's image of him, the child manages to repay that denigration with ironic justice by failing not only in the comparison in which the parent wants him to fail but also in that in which the parent wants him to be successful.

Reflection of Child's Emotional Conflicts. Other learning difficulties, however, originate more directly from emotional conflicts, in which case the problem in learning actually is kind of a solution to the neurotic conflict. For instance, the child may try to solve his conflicts by isolating his school life from his home life and by playing out the separate aspects of the conflict in the different locations. Thus, the child who is excessively suppressed and inhibited at home may find school to be the place where he can be impulsive and uncontrollable. Similarly, but perhaps less frequently, the child who experiences too little control at home may be unduly inhibited at school. In such cases, parents may find it difficult to recognize descriptions of their own child's behavior in school.

Other children may have conflicts about being competent insofar as this threatens their dependent relationship with the parent. Such children may fear accomplishment on their own, for this means they are capable of becoming independent and hence of surviving without the support of the parents. For some children, the idea of such separation from the parents is so painful and produces so much anxiety that they manage to make sure that they remain dependent—that is, that they do not learn.

Still other children may do poorly in school because they have emotional conflicts about competition. Some of these children will avoid competition—and hence learning, if they perceive it as being akin to competition—because they fear failure. Others avoid competition because they fear winning —or, rather, they fear that others will not like them if they do win. In either case, by removing themselves from the arena of competition, they avoid stirring up the emotional conflict.

Emotional conflicts can be expressed in more specific learning difficulties as well. Children with conflicts about incorporation, the earliest mode of behavior, may try to avoid them by refusing to absorb the material presented to them to learn. Children with conflicts about holding on and letting go, the dominant mode of the second stage of development, may try to handle them by refusing to part with whatever information they have acquired or, in other cases, by starting to work on a problem, changing their mind, starting again, and stopping again—that is, by making and unmaking, doing and undoing. In either case, the child is unable to produce and to part with a finished product.

Inhibition of Curiosity.   Learning difficulties may also be due to the child's inhibited curiosity. In order to learn, the child must be able to explore the world without being unduly hampered by anxieties about the unknown. Yet some children are severely limited in their capacity for the free expression of curiosity and are truly afraid to find out about anything new or different. Such a condition obviously interferes with learning.

Such inhibition of curiosity may have several different origins. One of the child's first experiences with the new or different occurs when he begins to differentiate between his mother's face and the faces of others. The range of the child's reactions to this new ability will depend on the nature of the previous mother-child relationship. When the relationship has produced a feeling of trust and confident expectation, the infant's new ability to recognize the difference between mother and others may produce a kind of inquisitive curiosity—that is, a pleasure in exploring and investigating the new. For other children, in which the feeling of trust is less well established, this new capacity for discriminative recognition may produce unusually strong feelings of stranger anxiety, with accompanying emotional upsets and withdrawal of attention from the disturbing new stimulus. In this case, the anxiety about the recognition of the stranger may produce a generalized anxiety about the new and different, and this feeling may carry over into later years and situations. That is, the earlier strong experience of anxiety in connection with the new may occur on subsequent occasions in which an encounter with the unknown is required. The content of the two situations may differ radically, but the problem is the same and so arouses the same anxiety.

The way the infant responds to this earlier experience with the unknown also affects the child's development when the intrusive mode becomes dominant. A child unencumbered by anxieties about the unknown will be relatively free to push out into the world and to explore. However, at this stage of development a new basis for inhibited curiosity may arise. The motivating force of exploration and intrusion at this period stems, in large part, from curiosity about the sexual differences between boys and girls. This curiosity in turn is connected with the child's desire for an exclusive relationship with one parent and a feeling of competition with the other. The intensification of both of these feelings eventually leads to a psychological crisis. The positive outcome of this crisis is that curiosity and intrusiveness are channeled into the development of initiative. However, the less favorable outcome is that the child may experience excessive guilt and anxiety as a reaction to his disturbing feelings toward his parents. This anxiety may then inhibit the use of the intrusive mode, which in turn inhibits curiosity and exploratory behavior. Subsequently, this inhibition of curiosity may become more general, with the result that the child actively avoids situations that are new or unknown.

This last statement is really at the center of understanding learning difficulties that are due to an inhibition of curiosity. Such children may appear to be apathetic or dull, apparently showing little interest in finding out about the world. The important thing, however, is to discern what purpose the apparent indifference serves. When lack of interest in the new is due to inhibited curiosity, the child is protecting himself from anxiety or guilt. It is not that he is uninterested in the material to be learned; rather, he wishes to avoid the anxiety that in the past has been associated with the free use of curiosity.

Finally, there are those children for whom failure in school provides a neurotic solution to the problem of dealing with excessive feelings of guilt. If, as a result of the inadequate resolution of the developmental crises, or as the outcome of certain life experiences, the child feels he is bad or unworthy, there may be a strong need to assuage this guilt by punishing himself. One way he can do this is to consistently fail at whatever activity he may undertake. For some children, failure in school is a way of alleviating the awful anxiety that stems from a stern and punishing superego.

Other Impediments to Intellectual Development

We have discussed how developmental imbalance will cause some ego functions to atrophy while others proliferate and how neurotic inhibition restricts intellectual development because learning has become associated with the expression of some prohibited instinctual impulse. Psychoanalytic theory also identifies several other impediments to intellectual development.

Restriction of the Ego. Another psychological problem that may impair cognitive development is restriction of ego functions. Such ego restriction, instead of protecting the individual from instinctual anxiety, wards off the pain of external sources. By limiting the areas in which he will encounter the world, by avoiding those situations that might remind him of past inadequacies, he can somewhat protect himself from objective anxiety. Whereas in neurotic inhibition certain kinds of learning activity are avoided, regardless of the situation, in ego restriction the learning activity itself is not avoided, but the individual considers whether performing the activity in the present context will produce anxiety. Thus, in the latter case, the individual may be able to develop cognitive capacities under some conditions but not others. This is obviously a more favorable situation for cognitive growth than is neurotic inhibition. Once it is understood that the child is not deficient in certain functions, but rather that he cannot perform them under certain conditions, then a sensitive teacher can change those conditions so as to remove the threat of pain—that is, he can create a more favorable external environment.

This way of avoiding psychic pain, through ego restriction, is a normal stage in the development of the child's ego.[32] His activities shift from one area to another, those giving pleasure being continued, those giving pain being abandoned.

Activity Overly Determined by Pleasure Principle.   The development of ego functions on the basis of the pleasure-pain dimension results in cognitive impairment only when it becomes, to an excessive degree, an exclusive basis for activity—that is, when activities are engaged in only if they are sure to provide pleasure and avoided if they will possibly produce pain.

We discussed the implications of the pleasure–pain dimension for the education of the child during the latency period (six to ten years). The fact that the child's instinctual drives are relatively dormant during this period means, on the one hand, that these drives serve as less of a motivating force for activity, and, on the other hand, that relatively less pleasure is derived from their expression. Rather, the primary source of pleasure and of pain is derived from the external situation, and the avoidance of objective anxiety becomes a primary motivating force. If the learning and life experiences of the child are left entirely to his own choosing, the selection will most often be made on the basis of what is easiest—what produces the least pain. This orientation may prevent him from ever discovering whole areas of ego functioning in which he might, with practice and experience, have considerable talent. To allow the child to always do what is easiest and most comfortable is to contribute to the potential impoverishment of his ego.

Interference with Reality Testing.   Cognitive development may also be impeded if the child is experiencing some interference with reality testing. The development of ego functions such as judgment, memory, logical thought, and problem solving all imply the continuing development of effective reality testing—the ability to make a match between the mental representation of the world and the world as it actually exists. Anything that interferes with this ability will obviously disrupt cognitive activities.

Interference with reality testing may occur in more or less severe forms. In extreme conditions, the individual may lose the ability to distinguish between ideas and perceptions—between what is in his mind and what is in the external world. Or, he may be able to separate idea from percept but attach an inappropriate, highly personalized meaning to the percept. Such breakdowns in reality testing are more characteristic of severe forms of mental disturbance. However, in less extreme form, such a disturbance is not infrequent among children and adults in everyday settings. It contributes to distortions and biases in what we are able to see and to the ways in which we think. Sometimes such distortions interfere with adequate cognitive development. Thinking becomes too much determined by subjective needs and wishes and too little based on objective reality.

Since reality testing requires a relative dominance of secondary process over primary process thinking, which in turn requires a curtailment of the immediate discharge of drives, it is thus dependent on the development of adequate functioning of defenses. This also means, however, that the failure of defenses—whether because of increased drive level or of the inadequacy of the defensive structure itself—will interfere with the capacity for reality testing. Similarly, the overuse of a defense—such as denial, projection, or reaction formation—can interfere with an individual's capacity to make adequate judgments about reality. Finally, inadequate reality testing may stem from the child's having learned certain distortions of reality from early experiences with significant adults. Because ego functions develop partly out of the interaction and identification with significant adults, they will have the same biases found in the adults' thinking. These distorting influences may also interfere with the child's capacity for adequate reality testing of himself—that is, they may lead to self-deceptions. The importance of the adult in determining the child's approach to reality has been succinctly stated by Hartmann: "The child learns [to adjust] to a world which is not only to a considerable extent man-made, but also man-thought."[33]

Loss of Ego Autonomy. We see, then, that the child's capacity for reality testing can be disrupted by the intrusion of drive-dominated wishes and needs into his thought and by ego functions developed out of identification with adults who themselves distort reality. These two conditions may be thought of more broadly as a loss of ego autonomy—on the one hand, the loss of autonomy from the id; on the other, the loss of autonomy from the environment. The ego functions best when independent of the drives—that is, when it is not drive-dominated—as well as when it is free of the slavish control of environmental stimuli. Psychoanalysis sees man's relative autonomy from the id as being guaranteed by the existence of the innately given ego functions that control drive discharge so that he can adapt to an average environment. Autonomy from the environment, on the other hand, is ensured by the existence of the innately determined drives. The reciprocal interaction of the two allows man to function relatively autonomously and to experience a feeling of free will.

Under certain situations, however, there may be a loss of the autonomy of the ego from the id. One such situation is the sudden intensification of drive strength, as is seen, for example, in puberty. This condition requires a counterintensification of defenses and thus may leave the ego depleted of energies for other cognitive functions. An example is the adolescent who denies himself any bodily pleasures, avoids contact with others, and withdraws his energies into himself. In using energy to deny pleasures, to avoid contact with possibly arousing situations, and to shut out external stimulation, he reduces the amount of energy available for cognitive functions.

Other conditions that can produce this kind of loss of autonomy are situations of stimulus deprivation and of hypnotism. People deprived of normal sensory stimulation for some time often report bizarre fantasies that are relatively direct representations of instinctual drives.[34] In some cases, they may even begin to act out these fantasies, which means that ego functions are being overly determined by drives; that is, the ego has lost its autonomy from the id.

Loss of autonomy from the environment may come about in several ways. Since the drives are the primary security of such autonomy, any condition that excessively blocks the discharge of instinctual drives will reduce that autonomy. An example is the person unable to take any independent action because he equates such action with being aggressive or hostile, and he is blocked in the expression of aggressive drives. Not being able to discharge aggressive drives in self-assertive channels, he depends entirely on others to tell him what to do, and so has lost his autonomy from the environment.

Loss of autonomy also occurs in situations that greatly enhance the importance of the environment—such as in circumstances of great needfulness, or danger, or social isolation—or which continually bombard the individual with a single track of information in the absence of any other stimulation, as occurs in brain-washing. Such situations can seriously impair the autonomy of the ego from the environment.

The maintenance of ego autonomy from drives and from environmental dominance is thus relative. A loss of autonomy from either direction will result in an impairment in cognitive functioning, resulting in thinking that is, on the one hand, overly drive-determined and pays too little heed to reality requirements or, on the other hand, too rigidly bound to the immediate external situation and robotlike in its conformity to external demands.

SUMMARY

In discussing some of the implications of psychoanalytic theory for education,[35] we stressed that the child's learning experiences must be considered in relation to his psychological stage of development. We noted that as the child's subjective sense of himself changes, the type of educational experiences most meaningful to him will also change. In addition, because the environmental experiences interacting with the innate maturational plan are so varied, inevitably children will be produced who differ considerably from each other. Thus, a teacher who tries to apply a single educational mold to teach such a widely varying group will undoubtedly have difficulty.

In discussing how several emotional factors affect learning, we noted that the child's relationship with his mother is very important, not only for the development of specific early cognitive functions, but also for producing a general orientation of wanting to find out about the world. The child's original "learning for love" changes into a "love of learning,"[36] and this pleasure derived from the learning process enhances the child's self-esteem. Frustration and conflict may both foster and impede learning, depending on the magnitude of the frustration and on the child's ability to cope with it.

A number of psychological problems may lead to learning difficulties —developmental imbalance, deprivation, and overgratification. Certain psychological symptoms and defenses may play an adaptive role in the child's development, but at other times they may interfere with his ability to learn. Specific developmental conflicts—such as of incorporation or curiosity—can also create learning difficulties. Some factors can interfere with reality testing, an essential ingredient of learning, and can produce a loss of ego autonomy and thus a loss of those ego functions on which learning depends.

The removal of psychological problems or symptoms is not easy. Both the problems and the methods of treatment are often complex, and the job of teachers is to teach, not to treat behavior disorders. However, without attempting to act as a therapist, the teacher can be aided by recognizing and understanding certain aspects of a child's behavior from a clinical point of view. Recognizing that certain types of behavior are not just disruptive, or babyish, or withdrawn but that they serve a defensive function for the child can alert the teacher that the child is anxious about something. Although often unable to do anything directly about the underlying psychological problem or the defensive maneuver, the teacher can try to work around them by minimizing the anxiety that the child experiences in the situation.

More generally, an understanding of psychoanalytic theory should help the teacher understand more about the meaning of the child's behavior for the child. Such an understanding should make it possible for the teacher to communicate more effectively with the child, and, ultimately, to teach him more successfully.

NOTES

PART 1. THE STIMULUS-RESPONSE APPROACH TO INTELLECTUAL DEVELOPMENT

Chapter 2. The Stimulus-Response Point of View

[1]More extensive discussions of the historical background of the S-R tradition are provided in Boring (1950), Hilgard and Bower (1966), and Murphy (1949).

[2]Hilgard and Bower (1966) is a secondary source that offers systematic accounts of the contributions made by Pavlov and Thorndike. Representative primary sources are Pavlov (1927) and Thorndike (1911).

[3]A clear statement of the structuralist position may be found in Titchener (1902).

[4]The Gestalt approach is presented in Köhler (1929).

[5]Watson (1913), p. 158.

[6]A systematic discussion of the role of internal conditions is presented in Osgood (1953), pp. 392–412.

[7]Skinner (1968).

Chapter 3. Basic Concepts and Principles in Stimulus-Response Theory

[1]A systematic treatment of the topic of reinforcement may be found in Skinner (1953). See Skinner (1958) for a more recent statement and Glaser (1971) for discussions of a variety of issues concerning reinforcement.

[2]A clear analysis of issues and disputes about the effects of punishment is presented by Solomon (1964). Additional discussion may be found in Sulzer and Mayer (1972).

Chapter 4. A Stimulus-Response Model of Behavior

[1]All of that portion of this chapter concerned with varieties of learning has been adapted from Gagné (1970).

Chapter 5. The Character and Causes of Development

[1]For extensive reviews of research that has produced information about physical growth, see Eichorn (1970) and Tanner (1970).

Chapter 6. Some Major Areas of Intellectual Development

[1]Using an S-R framework, Stevenson (1970) and White (1970) trace the history and present status of research and theory on intellectual development in children.

[2]For an extensive review of the results of research concerning conditioning in children, see Reese and Lipsitt (1970), pp. 65–149.

[3]Stevenson (1970), p. 855.

[4]White (1965), p. 198.

[5]Stevenson, Iscoe, and McConnell (1955).

[6]Mednick and Lehtinen (1957).

[7]Jeffrey and Skager (1962). For a discussion of developmental changes in stimulus generalization in children, see Stevenson (1970), pp. 863–865.

[8]Jensen and Rohwer (1965).

[9]See Saltz (1971), pp. 313–341, and Reese and Lipsitt (1970), pp. 195–218.

[10]See Postman and Goggin (1966).

[11]See, for example, Wicklund (1964).

[12]See, for example, Postman (1962).

[13]Gagné (1970), pp. 155–171.

[14]Keppel, Postman, and Zavortink (1968).

[15]Rohwer and Bean (1973).

[16]Koppenaal, Krull, and Katz (1964).

[17]Odom (1966).

[18]Zaporozhets (1965).

[19]See, for example, Levinson and Reese (1967).

[20]See Stevenson (1970) for a review of research on oddity-task performance.

[21]Stevenson (1970), pp. 882–892.

[22]For a review of this topic, see Reese and Lipsitt (1970), pp. 230–250, 295–309.

[23]For a review of research generated by an alternative approach to individual differences in intellectual development, see Kagan and Kogan (1970).

Chapter 7. Implications of Stimulus-Response Theory for Education

[1]After providing a comparative analysis of psychological theories, Kohlberg and Mayer (1972) advance the proposition that such theories should include principles that imply prescriptions for educational objectives.

[2]For a description of additional analyses of instruction from an S-R viewpoint, see Gagné (1970) and Skinner (1968).

[3]Reviews of research on external conditions that affect concept learning may be found in Reese and Lipsitt (1970), pp. 238–245, 270–278, 295–309, and in Stevenson (1970), pp. 899–902.

[4]See Gagné (1970), pp. 302–344.

[5]Sulzer and Mayer (1972) and Reese and Lipsitt (1970), pp. 643–672, provide a more comprehensive discussion of the principles and practice of behavior modification.

[6]See Gagné and Rohwer (1969), pp. 398–401.

[7]This table is drawn from Gagné (1970), pp. 321–322.

[8]Extended discussions of the topic of evaluation may be found in Wittrock and Wiley (1970).

[9]See Sulzer and Mayer (1972).

[10]For descriptions and analyses of the effects of punishment, see Solomon (1964) and Sulzer and Mayer (1972).

PART 2. THE COGNITIVE APPROACH TO INTELLECTUAL DEVELOPMENT

Chapter 8. The Cognitive Point of View

[1]The term "mental structure" or "cognitive structure" is defined in this chapter simply as "a way of thinking," but it will be discussed at length in Chapter 9.

[2]The assertion that later structures depend on earlier structures does not necessarily follow from the assumption that cognition intervenes between the situation and behavior or from the assumption that cognitive structures cannot be reduced to previous experience with the environment. One can imagine the possibility of a series of structures emerging in development quite independent of one another. However, that is not the position of the cognitive theorists, principally Jean Piaget, whose ideas form the basis for the present discussion.

[3]The term *constructivism* has not been as widely used in philosophical and psychological discussions of epistemology as the terms empiricism, nativism, and interactionism. However, Piaget (for example, 1970b) has used the term and it does seem to be a good name for the particular type of interactionism that has been most prominent in cognitive theory.

[4]Miller (1967), p. 51.

[5]Piaget (1960), pp. 97–98. A good discussion of the clinical method can be found in Ginsburg and Opper (1969), pp. 94–98.

[6]Piaget (1971a) has devoted an entire book to the relationship between biology and cognitive theory.

[7]For a general discussion of the relationship between computers and the study of cognitive processes, see Newell, Shaw, and Simon (1958).

Chapter 9. Basic Concepts and Principles in Cognitive Theory

[1]Bruner (1964).

[2]Piaget (1965a).

[3]For example, Chomsky (1965).

[4]The distinction between competence and performance has come to the fore in the writings of linguists who have attempted to separate the study of what a person *knows*

about his language from the study of how the person *uses* language. The term "process" has figured in some of the same discussions as a name for the mental events involved in language behavior. Unfortunately, there are now as many different definitions of these terms as there are people writing about the various distinctions involved. For a recent discussion of competence in relation to cognitive psychology, see Pylyshyn (1973).

[5] For example, see Kohlberg and Turiel (1971).

[6] Piaget (1954), chap. 1.

[7] The attainment of objectivity has been discussed by Baldwin (1955).

[8] Actually Piaget has defined the "field" of equilibrium somewhat more narrowly than we have here. However, our notion of the broadening field of equilibrium seems generally consistent with Piaget's ideas about developmental changes in equilibrium. For further discussion pertaining to equilibrium, see Ginsburg and Opper (1969), p. 173.

[9] Piaget (1967).

Chapter 10. A Cognitive Model of Behavior

[1] This model was constructed to represent some common themes in cognitive theory. Although it was suggested by some other models (principally the one described by Baldwin, 1955), we have simplified the present model a great deal in order to focus on the most basic ideas regarding behavior as seen from the cognitive point of view.

[2] The model is restricted to goal-directed behavior because cognitive theorists have not shown much interest in behavior that is purely reflexive or expressive. It is in goal-directed behavior that man's intellect reveals itself most clearly. One might argue that *art* is expressive behavior and that it certainly involves man's intellect too. But art is also goal-directed behavior in that the artist deliberately sets out to express a particular emotion or idea.

[3] Guthrie (1952), p. 143.

[4] Miller, Galanter, and Pribram (1960), chap. 2.

[5] Pascual-Leone (1970) has suggested that there is a basic capacity for processing information that increases with age as a function of maturation, but this still leaves open the question of how the child *uses* whatever capacity he has.

[6] For example, Mosher and Hornsby (1966).

[7] Piaget (1963).

[8] Weir (1962), p. 115.

[9] Since there are *non*cognitive sources of motivation too, it is possible that some sort of aggressive disposition, for example, affects the behavior in question, along with the cognitive factors suggested in the remainder of the present summary. People often do the same thing for a number of reasons.

Chapter 11. The Character and Causes of Development

[1] For recent summaries of Piaget's theory, see Piaget (1970b) and Piaget and Inhelder (1969). A good secondary source is Ginsburg and Opper (1969), which goes into somewhat more detail than the present treatment of Piaget.

[2] The original research on object permanence is reported in Piaget (1954).

[3] Piaget (1963), chap. 5.

[4] For those readers concerned about the possibility of bias with such a small and select sample, it can be reported that many of Piaget's findings have been corroborated by other investigators studying other children (for example, Gouin-Decarie, 1965; Uzgiris and Hunt, 1966).

[5]For example, Piaget (1970b).

[6]This period is sometimes referred to as the first phase of the next period, that is, the period of concrete operations.

[7]The primary reference on this topic is Piaget (1962b). There and elsewhere, Piaget uses the term "symbolic function" for what he now calls the "semiotic function." The word "symbol" has a rather specific meaning for Piaget (see below), so recently he has expressed a preference for "semiotic" as the more general term (for example, Piaget, 1970b).

[8]Unfortunately, Piaget's use of the word "symbol" is incompatible with Bruner's notion of a "symbolic" mode of representation (see Chapter 9). For Bruner, symbols do not resemble the things they represent, so they correspond to what Piaget calls "signs." In fact, Piaget's definitions of "sign" and "symbol" are reversed by several authors in other fields, such as psycholinguistics and ethology.

[9]Hunt (1961), p. 186.

[10]Piaget (1965a), chap. 1.

[11]In such a case, Piaget would simply argue that the child has already begun to move into the next developmental period, where conservation is understood. Had the child been tested earlier, we would have found him to be a nonconserver.

[12]Piaget (1965a), chap. 7.

[13]Inhelder and Piaget (1958), chap. 2.

[14]Until recently, Piaget referred to these behaviors as sensorimotor *schemata* (plural of *schema*). Now he prefers to use the term *scheme* for the dynamic or "operative" aspect of cognition, while *schema* is used for the more static or "figurative" aspect of cognition, as in imagery, for example. In reading Piaget's older works, it should be recalled that he had not yet made this distinction between scheme and schema.

[15]Flavell (1970) cites a large number of studies inspired by Piaget's theory. Although it certainly is not the case that all of these studies confirm Piaget's work in every detail, the amount of general support for his theory of stages is impressive.

[16]The reasons that we have in mind here are such factors as mental retardation and cultural differences in environmental opportunities for development to occur. With regard to the latter factor, see Dasen (1972).

[17]This example is discussed in Piaget (1964).

[18]See Itard (1932).

Chapter 12. Some Major Areas of Intellectual Development

[1]Piaget (1960a, 1965b).

[2]Piaget's conclusions about "precausal" thinking have met with a great deal of criticism. However, Laurendeau and Pinard (1962) have pointed out that many studies which appear to conflict with Piaget's have used different methods of examination, questions with different content, different types of subjects, and different techniques of analysis.

[3]Inhelder and Piaget (1958), p. 22.

[4]*Ibid.*, chap. 3.

[5]Flavell (1963), p. 299.

[6]This section is based largely on Piaget and Inhelder (1967).

[7]Laurendeau and Pinard (1970).

[8]Piaget, Inhelder, and Szeminska (1964).

[9]The studies described in this section are reported in Piaget (1970a, 1971b).

[10]This section is based on Inhelder and Piaget (1964).

[11]Vygotsky (1962), chap. 5.

[12]Langer (1969a) reports a study in which children were actually asked to perform these incompatible actions.

[13]This example is given by E. Lunzer in his introduction to Inhelder and Piaget (1964).

[14]Inhelder and Piaget (1964), chap. 9.

[15]Based on Piaget (1965a).

[16]Based on Inhelder and Piaget (1958).

[17]Theoretically, there were 16 possible ways to fill in the truth table at the outset, including the possibility of filling the table with four zeros. The 16 possibilities correspond to the 16 "binary operations" discussed by Inhelder and Piaget (1958).

[18]This discussion is based on an actual study carried out by Marascuilo and McSweeney (1972). However, we have altered the details for present purposes.

[19]Inhelder and Piaget (1958).

[20]Piaget and Inhelder (1969), p. 145.

[21]Reported in Piaget (1962a).

[22]Based largely on Kohlberg (1969).

[23]Baldwin, Baldwin, Hilton, and Lambert (1969). We have modified the details of this research slightly for the sake of convenience in the present discussion.

[24]For a comprehensive introduction to the area of language development, see Dale (1972).

[25]McNeill (1966), p. 18.

[26]Clark (1973).

[27]Donaldson and Balfour (1968).

[28]Based on Ervin (1964).

[29]Berko (1958).

[30]This section is based on Bellugi (1967). This work is summarized in McNeill (1966), pp. 53–62.

[31]Actually, Brown (for example, in 1973) has discussed broader stages in early language acquisition. Although these stages were at first defined arbitrarily in terms of the mean length of a child's utterances, the stages may actually have structural coherence. However, it is not clear that each of Brown's stages fits the general description of a developmental stage, as presented in Chapter 11.

Chapter 13. Implications of a Cognitive Theory for Education

[1]The developments during the 1960s in psychology and education did not come from out of the blue. The basic ideas of Piaget's theory, for example, were already evident in his writings during the 1930s (although many of these were not translated into English until much later). At about the same time, the progressive education movement, inspired by John Dewey, was enjoying popularity in the United States. In fact, in 1935 Piaget published an essay that related the "new" methods of education to developmental psychology (see Piaget, 1970c). Moreover, his ideas and the ideas of progressive education can be traced back to earlier generations of thinkers about development and education.

[2]For example, see Duckworth (1964).

[3]One may decide for himself whether the implications we discuss actually follow logically from cognitive theory as we have presented it in the preceding chapters.

[4]See Piaget (1970c).

[5]Pascual-Leone (1972) proposed an explanation of the horizontal decalage that occurs with respect to the conservation of amount, weight, and volume. However, there is some question as to whether his explanation is derived from a *structural* analysis.

[6]Langer (1969b) *has* discussed the need for a structural analysis of the environment.

[7]See Piaget (1972).

[8]Studies in which conservation has been taught successfully are discussed by Brainerd and Allen (1971). For similar research on moral judgment and language development, see Turiel (1969) and Ammon (1966), respectively.

[9]Aside from biologically based critical periods, there may be critical periods that are imposed by the social environment. Suppose a child does not acquire some particular knowledge or skill by the age society expects him to have done so. The child may then be stigmatized by his teachers, parents, or peers. The emotional upset that results from this stigma may inhibit later acquisition of the knowledge or skill in question, even though the child is perfectly capable of learning, from a biological standpoint.

[10]See Kuhn, Langer, Kohlberg, and Hahn (in press).

[11]A similar point of view has been expressed by Piaget (in Duckworth, 1964) and by Kohlberg (1973).

[12]This example is taken from Turiel (1969), with superficial modifications to make it more congruent with our discussion of moral judgment in Chapter 12.

[13]This procedure was suggested by Langer (1969a).

[14]See Langer (1969a).

[15]See Turiel (1969).

[16]On the other hand, there is some evidence that children with high IQ scores do not necessarily attain more advanced cognitive structures sooner than other children; rather, they seem to make more flexible use of the structures they have. See Lovell (1968).

[17]Some of the work on developmental tests is discussed in Green, Ford, and Flamer (1971).

PART 3. THE PSYCHOANALYTIC APPROACH TO INTELLECTUAL DEVELOPMENT

Chapter 14. The Psychoanalytic Point of View

[1]Hartmann (1964), p. 257.

[2]S. Freud (1900), p. 613.

[3]S. Freud (1911), p. 14. Also see S. Freud (1900), p. 566, p. 599, p. 602.

[4]See Hartmann (1939).

[5]For a discussion of the historical development of psychoanalytic ego psychology, see D. Rapaport (1959a).

[6]See D. Rapaport (1959a and 1956) for a discussion of the contributions of these three men.

[7]D. Rapaport (1960c), p. 39.

[8]S. Freud (1900), pp. 514–515, p. 593.

[9]Erikson (1939), pp. 131–132; (1950), p. 52; (1959), p. 52.

[10]Klein (1968), pp. 19–20; D. Rapaport (1959a), pp. 12–14.

[11]See *The Psychoanalytic Study of the Child*, vols. 1–27, and *Psychological Issues*, vols. 1–7.

[12]S. Freud (1900), p. 608.

[13]See especially *The Psychoanalytic Study of the Child*, vols. 1–27; *Annual Progress in Child Psychiatry and Child Development*, vols. 1–5; and Axelrad and Brody (1970).

[14]D. Rapaport (1960a), p. 822.

[15]See note 9, above.

[16]D. Rapaport (1960a), p. 833.

[17]Erikson (1950) has provided an excellent example of this in his description of the different character structure of children in the Yurok and the Sioux societies.

Chapter 15. Basic Concepts and Principles in Psychoanalytic Theory

[1]Rapaport and Gill (1959).

[2]See note 12, below.

[3]Erikson (1950).

[4]*Ibid.*

[5]For a discussion of critical periods of development, of the emergence of new levels of development, and of developmental imbalance, see Spitz (1959), pp. 76–77, p. 93 ff; (1965), pp. 118–119.

[6]S. Freud (1915a), p. 65.

[7]D. Rapaport (1953), for example, pp. 537–540.

[8]S. Freud (1900), p. 593; D. Rapaport (1959b), p. 781.

[9]Working in a different context, this assumption has been demonstrated empirically by Miller (1956), who found the attentional limit to be seven "bits" of information, plus or minus two.

[10]Note, however, that pleasure does not equal the elimination of drive tension, merely its reduction. This is an important difference between the drive theory of S-R psychology and that of psychoanalysis.

[11]See, for example, D. Rapaport (1956), p. 620.

[12]The concepts of unconscious, preconscious, and conscious do not involve psychological structures, but they are discussed here for three reasons: (1) this topographical approach was the historical forerunner of the structural approach in psychoanalytic theory; (2) newcomers to the theory sometimes equate id with unconscious, and ego and superego with preconscious and conscious; (3) insofar as conscious *ness* is conceptualized as being similar to a sense organ (see Chapter 18) or as the mental mechanism related to the organ (Rapaport and Gill, 1959, p. 5), it is a psychological structure and thus should be discussed here. This also seemed a good place to distinguish between the concepts of conscious and consciousness.

[13]The term consciousness also refers to a subjective experience, in psychoanalytic theory. However, for the purposes of the present work, the role of consciousness in ego functioning is most important.

Chapter 17. The Character and Causes of Development

[1]The discussion of zones and modes is based on Erikson (1950), p. 72 ff.

[2]This discussion is based on Fenichel (1945), p. 42, and D. Rapaport (1957a), p. 705; (1957b), p. 739; (1960a), p. 830.

[3]See Erikson (1950).

[4]Unless otherwise noted, the discussion of these three phases is based on Spitz (1965). The integration of the material, however, does not necessarily follow Spitz.

[5]Quoted in McCandless (1967), p. 30.

[6]S. Freud (1900), pp. 565–566.

[7]*Ibid.* (1925), p. 183.

[8]Spitz (1957), p. 113.

[9]Spitz (1965, p. 104) places the age for formation of a rudimentary ego at three months.

[10]Although Spitz (1965, p. 103) believes that the existence of a memory trace of the face indicates a division of the mental apparatus into conscious, preconscious, and

unconscious, Freud (1915c) would not necessarily have arrived at this conclusion. This is because, for Freud, unconscious ideas were memories of the thing alone (for example, a concrete image of the face), whereas preconscious ideas consisted of both the thing and the verbal symbol that represents the thing. Since the infant has only the concrete image, but no verbal label for it, the memory of the face would qualify as an unconscious idea, and thus the existence of preconscious and conscious mental processes need not be assumed.

[11]Although this is a simple form of thought, the shifting of mental energy from one memory trace to an associated trace meets the psychoanalytic definition of thought. See S. Freud, 1900, pp. 533–536; 1925, p. 183; and R. Spitz (1965), p. 103. A forerunner of this is the establishment of an association between rising instinctual tension and the drive object that satisfies that tension (see Figure 16.4). The mental process involved in this latter case is referred to as *ideation* (see D. Rapaport, 1951, p. 325).

[12]Although Spitz (1965) places recognition of the mother's face at eight months, it seems quite likely that this may occur earlier for many children.

[13]Stranger anxiety is thus a special case of separation anxiety. While the view discussed in Chapter 17 is that of Spitz, A. L. Baldwin (personal communication) has pointed out that J. Benjamin has reported data indicating that stranger anxiety and mother-absent anxiety are not the same.

[14]Although Spitz does not use such terms as *recognition memory* (the ability to recognize an external stimulus as corresponding to an internal memory) or *discrimination learning* (the ability to distinguish between two external stimuli, and to associate reward or pleasure with one of them), his meaning indicates that these are the processes involved.

[15]Erikson (1950), p. 82.

[16]Although the building of structures also requires energy, once they are in existence, relatively little energy is required for their maintenance. See D. Rapaport (1959b), p. 788.

[17]Erikson (1959), p. 70.

[18]This statement combines the focus of Erikson on autonomy and of Spitz on communication.

[19]Spitz (1965), p. 183.

[20]S. Freud (1915c), pp. 133–134.

[21]As we have seen (note 10, above) Spitz believes that the differentiation of conscious, preconscious, and unconscious occurs around two months of age, insofar as there is evidence that memory traces of the human face have been laid down.

[22]See, for example, Lynch and Rohwer (1972).

[23]R. Brown (1965), p. 334.

[24]Hartmann (1964), p. 83.

[25]The reasons for this are discussed in Chapter 18.

[26]The following discussion of Stages 3 and 4 relies most heavily on Erikson (1950), although again the integration of the material is the responsibility of the author.

[27]A. Freud (1936), p. 180.

[28]A. Freud (1936), p. 177, p. 181.

[29]Blos (1962), p. 2.

[30]This approach to adolescence draws heavily on Blos (1962).

[31]P. Blos (1962), p. 175.

[32]A. Freud (1936), p. 152, points out that this is similar to the situation in childhood.

[33]Blos (1962), p. 118, adds to these the defense of "uniformism," which he sees as characteristic of American adolescents. A. Freud (1958), p. 274, has also included the defense of being "uncompromising."

[34]Blos (1962), p. 115.

[35]The following discussion is based on A. Freud (1958).

[36]Blos (1962), p. 183.

[37]Erikson (1959), p. 129 ff.
[38]Erikson (1950), p. 261 ff.
[39]Erikson (1959), p. 116 ff.
[40]A. Freud (1936), pp. 173–174.
[41]Blos (1962), p. 126.
[42]*Ibid.,* p. 188.
[43]*Ibid.,* p. 183.
[44]This and the following four definitions of self are taken from Erikson (1959).
[45]Spitz (1965), p. 119.
[46]A. Freud (1936), p. 179.

Chapter 18. Some Major Areas of Intellectual Development

[1]Blos (1962); D. Rapaport (1960a, 1960b). For excellent comparisons of the two theories, see Wolff (1960) and W. G. Cobliner (1965).

[2]Spitz (1965).

[3]For a discussion of the concept of delay, see D. Rapaport (1951), p. 690, p. 693.

[4]For a discussion of the concept of detour, see S. Freud (1900), p. 602; (1940), p. 114; and D. Rapaport (1951), p. 697.

[5]S. Freud (1915b); D. Rapaport (1951) p. 702. Additional factors that contribute to the internal-external distinction include (1) that which was felt inside and is now seen outside (R. Spitz, 1957, p. 113), and (2) that which tastes good versus that which tastes bad, and is therefore spat out (S. Freud, 1925, p. 183).

[6]See also note 10, Chapter 17, for the idea of dual organization of memories, based on the acquisition of language.

[7]S. Freud (1915a, 1915b).

[8]Although the predefenses are eventually replaced by the true defenses, the instinctual vicissitudes continue unchanged.

[9]This discussion is based on A. Freud (1936).

[10]This, and the subsequent discussion of denial in word and fantasy, are based on A. Freud (1936). The statement that denial in act represents conscious, intentional behavior is based on Spitz (1965).

[11]It may be noted that the child's lack of understanding about object permanence must contribute to this defense.

[12]S. Freud (1915b), p. 85.

[13]*Ibid.,* p. 84.

[14]*Ibid.,* p. 86.

[15]*Ibid.,* p. 88.

[16]S. Freud (1915c), p. 119. As will be apparent from the examples that follow, the development of this function is closely tied up with the development of "No" and the period of oppositionalism and obstinacy in the child—that is, the period of holding on and letting go.

[17]A. Freud (1936), p. 100 ff.

[18]*Ibid.,* p. 110.

[19]*Ibid.,* p. 155.

[20]*Ibid.,* p. 117 ff.

[21]*Ibid.,* p. 117 ff.

[22]Fenichel (1945), p. 146.

[23]A. Freud (1936), p. 132 ff.

[24]Fenichel (1945), p. 154. Hartmann (1964), p. 225, does not agree with Fenichel's formulation. Hartmann sees any defense mechanism that performs its function as successful. He does not consider the long-range outcome relevant.

[25]Fenichel (1945).

[26]S. Freud: (1912), p. 216; (1940), p. 114.

[27]Spitz, 1965, p. 65.

[28]For example, Fantz (1961, 1966); Fantz and Nevis (1967); Haaf and Bell (1967); Kagan (1970); Lewis (1969). It should be pointed out that not all investigators of this topic have reached the same conclusion; cf., for example, Koopman and Ames (1968).

[29]S. Freud (1925), p. 183.

[30]Spitz (1965), pp. 183–184.

[31]*Ibid.*, (1957), p. 66. See also footnote 4.

[32]*Ibid.*, p. 66, p. 91.

[33]Spitz (1965), p. 195.

[34]However, there is a "change of function" involved in head nodding, in that it was originally a consummatory behavior and changes to function as a detour behavior.

[35]Spitz (1957), p. 91.

[36]S. Freud (1925), p. 184.

[37]D. Rapaport (1960c), pp. 34–35.

[38]D. Rapaport (1951), p. 696 ff.

[39]S. Freud (1900), p. 539.

[40]The following discussion of structure building is based on D. Rapaport (1957a, 1959b).

[41]Although this does not mean that they are *un*conscious—a position none of these theories would acknowledge.

[42]This discussion is based on Rapaport (1960b), p. 906 ff.

[43]S. Freud (1900), p. 574; (1925), p. 185.

[44]S. Freud (1911), p. 15.

[45]*Ibid.*

[46]Hartmann (1964), p. 171 ff, p. 235 ff; D. Rapaport (1960b).

[47]D. Rapaport (1951), p. 700 ff; Rapaport and Gill (1959), p. 6.

[48]Hartmann (1964), p. 229 ff; D. Rapaport (1960b), p. 899.

[49]S. Freud (1895), p. 369 ff; (1900), p. 617; (1923), p. 10.

[50]See Chap. 17, note 10.

[51]D. Rapaport (1960b), p. 898.

[52]S. Freud (1900), p. 593; D. Rapaport (1960b), p. 898.

[53]As discussed earlier, there may be some memories that, owing to repression, cannot attract attentional energy, that is, cannot become conscious.

[54]See Chapter 15, notes 7 and 8.

[55]For a discussion of this point, see D. Rapaport (1959b), p. 784, p. 786.

[56]S. Freud (1900), p. 594.

[57]In this connection, see the "plan" of Chapter 15.

[58]S. Freud (1901), p. 55.

[59]It should be pointed out that there is a lack of clarity, within psychoanalytic theory, as to whether there is a single storehouse of associated cognitive structures that can be differentially activated according to the source of energy used for the activation (neutralized attentional, or drive), or whether there are separate memory organizations and structures, one for conceptual, secondary process thought and one for drive related, primary process thought. For discussions of this issue, see S. Freud (1915c), pp. 106–109, and Spitz (1965), footnote, pp. 186–187.

Chapter 19. Implications of Psychoanalytic Theory for Education

[1]Erikson (1939).

[2]For a discussion of personality traits characteristic of different cultures, see Benedict (1934); Erikson (1939, 1950); Whiting and Child (1953). For differences within our own culture, see Sears, Maccoby, and Levin (1956).

[3]For a discussion of thought forms in different societies, see Werner (1948); Whorf (1956).

[4]See, for example, Hess (1959), Lorenz (1935), Scott (for instance, 1950, 1968).

[5]See, for example, Cronbach (1962), pp. 88–267.

[6]A. Freud (1936), p. 91 ff, discusses this point.

[7]Erikson (1959), pp. 22–23.

[8]*Ibid.,* p. 41.

[9]For an excellent treatment of this topic, from which some of the following discussion is drawn, see Kessler (1966), p. 208 ff.

[10]For example, Goldfarb (1945, 1958); Skeels and Dye (1939); Spitz (1949, 1965). Spitz (1957), p. 135, notes that affect-deprived infants have difficulty in learning and that they can only learn from gratifying experiences, not from punishment.

[11]Kessler (1966), p. 82.

[12]Ekstein and Motto (1969).

[13]This point is discussed by Katan (1961), pp. 185–186.

[14]Spitz (1959), pp. 76–77.

[15]This discussion is based on A. Freud (1965), pp. 81–82.

[16]Fenichel (1945), p. 160.

[17]A. Freud (1936), pp. 111–12, has discussed this problem.

[18]The idea of bringing the child's behavior under the control of the stimulus (Skinner, 1971) is not the view of all behaviorists or S-R theorists; Gagné (1970) has a different type of behavioristic learning theory.

[19]Cf. Birns (1965), Escalona (1963). For a review of these and other studies, see Korner (1971).

[20]For example, Burlingham (1961), S. Rappaport (1961). For other investigations of these topics, see vols. 1–27 of *The Psychoanalytic Study of the Child.*

[21]Cases of developmental imbalance have been discussed by Spitz (1965).

[22]For further discussion of this point, see A. Freud (1965), for example, p. 87.

[23]The idea of developmental imbalance and portions of the following discussion are based on Spitz (1965).

[24]Spitz (1945).

[25]W. Dennis (1960) has provided extensive evidence of this physical deterioration of infants in orphanages. He stresses the lack of physical handling of these infants as the critical causal factor.

[26]Spitz (1957), pp. 12–14.

[27]*Ibid.,* pp. 70–85, gives a fascinating account of such development in a baby girl who was fed for the first 21 months of her life via a gastric fistula. In the absence of rooting and oral gratification, the three stages in semantic development were deviant, insofar as they were based on the experiences with the fistula and hand gestures related to it.

[28]The term "fake progression" has been used by Erikson (1959, p. 68), to describe this state of affairs.

[29]Kessler (1966), p. 201.

[30]D. Rapaport (1960b), p. 899.

[31]Parts of the following discussion are based on Kessler (1966), p. 211 ff.

[32]A. Freud (1936), pp. 100–113.

[33]Hartmann (1964), p. 257.

[34]Goldberger and Holt (1958); D. Rapaport (1957b), p. 728.

[35]The interested reader is also referred to Ekstein and Motto (1969), and to A. Freud (1931, 1954).

REFERENCES

PART 1. THE STIMULUS RESPONSE APPROACH TO INTELLECTUAL DEVELOPMENT

Boring, E. G. *A history of experimental psychology.* New York: Appleton-Century-Crofts, 1950.

Eichorn, D. Physiological development. In P. H. Mussen (Ed.), *Carmichael's manual of child psychology.* New York: Wiley, 1970, pp. 157–283.

Gagné, R. M. *The conditions of learning.* New York: Holt, Rinehart, and Winston, 1970.

Gagné, R. M., & Rohwer, W. D., Jr. Instructional psychology. *Annual Review of Psychology,* 1969, **20,** 381–418.

Glaser, R. (Ed.) *The nature of reinforcement.* New York: Academic Press, 1971.

Hilgard, E. R., & Bower, G. H. *Theories of learning.* New York: Appleton-Century-Crofts, 1966.

Jeffrey, W. E., & Skager, R. W. Effect of incentive conditions on stimulus generalization in children. *Child Development,* 1962, **33,** 865–870.

Jensen, A. R., & Rohwer, W. D., Jr. Syntactical mediation of serial and paired-associate learning as a function of age. *Child Development,* 1965, **36,** 601–608.

Kagan, J., & Kogan, N. Individual variation in cognitive processes. In P. H. Mussen (Ed.) *Carmichael's manual of child psychology.* New York: Wiley, 1970.

Keppel, G., Postman, L. J., & Zavortink, B. Studies of learning to learn: VIII. The influence of massive amounts of training upon the learning and retention of paired-associate lists. *Journal of Verbal Learning and Verbal Behavior,* 1968, **7,** 790–796.

Kohlberg, L., & Mayer, R. Development as the aim of education. *Harvard Educational Review,* 1972, **42,** 449–496.

Köhler, W. *Gestalt psychology.* New York: Liveright, 1929.

Koppenaal, R. J., Krull, A., & Katz, H. Age, interference, and forgetting. *Journal of Experimental Child Psychology,* 1964, **1,** 360–375.

Levinson, B., & Reese, H. W. Patterns of discrimination learning set in preschool children, fifth-graders, college freshmen, and the aged. *Monographs of the Society for Research in Child Development,* 1967, **32**(7, Whole No. 115).

Mednick, S. A., & Lehtinen, L. C. Stimulus generalization as a function of age in children. *Journal of Experimental Psychology,* 1957, **53,** 180–183.

Murphy, G. *Historical introduction to modern psychology.* New York: Harcourt, Brace, 1949.

Odom, R. D. Concept identification and utilization among children of different ages. *Journal of Experimental Child Psychology,* 1966, **4,** 309–316.

Osgood, C. E. *Method and theory in experimental psychology.* New York: Oxford University Press, 1953.

Pavlov, I. P. *Conditioned reflexes.* London: Oxford Press, 1927.

Postman, L. J. The effects of language habits on the acquisition and retention of verbal associations. *Journal of Experimental Psychology,* 1962, **64,** 7–19.

Postman, L. J., & Goggin, J. Whole versus part learning of paired-associate lists. *Journal of Experimental Psychology,* 1966, **71,** 867–877.

Reese, H. W., & Lipsitt, L. P. *Experimental child psychology.* New York: Academic Press, 1970.

Rohwer, W. D., Jr., & Bean, J. P. Sentence effects and noun-pair learning: A developmental interaction during adolescence. *Journal of Experimental Child Psychology,* 1973, **15,** 521–533.

Saltz, E. *The cognitive bases of human learning.* Homewood, Ill.: Dorsey Press, 1971.

Skinner, B. F. *Science and human behavior.* New York: Macmillan, 1953.

Skinner, B. F. Reinforcement today. *American Psychologist,* 1958, **13,** 94–99.

Skinner, B. F. *The technology of teaching.* New York: Appleton-Century-Crofts, 1968.

Solomon, R. L. Punishment. *American Psychologist,* 1964, **19,** 239–253.

Stevenson, H. W. Learning in children. In P. H. Mussen (Ed.), *Carmichael's manual of child psychology.* New York: Wiley, 1970.

Stevenson, H. W., Iscoe, I., & McConnell, C. A developmental study of transposition. *Journal of Experimental Psychology,* 1955, **49,** 278–280.

Sulzer, B., & Mayer, G. R. *Behavior modification procedures for school personnel.* Hindsdale, Ill.: Dryden Press, 1972.

Tanner, J. M. Physical growth. In P. H. Mussen (Ed.), *Carmichael's manual of child psychology.* New York: Wiley, 1970. Pp. 77–155.

Thorndike, E. L. *Animal intelligence: Experimental studies.* New York: Macmillan, 1911.

Titchener, E. B. *An outline of psychology.* New York: Macmillan, 1902.

Watson, J. B. Psychology as the behaviorist views it. *Psychological Review,* 1913, **20,** 158–177.

White, S. H. Evidence for a hierarchical arrangement of learning processes. In L. P. Lipsitt & C. C. Spiker (Eds.), *Advances in child development and behavior.* New York: Academic Press, 1965.

White, S. H. The learning theory tradition and child psychology. In P. H. Mussen (Ed.), *Carmichael's manual of child psychology.* New York: Wiley, 1970.

Wicklund, D. A. Paired-associate learning in children as a function of free association strength and type of associative response hierarchy at four grade levels. Unpublished doctoral dissertation, University of Minnesota, 1964.

Wittrock, M. C., & Wiley, D. (Eds.) *The evaluation of instruction: Issues and problems.* New York: Holt, Rinehart, and Winston, 1970.
Zaporozhets, A. V. The development of perception in the preschool child. In P. H. Mussen (Ed.), European research in cognitive development. *Monographs of the Society for Research in Child Development,* 1965, **30**(2, Whole No. 100), 82–101.

PART 2. THE COGNITIVE APPROACH TO INTELLECTUAL DEVELOPMENT

Ammon, M. S. Experimental acceleration of children's grammatical rules. Unpublished M.S. thesis, Cornell University, 1966.
Baldwin, A. L. *Behavior and development in childhood.* New York: Holt, Rinheart and Winston, 1955.
Baldwin, A. L., Baldwin, C. P., Hilton, I. R., & Lambert, N. W. The measurement of social expectations and their development in children. *Monographs of the Society for Research in Child Development,* 1969, **34**(Whole No. 4).
Bellugi, U. The acquisition of negation. Unpublished doctoral dissertation, Graduate School of Education, Harvard University, 1967.
Berko, J. The child's learning of English morphology. *Word,* 1958, **14,** 150–177.
Brainerd, C. J., & Allen, T. W. Experimental inductions of the conservation of "first-order" quantitative invariants. *Psychological Bulletin,* 1971, **75,** 128–144.
Brown, R. *A first language.* Cambridge, Mass.: Harvard University Press, 1973.
Bruner, J. S. The course of cognitive growth. *American Psychologist,* 1964, **19,** 1–15.
Chomsky, N. *Aspects of the theory of syntax.* Cambridge, Mass.: M.I.T. Press, 1965.
Clark, E. V. What's in a word? On the child's acquisition of semantics in his first language. In T. E. Moore (Ed.), *Cognitive development and the acquisition of language.* New York: Academic Press, 1973.
Dale, P. S. *Language development.* Hinsdale, Ill.: Dryden Press, 1972.
Dasen, P. R. Cross-cultural Piagetian research: A summary. *Journal of Cross-cultural Psychology,* 1972, **3,** 23–39.
Donaldson, M., & Balfour, G. Less is more: A study of language comprehension in children. *British Journal of Psychology,* 1968, **59,** 461–471.
Duckworth, E. Piaget rediscovered. In R. E. Ripple & V. N. Rockcastle (Eds.), *Piaget rediscovered.* Ithaca, N.Y.: Cornell University School of Education, 1964.
Ervin, S. Imitation and structural change in children's language. In E. H. Lenneberg (Ed.), *New directions in the study of language.* Cambridge, Mass.: M.I.T. Press, 1964.
Flavell, J. H. *The developmental psychology of Jean Piaget.* Princeton, N.J.: Van Nostrand, 1963.
Flavell, J. H. Concept development. In P. H. Mussen (Ed.), *Carmichael's manual of child psychology.* (3rd ed.) Vol. 1. New York: Wiley, 1970.
Ginsburg, H., & Opper, S. *Piaget's theory of intellectual development.* Englewood Cliffs, N.J.: Prentice-Hall, 1969.
Gouin-Decarie, T. *Intelligence and affectivity in early childhood.* New York: International Universities Press, 1965.
Green, D. R., Ford, M. P., & Flamer, G. B. (Eds.), *Measurement and Piaget,* New York: McGraw-Hill, 1971.
Guthrie, E. R. *The psychology of learning.* (Rev. ed.) New York: Harper, 1952.
Hunt, J. McV. *Intelligence and experience.* New York: Ronald Press, 1961.
Inhelder, B., & Piaget, J. *The growth of logical thinking from childhood to adolescence.* New York: Basic Books, 1958.

Inhelder, B., & Piaget, J. *The early growth of logic in the child.* New York: Norton, 1964.

Itard, J. M. G. *The wild boy of Aveyron.* New York: Century, 1932.

Kohlberg, L. Stage and sequence: The cognitive-developmental approach to socialization. In D. Goslin (Ed.), *Handbook of socialization theory and research.* Chicago: Rand McNally, 1969.

Kohlberg, L. Implications of developmental psychology for education: Examples from moral development. *Educational Psychologist,* 1973, **10**, 2–14.

Kohlberg, L., & Turiel, E. Moral development and moral education. In G. Lesser (Ed.), *Psychology and educational practice.* Glenview, Ill.: Scott, Foresman, 1971.

Kuhn, D., Langer, J., Kohlberg, L., & Haan, N. S. Operational thought structures in adolescence and adulthood. *Genetic Psychology Monographs,* in press.

Langer, J. (1969a) Disequilibrium as a source of development. In P. H. Mussen, J. Langer, & M. Covington (Eds.), *Trends and issues in developmental psychology.* New York: Holt, Rinehart and Winston, 1969.

Langer, J. (1969b) *Theories of development.* New York: Holt, Rinehart and Winston, 1969.

Laurendeau, M., & Pinard, A. *Causal thinking in the child.* New York: International Universities Press, 1962.

Laurendeau, M., & Pinard, A. *The development of the concept of space in the child.* New York: International Universities Press, 1970.

Lovell, K. Some recent studies in cognitive and language development. *Merrill-Palmer Quarterly,* 1968, **14**, 123–138.

Lunzer, E. A. Translator's introduction. In B. Inhelder & J. Piaget, *The early growth of logic in the child.* New York: Norton, 1964.

Marascuilo, L. A., & McSweeney, M. Tracking and minority student attitudes and performance. *Urban Education,* 1972, **6**, 303–319.

McNeill, D. Developmental psycholinguistics. In F. Smith & G. A. Miller (Eds.), *The genesis of language.* Cambridge, Mass.: M.I.T. Press, 1966.

Miller, G. A. Psycholinguistic approaches to the study of communication. In D. L. Arm (Ed.), *Journeys in science: Small steps—great strides.* Albuquerque: University of New Mexico Press, 1967.

Miller, G. A., Galanter, E., & Pribram, K. H. *Plans and the structure of behavior.* New York: Holt-Dryden, 1960.

Mosher, F. A., & Hornsby, J. R. On asking questions. In J. S. Bruner, R. R. Olver, P. M. Greenfield, *et al., Studies in cognitive growth.* New York: Wiley, 1966.

Newell, A., Shaw, J. C., & Simon, H. A. Elements of a theory of human problem solving. *Psychological Review,* 1958, **65**, 151–166.

Pascual-Leone, J. A mathematical model for the transition rule in Piaget's developmental stages. *Acta Psychologica,* 1970, **63**, 301–345.

Pascual-Leone, J. A theory of constructive operators, a neo-Piagetian model of conservation, and the problem of horizontal décalages. Paper presented at the annual meeting of the Canadian Psychological Association, Montreal, June, 1972.

Piaget, J. *The construction of reality in the child.* New York: Basic Books, 1954.

Piaget, J. *The child's conception of the world.* Paterson, N.J.: Littlefield, Adams, 1960.

Piaget, J. (1962a) *The moral judgment of the child.* New York: Collier, 1962.

Piaget, J. (1962b) *Play, dreams, and imitation in childhood.* New York: Norton, 1962.

Piaget, J. *The origins of intelligence in children.* New York: Norton, 1963.

Piaget, J. Development and learning. In R. E. Ripple & V. N. Rockcastle (Eds.), *Piaget Rediscovered.* Ithaca, N.Y.: Cornell University School of Education, 1964.

Piaget, J. (1965a) *The child's conception of number.* New York: Norton, 1965.

Piaget, J. (1965b) *The child's conception of physical causality.* Paterson, N.J.: Littlefield, Adams, 1965.

Piaget, J. *Six psychological studies.* New York: Random House, 1967.
Piaget, J. (1970a) *The child's conception of movement and speed.* New York: Basic Books, 1970.
Piaget, J. (1970b) Piaget's theory. In P. H. Mussen (Ed.), *Carmichael's manual of child psychology.* (3rd ed.) vol. 1. New York: Wiley, 1970.
Piaget, J. (1970c) *Science of education and the psychology of the child.* New York: Orion, 1970.
Piaget, J. (1971a) *Biology and knowledge.* Chicago: University of Chicago Press, 1971.
Piaget, J. (1971b) *The child's conception of time.* New York: Ballantine, 1971.
Piaget, J. Intellectual evolution from adolescence to adulthood. *Human Development,* 1972, **15,** 1–12.
Piaget, J., & Inhelder, B. *The child's conception of space.* New York: Norton, 1967.
Piaget, J., & Inhelder, B. *The psychology of the child.* New York: Basic Books, 1969.
Piaget, J., Inhelder, B., & Szeminska, A. *The child's conception of geometry.* New York: Harper & Row, 1964.
Pylyshyn, Z. W. The role of competence theories in cognitive psychology. *Journal of Psycholinguistic Research,* 1973, **2,** 21–50.
Turiel, E. Developmental processes in the child's moral thinking. In P. H. Mussen, J. Langer, & M. Covington (Eds.), *Trends and issues in developmental psychology,* New York: Holt, Rinehart and Winston, 1969.
Uzgiris, I. C., & Hunt, J. McV. Ordinal scales of infant development. Paper read at XVIII International Congress of Psychology, Moscow, August, 1966.
Vygotsky, L. S. *Thought and language.* Cambridge, Mass.: M.I.T. Press, 1962.
Weir, R. *Language in the crib.* The Hague: Mouton, 1962.

PART 3. THE PSYCHOANALYTIC APPROACH TO INTELLECTUAL DEVELOPMENT

Axelrad, S., & Brody, S. *Anxiety and Ego Formation in Infancy.* New York: International Universities Press, 1970.
Benedict, R. *Patterns of Culture.* Boston: Houghton Mifflin, 1934.
Birns, B. Individual differences in human neonates' responses to stimulation. *Child Development,* 1965, **36,** 249–256.
Blos, P. *On Adolescence: A Psychoanalytic Interpretation.* New York: Free Press, 1962.
Brown, R. *Social Psychology.* New York: Free Press, 1965.
Burlingham, D. Some notes on the development of the blind. *The Psychoanalytic Study of the Child,* 1961, **16,** 121–145.
Cobliner, W. The Geneva school of genetic psychology and psychoanalysis: parallels and counterparts. In R. Spitz, *The First Year of Life.* New York: International Universities Press, 1965. Pp. 301–356.
Cronbach, L. J. *Educational Psychology.* (2nd ed.) New York: Harcourt, Brace and World, 1962.
Dennis, W. Causes of retardation among institutional children: Iran. *Journal of Genetic Psychology,* 1960, **96,** 47–59.
Ekstein, R. & Motto, R. L. *From Learning for Love to Love of Learning.* New York: Brunner/Mazel, 1969.
Erikson, E. H. Observations on Sioux education. *Journal of Psychology,* 1939, **7,** 101–156.
Erikson, E. H. *Childhood and Society.* (2nd ed.) New York: Norton, 1950.
Erikson, E. H. Identity and the life cycle. *Psychological Issues,* 1959, **1**(1), 18–171.
Escalona, S. Patterns of infantile experience and the developmental process. *The Psychoanalytic Study of the Child,* 1963, **18,** 197–244.

Fantz, R. L. The origin of form perception. *Scientific American,* 1961, **204,** 66–72.

Fantz, R. L. Pattern discrimination and selective attention as determinants of perceptual development from birth. In A. H. Kidd and J. L. Rivoire (Eds.), *Perceptual Development in Children.* New York: International Universities Press, 1966. Pp. 143–173.

Fantz, R. L., & Nevis, S. Pattern preferences and perceptual-cognitive development in early infancy. *Merrill-Palmer Quarterly,* 1967, **13,** 77–108.

Fenichel, O. *The Psychoanalytic Theory of Neurosis.* New York: Norton, 1945.

Freud, A. *Introduction to Psychoanalysis for Teachers.* London: Allen and Unwin, 1931.

Freud, A. (1936) *The Ego and the Mechanisms of Defense.* New York: International Universities Press, 1946.

Freud, A. Psychoanalysis and education. *The Psychoanalytic Study of the Child,* 1954, **9,** 9–15.

Freud, A. Adolescence. *The Psychoanalytic Study of the Child,* 1958, **13,** 255–278.

Freud, A. *Normality and Pathology in Childhood.* New York: International Universities Press, 1965.

Freud, S. Project for a scientific psychology. (1895) In M. Bonaparte, A. Freud, E. Kris (Eds.), *The Origins of Psychoanalysis. Letters to Wilhelm Fliess, Drafts and Notes: 1887–1902.* New York: Basic Books, 1954.

Freud, S. (1900) *The Interpretation of Dreams.* (trans. J. Strachey). New York: Basic Books.

Freud, S. (1901) The psychopathology of everyday life. In *Standard Edition.* Vol. VI. London: Hogarth Press, 1960.

Freud, S. (1911) Formulations regarding the two principles in mental functioning. In *Collected Papers.* Vol. IV. New York: Basic Books, 1959, Pp. 13–21.

Freud, S. (1912) The most prevalent form of degradation in erotic life. In *Collected Papers.* Vol. IV. New York: Basic Books, 1959, Pp. 203–216.

Freud, S. (1915a) Instincts and their vicissitudes. In *Collected Papers.* Vol. IV. New York: Basic Books, 1959. Pp. 60–83.

Freud, S. (1915b) Repression. In *Collected Papers.* Vol. IV. New York: Basic Books, 1959. Pp. 84–97.

Freud, S. (1915c) The unconscious. In *Collected Papers.* Vol. IV. New York: Basic Books, 1959. Pp. 98–136.

Freud, S. (1923) *The Ego and the Id.* (Ed. J. Strachey; Trans. Joan Riviere) New York: Norton, 1960.

Freud, S. (1925) Negation. In *Collected Papers.* Vol. V. New York: Basic Books. Pp. 181–185.

Freud, S. (1940) *An Outline of Psychoanalysis.* (Trans. J. Strachey) New York: Norton, 1949.

Gagné, R. M. *The Conditions of Learning.* New York: Holt, Rinehart and Winston, 1970.

Goldberger, L., & Holt, R. R. Experimental interference with reality contact (perceptual isolation): Method and group results. *Journal of Nervous and Mental Disease,* 1958, **127,** 99–112.

Goldfarb, W. Effects of psychological deprivation in infancy and subsequent stimulation. *American Journal of Psychiatry,* 1945, **102,** 18–33.

Goldfarb, W. Emotional and intellectual consequences of psychologic deprivation in infancy: A re-evaluation. In P. Hoch & J. Zubin (Eds.), *Psychopathology of Childhood.* New York: Grune and Stratton, 1958.

Haaf, R. A., & Bell, R. Q. A facial dimension in visual discrimination by human infants. *Child Development,* 1967, **38,** 893–899.

Hartmann, H. (1939) *Ego Psychology and the Problem of Adaptation.* New York: International Universities Press, 1958.

Hartmann, H. *Essays on Ego Psychology.* New York: International Universities Press, 1964.

Hess, E. H. Imprinting: An effect of early experience. *Science,* 1959, **130,** 133–141.

Kagan, J. Attention and psychological change in the young child. *Science,* 1970, **170,** 826–832.

Katan, A. Some thoughts about the role of verbalization in early childhood. *The Psychoanalytic Study of the Child,* 1961, **16,** 184–188.

Kessler, J. *Psychopathology of Childhood.* Englewood Cliffs, New Jersey: Prentice-Hall, 1966.

Klein, G. S. Psychoanalysis: Ego psychology. Vol. 13. *International Encyclopedia of the Social Sciences.* New York: Macmillan and Free Press, 1968.

Koopman, P. R., & Ames, E. W. Infants' preferences for facial arrangements: A failure to replicate. *Child Development,* 1968, **39,** 481–487.

Korner, A. F. Individual differences at birth. Implications for early experience and later development. *American Journal of Orthopsychiatry,* 1971, **41,** 608–619.

Lewis, M. Infant's responses to facial stimuli during the first year of life. *Developmental Psychology,* 1969, **1,** 75–86.

Lorenz, K. (1935) Companionship in bird life. In C. Schiller (Ed. and Trans.), *Instinctive Behavior.* New York: International Universities Press, 1957.

Lynch, S. & Rohwer, W. D. Grade interaction with words and pictures in a paired-associate task: A proposed explanation. *Journal of Experimental Child Psychology,* 1972, **13,** 413–421.

McCandless, B. R. *Children Behavior and Development.* (2nd ed.) New York: Holt, Rinehart and Winston, 1967.

Miller, G. The magical number seven, plus or minus two: Some limits on our capacity for processing information. *Psychological Review,* 1956, **63,** 81–97.

Rapaport, D. Toward a theory of thinking. In D. Rapaport, *Organization and Pathology of Thought.* New York: Columbia University Press, 1951.

Rapaport, D. *Organization and Pathology of Thought.* New York: Columbia University Press, 1951.

Rapaport, D. (1953) Some metapsychological considerations concerning activity and passivity. In M. M. Gill (Ed.), *The Collected Papers of David Rapaport.* New York: Basic Books, 1967. Pp. 530–568.

Rapaport, D. (1957a) A theoretical analysis of the superego concept. In M. M. Gill (Ed.), *The Collected Papers of David Rapaport.* New York: Basic Books, 1967, Pp. 685–709.

Rapaport, D. (1957b) The theory of ego autonomy: A generalization. In M. M. Gill (Ed.), *The Collected Papers of David Rapaport.* New York: Basic Books, 1967. Pp. 722–744.

Rapaport, D. (1956) Present-day ego psychology. In M. M. Gill (Ed.), *The Collected Papers of David Rapaport.* New York: Basic Books, 1967. Pp. 594–623.

Rapaport, D. (1957a) Cognitive structures. In M. M. Gill (Ed.), *The Collected Papers of David Rapaport.* New York: Basic Books, 1967. Pp. 631–664.

Rapaport, D. (1957b) The theory of ego autonomy: A generalization. In M. M. Gill (Ed.), *The Collected Papers of David Rapaport.* New York: Basic Books, 1967. Pp. 722–744.

Rapaport, D. Historical survey of psychoanalytic ego psychology. In E. H. Erikson, Identity and the life cycle. *Psychological Issues,* 1959a, **1**(1), 5–17.

Rapaport, D. (1959b) The theory of attention cathexis: An economic and structural attempt at the explanation of cognitive processes. In M. M. Gill (Ed.), *The*

Collected Papers of David Rapaport. New York: Basic Books, 1967. Pp. 778–794.

Rapaport, D. (1960a) Psychoanalysis as developmental psychology. In M. M. Gill (Ed.), *The Collected Papers of David Rapaport.* New York: Basic Books, 1967. Pp. 820–852.

Rapaport, D. (1960b) On the psychoanalytic theory of motivation. In M. M. Gill (Ed.), *The Collected Papers of David Rapaport.* New York: Basic Books, 1967. Pp. 853–915.

Rapaport, D. The structure of psychoanalytic theory: A systematizing attempt. *Psychological Issues,* 1960c, **2**(2), 7–158.

Rapaport, D., & Gill, M. M. The points of view and assumptions of metapsychology. *International Journal of Psychoanalysis,* 1959, **40**, 1–10.

Rappaport, S. R. Behavior disorder and ego development in a brain-injured child. *The Psychoanalytic Study of the Child,* 1961, **16**, 423–450.

Scott, J. P. *Early Experience and the Organization of Behavior.* Belmont, Calif.: Wadsworth, 1968.

Scott, J. P., & Marston, M. Critical periods affecting the development of normal and maladjusted social behavior of puppies. *Journal of Genetic Psychology,* 1950, **77**, 26–60.

Sears, R. R., Maccoby, E. E., & Levin, H. *Patterns of Child Rearing.* New York: Harper & Row, 1956.

Skeels, H. M., & Dye, H. B. A study of the effects of differential stimulation on mentally retarded children. *Proceedings of the American Association for Mental Deficiency,* 1939, **44**, 114–136.

Skinner, B. F. *Beyond Freedom and Dignity.* New York: Knopf, 1971.

Spitz, R. A. Hospitalism: An inquiry into the genesis of psychiatric conditions in early childhood. *The Psychoanalytic Study of the Child,* 1945, **1**, 53–74.

Spitz, R. A. The role of ecological factors in emotional development in infancy. *Child Development,* 1949, **20**, 145–155.

Spitz, R. A. *No and Yes.* New York: International Universities Press, 1957.

Spitz, R. A. *A Genetic Field Theory of Ego Formation.* New York: International Universities Press, 1959.

Spitz, R. A. *The First Year of Life.* New York: International Universities Press, 1965.

Werner, H. *Comparative Psychology of Mental Development.* New York: International Universities Press, 1948.

Whiting, J. W. M., & Child, I. L. *Child Training and Personality: A Cross-cultural Study.* New Haven: Yale University Press, 1953.

Whorf, B. L. *Language, Thought, and Reality.* (Ed. J. B. Carroll) Cambridge, Mass.: M.I.T. Press, 1956.

Wolff, P. H. The developmental psychologies of Jean Piaget and psychoanalysis. *Psychological Issues,* 1960, **2**(1), 7–181.

INDEX